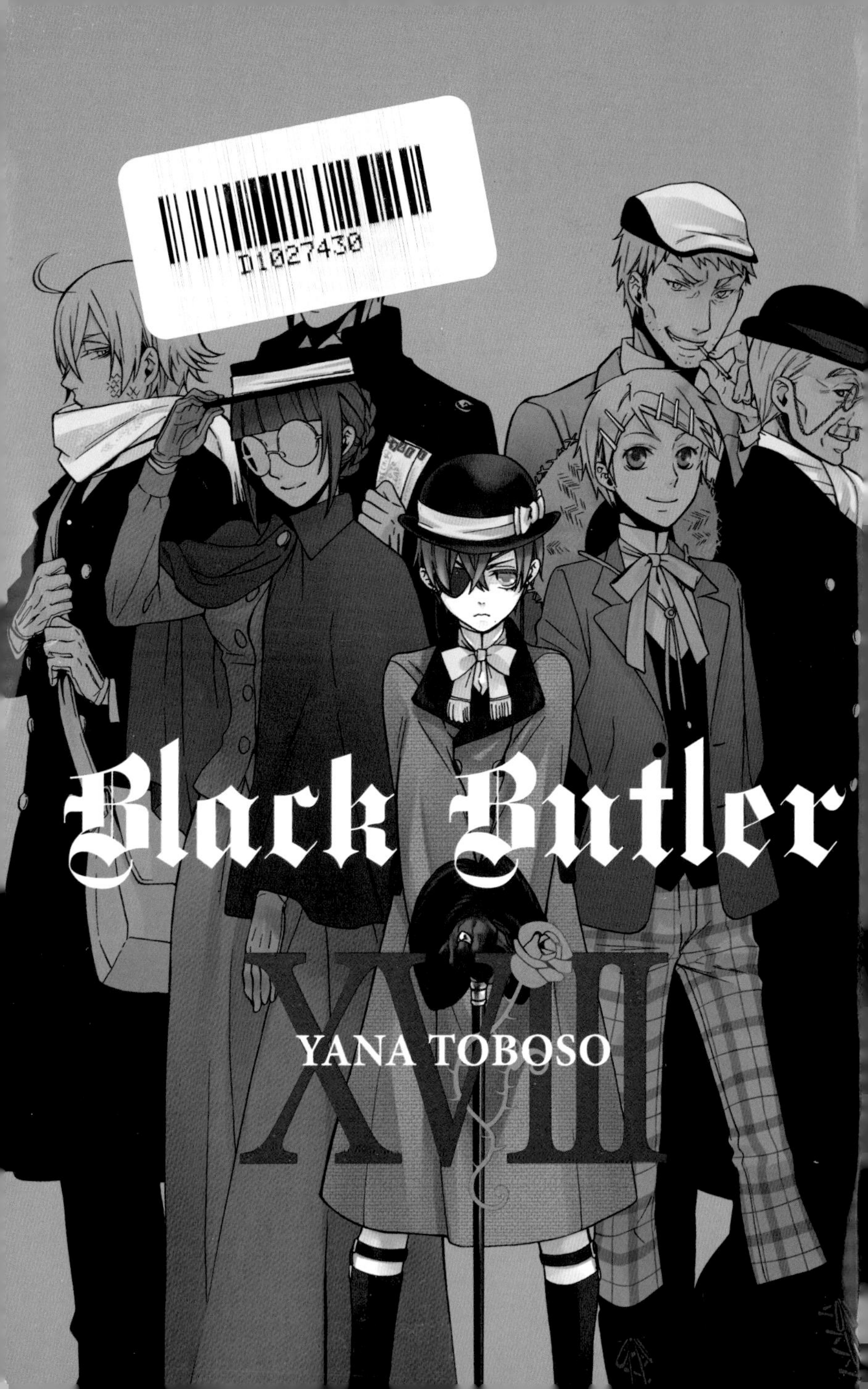
D1027430
Black Butler
XVIII
YANA TOBOSO

Contents

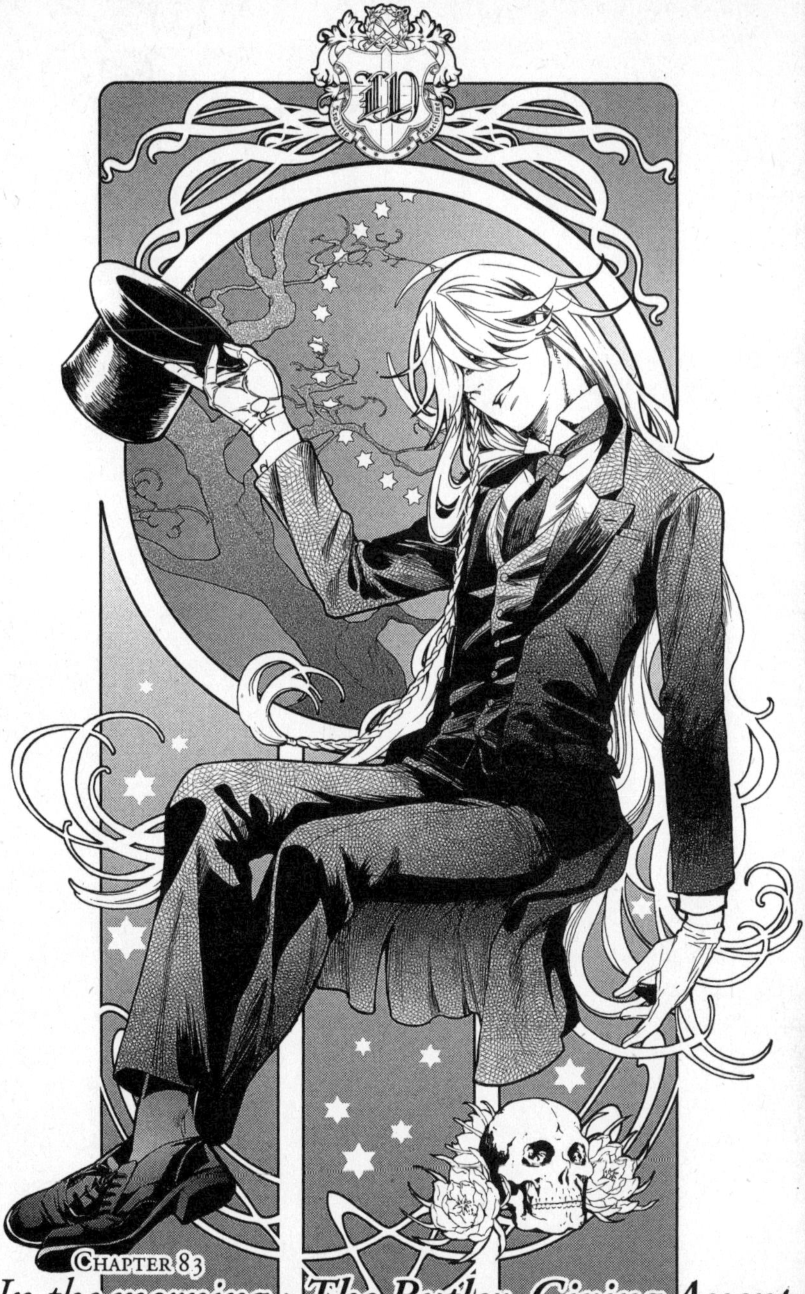

CHAPTER 83

In the morning : The Butler, Giving Assent

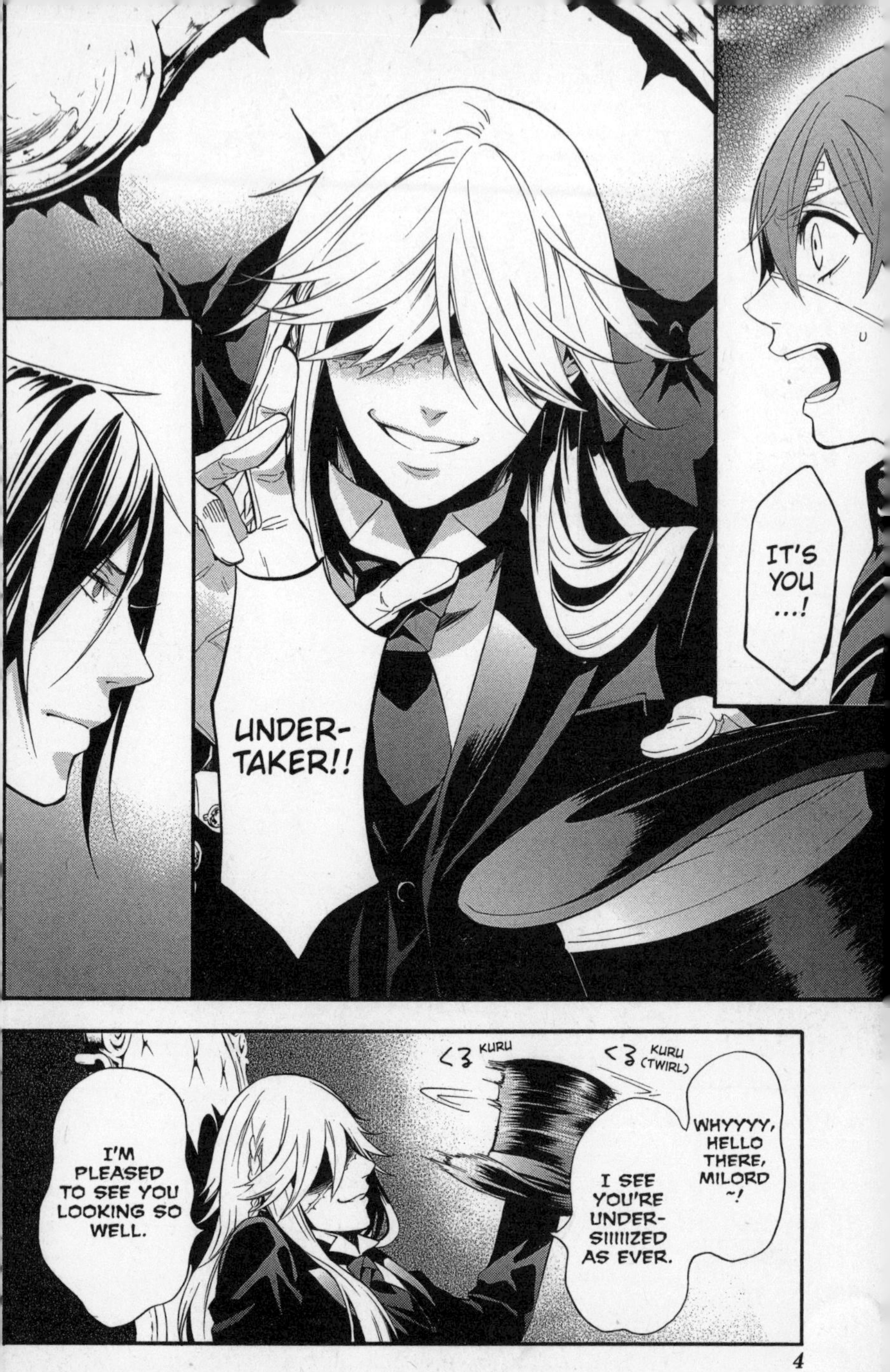
IT'S YOU ...!
UNDER-TAKER!!
くる KURU (TWIRL)
くる KURU
WHYYYY, HELLO THERE, MILORD ~!
I SEE YOU'RE UNDER-SIIIIIIZED AS EVER.
I'M PLEASED TO SEE YOU LOOKING SO WELL.

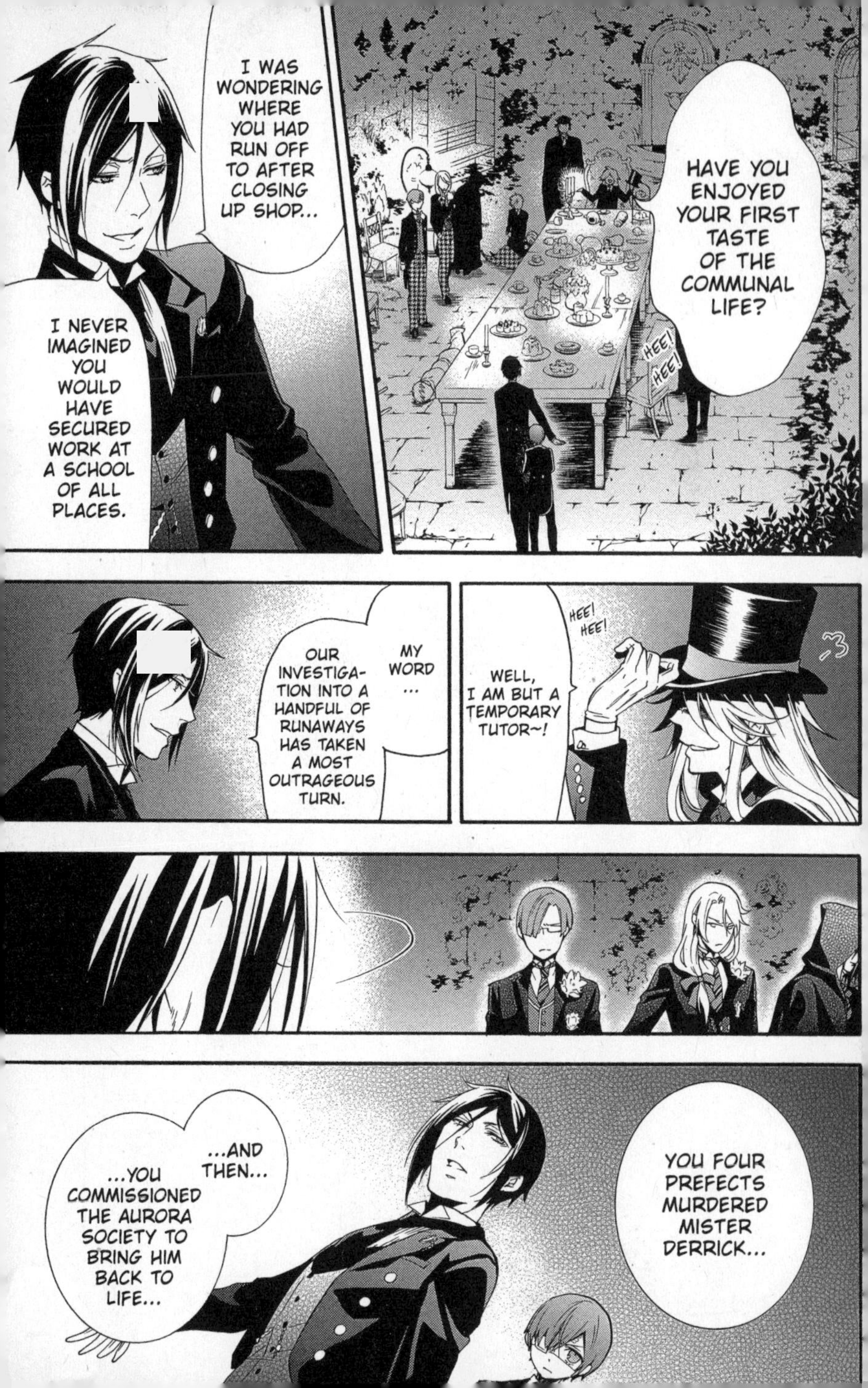
HAVE YOU ENJOYED YOUR FIRST TASTE OF THE COMMUNAL LIFE?
HEE! HEE!
I WAS WONDERING WHERE YOU HAD RUN OFF TO AFTER CLOSING UP SHOP...
I NEVER IMAGINED YOU WOULD HAVE SECURED WORK AT A SCHOOL OF ALL PLACES.
HEE! HEE!
WELL, I AM BUT A TEMPORARY TUTOR~!
MY WORD...
OUR INVESTIGA-TION INTO A HANDFUL OF RUNAWAYS HAS TAKEN A MOST OUTRAGEOUS TURN.
YOU FOUR PREFECTS MURDERED MISTER DERRICK...
...AND THEN...
...YOU COMMISSIONED THE AURORA SOCIETY TO BRING HIM BACK TO LIFE...

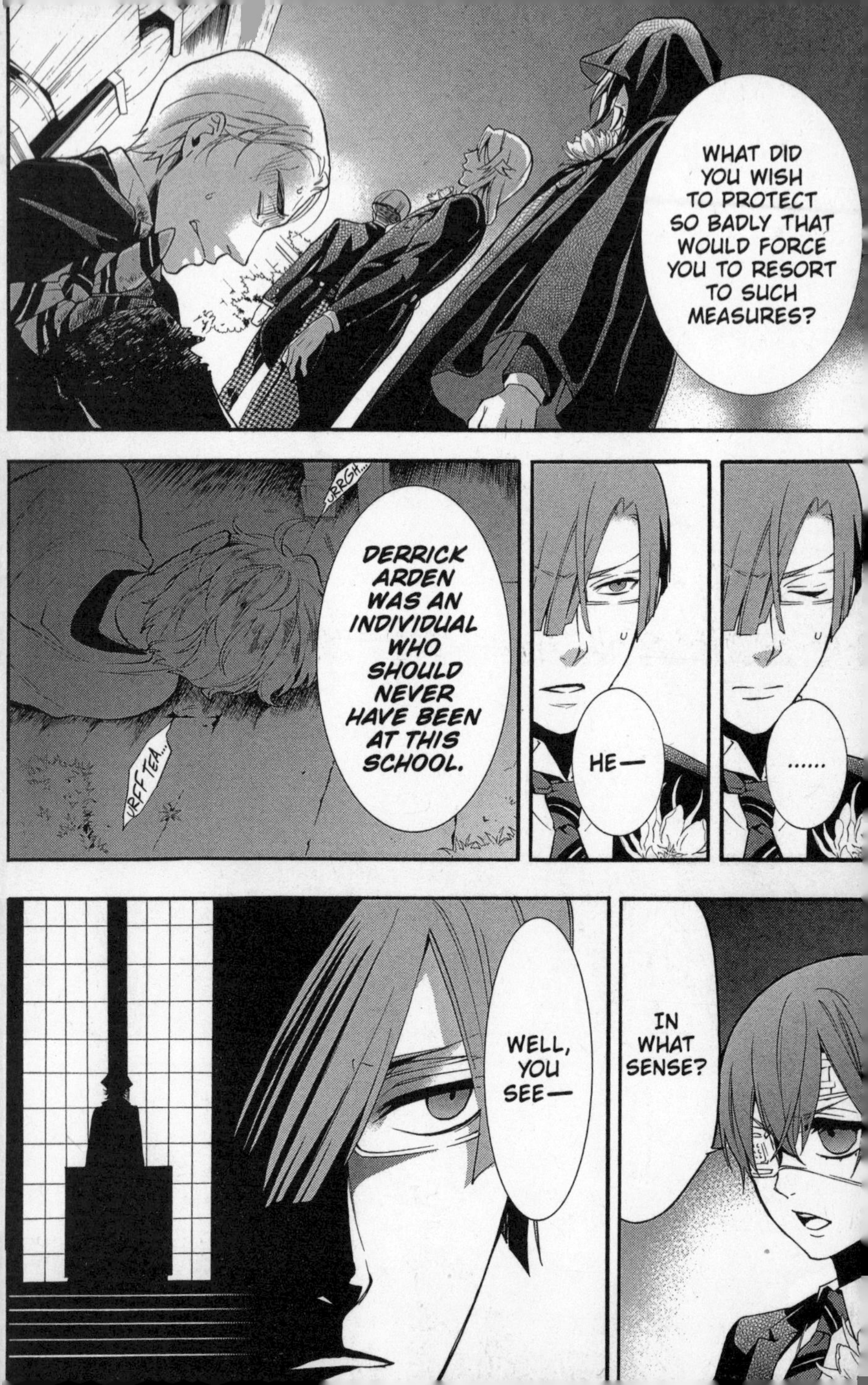
WHAT DID YOU WISH TO PROTECT SO BADLY THAT WOULD FORCE YOU TO RESORT TO SUCH MEASURES?
......
HE—
URRGH...
DERRICK ARDEN WAS AN INDIVIDUAL WHO SHOULD NEVER HAVE BEEN AT THIS SCHOOL.
URFF TEA...
IN WHAT SENSE?
WELL, YOU SEE—

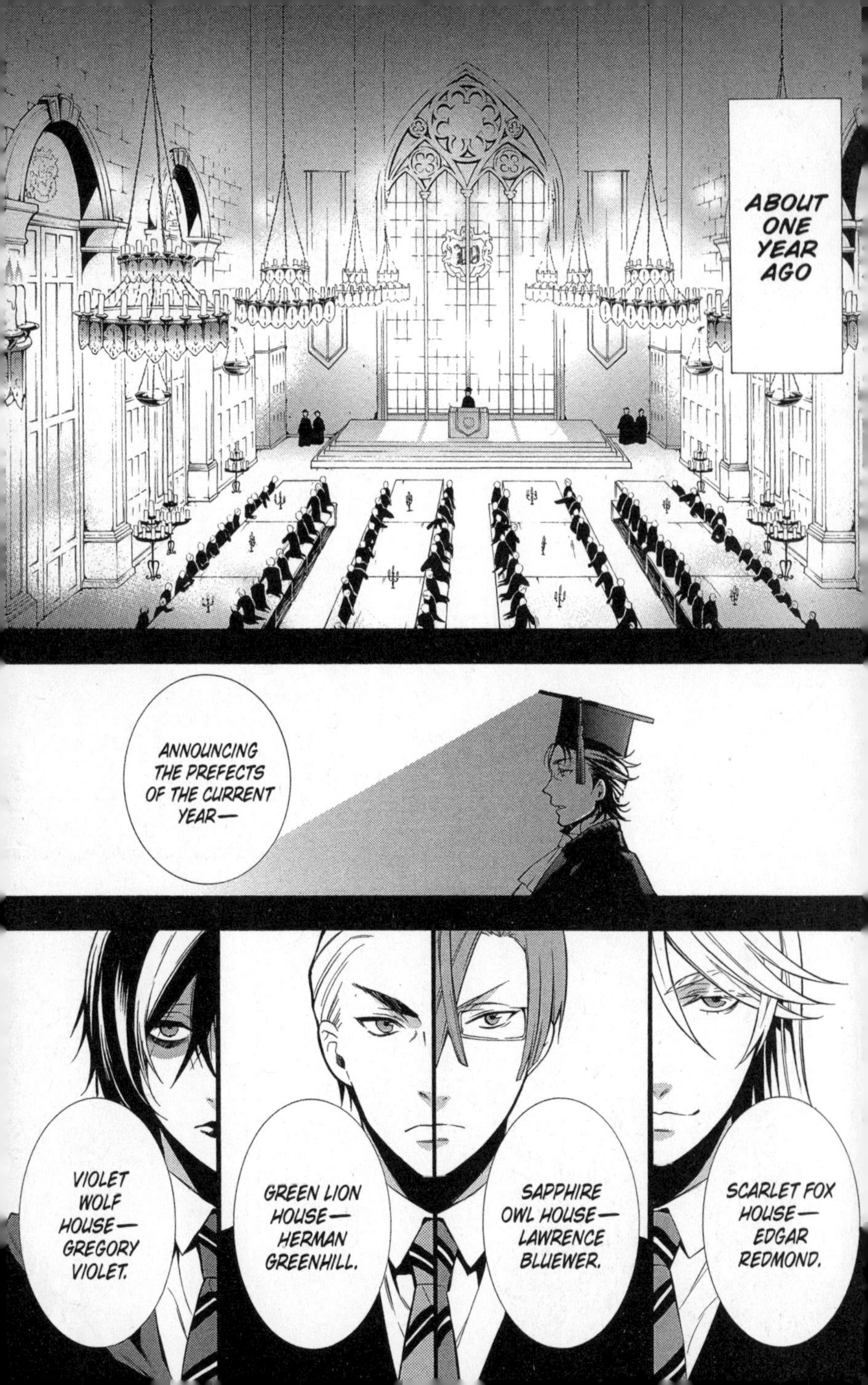
ABOUT ONE YEAR AGO
ANNOUNCING THE PREFECTS OF THE CURRENT YEAR—
SCARLET FOX HOUSE—EDGAR REDMOND.
SAPPHIRE OWL HOUSE—LAWRENCE BLUEWER.
GREEN LION HOUSE—HERMAN GREENHILL.
VIOLET WOLF HOUSE—GREGORY VIOLET.

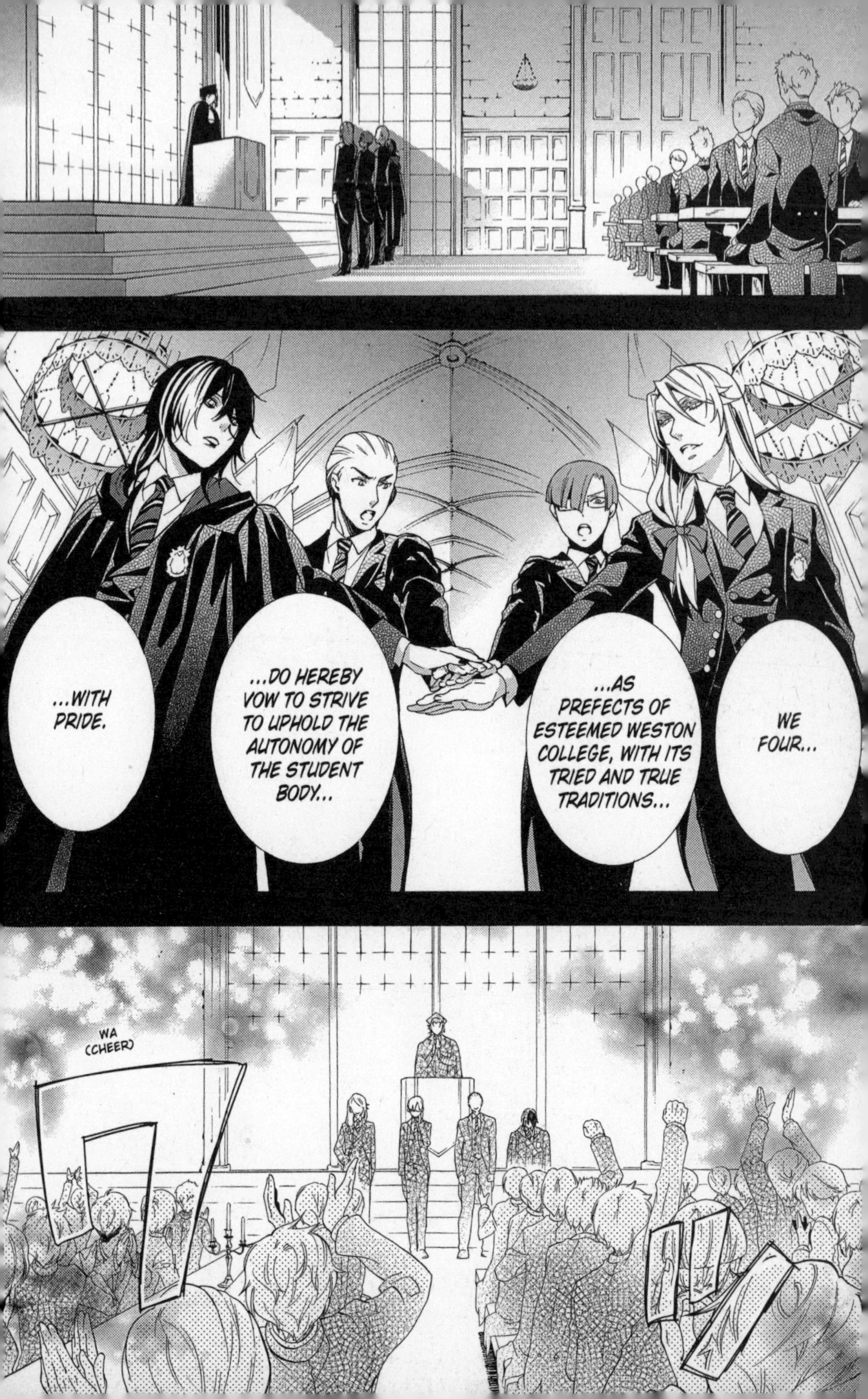
WE FOUR...
...AS PREFECTS OF ESTEEMED WESTON COLLEGE, WITH ITS TRIED AND TRUE TRADITIONS...
...DO HEREBY VOW TO STRIVE TO UPHOLD THE AUTONOMY OF THE STUDENT BODY...
...WITH PRIDE.
WA (CHEER)

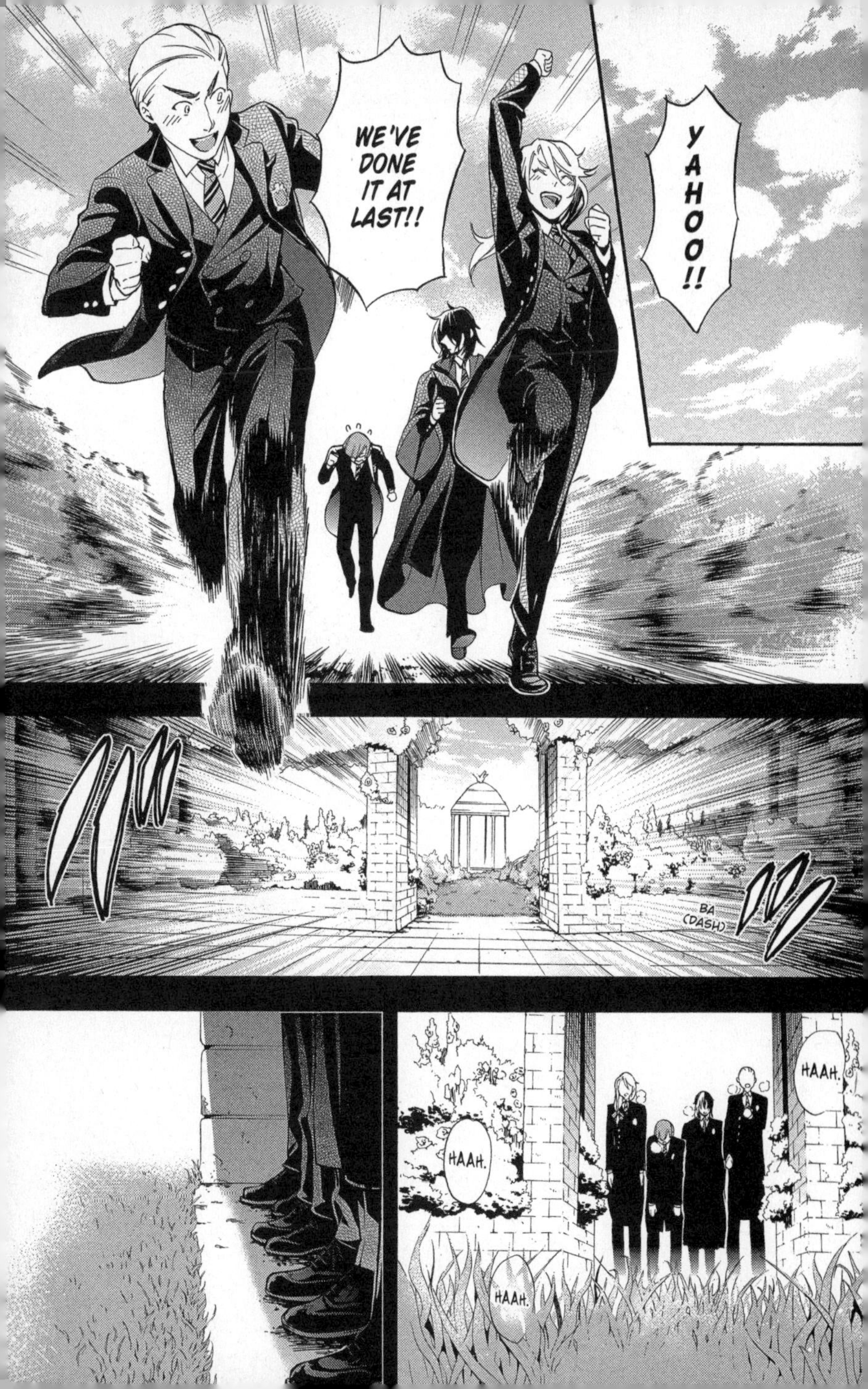
YAHOO!!
WE'VE DONE IT AT LAST!!
BA (DASH)
HAAH.
HAAH.
HAAH.

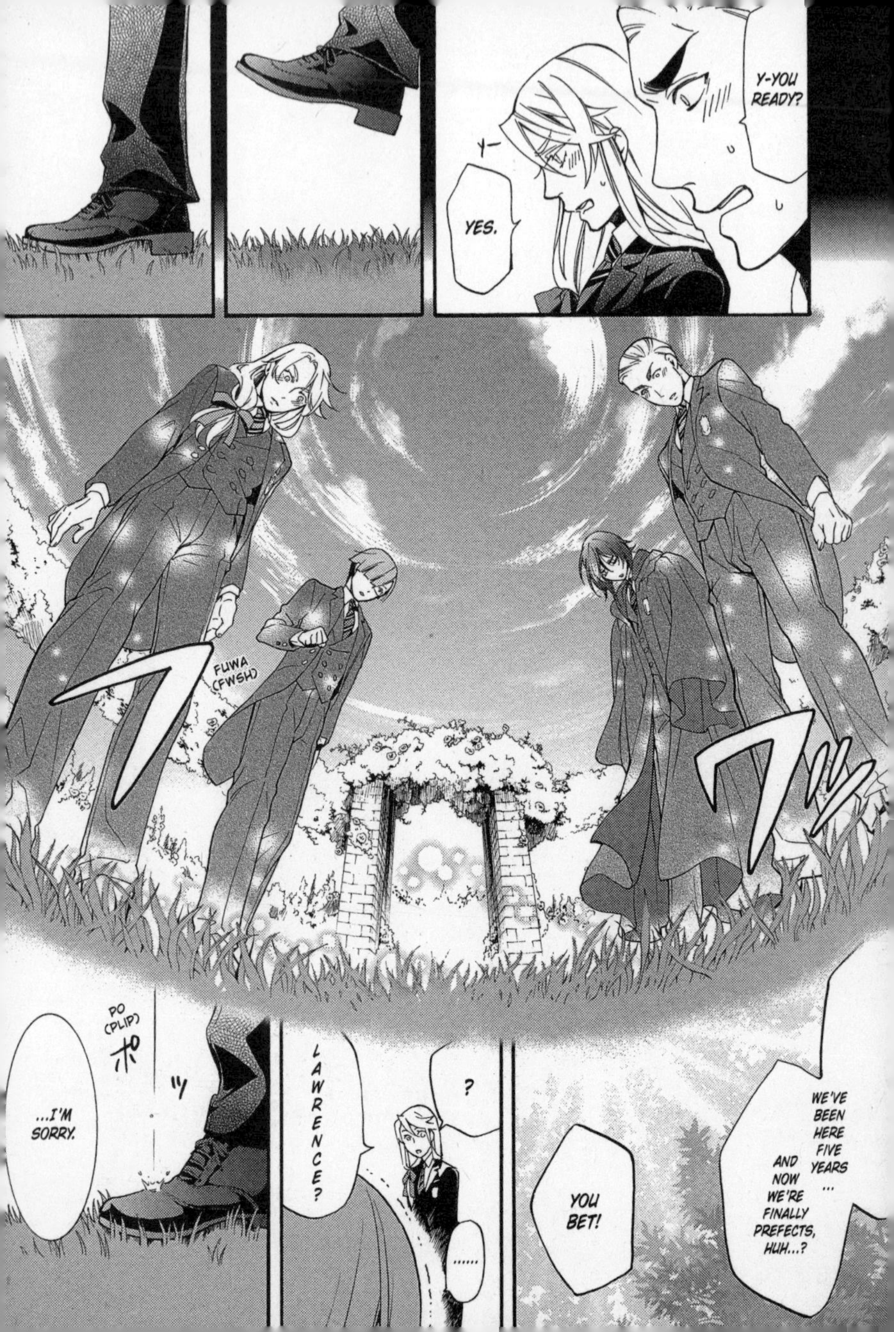
Y-YOU READY?
Y-
YES.
FUWA (FWSH)
WE'VE BEEN HERE FIVE YEARS...
AND NOW WE'RE FINALLY PREFECTS, HUH...?
YOU BET!
?
LAWRENCE?
......
PO (PLIP)
...I'M SORRY.

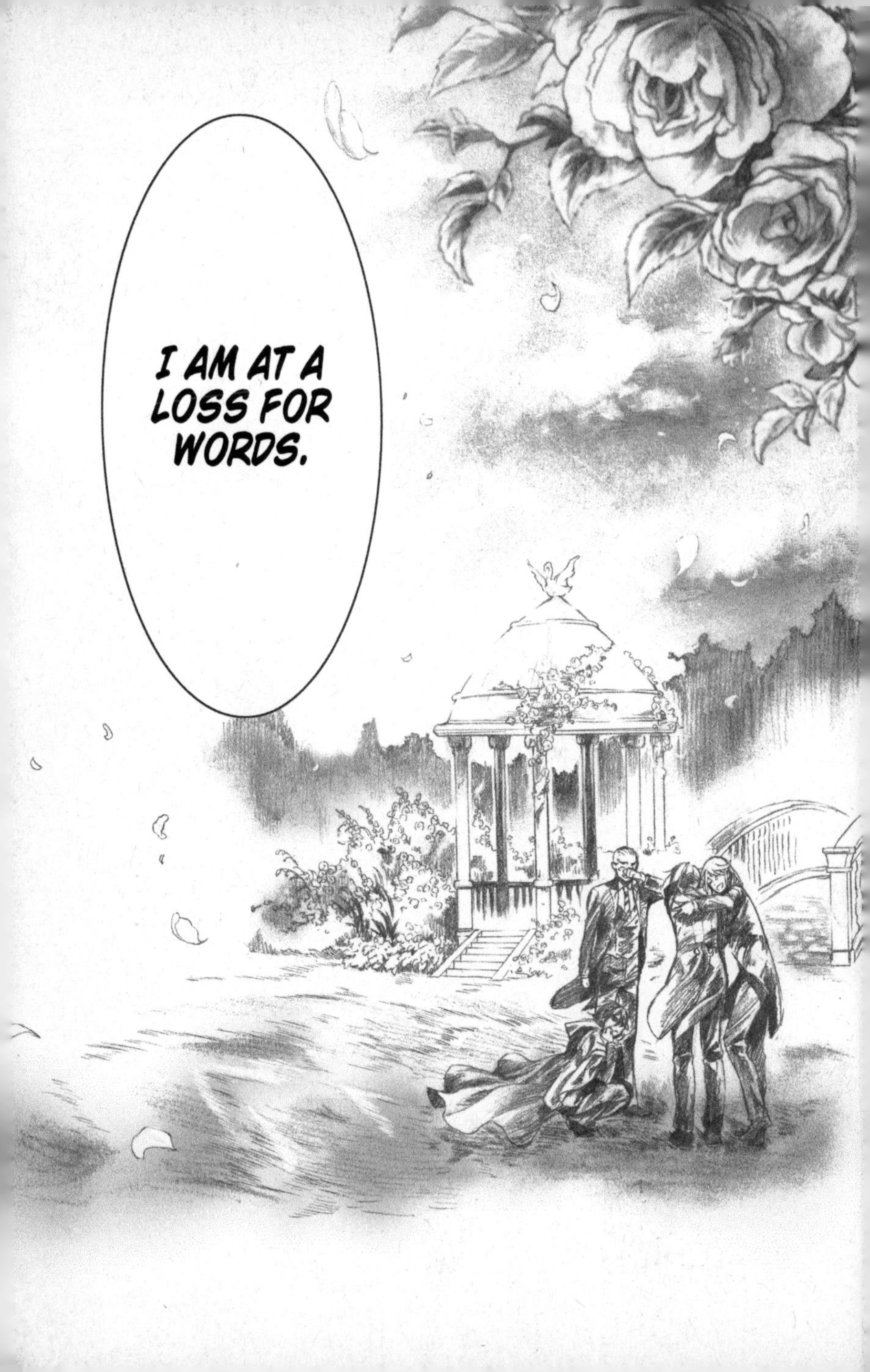
I AM AT A LOSS FOR WORDS.

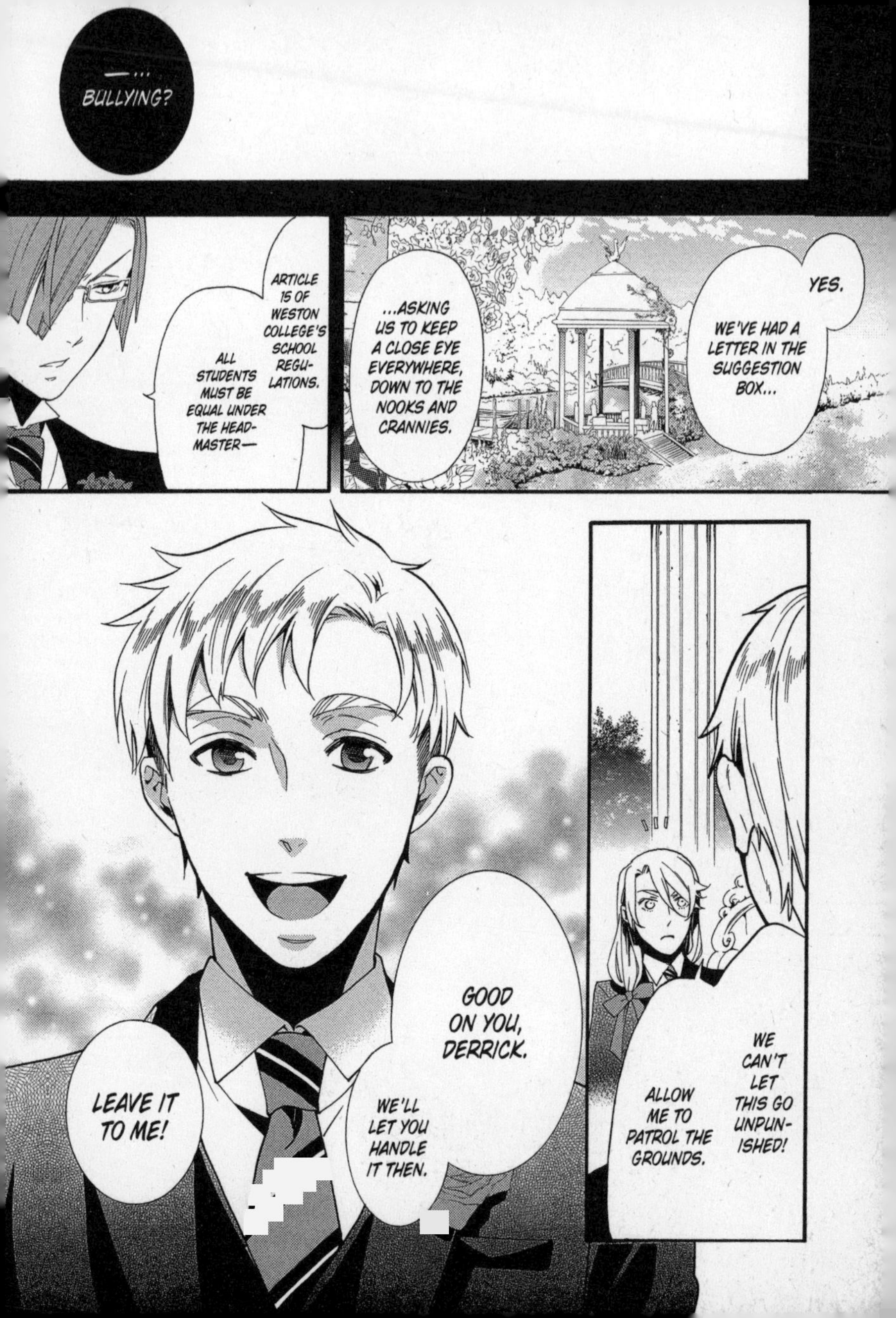
—... BULLYING?
YES.
WE'VE HAD A LETTER IN THE SUGGESTION BOX...
...ASKING US TO KEEP A CLOSE EYE EVERYWHERE, DOWN TO THE NOOKS AND CRANNIES.
ARTICLE 15 OF WESTON COLLEGE'S SCHOOL REGULATIONS.
ALL STUDENTS MUST BE EQUAL UNDER THE HEADMASTER—
WE CAN'T LET THIS GO UNPUNISHED!
ALLOW ME TO PATROL THE GROUNDS.
GOOD ON YOU, DERRICK.
WE'LL LET YOU HANDLE IT THEN.
LEAVE IT TO ME!

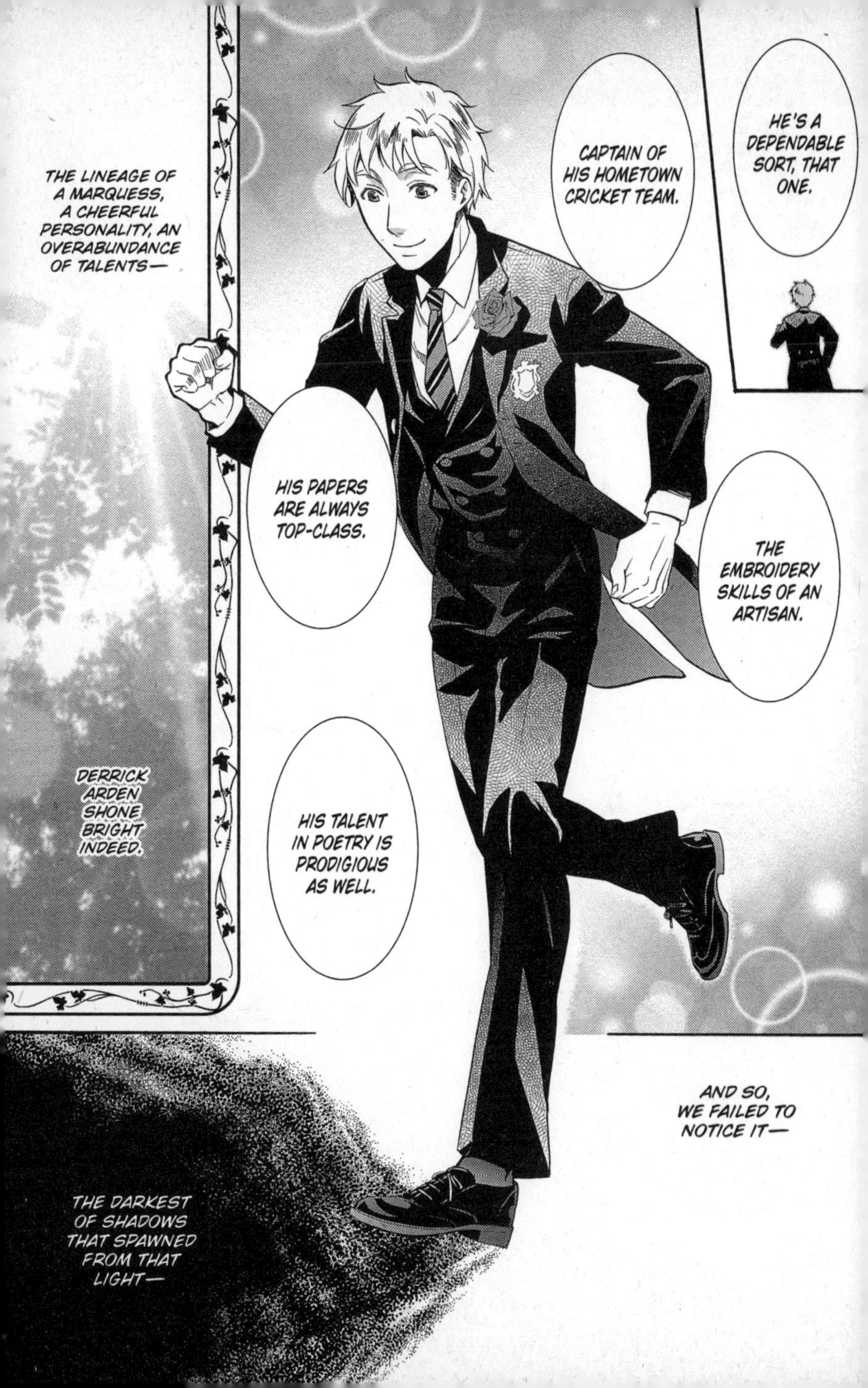
HE'S A DEPENDABLE SORT, THAT ONE.
CAPTAIN OF HIS HOMETOWN CRICKET TEAM.
THE LINEAGE OF A MARQUESS, A CHEERFUL PERSONALITY, AN OVERABUNDANCE OF TALENTS—
THE EMBROIDERY SKILLS OF AN ARTISAN.
HIS PAPERS ARE ALWAYS TOP-CLASS.
HIS TALENT IN POETRY IS PRODIGIOUS AS WELL.
DERRICK ARDEN SHONE BRIGHT INDEED.
AND SO, WE FAILED TO NOTICE IT—
THE DARKEST OF SHADOWS THAT SPAWNED FROM THAT LIGHT—

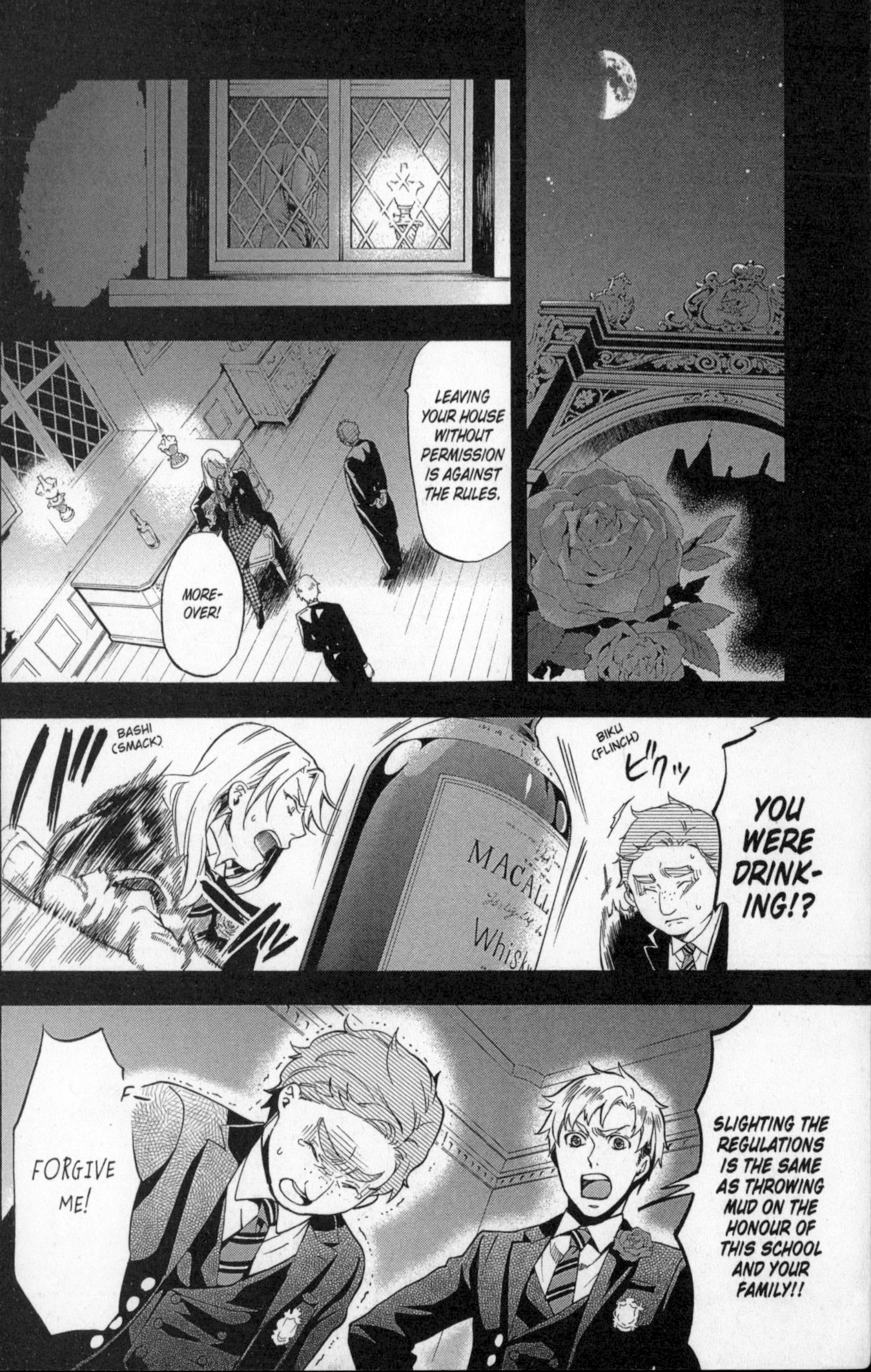
LEAVING YOUR HOUSE WITHOUT PERMISSION IS AGAINST THE RULES.
MORE-OVER!
BIKU (FLINCH)
ビクッ
YOU WERE DRINK-ING!?
BASHI (SMACK)
MACALL
Whisk
SLIGHTING THE REGULATIONS IS THE SAME AS THROWING MUD ON THE HONOUR OF THIS SCHOOL AND YOUR FAMILY!!
F—
FORGIVE ME!

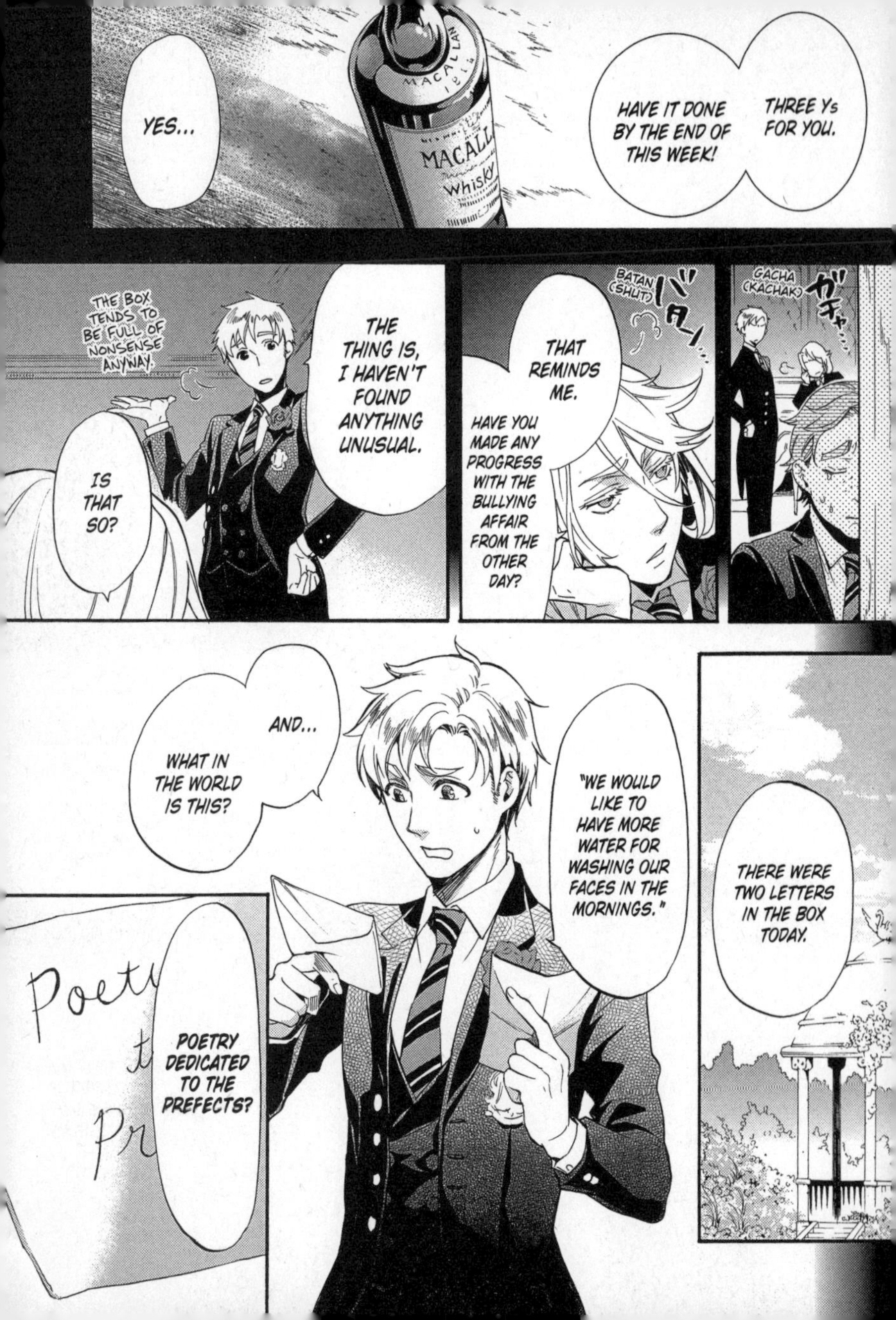
THREE Ys FOR YOU.
HAVE IT DONE BY THE END OF THIS WEEK!
YES...
GACHA (KACHAK)
BATAN (SHUT)
THAT REMINDS ME.
HAVE YOU MADE ANY PROGRESS WITH THE BULLYING AFFAIR FROM THE OTHER DAY?
THE THING IS, I HAVEN'T FOUND ANYTHING UNUSUAL.
THE BOX TENDS TO BE FULL OF NONSENSE ANYWAY.
IS THAT SO?
THERE WERE TWO LETTERS IN THE BOX TODAY.
"WE WOULD LIKE TO HAVE MORE WATER FOR WASHING OUR FACES IN THE MORNINGS."
AND...
WHAT IN THE WORLD IS THIS?
POETRY DEDICATED TO THE PREFECTS?

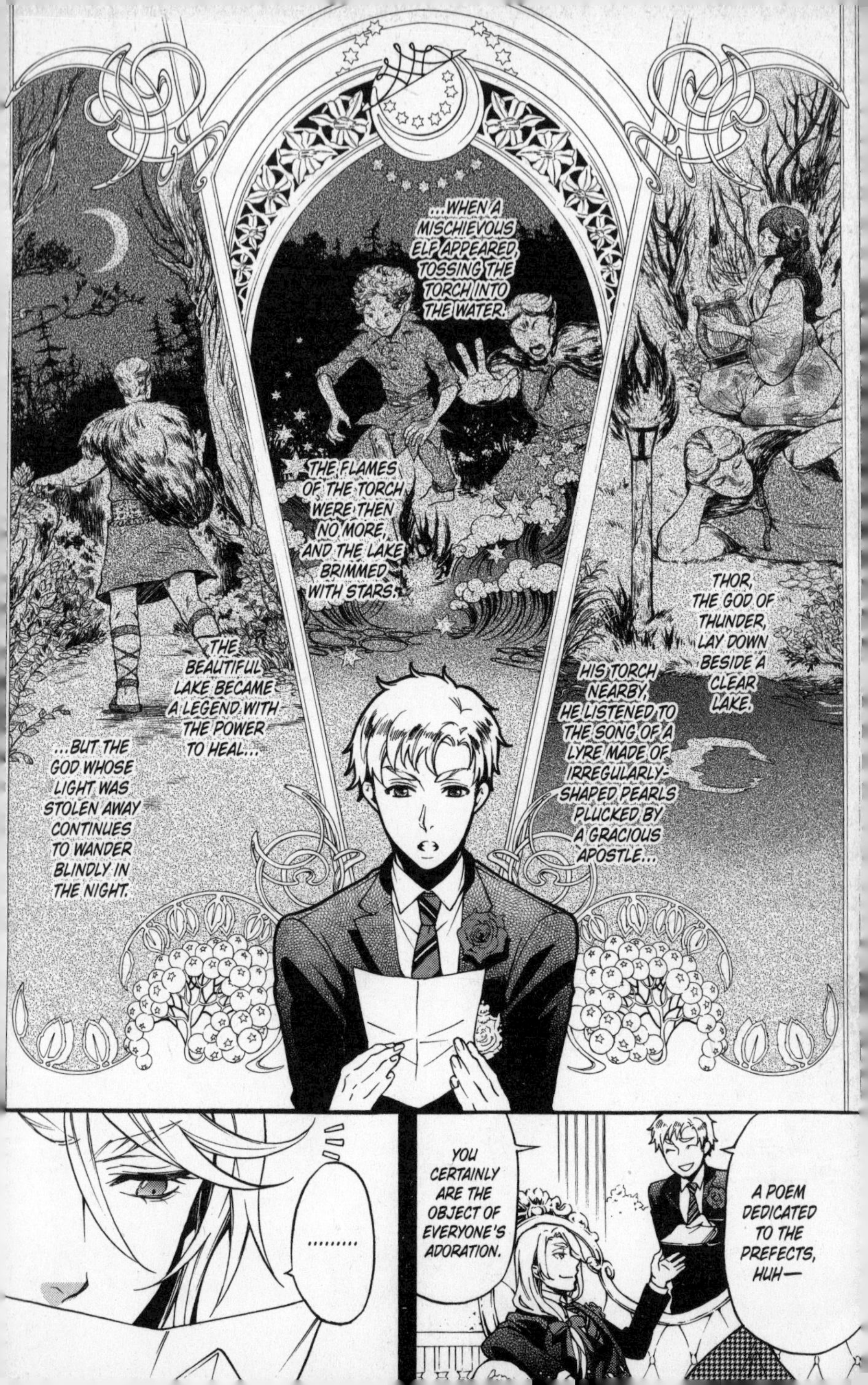
THOR, THE GOD OF THUNDER, LAY DOWN BESIDE A CLEAR LAKE.
HIS TORCH NEARBY, HE LISTENED TO THE SONG OF A LYRE MADE OF IRREGULARLY-SHAPED PEARLS PLUCKED BY A GRACIOUS APOSTLE...
...WHEN A MISCHIEVOUS ELF APPEARED, TOSSING THE TORCH INTO THE WATER.
THE FLAMES OF THE TORCH WERE THEN NO MORE, AND THE LAKE BRIMMED WITH STARS.
THE BEAUTIFUL LAKE BECAME A LEGEND WITH THE POWER TO HEAL...
...BUT THE GOD WHOSE LIGHT WAS STOLEN AWAY CONTINUES TO WANDER BLINDLY IN THE NIGHT.
A POEM DEDICATED TO THE PREFECTS, HUH—
YOU CERTAINLY ARE THE OBJECT OF EVERYONE'S ADORATION.
....

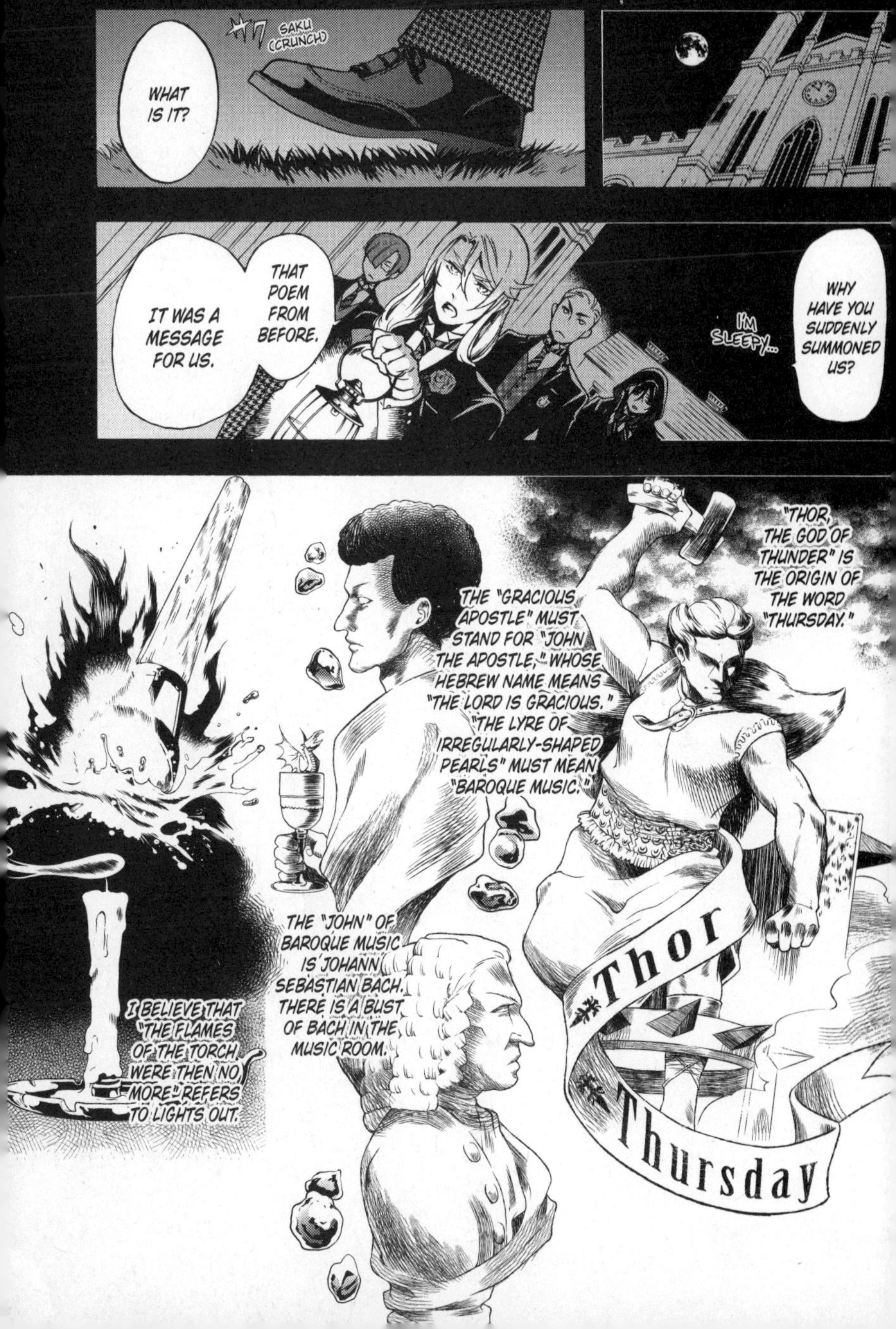
SAKU (CRUNCH)
WHAT IS IT?
WHY HAVE YOU SUDDENLY SUMMONED US?
I'M SLEEPY...
THAT POEM FROM BEFORE.
IT WAS A MESSAGE FOR US.
"THOR, THE GOD OF THUNDER" IS THE ORIGIN OF THE WORD "THURSDAY."
THE "GRACIOUS APOSTLE" MUST STAND FOR "JOHN THE APOSTLE," WHOSE HEBREW NAME MEANS "THE LORD IS GRACIOUS." "THE LYRE OF IRREGULARLY-SHAPED PEARLS" MUST MEAN "BAROQUE MUSIC."
THE "JOHN" OF BAROQUE MUSIC IS JOHANN SEBASTIAN BACH. THERE IS A BUST OF BACH IN THE MUSIC ROOM.
I BELIEVE THAT "THE FLAMES OF THE TORCH WERE THEN NO MORE" REFERS TO LIGHTS OUT.
Thor
Thursday

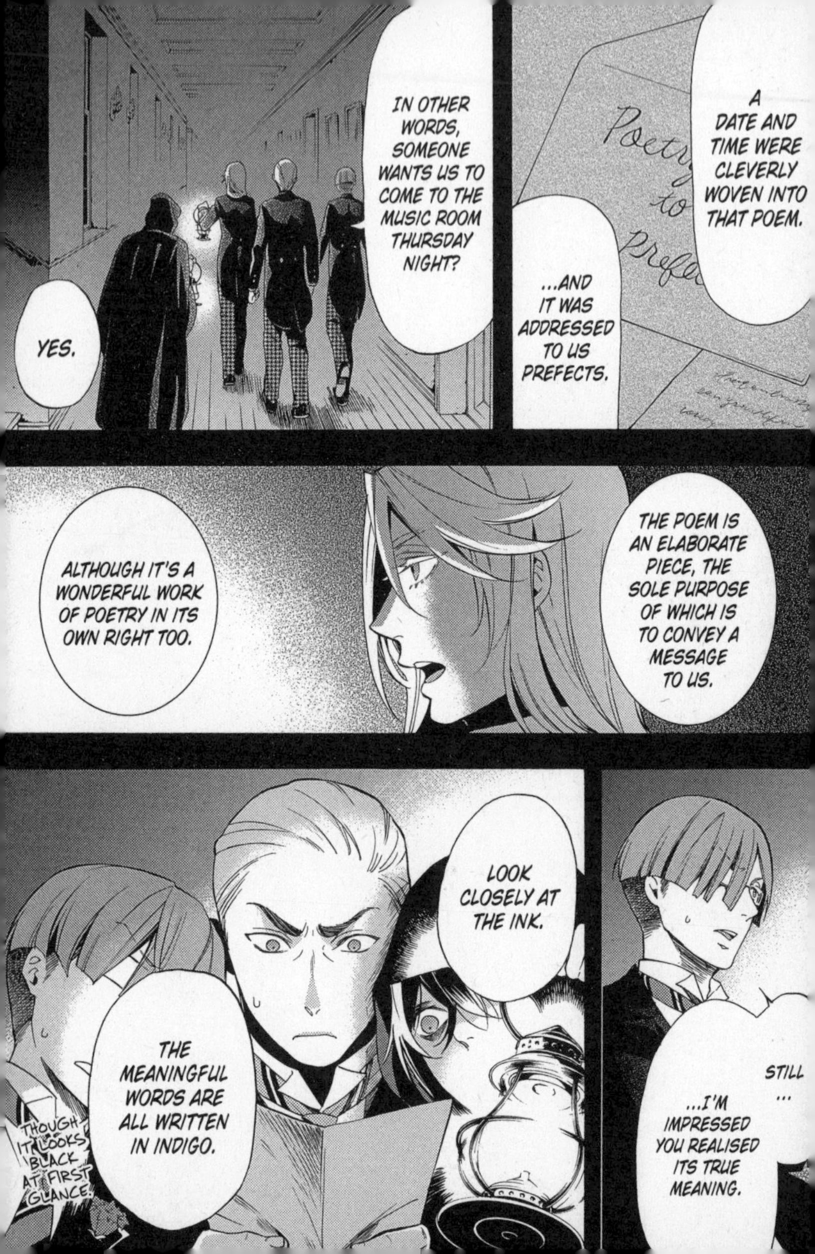
A DATE AND TIME WERE CLEVERLY WOVEN INTO THAT POEM.
...AND IT WAS ADDRESSED TO US PREFECTS.
IN OTHER WORDS, SOMEONE WANTS US TO COME TO THE MUSIC ROOM THURSDAY NIGHT?
YES.
THE POEM IS AN ELABORATE PIECE, THE SOLE PURPOSE OF WHICH IS TO CONVEY A MESSAGE TO US.
ALTHOUGH IT'S A WONDERFUL WORK OF POETRY IN ITS OWN RIGHT TOO.
STILL...
...I'M IMPRESSED YOU REALISED ITS TRUE MEANING.
LOOK CLOSELY AT THE INK.
THE MEANINGFUL WORDS ARE ALL WRITTEN IN INDIGO.
THOUGH IT LOOKS BLACK AT FIRST GLANCE.

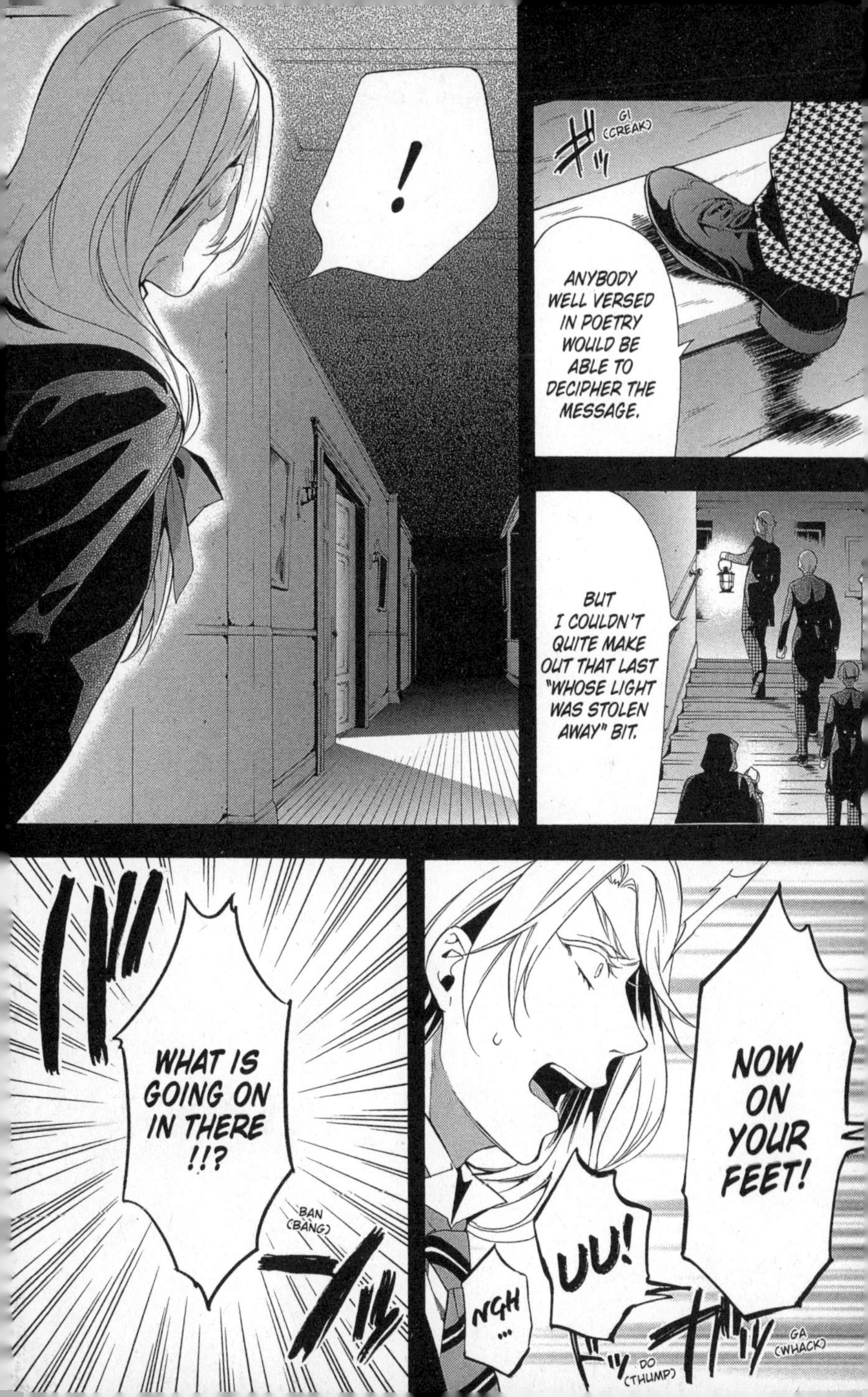
GI (CREAK)
ANYBODY WELL VERSED IN POETRY WOULD BE ABLE TO DECIPHER THE MESSAGE.
BUT I COULDN'T QUITE MAKE OUT THAT LAST "WHOSE LIGHT WAS STOLEN AWAY" BIT.
!
NOW ON YOUR FEET!
GA (WHACK)
UU!
DO (THUMP)
NGH ...
WHAT IS GOING ON IN THERE !!?
BAN (BANG)

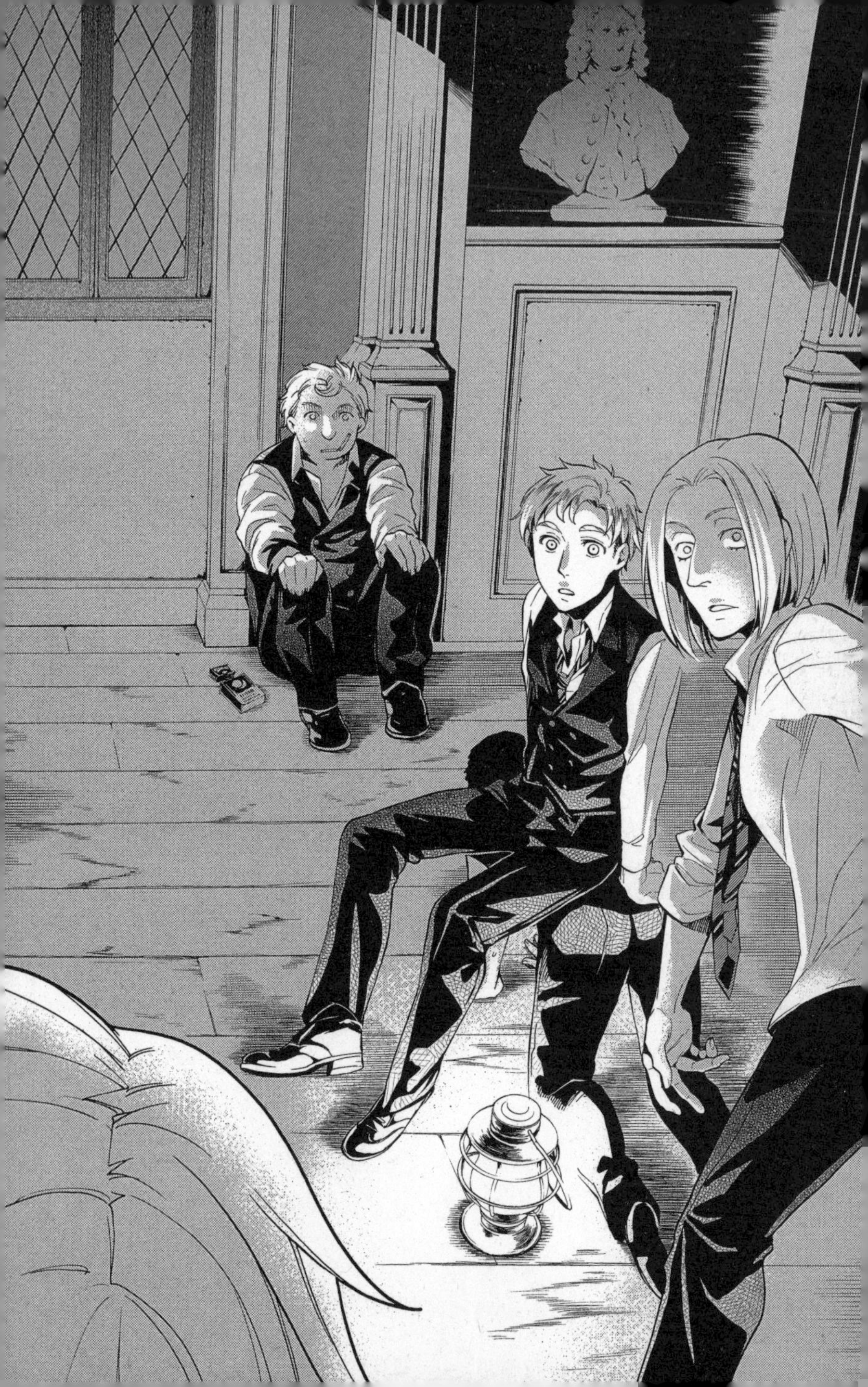

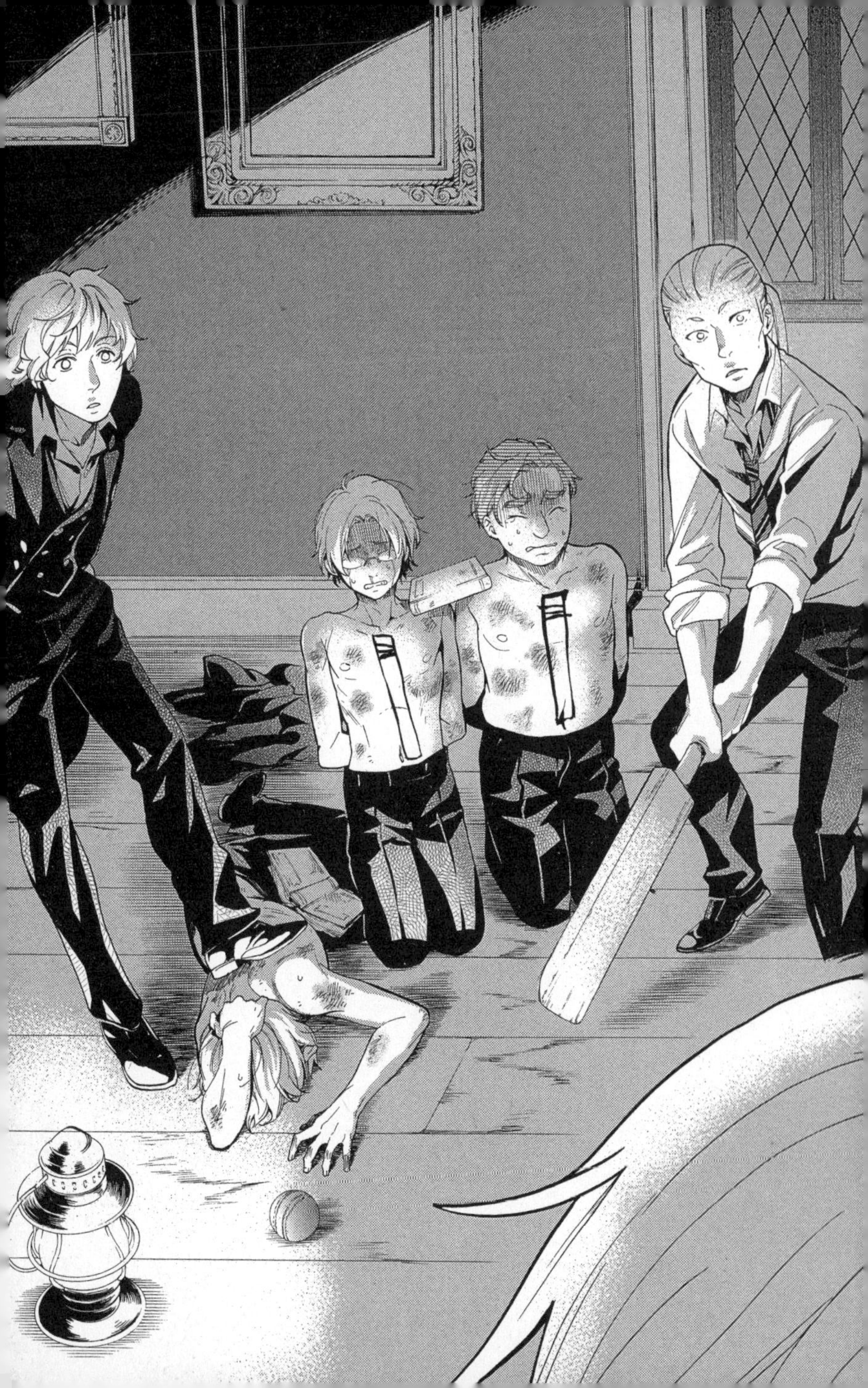

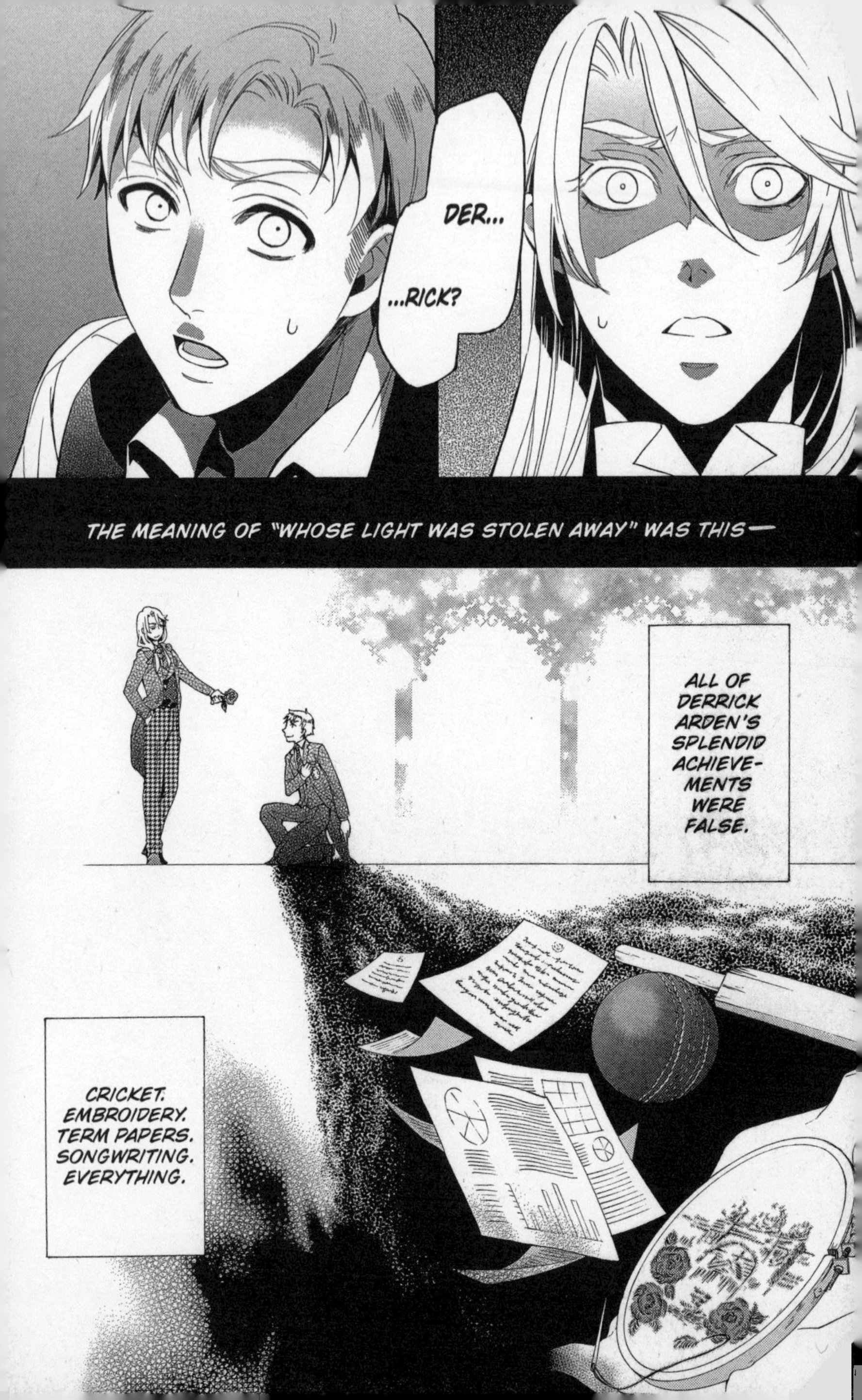
DER...
...RICK?
THE MEANING OF "WHOSE LIGHT WAS STOLEN AWAY" WAS THIS—
ALL OF DERRICK ARDEN'S SPLENDID ACHIEVEMENTS WERE FALSE.
CRICKET. EMBROIDERY. TERM PAPERS. SONGWRITING. EVERYTHING.

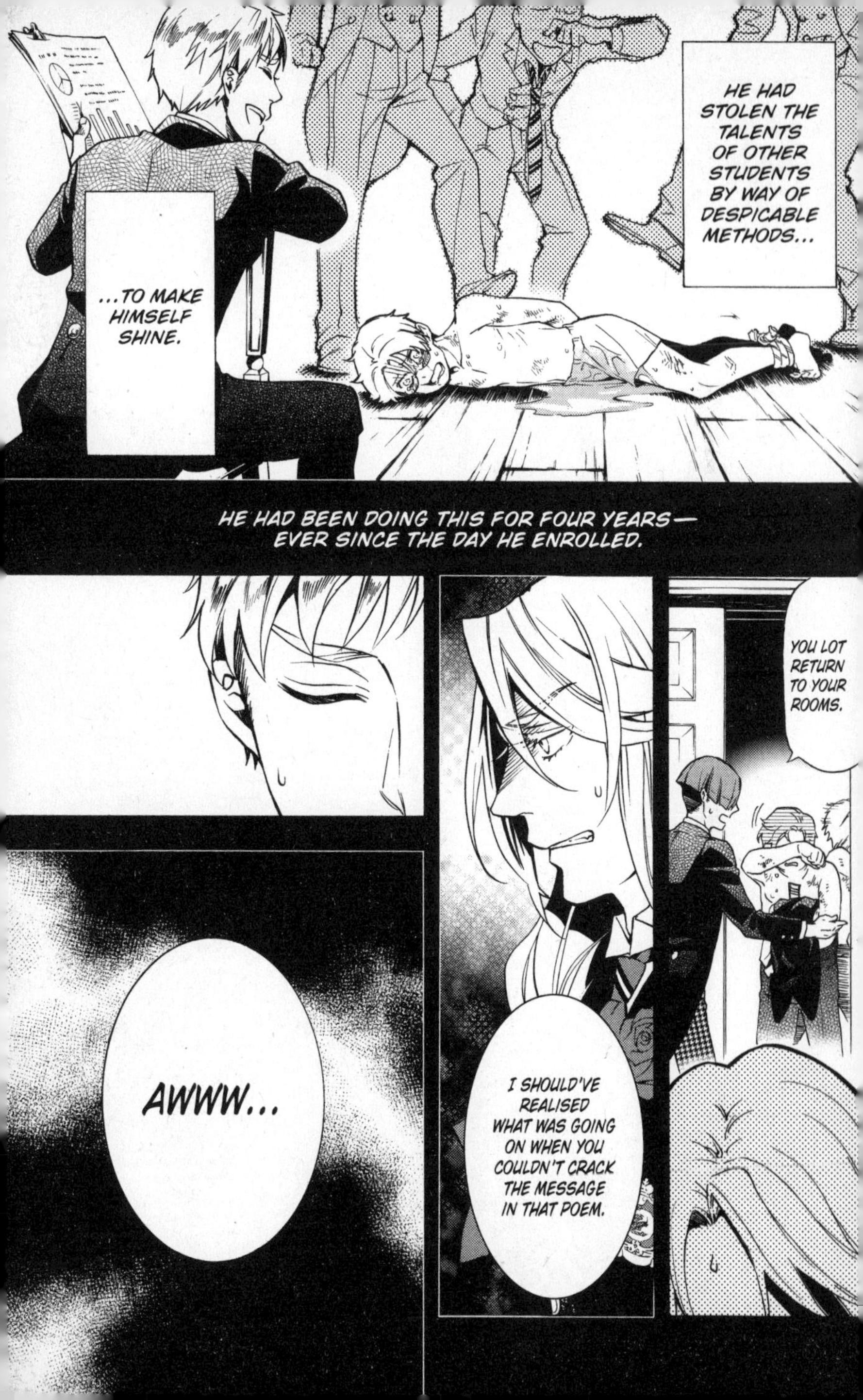
HE HAD STOLEN THE TALENTS OF OTHER STUDENTS BY WAY OF DESPICABLE METHODS...
...TO MAKE HIMSELF SHINE.
HE HAD BEEN DOING THIS FOR FOUR YEARS— EVER SINCE THE DAY HE ENROLLED.
YOU LOT RETURN TO YOUR ROOMS.
I SHOULD'VE REALISED WHAT WAS GOING ON WHEN YOU COULDN'T CRACK THE MESSAGE IN THAT POEM.
AWWW...

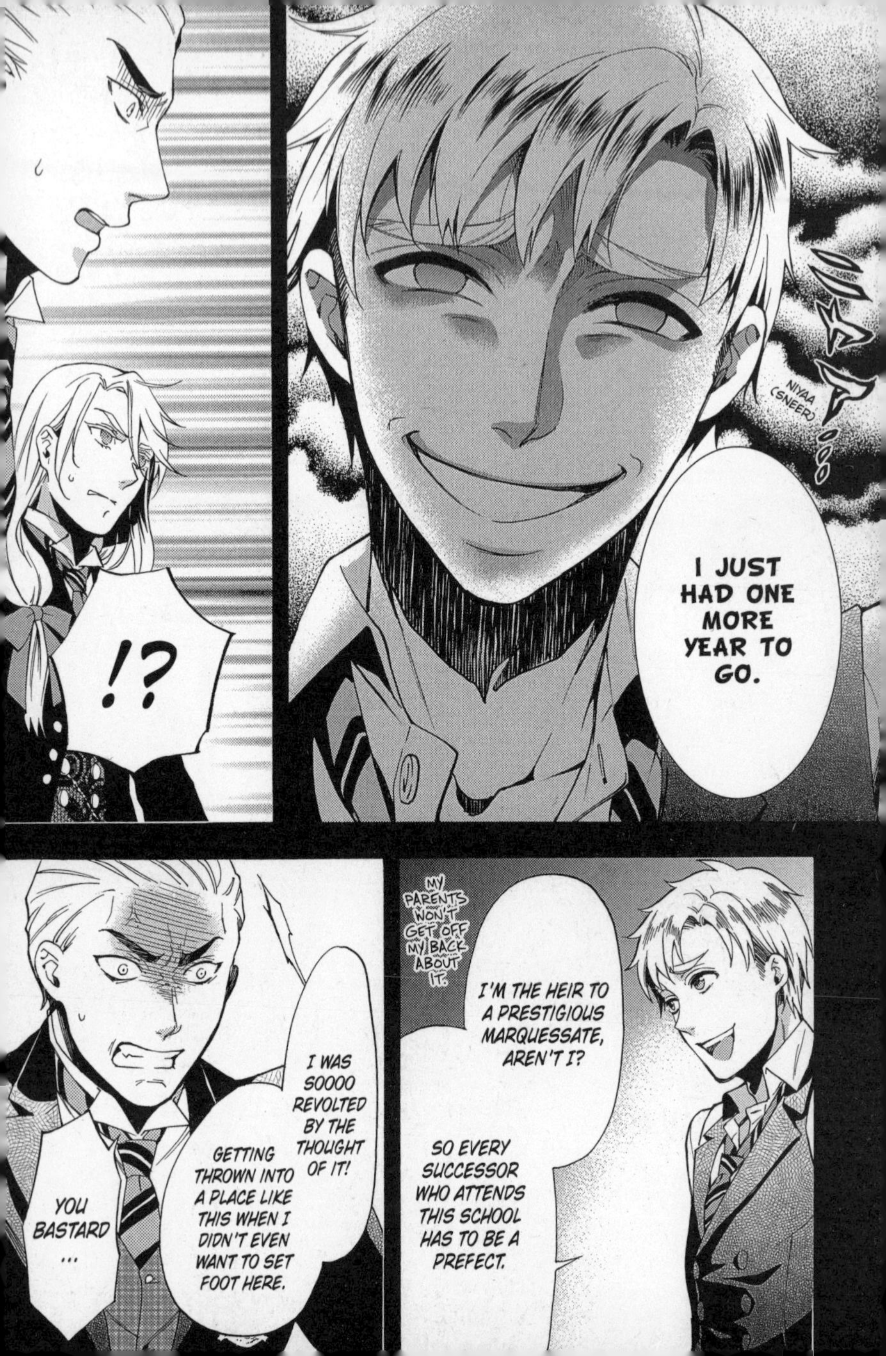
NIYAA (SNEER)
I JUST HAD ONE MORE YEAR TO GO.
!?
MY PARENTS WON'T GET OFF MY BACK ABOUT IT.
I'M THE HEIR TO A PRESTIGIOUS MARQUESSATE, AREN'T I?
SO EVERY SUCCESSOR WHO ATTENDS THIS SCHOOL HAS TO BE A PREFECT.
I WAS SOOOO REVOLTED BY THE THOUGHT OF IT!
GETTING THROWN INTO A PLACE LIKE THIS WHEN I DIDN'T EVEN WANT TO SET FOOT HERE.
YOU BASTARD ...

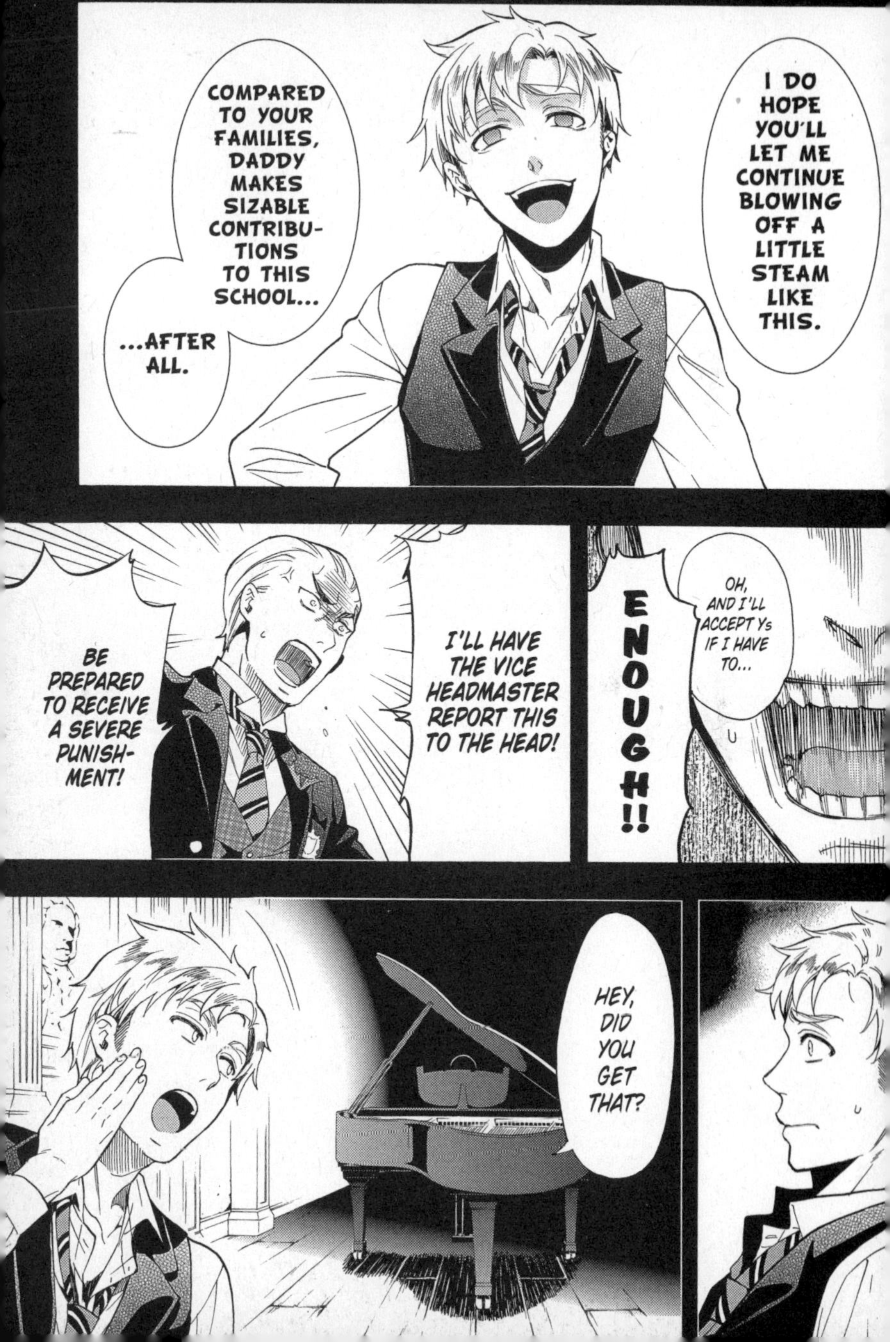

I DO HOPE YOU'LL LET ME CONTINUE BLOWING OFF A LITTLE STEAM LIKE THIS.
COMPARED TO YOUR FAMILIES, DADDY MAKES SIZABLE CONTRIBU-TIONS TO THIS SCHOOL...
...AFTER ALL.
OH, AND I'LL ACCEPT Ys IF I HAVE TO...
ENOUGH!!
I'LL HAVE THE VICE HEADMASTER REPORT THIS TO THE HEAD!
BE PREPARED TO RECEIVE A SEVERE PUNISH-MENT!
HEY, DID YOU GET THAT?

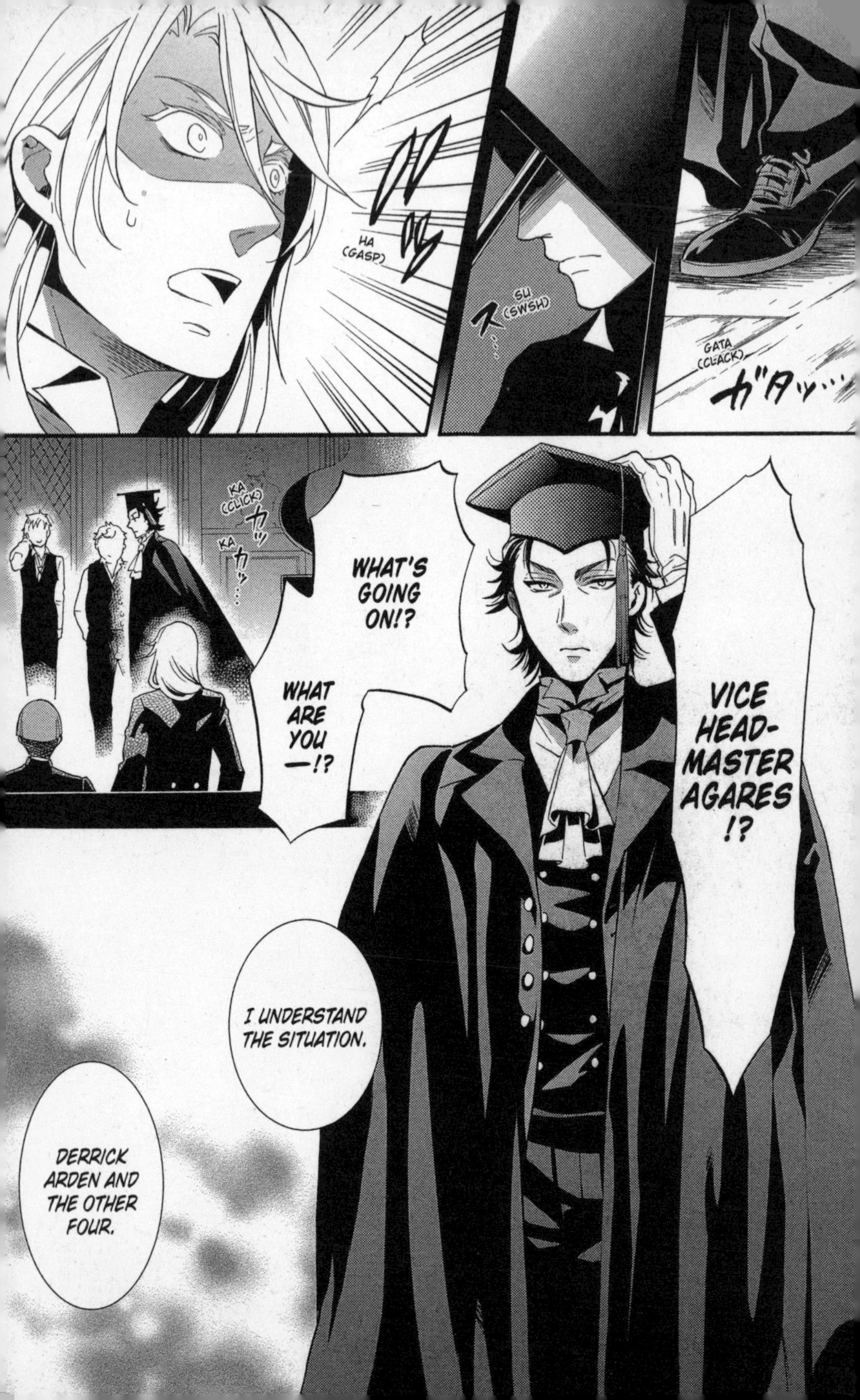
GATA (CLACK)
ガタッ…
SU (SWSH)
ス…
HA (GASP)
ハッ
VICE HEAD-MASTER AGARES!?
WHAT'S GOING ON!?
WHAT ARE YOU—!?
KA (CLICK)
カッ
KA
カッ…
I UNDERSTAND THE SITUATION.
DERRICK ARDEN AND THE OTHER FOUR.

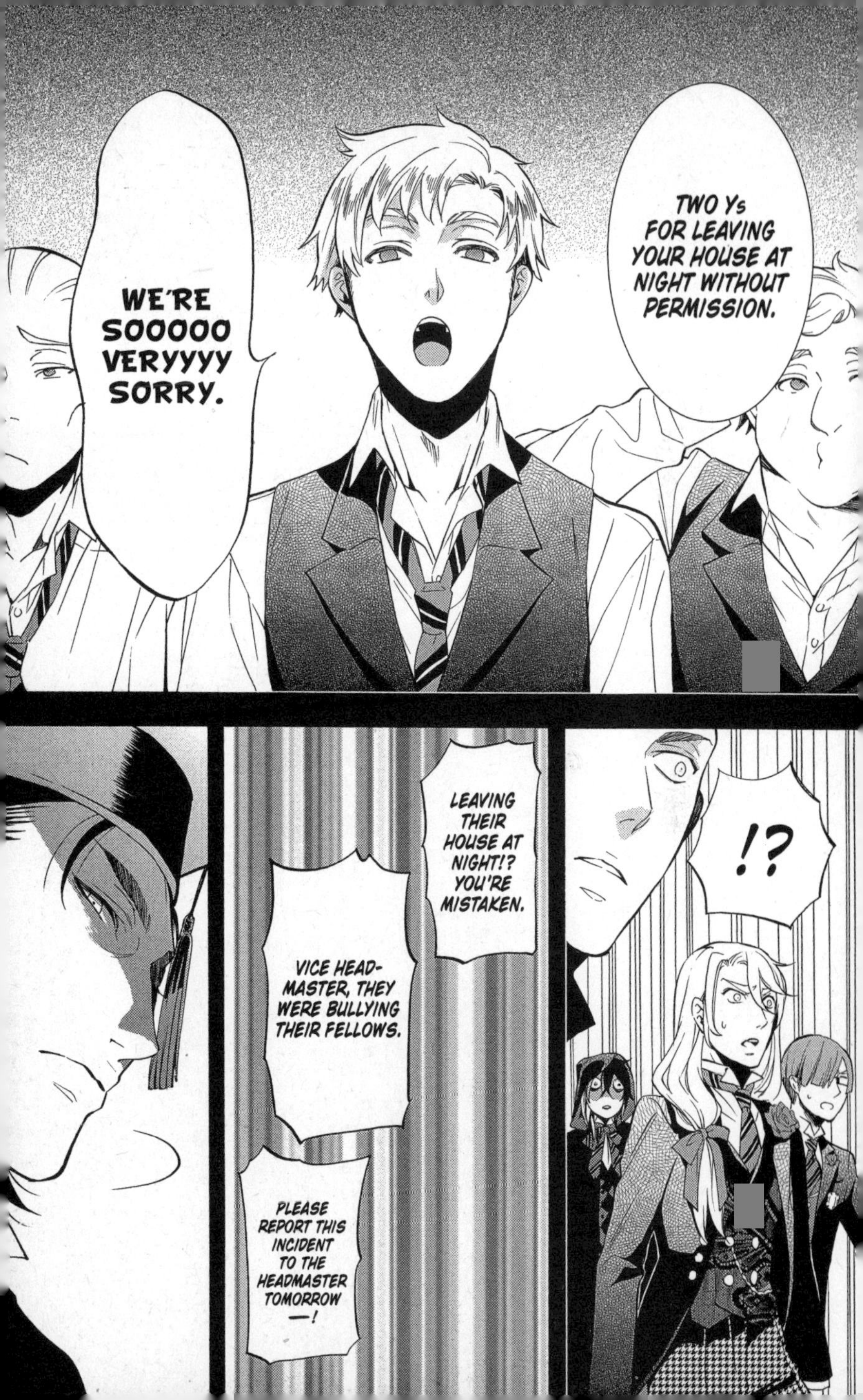
TWO Ys FOR LEAVING YOUR HOUSE AT NIGHT WITHOUT PERMISSION.
WE'RE SOOOOO VERYYYY SORRY.
!?
LEAVING THEIR HOUSE AT NIGHT!? YOU'RE MISTAKEN.
VICE HEAD-MASTER, THEY WERE BULLYING THEIR FELLOWS.
PLEASE REPORT THIS INCIDENT TO THE HEADMASTER TOMORROW —!

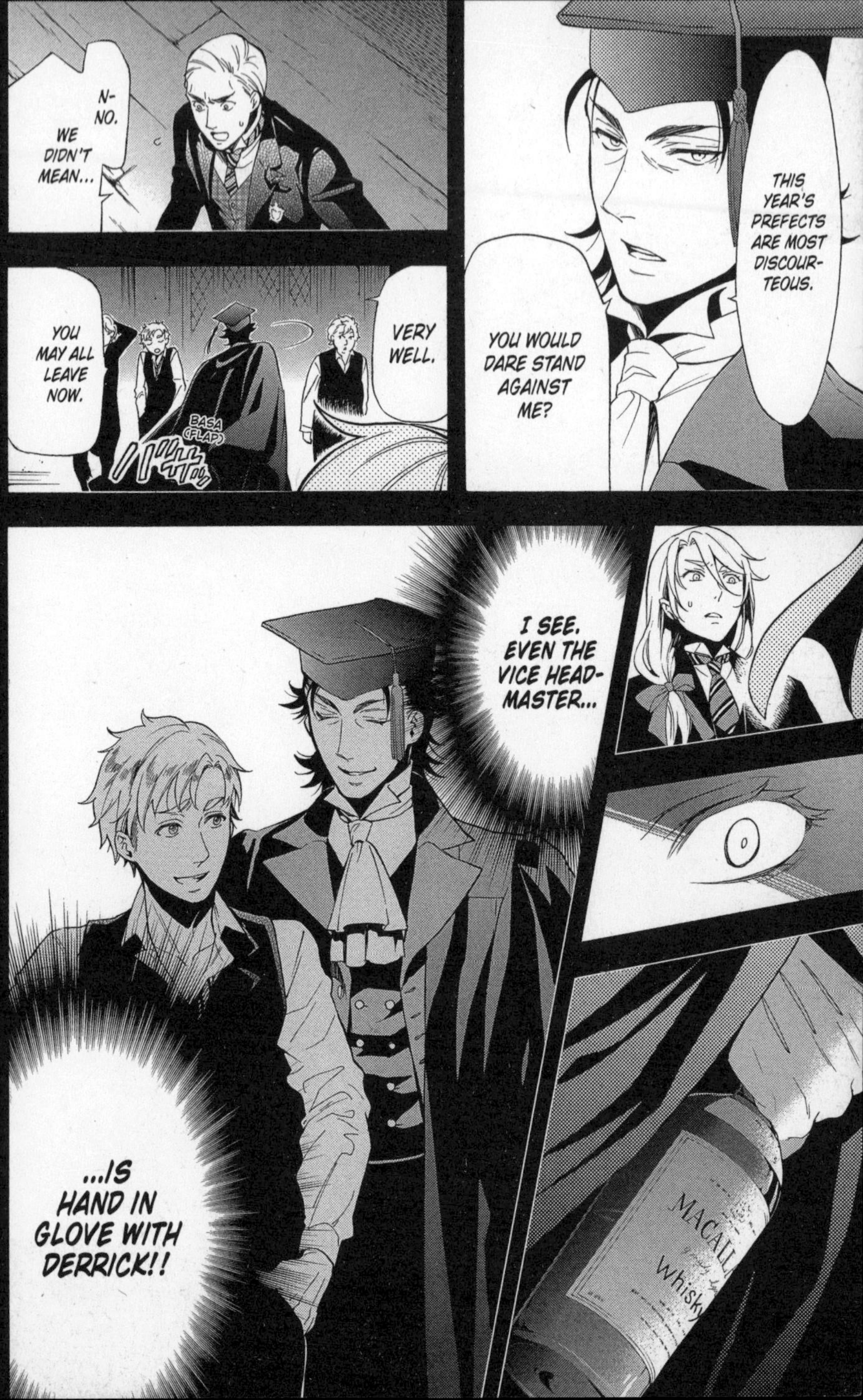
THIS YEAR'S PREFECTS ARE MOST DISCOURTEOUS.
YOU WOULD DARE STAND AGAINST ME?
N-NO. WE DIDN'T MEAN...
VERY WELL.
YOU MAY ALL LEAVE NOW.
BASA (FLAP)
I SEE. EVEN THE VICE HEAD-MASTER...
...IS HAND IN GLOVE WITH DERRICK!!
MACALL
Whisky

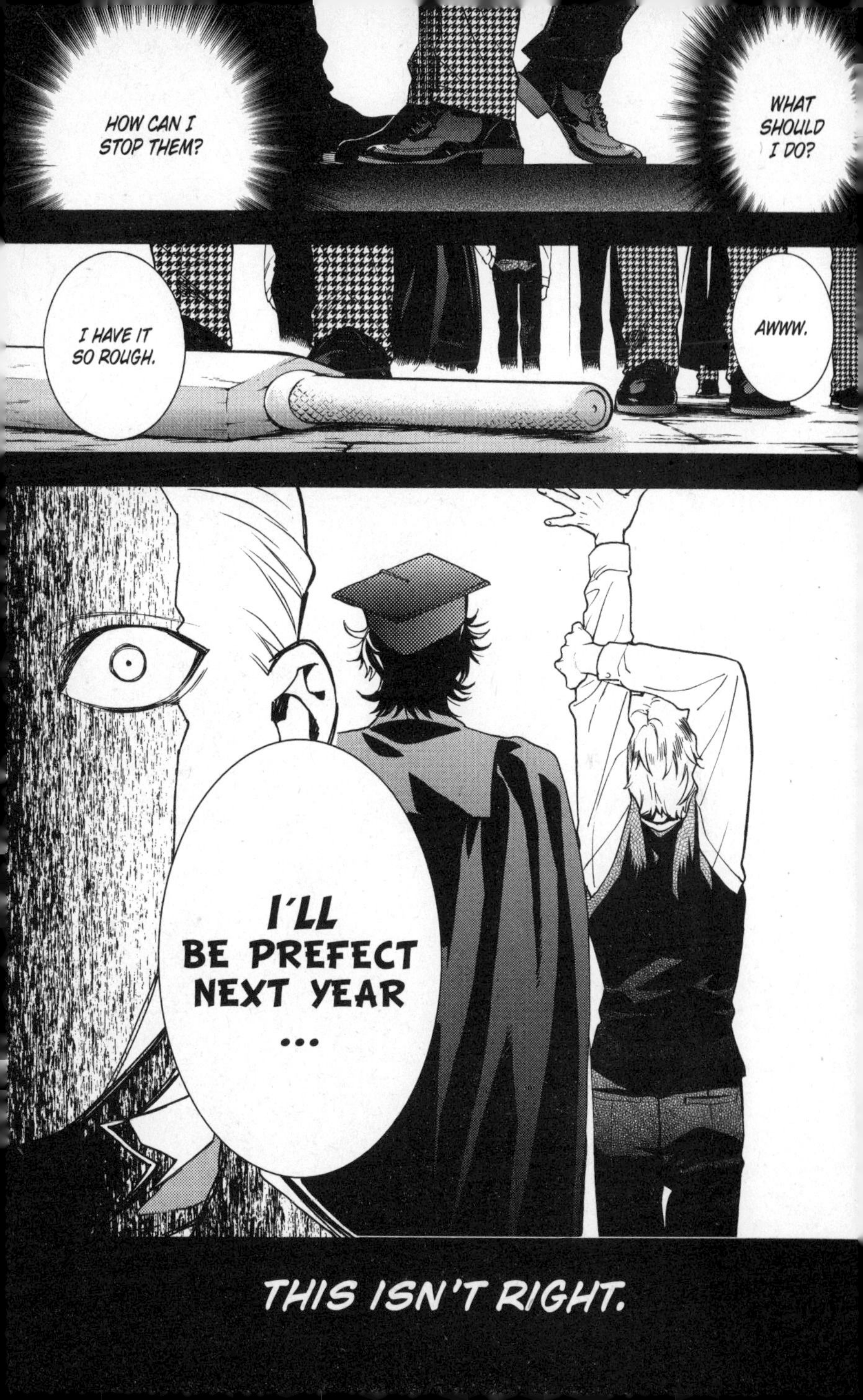
WHAT SHOULD I DO?
HOW CAN I STOP THEM?
AWWW.
I HAVE IT SO ROUGH.
I'LL BE PREFECT NEXT YEAR ...
THIS ISN'T RIGHT.

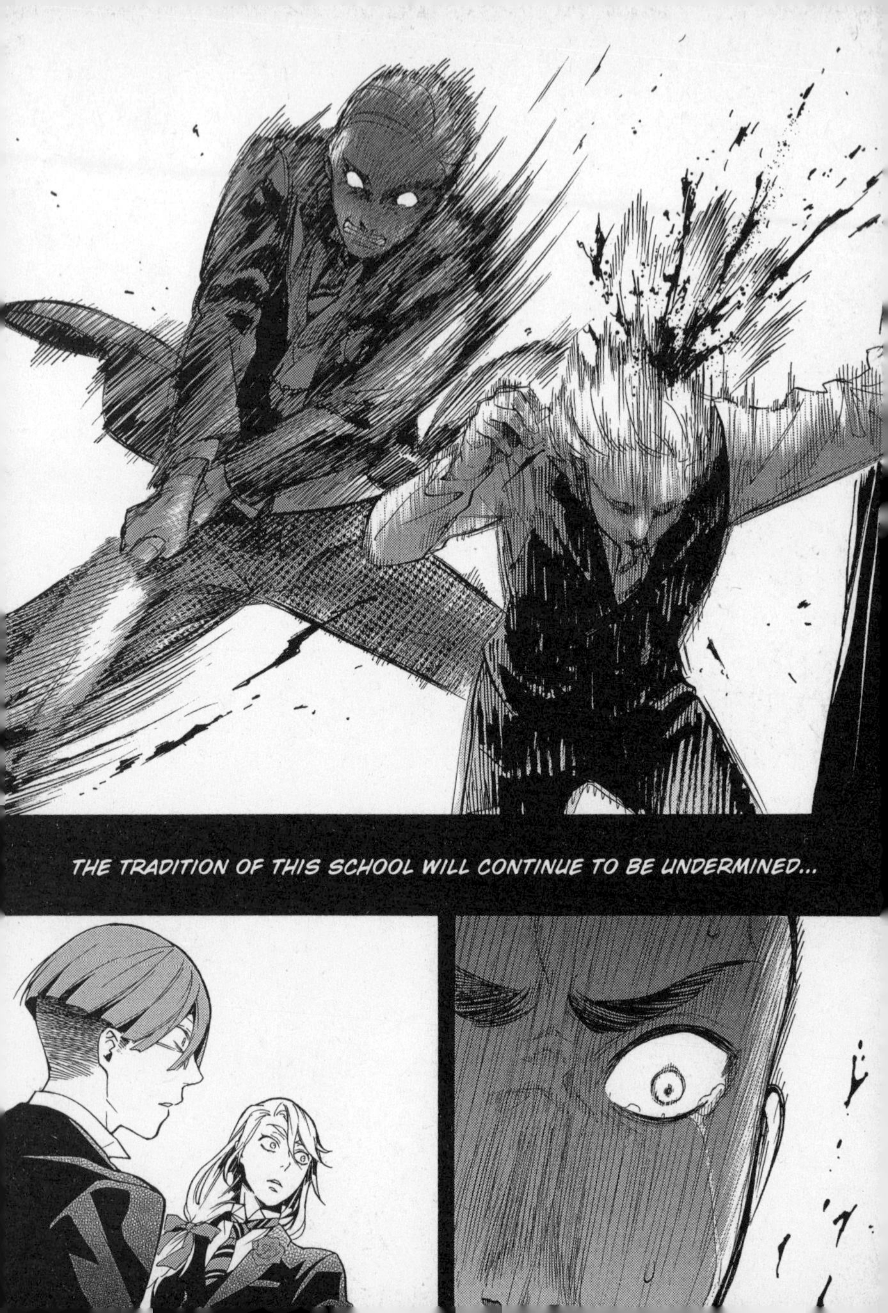
THE TRADITION OF THIS SCHOOL WILL CONTINUE TO BE UNDERMINED...

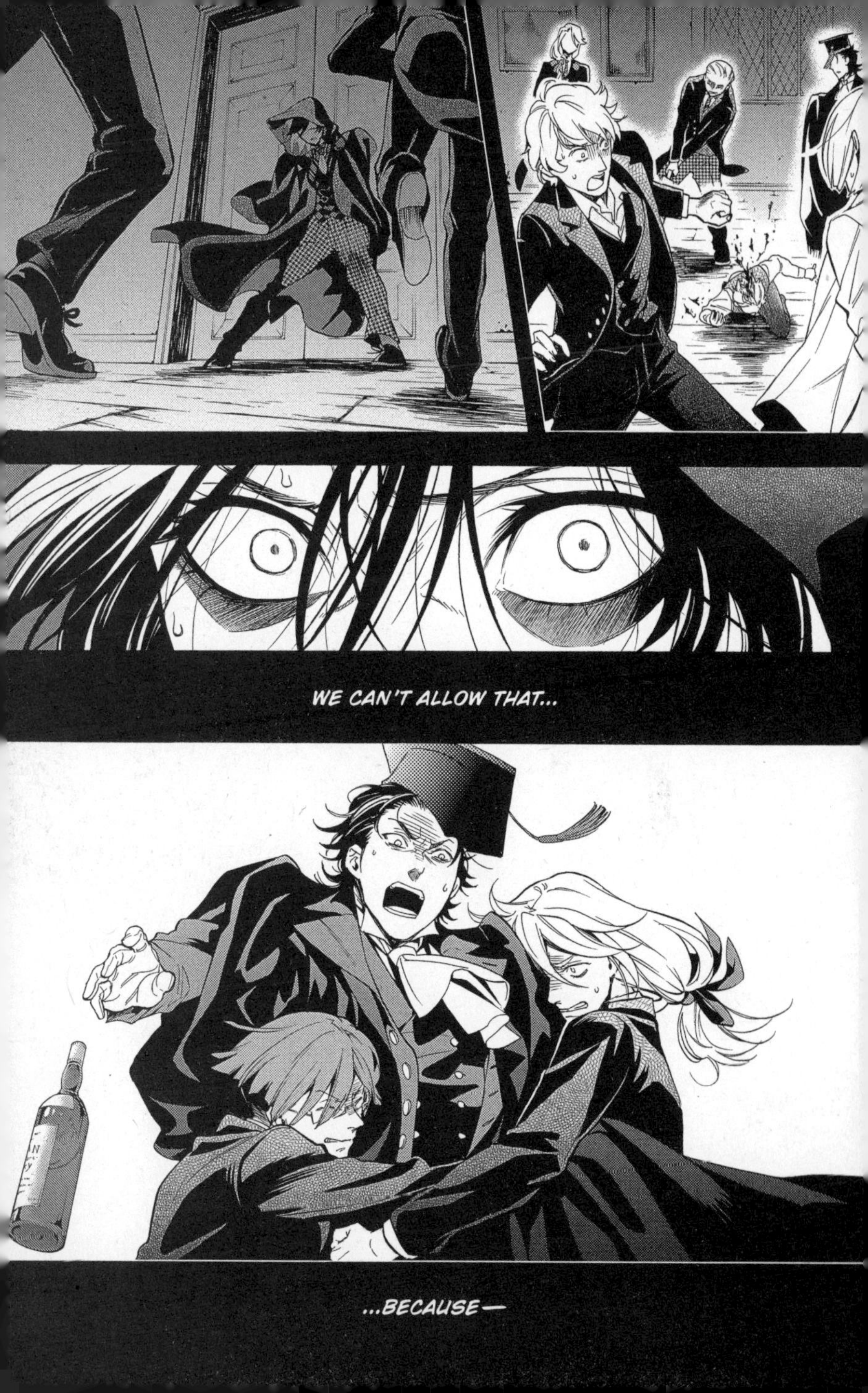
WE CAN'T ALLOW THAT...
...BECAUSE—

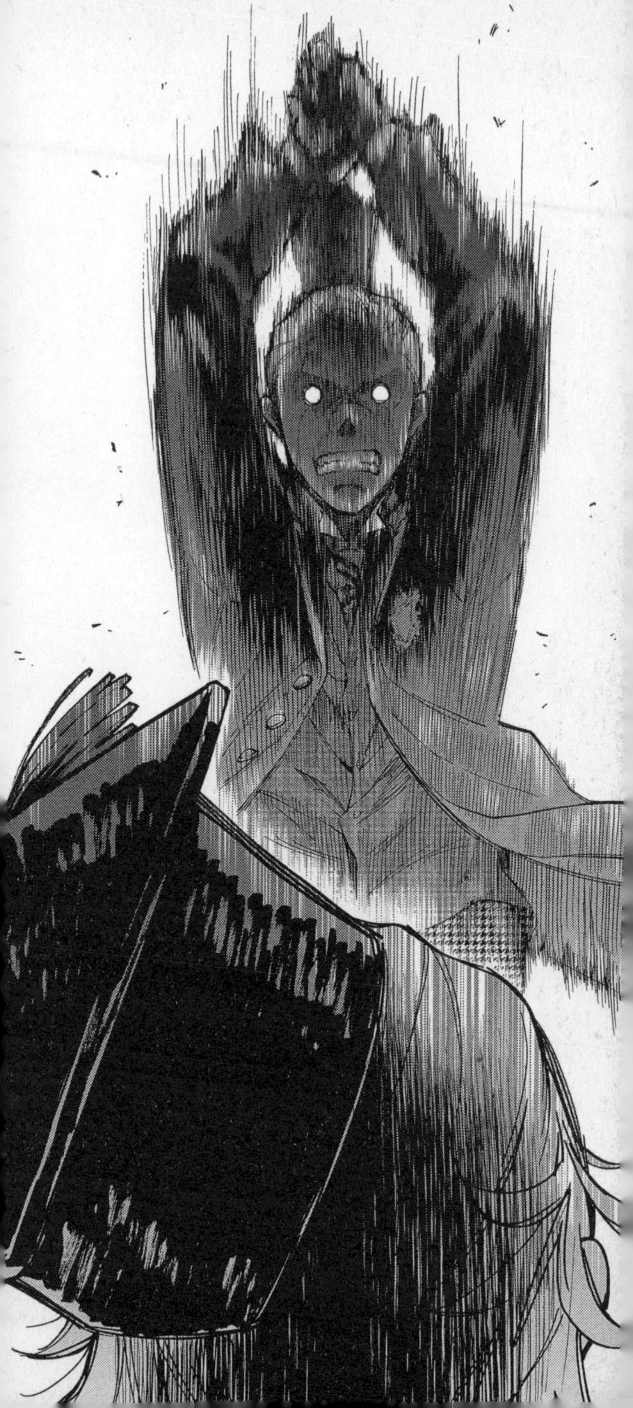

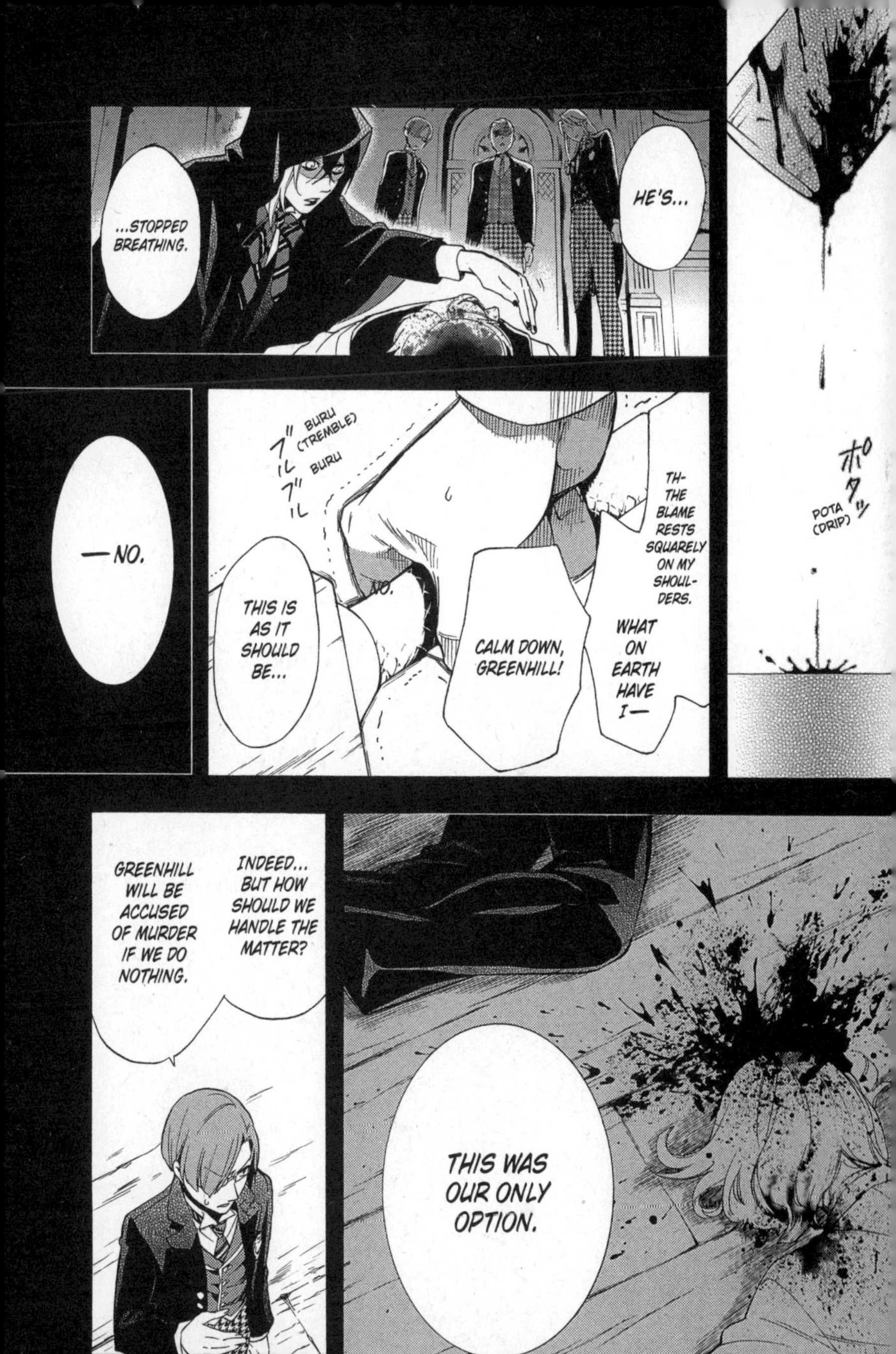
ポタッ
POTA (DRIP)
HE'S...
...STOPPED BREATHING.
TH-THE BLAME RESTS SQUARELY ON MY SHOULDERS.
WHAT ON EARTH HAVE I—
CALM DOWN, GREENHILL!
ブル BURU (TREMBLE)
ブル BURU
NO.
THIS IS AS IT SHOULD BE...
—NO.
THIS WAS OUR ONLY OPTION.
INDEED... BUT HOW SHOULD WE HANDLE THE MATTER?
GREENHILL WILL BE ACCUSED OF MURDER IF WE DO NOTHING.

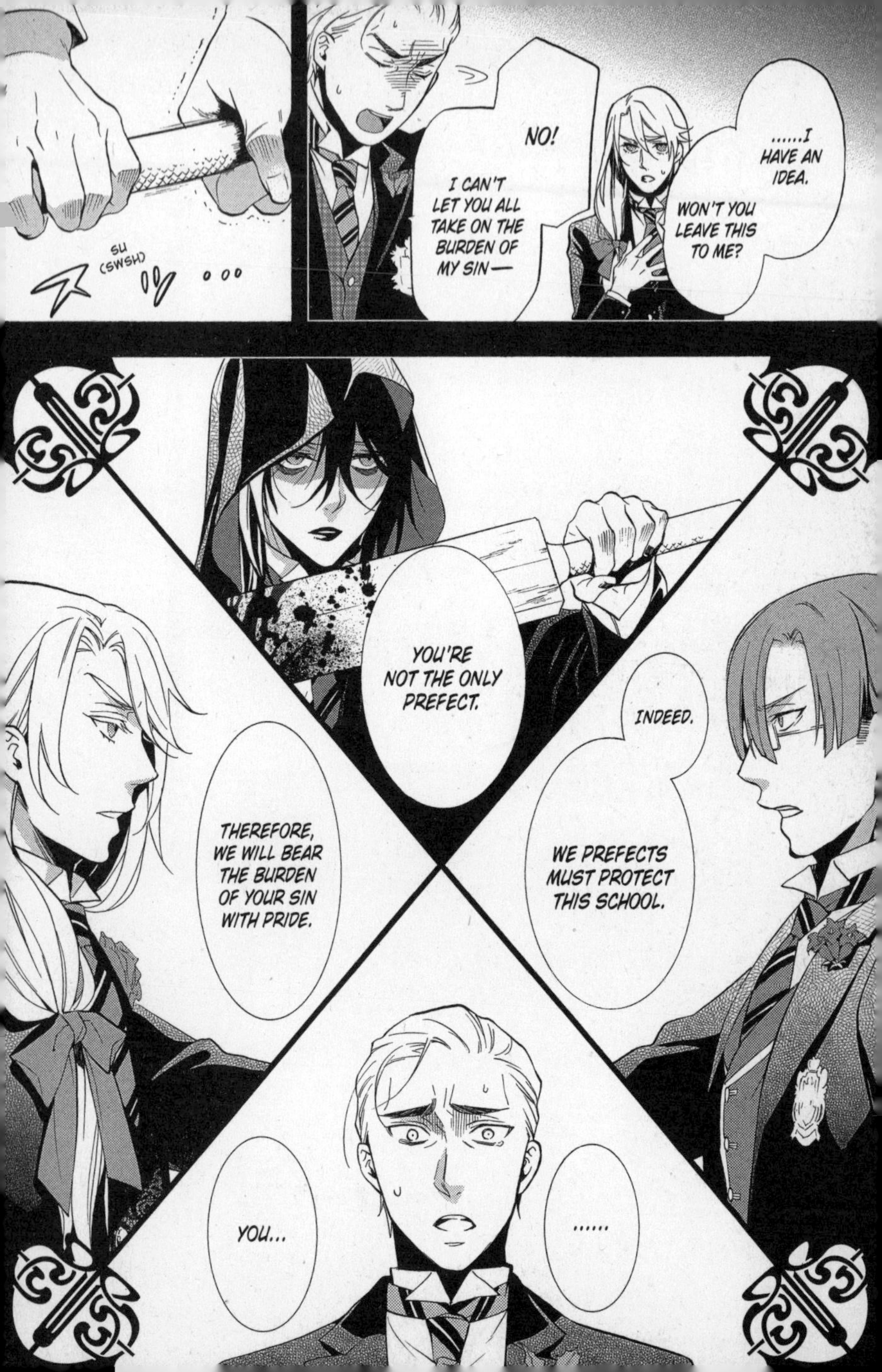
......I HAVE AN IDEA.
WON'T YOU LEAVE THIS TO ME?
NO!
I CAN'T LET YOU ALL TAKE ON THE BURDEN OF MY SIN—
SU (SWSH)
YOU'RE NOT THE ONLY PREFECT.
INDEED.
WE PREFECTS MUST PROTECT THIS SCHOOL.
THEREFORE, WE WILL BEAR THE BURDEN OF YOUR SIN WITH PRIDE.
......
YOU...

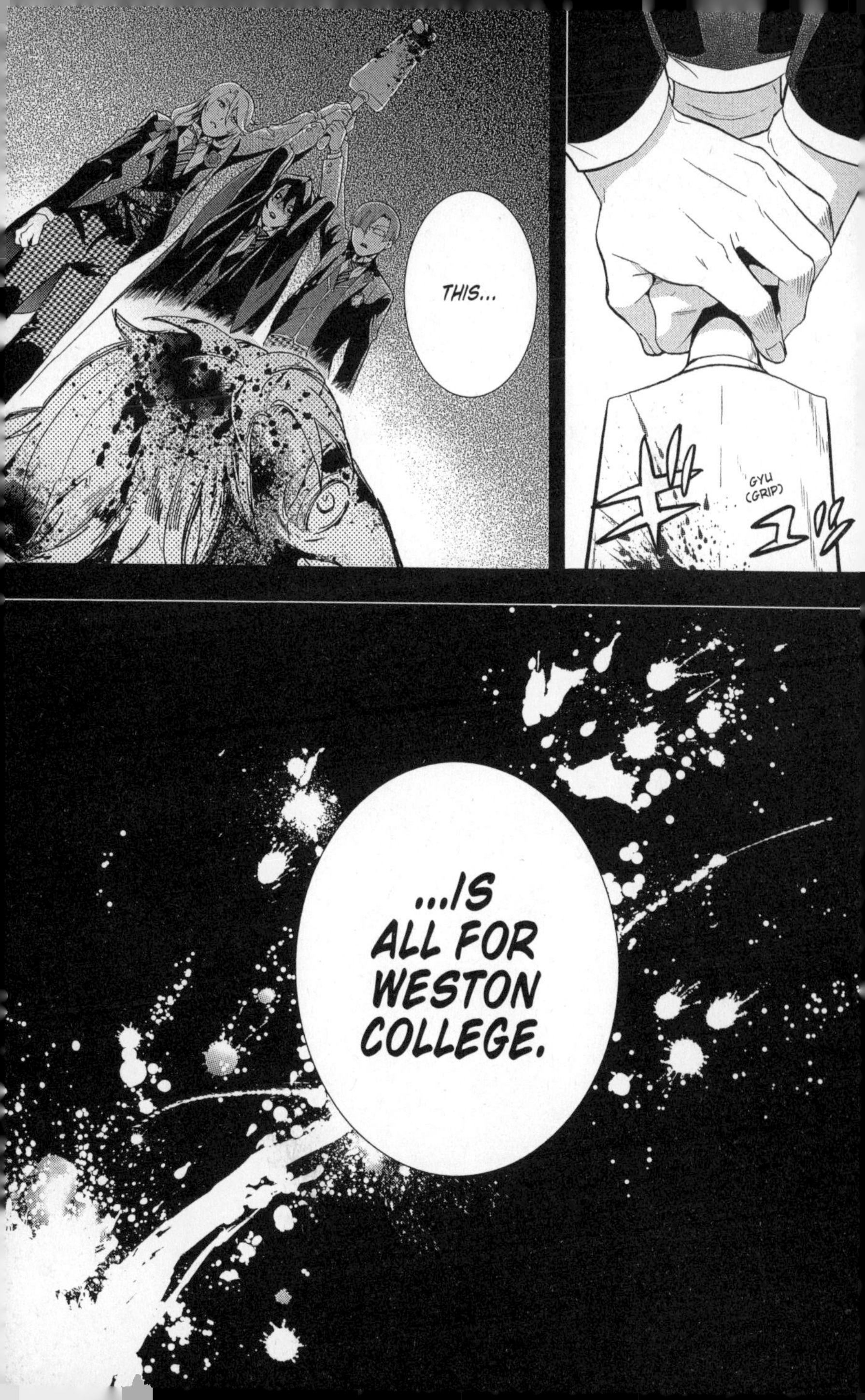
GYU
(GRIP)
THIS...
...IS ALL FOR WESTON COLLEGE.

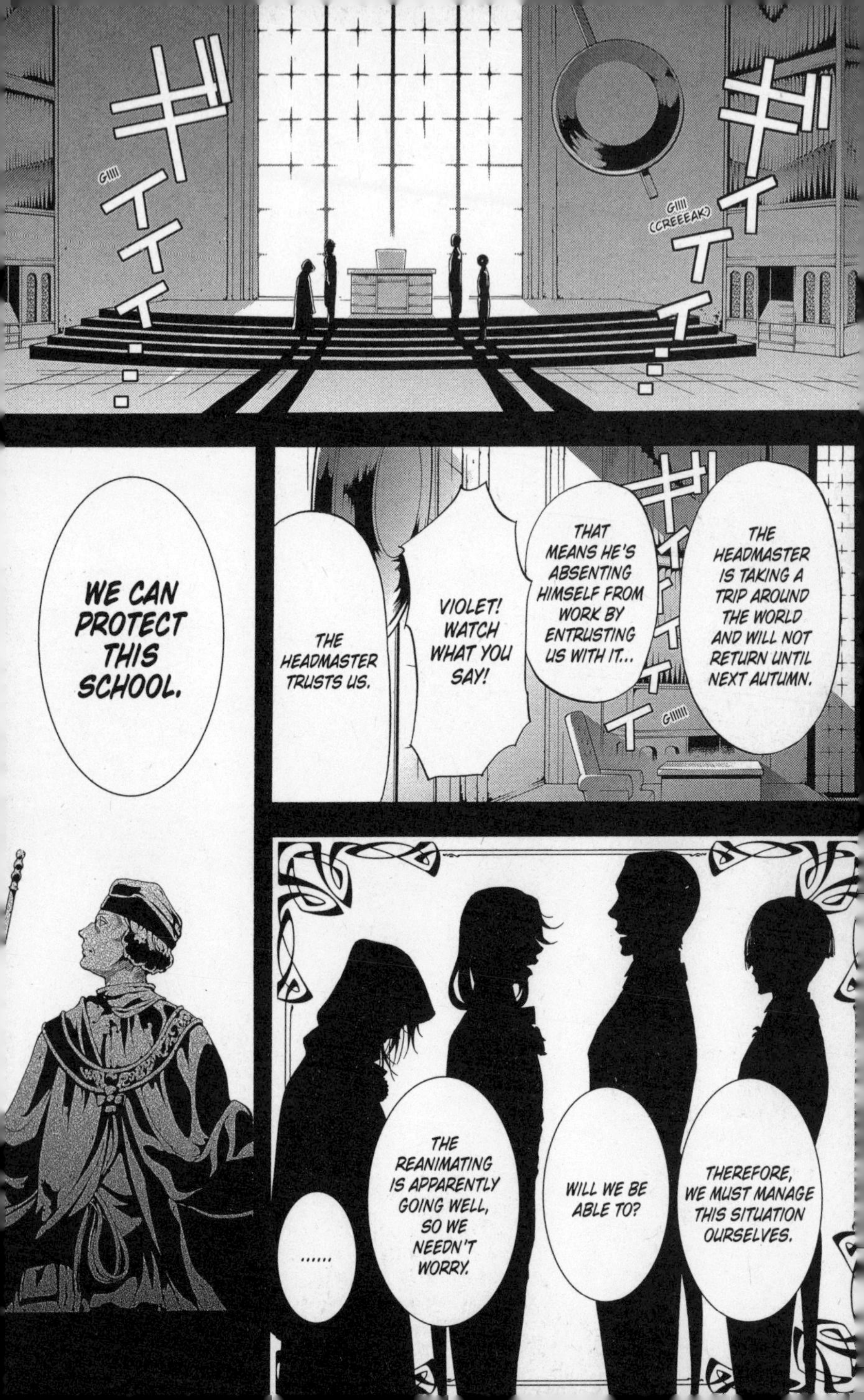
GIIII (CREEEAK)
GIIII
THE HEADMASTER IS TAKING A TRIP AROUND THE WORLD AND WILL NOT RETURN UNTIL NEXT AUTUMN.
GIIIII
THAT MEANS HE'S ABSENTING HIMSELF FROM WORK BY ENTRUSTING US WITH IT...
VIOLET! WATCH WHAT YOU SAY!
THE HEADMASTER TRUSTS US.
THEREFORE, WE MUST MANAGE THIS SITUATION OURSELVES.
WILL WE BE ABLE TO?
THE REANIMATING IS APPARENTLY GOING WELL, SO WE NEEDN'T WORRY.
......
WE CAN PROTECT THIS SCHOOL.

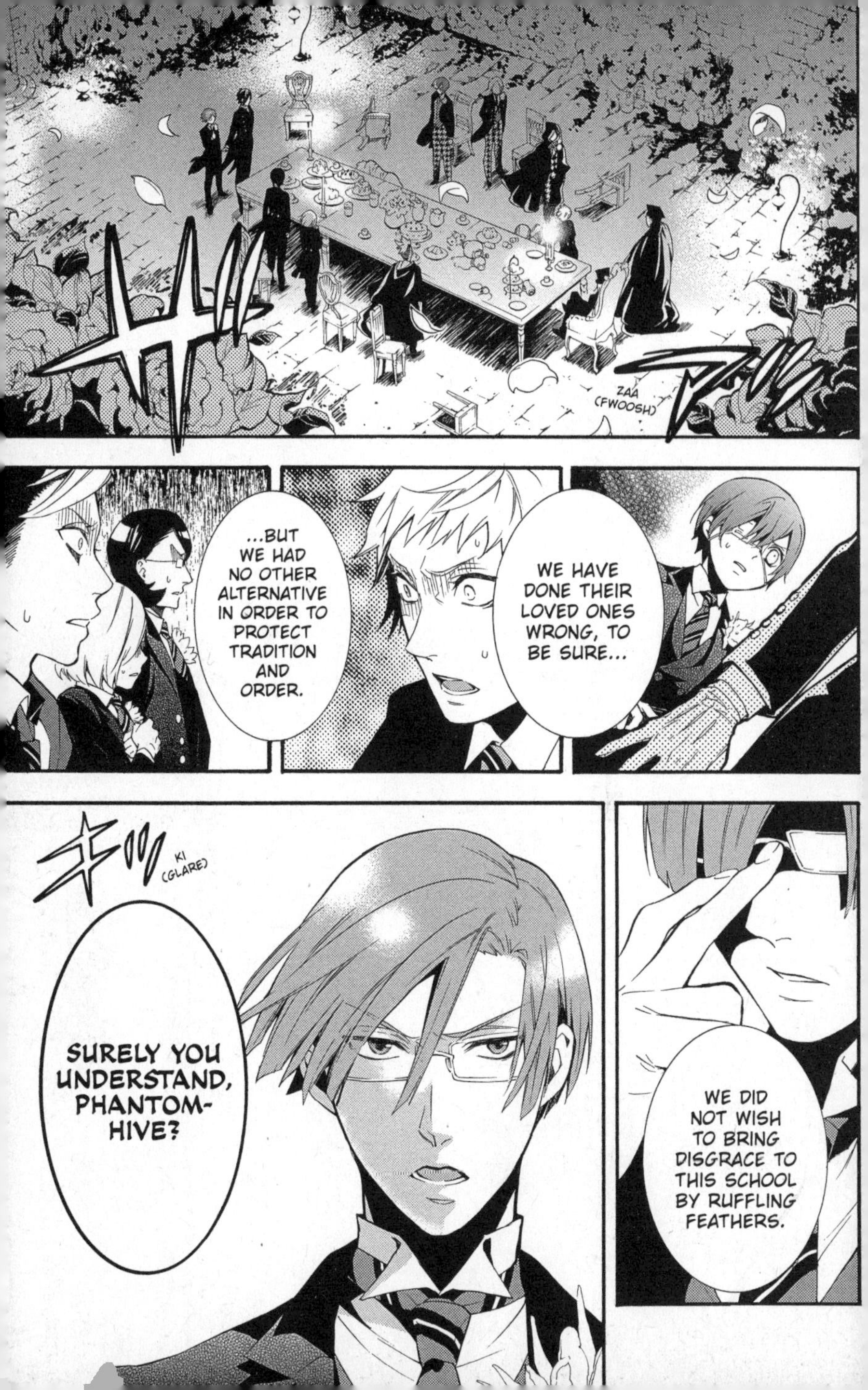
ZAA (FWOOSH)
WE HAVE DONE THEIR LOVED ONES WRONG, TO BE SURE...
...BUT WE HAD NO OTHER ALTERNATIVE IN ORDER TO PROTECT TRADITION AND ORDER.
WE DID NOT WISH TO BRING DISGRACE TO THIS SCHOOL BY RUFFLING FEATHERS.
KI (GLARE)
SURELY YOU UNDERSTAND, PHANTOM-HIVE?

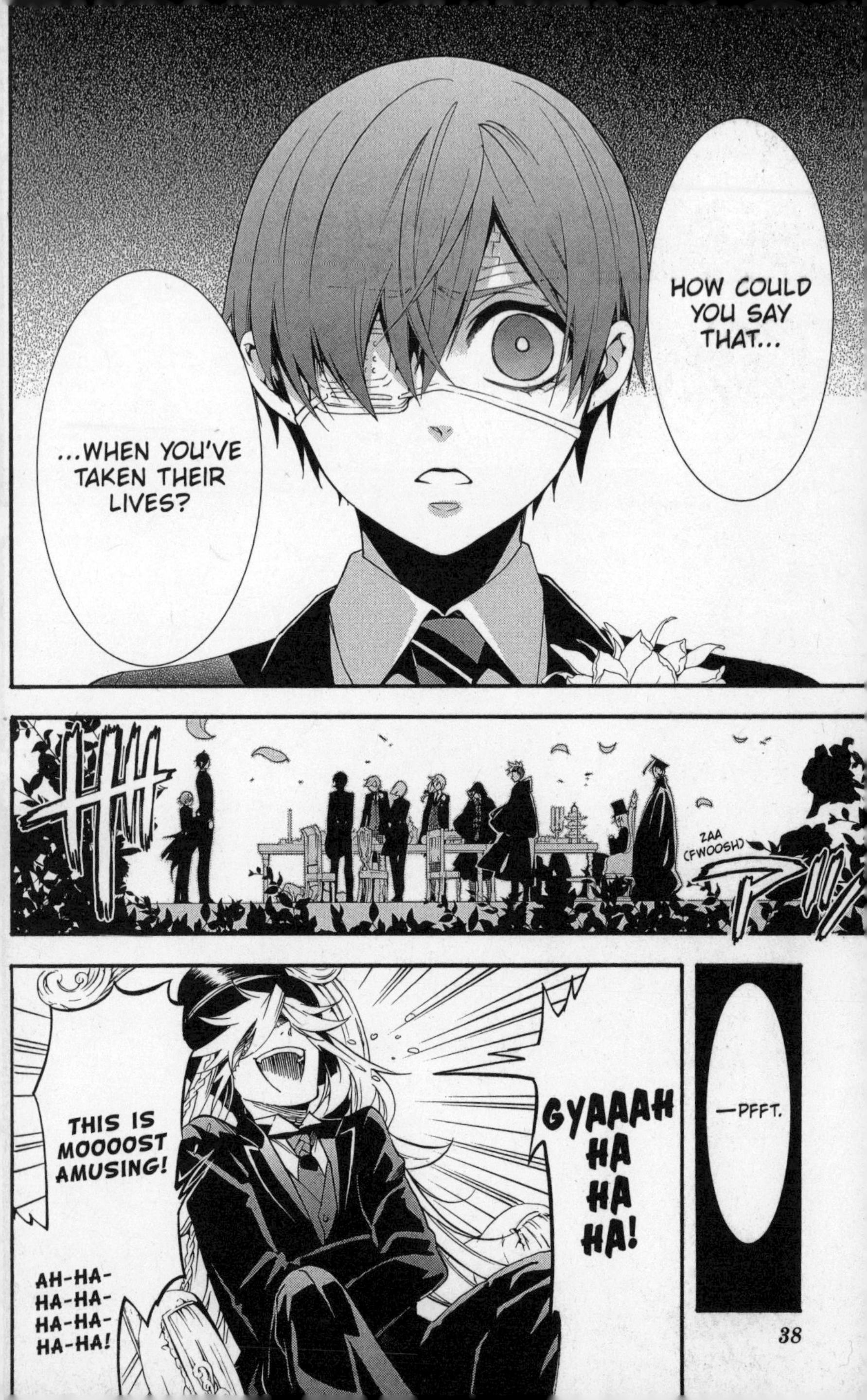
HOW COULD YOU SAY THAT...
...WHEN YOU'VE TAKEN THEIR LIVES?
ZAA (FWOOSH)
—PFFT.
GYAAAH HA HA HA!
THIS IS MOOOOST AMUSING!
AH-HA-HA-HA-HA-HA-HA-HA!

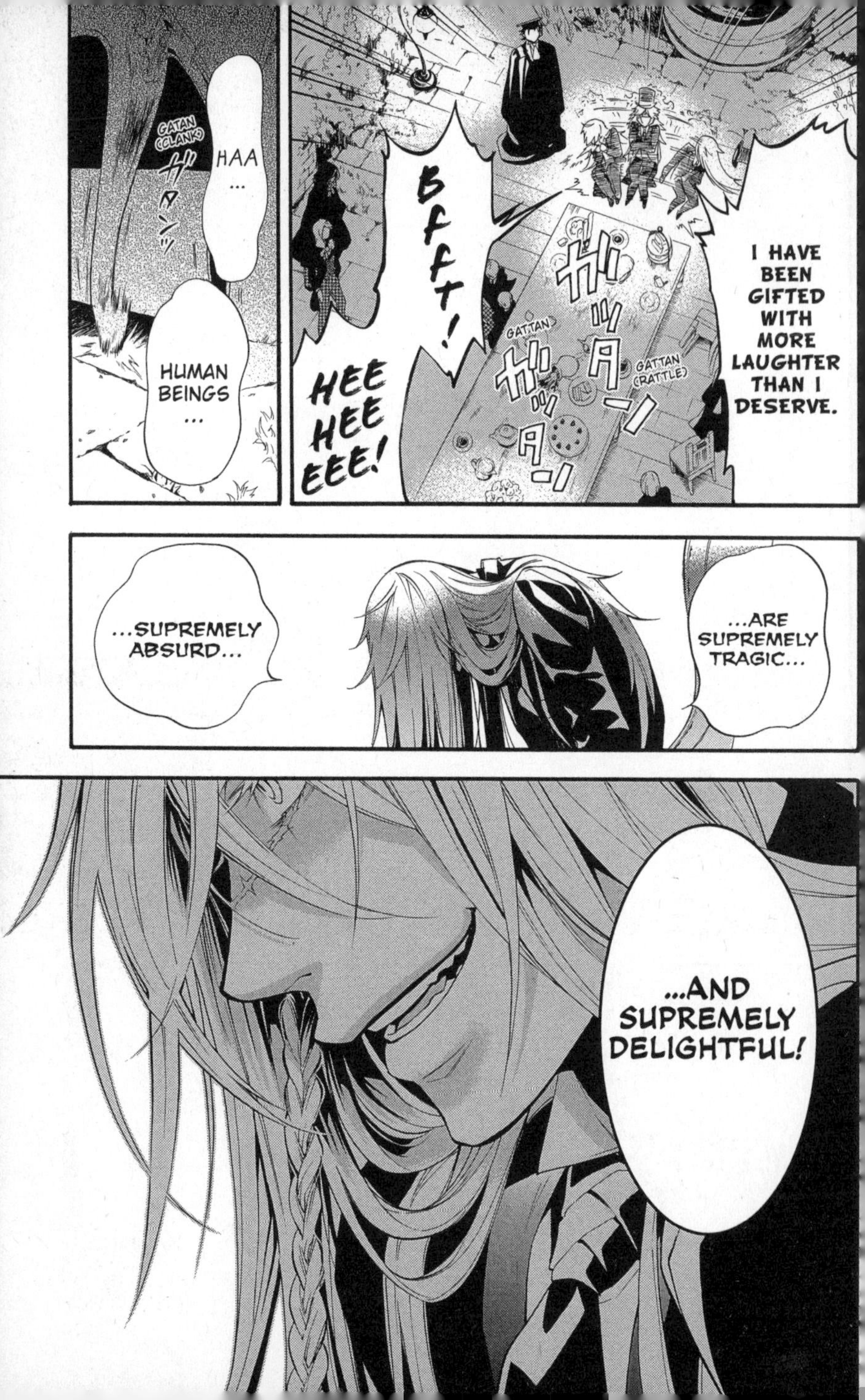
I HAVE BEEN GIFTED WITH MORE LAUGHTER THAN I DESERVE.
BFFT!
HEE HEE EEE!
GATTAN (RATTLE)
GATTAN
GATAN (CLANK)
HAA...
HUMAN BEINGS...
...ARE SUPREMELY TRAGIC...
...SUPREMELY ABSURD...
...AND SUPREMELY DELIGHTFUL!

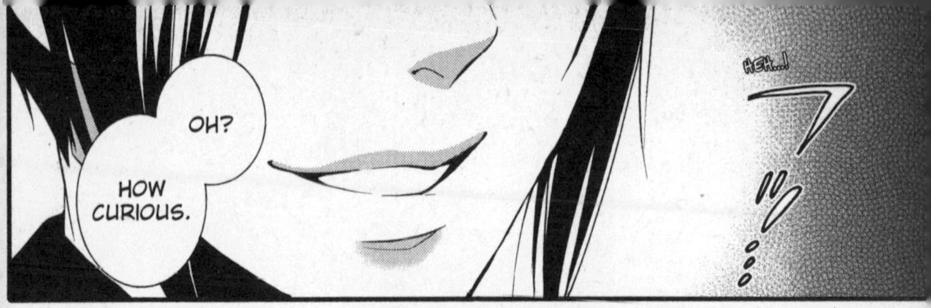
HEH...!
OH?
HOW CURIOUS.
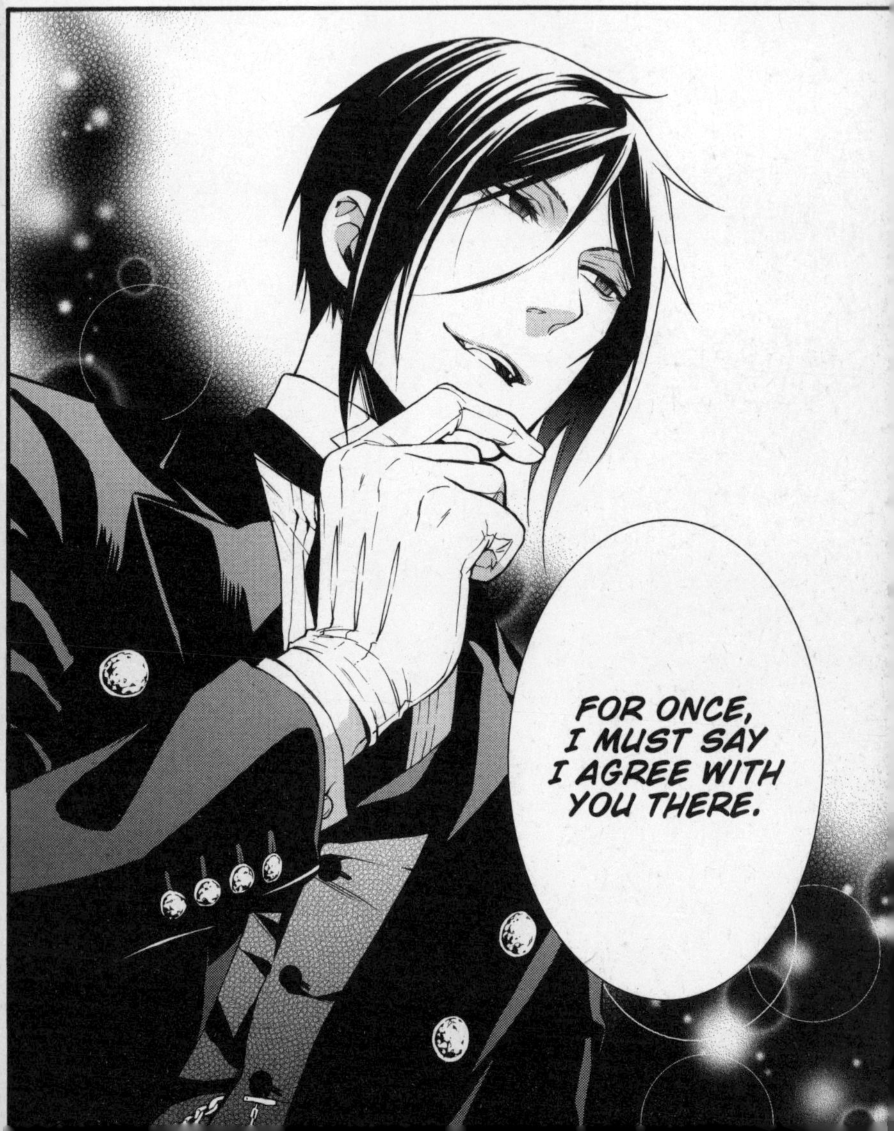
FOR ONCE, I MUST SAY I AGREE WITH YOU THERE.

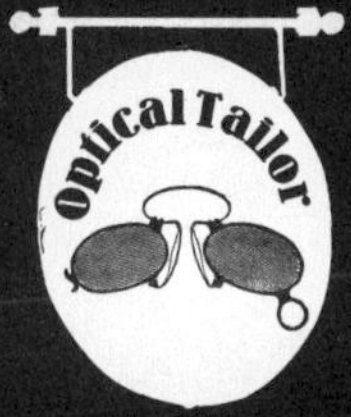
Optical Tailor

Black Butler

Chapter 84

At noon : The Butler, Speculating

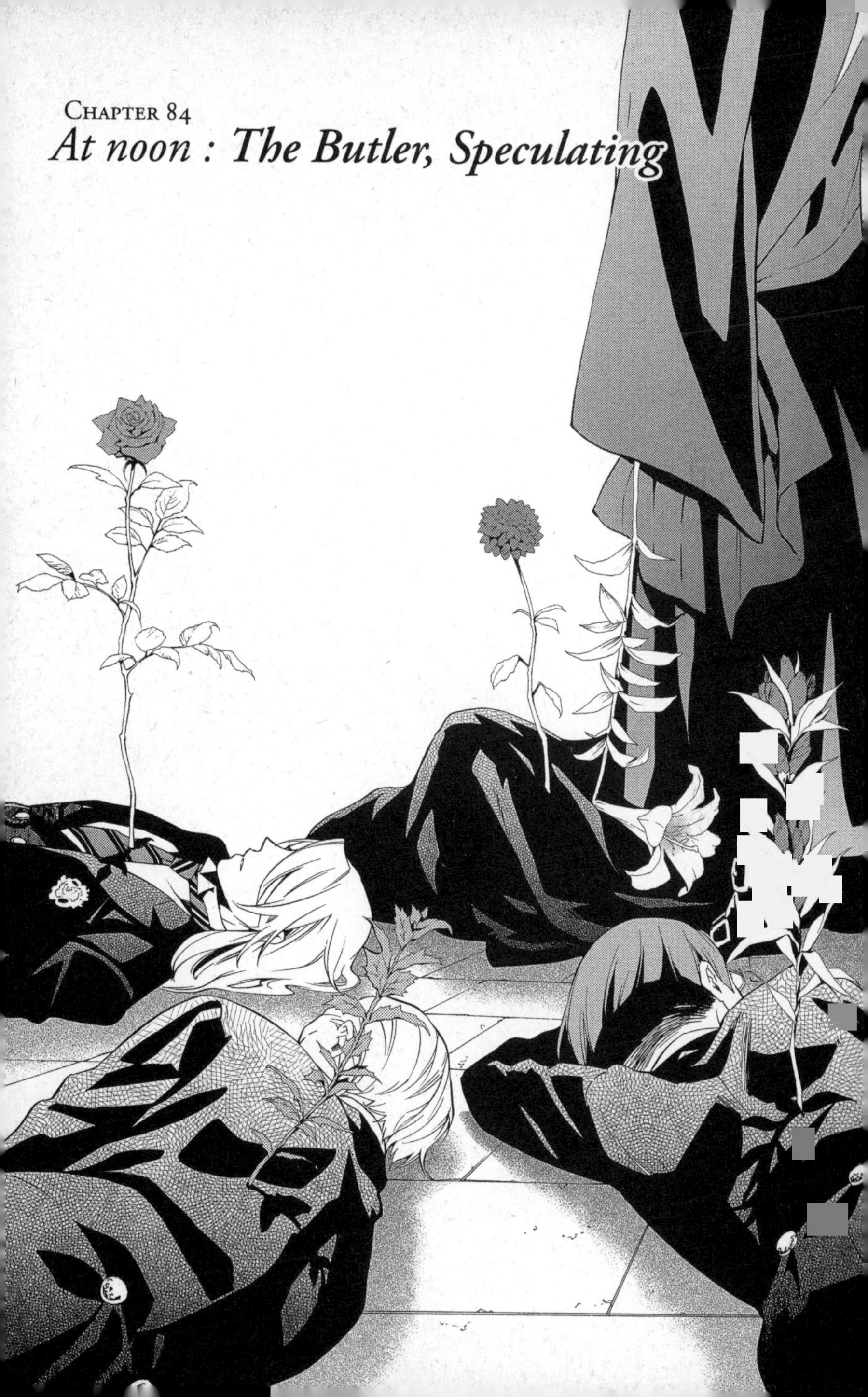

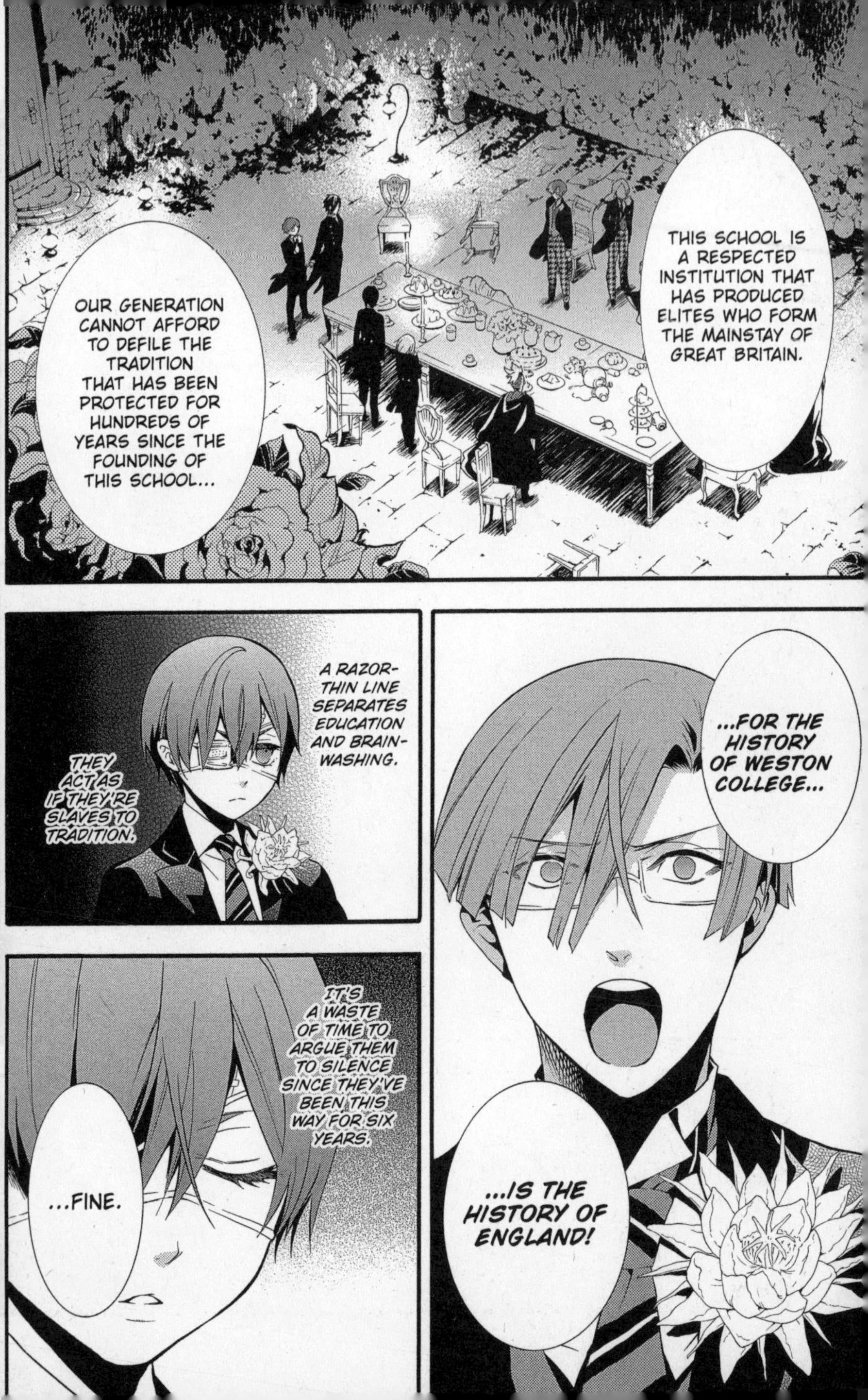
THIS SCHOOL IS A RESPECTED INSTITUTION THAT HAS PRODUCED ELITES WHO FORM THE MAINSTAY OF GREAT BRITAIN.
OUR GENERATION CANNOT AFFORD TO DEFILE THE TRADITION THAT HAS BEEN PROTECTED FOR HUNDREDS OF YEARS SINCE THE FOUNDING OF THIS SCHOOL...
...FOR THE HISTORY OF WESTON COLLEGE...
...IS THE HISTORY OF ENGLAND!
A RAZOR-THIN LINE SEPARATES EDUCATION AND BRAIN-WASHING.
THEY ACT AS IF THEY'RE SLAVES TO TRADITION.
IT'S A WASTE OF TIME TO ARGUE THEM TO SILENCE SINCE THEY'VE BEEN THIS WAY FOR SIX YEARS.
...FINE.

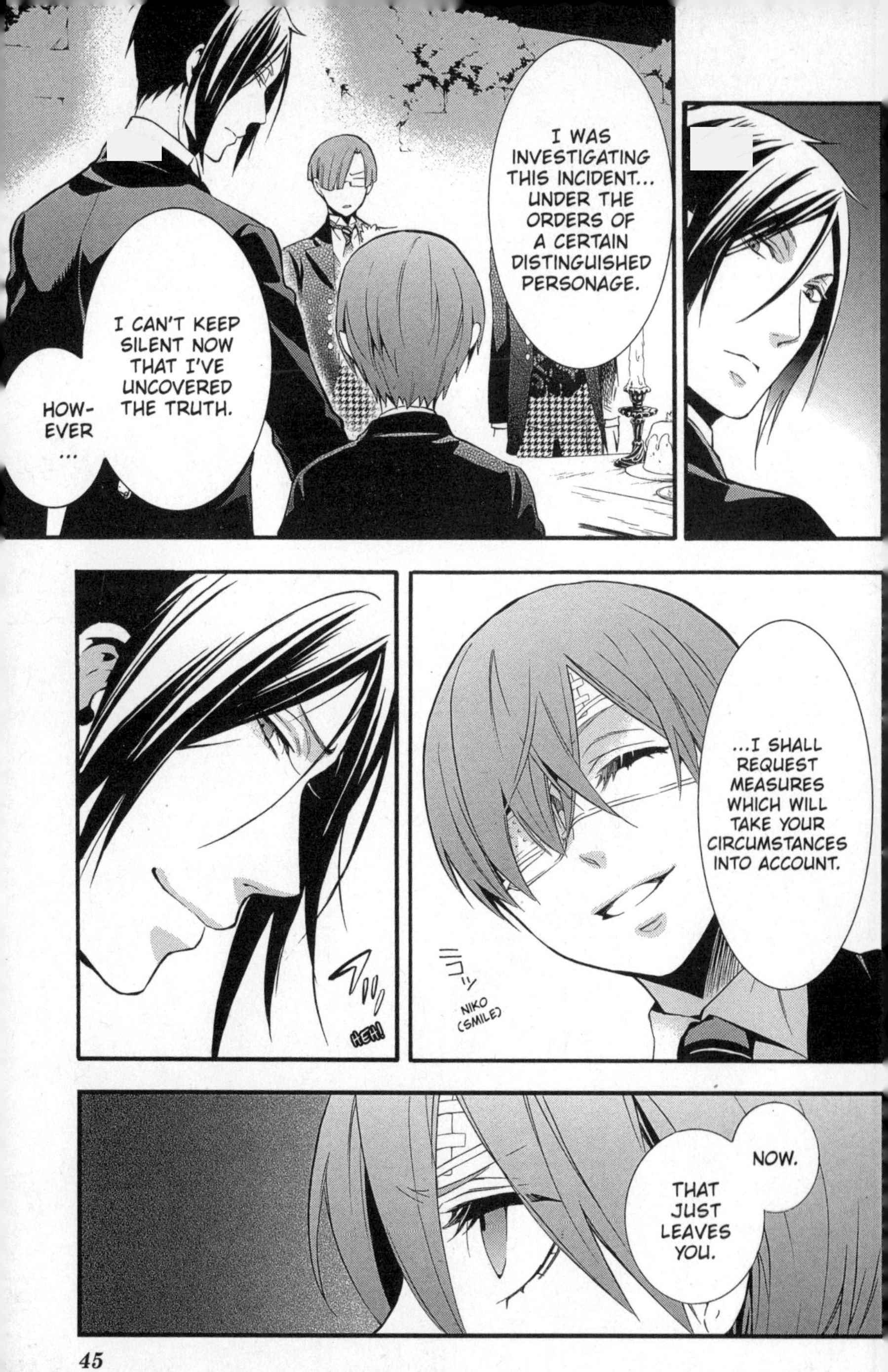
I WAS INVESTIGATING THIS INCIDENT... UNDER THE ORDERS OF A CERTAIN DISTINGUISHED PERSONAGE.
I CAN'T KEEP SILENT NOW THAT I'VE UNCOVERED THE TRUTH.
HOW-EVER...
...I SHALL REQUEST MEASURES WHICH WILL TAKE YOUR CIRCUMSTANCES INTO ACCOUNT.
ニコッ
NIKO (SMILE)
HEH!
NOW.
THAT JUST LEAVES YOU.

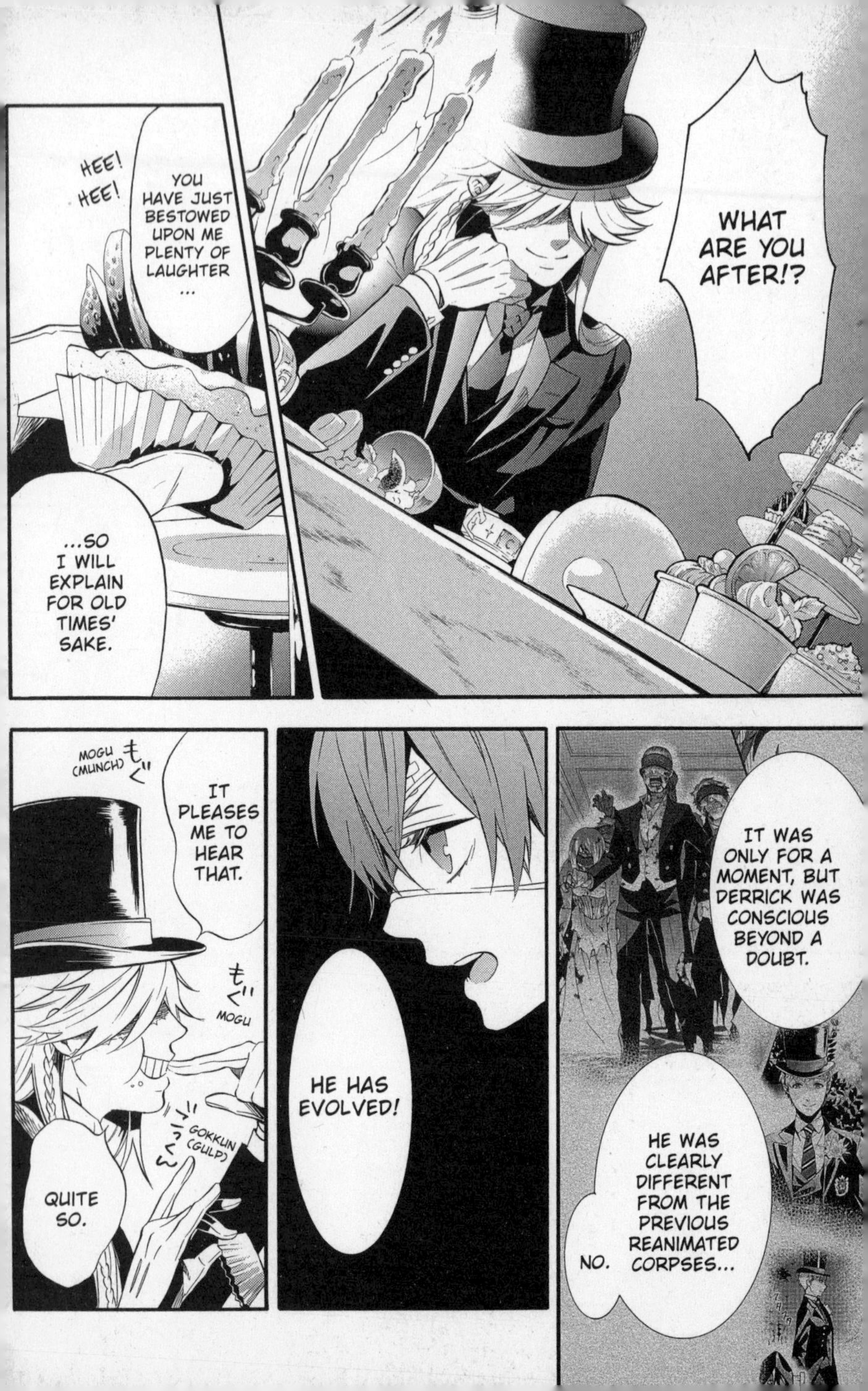
WHAT ARE YOU AFTER!?
HEE! HEE!
YOU HAVE JUST BESTOWED UPON ME PLENTY OF LAUGHTER ...
...SO I WILL EXPLAIN FOR OLD TIMES' SAKE.
IT WAS ONLY FOR A MOMENT, BUT DERRICK WAS CONSCIOUS BEYOND A DOUBT.
NO.
HE WAS CLEARLY DIFFERENT FROM THE PREVIOUS REANIMATED CORPSES...
HE HAS EVOLVED!
MOGU (MUNCH)
IT PLEASES ME TO HEAR THAT.
MOGU
GOKKUN (GULP)
QUITE SO.

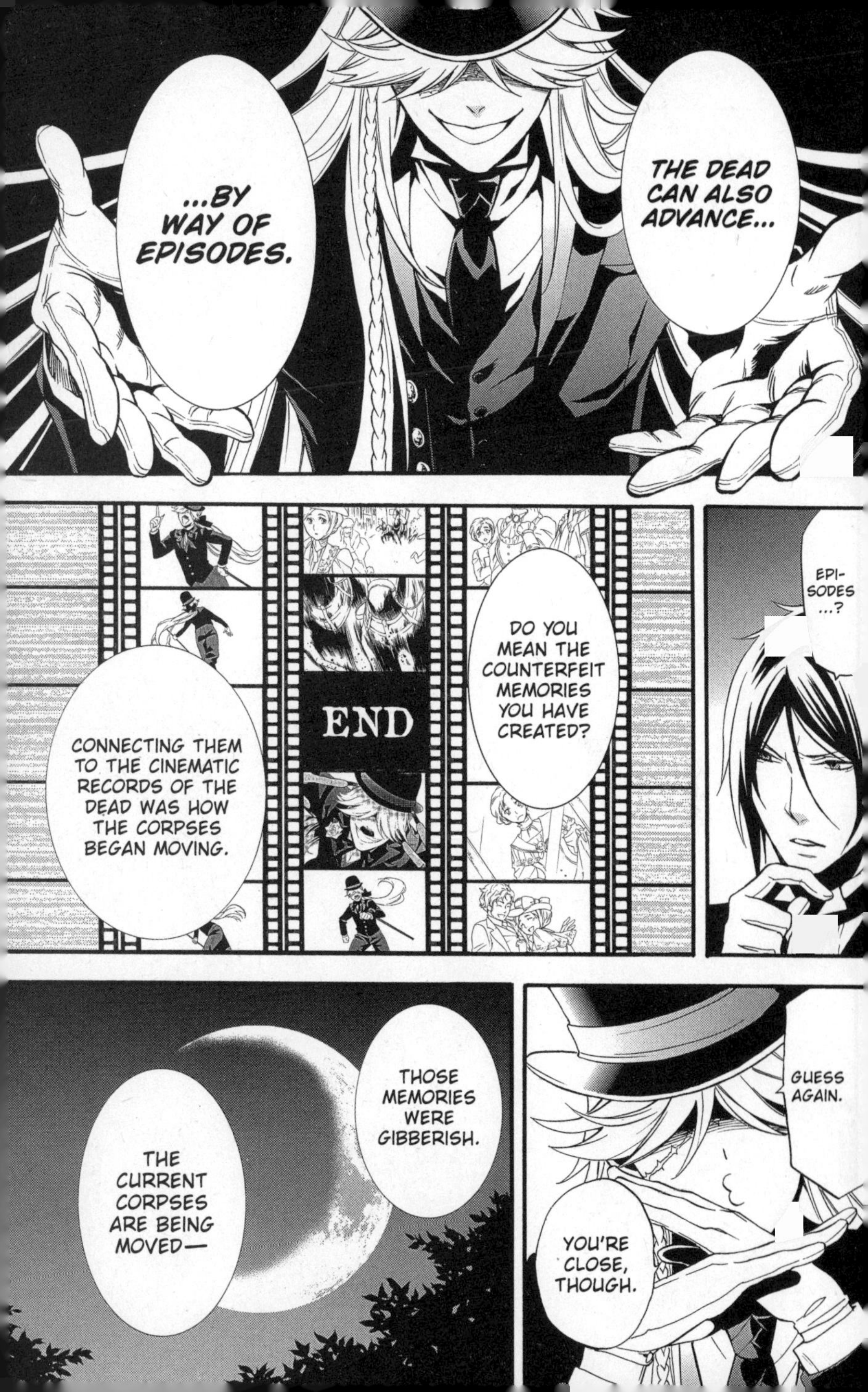
THE DEAD CAN ALSO ADVANCE...
...BY WAY OF EPISODES.
EPI-SODES ...?
DO YOU MEAN THE COUNTERFEIT MEMORIES YOU HAVE CREATED?
END
CONNECTING THEM TO THE CINEMATIC RECORDS OF THE DEAD WAS HOW THE CORPSES BEGAN MOVING.
GUESS AGAIN.
YOU'RE CLOSE, THOUGH.
THOSE MEMORIES WERE GIBBERISH.
THE CURRENT CORPSES ARE BEING MOVED—

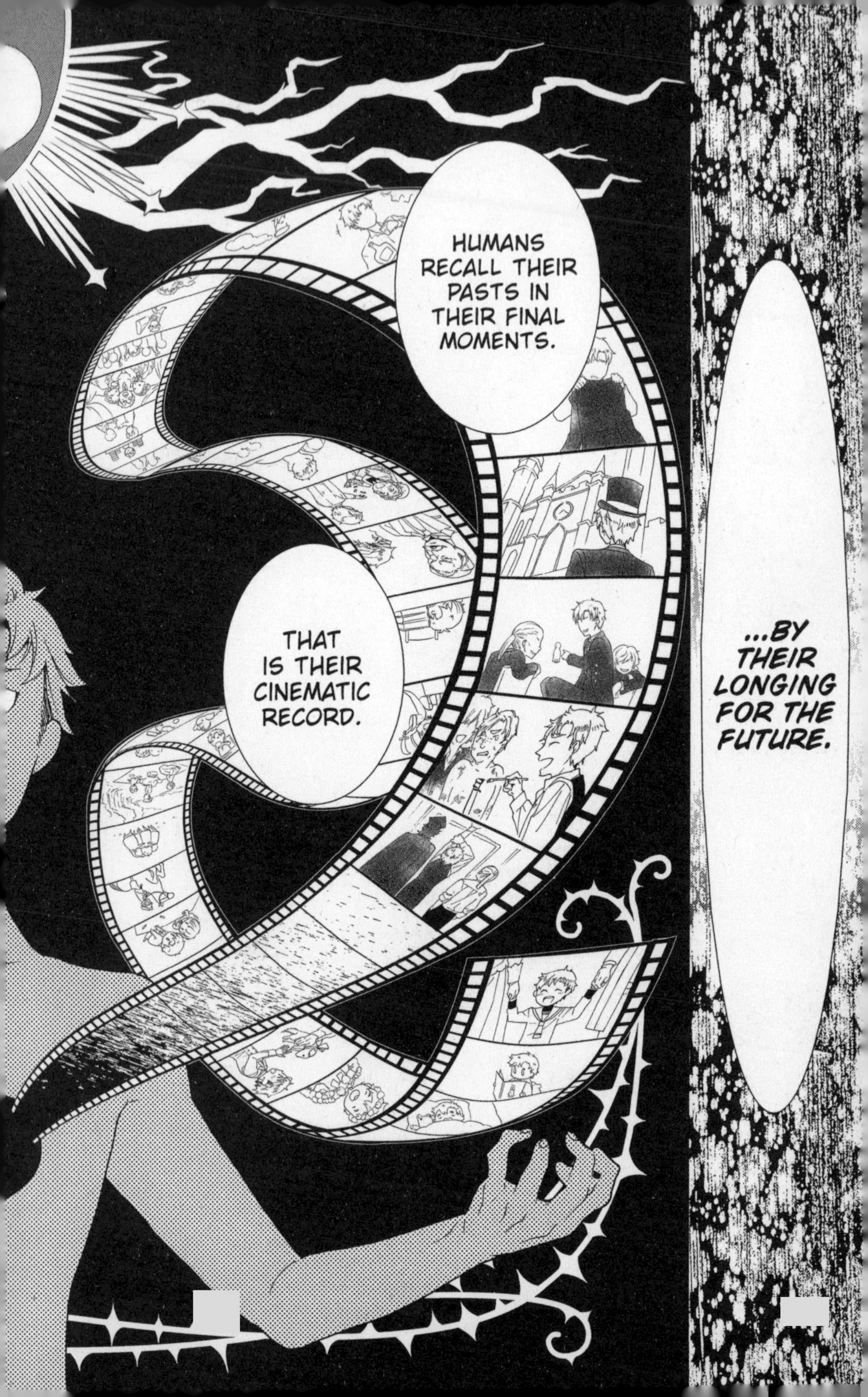
...BY THEIR LONGING FOR THE FUTURE.
HUMANS RECALL THEIR PASTS IN THEIR FINAL MOMENTS.
THAT IS THEIR CINEMATIC RECORD.

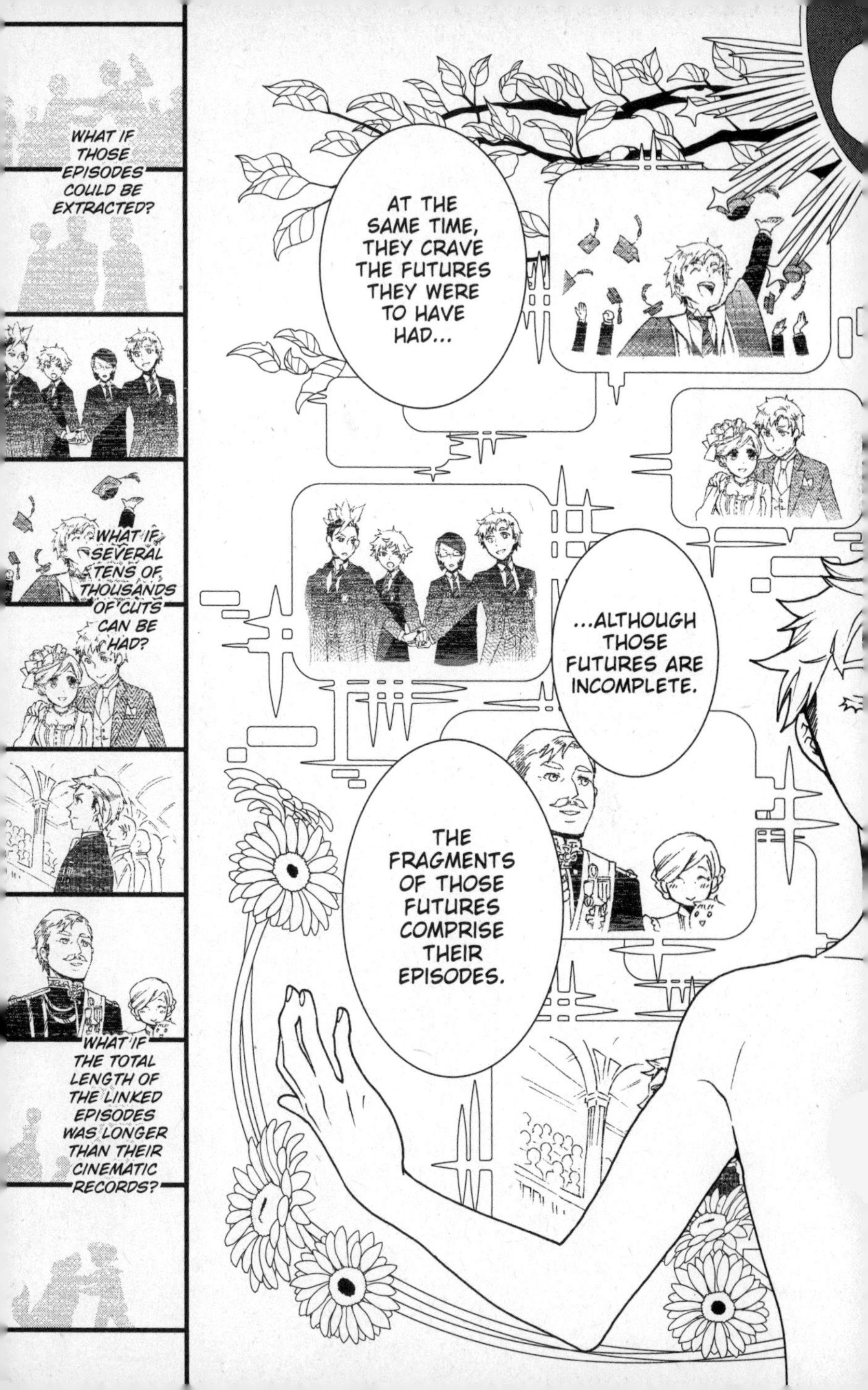
AT THE SAME TIME, THEY CRAVE THE FUTURES THEY WERE TO HAVE HAD...
...ALTHOUGH THOSE FUTURES ARE INCOMPLETE.
THE FRAGMENTS OF THOSE FUTURES COMPRISE THEIR EPISODES.
WHAT IF THOSE EPISODES COULD BE EXTRACTED?
WHAT IF SEVERAL TENS OF THOUSANDS OF CUTS CAN BE HAD?
WHAT IF THE TOTAL LENGTH OF THE LINKED EPISODES WAS LONGER THAN THEIR CINEMATIC RECORDS?

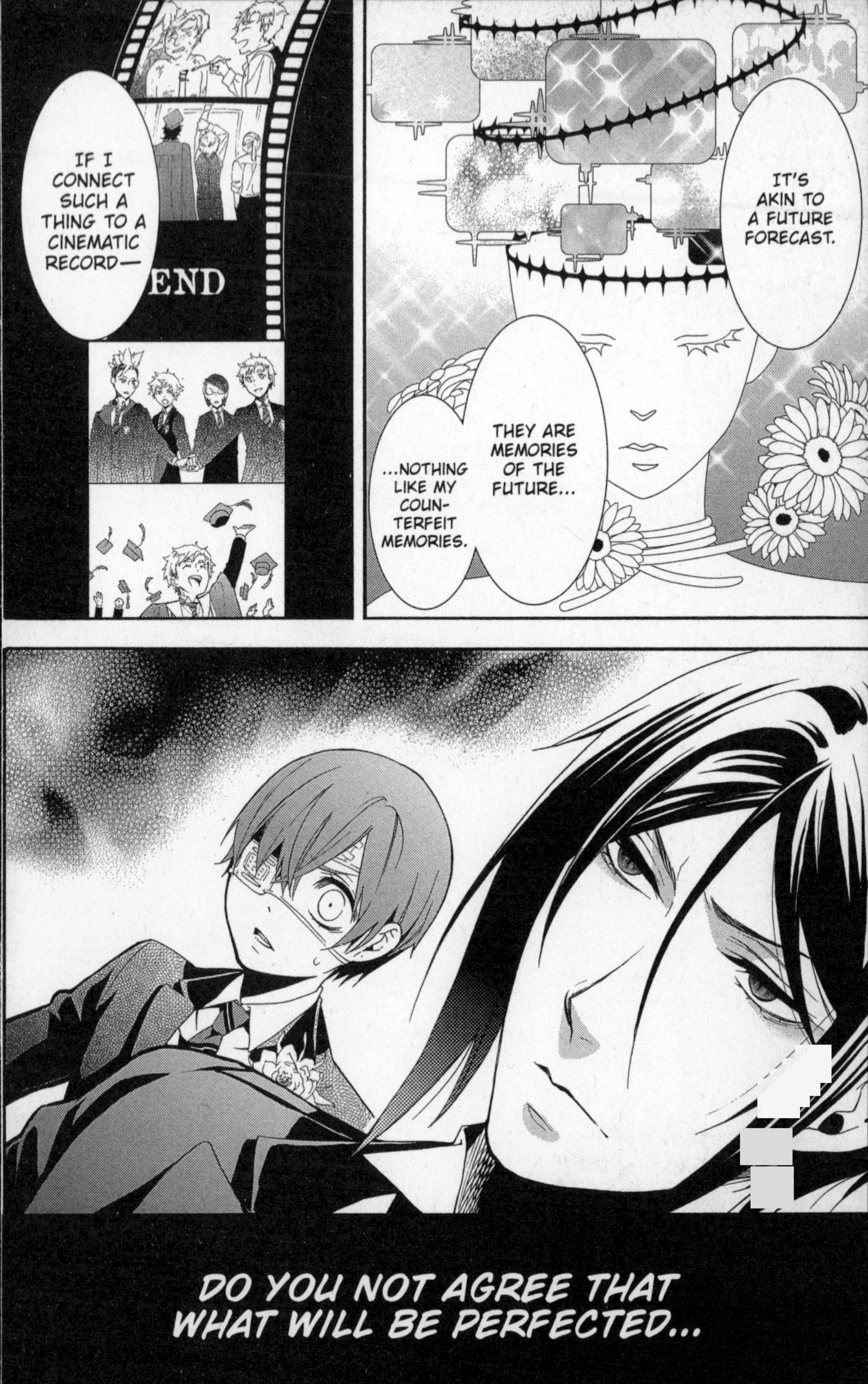
IT'S AKIN TO A FUTURE FORECAST.
THEY ARE MEMORIES OF THE FUTURE...
...NOTHING LIKE MY COUNTERFEIT MEMORIES.
IF I CONNECT SUCH A THING TO A CINEMATIC RECORD—
END
DO YOU NOT AGREE THAT WHAT WILL BE PERFECTED...

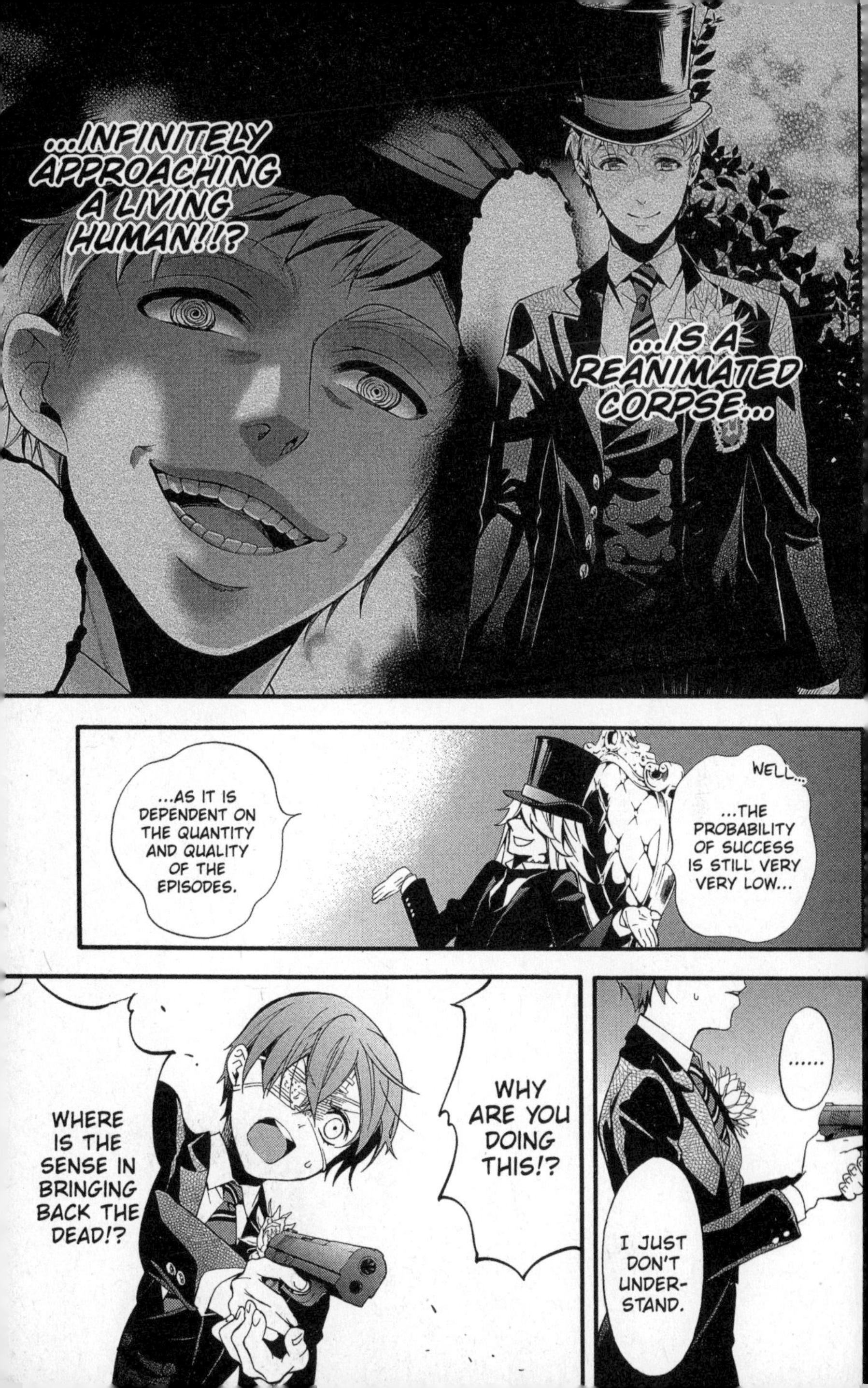
...IS A REANIMATED CORPSE...
...INFINITELY APPROACHING A LIVING HUMAN!!?
WELL...
...THE PROBABILITY OF SUCCESS IS STILL VERY VERY LOW...
...AS IT IS DEPENDENT ON THE QUANTITY AND QUALITY OF THE EPISODES.
......
I JUST DON'T UNDER-STAND.
WHY ARE YOU DOING THIS!?
WHERE IS THE SENSE IN BRINGING BACK THE DEAD!?

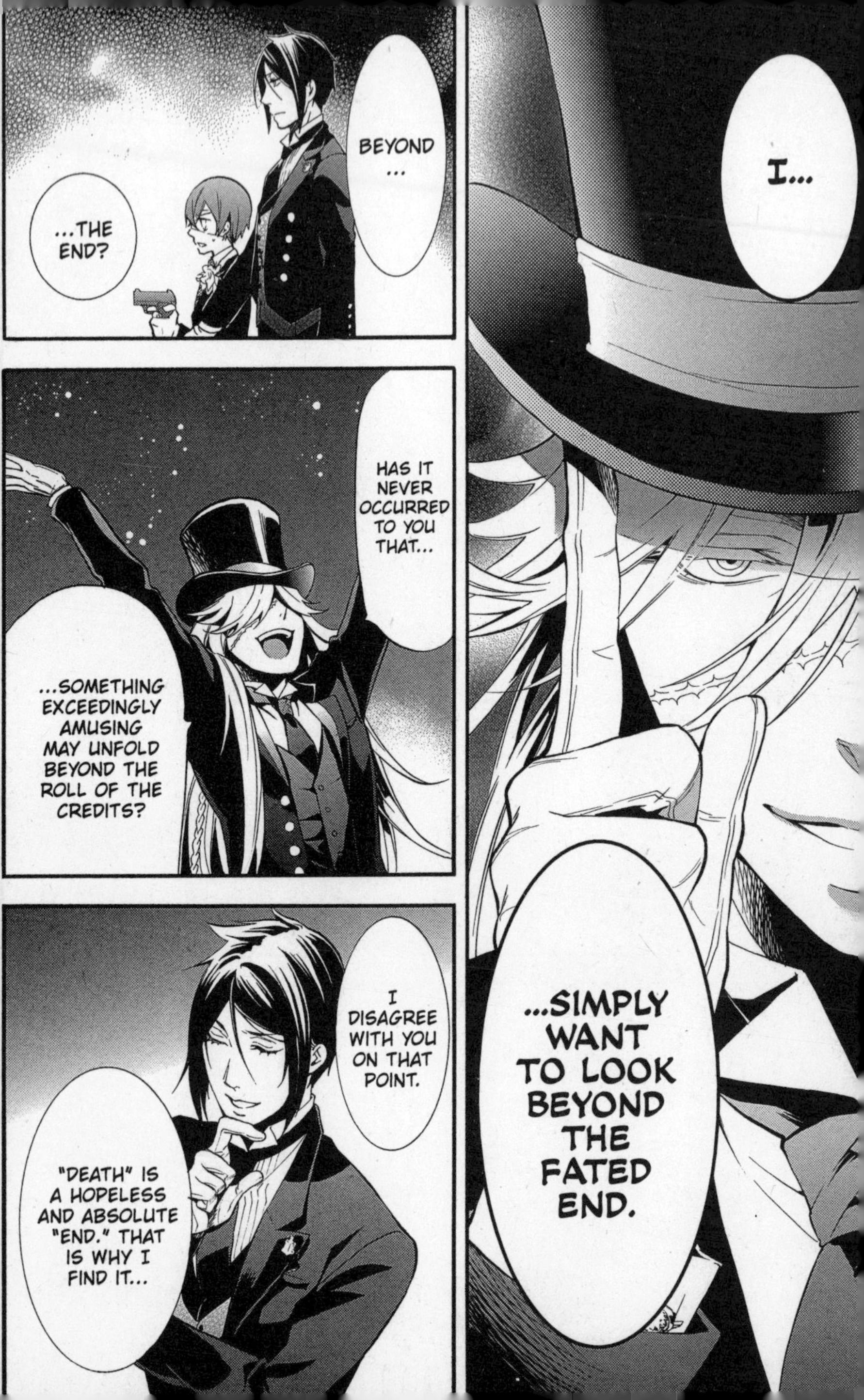
I...
...SIMPLY WANT TO LOOK BEYOND THE FATED END.
BEYOND ...
...THE END?
HAS IT NEVER OCCURRED TO YOU THAT...
...SOMETHING EXCEEDINGLY AMUSING MAY UNFOLD BEYOND THE ROLL OF THE CREDITS?
I DISAGREE WITH YOU ON THAT POINT.
"DEATH" IS A HOPELESS AND ABSOLUTE "END." THAT IS WHY I FIND IT...

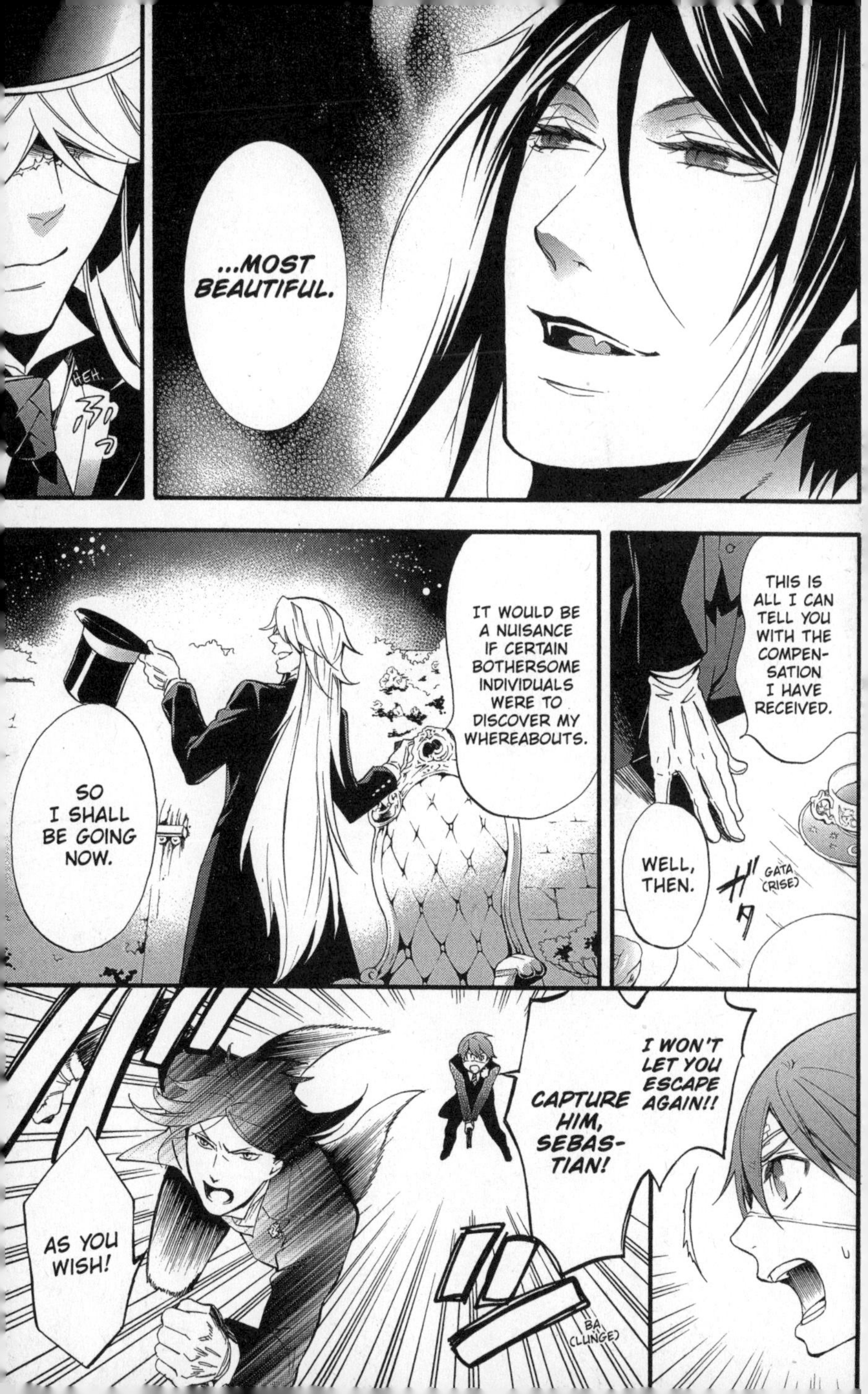
...MOST BEAUTIFUL.
HEH.
THIS IS ALL I CAN TELL YOU WITH THE COMPEN-SATION I HAVE RECEIVED.
WELL, THEN.
GATA (RISE)
IT WOULD BE A NUISANCE IF CERTAIN BOTHERSOME INDIVIDUALS WERE TO DISCOVER MY WHEREABOUTS.
SO I SHALL BE GOING NOW.
I WON'T LET YOU ESCAPE AGAIN!!
CAPTURE HIM, SEBAS-TIAN!
AS YOU WISH!
BA (LUNGE)

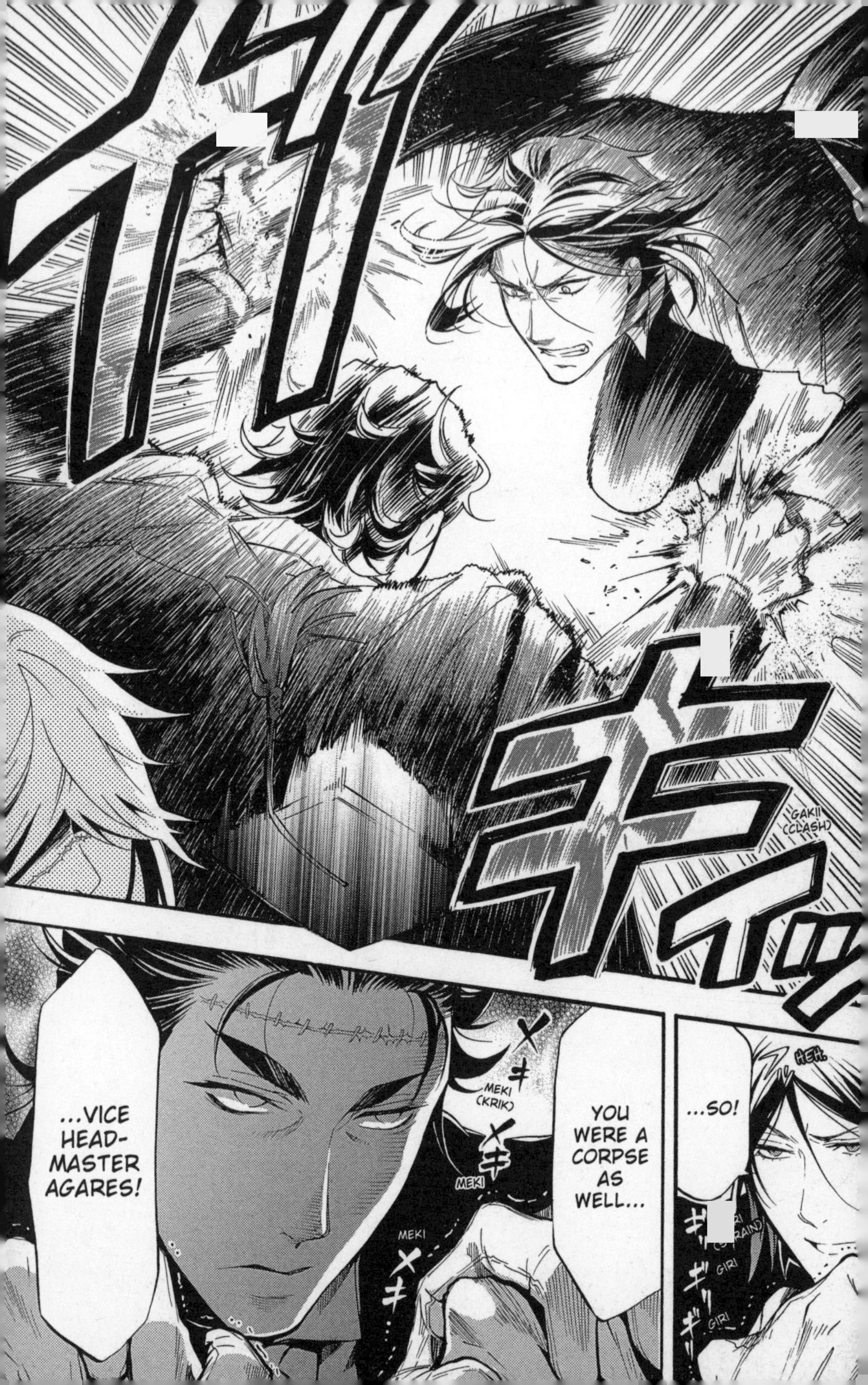
GAKI (CLASH)
HEH.
...SO!
GIRI
GIRI
GIRI
YOU WERE A CORPSE AS WELL...
MEKI (KRIK)
MEKI
MEKI
...VICE HEAD-MASTER AGARES!

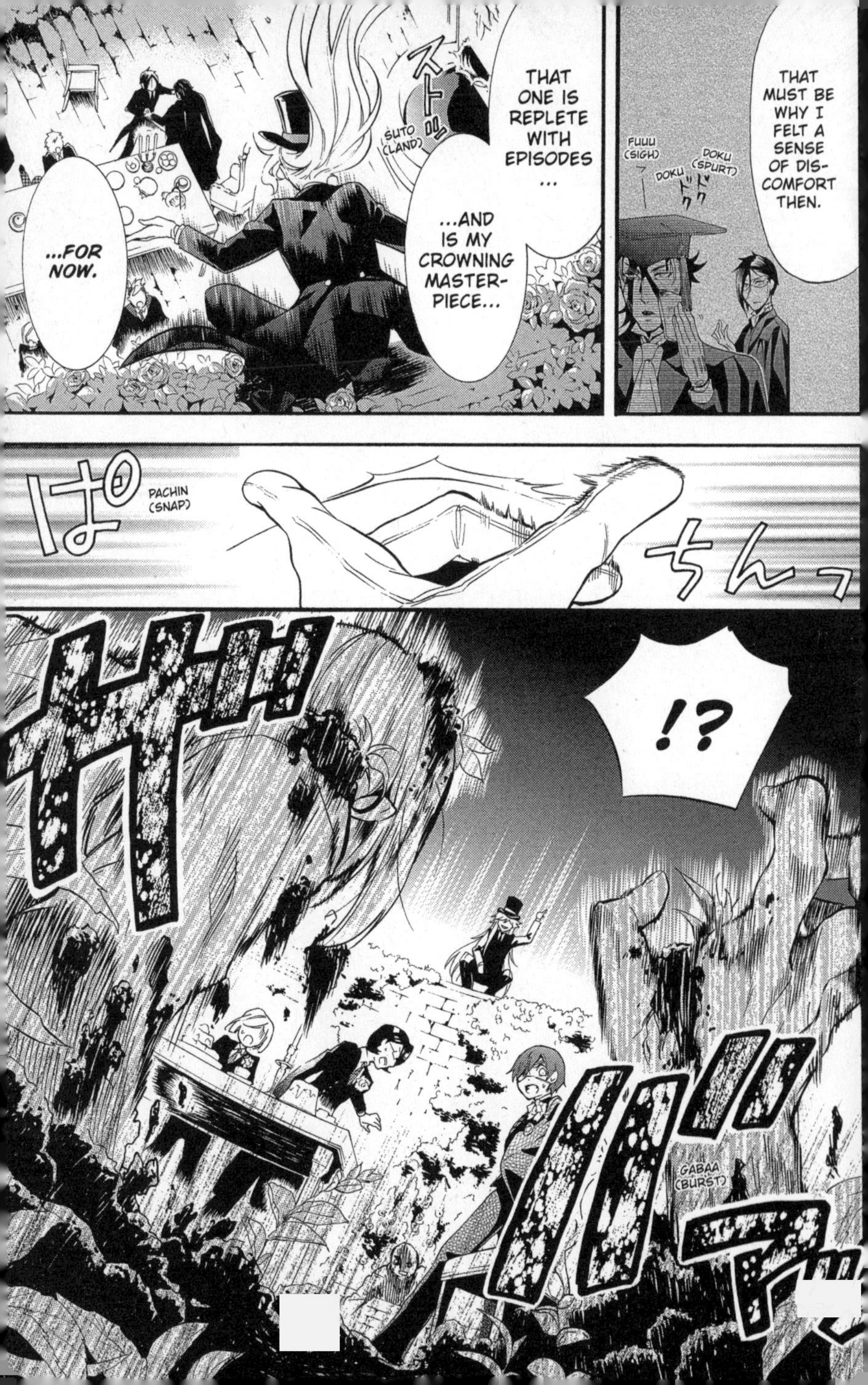
THAT MUST BE WHY I FELT A SENSE OF DIS-COMFORT THEN.
FUUU (SIGH)
DOKU DOKU (SPURT)
THAT ONE IS REPLETE WITH EPISODES ...
...AND IS MY CROWNING MASTER-PIECE...
SUTO (LAND)
...FOR NOW.
PACHIN (SNAP)
!?
GABAA (BURST)

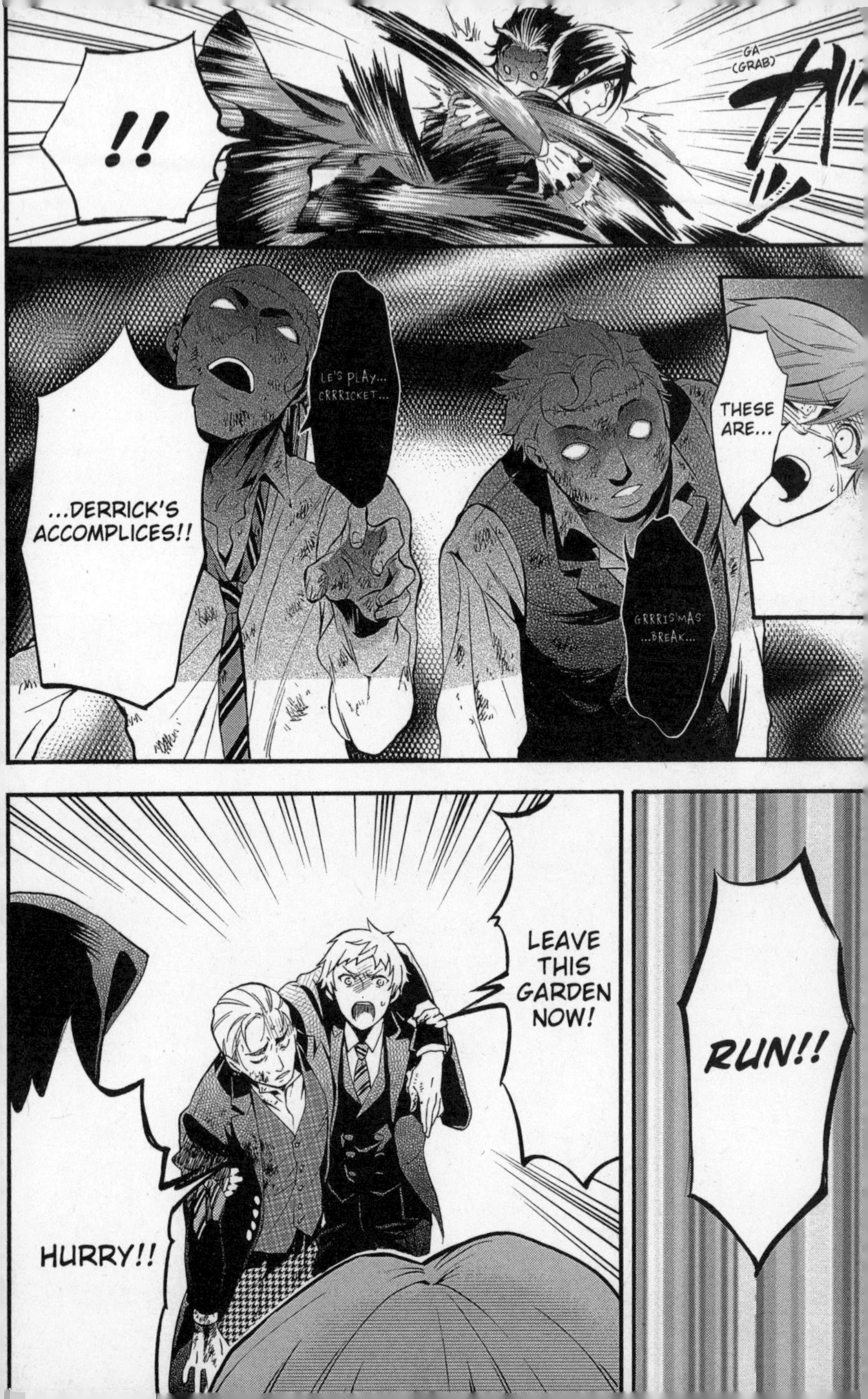
GA (GRAB)
!!
THESE ARE...
LE'S PLAY... CRRRICKET...
GRRRIS'MAS ...BREAK...
...DERRICK'S ACCOMPLICES!!
RUN!!
LEAVE THIS GARDEN NOW!
HURRY!!

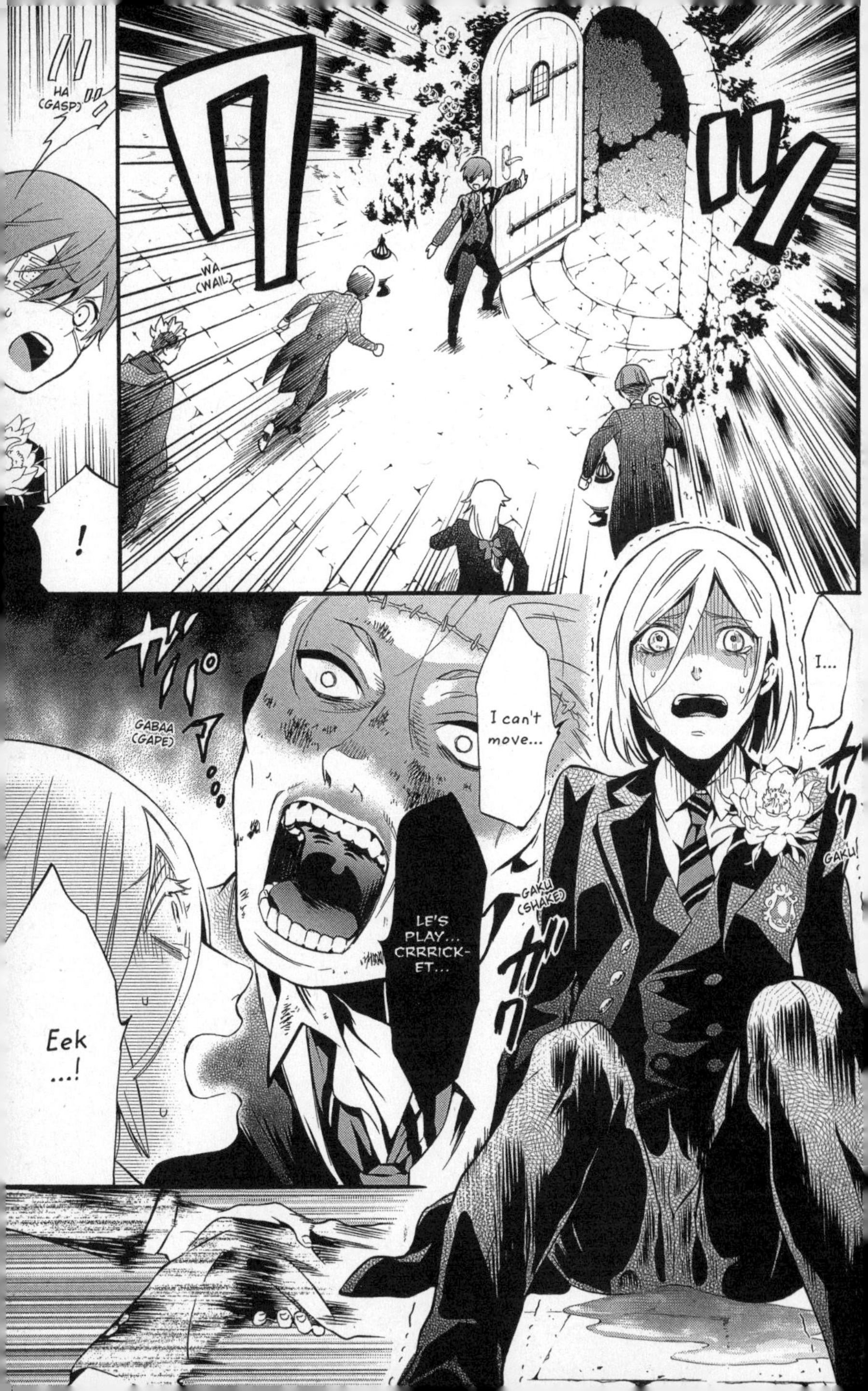
WA (WAIL)
HA (GASP)
!
I...
I can't move...
GAKU!
GAKU (SHAKE)
GABAA (GAPE)
LE'S PLAY... CRRRICK-ET...
Eek ...!

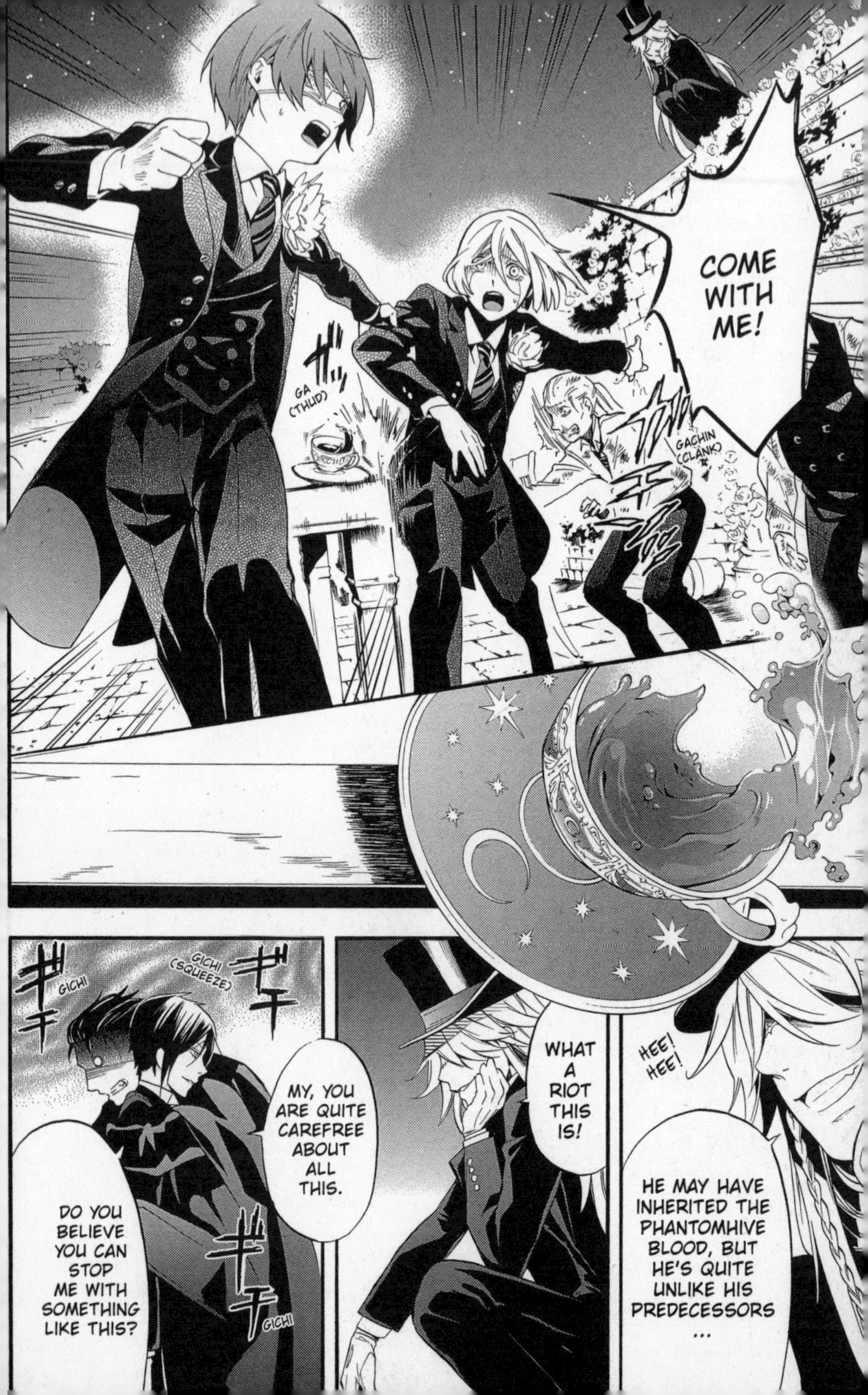
COME WITH ME!
GACHIN (CLANK)
GA (THUD)
HEE! HEE!
HE MAY HAVE INHERITED THE PHANTOMHIVE BLOOD, BUT HE'S QUITE UNLIKE HIS PREDECESSORS ...
WHAT A RIOT THIS IS!
MY, YOU ARE QUITE CAREFREE ABOUT ALL THIS.
GICHI (SQUEEZE)
GICHI
DO YOU BELIEVE YOU CAN STOP ME WITH SOMETHING LIKE THIS?
GICHI

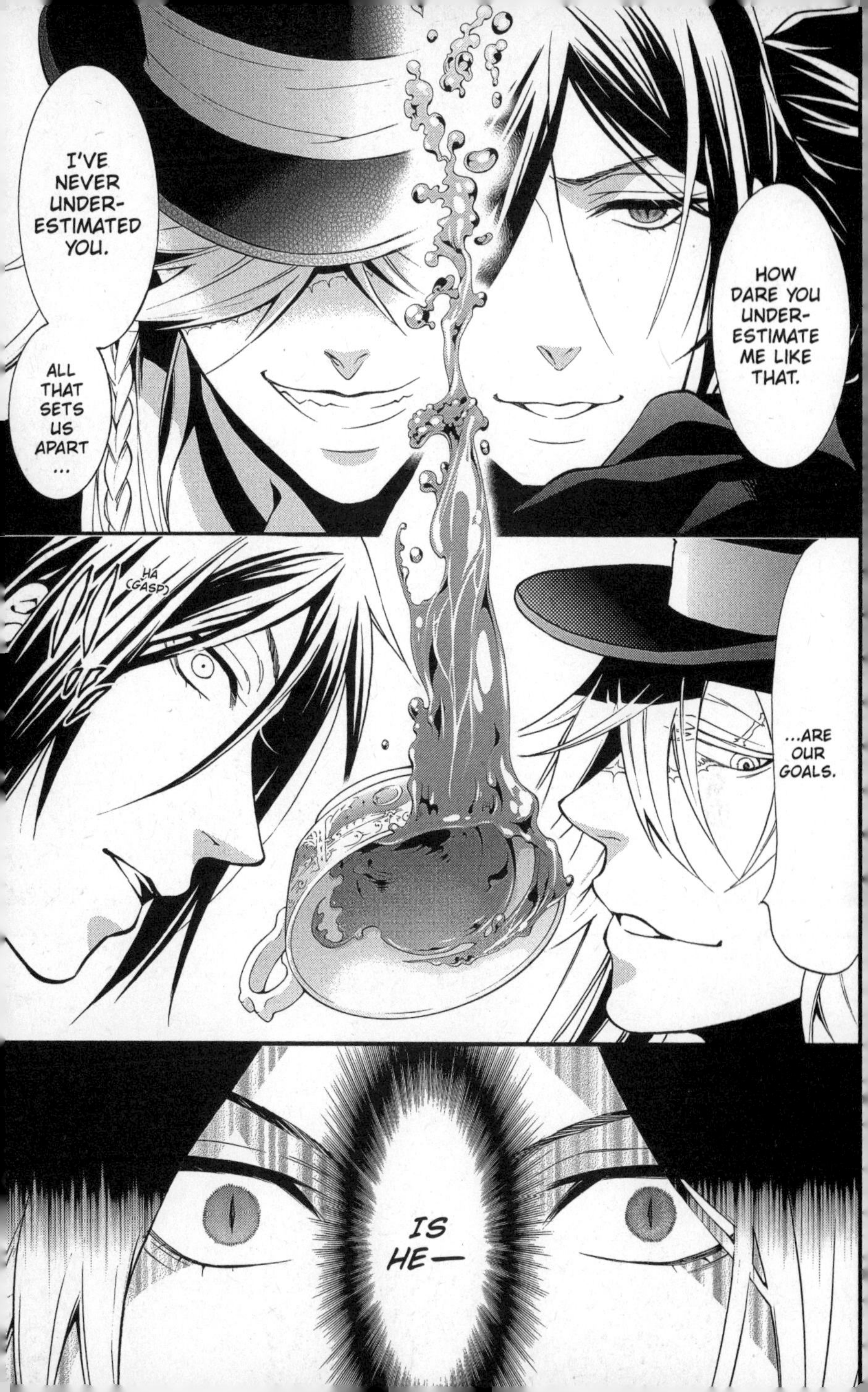
HOW DARE YOU UNDER-ESTIMATE ME LIKE THAT.
I'VE NEVER UNDER-ESTIMATED YOU.
ALL THAT SETS US APART ...
...ARE OUR GOALS.
HA (GASP)
IS HE—

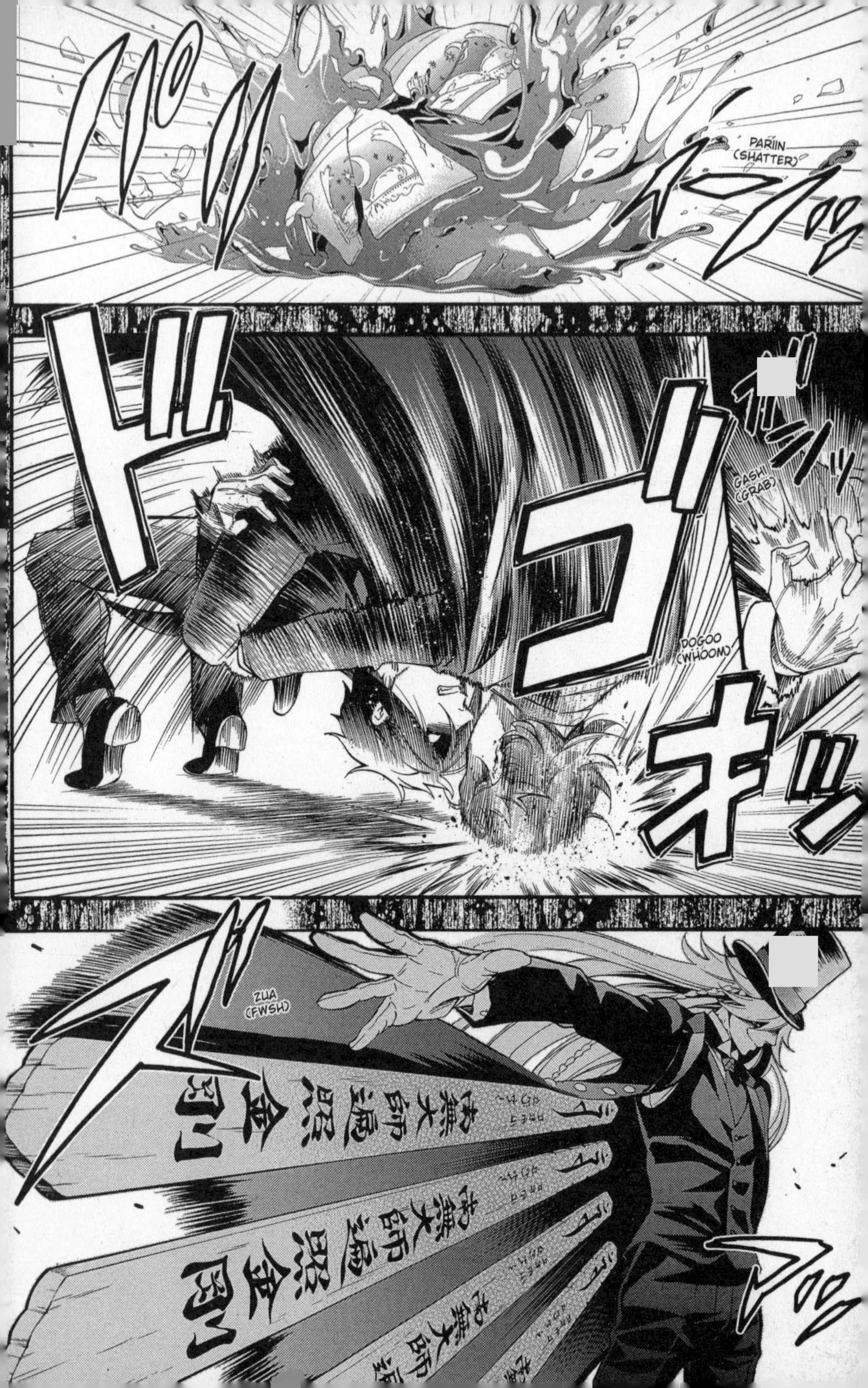
PARIIN
(SHATTER)
GASH
(GRAB)
DOGOO
(WHOOM)
ZUA
(FWSH)
南無大師遍照金剛
南無大師遍照金剛
南無大師遍照金剛

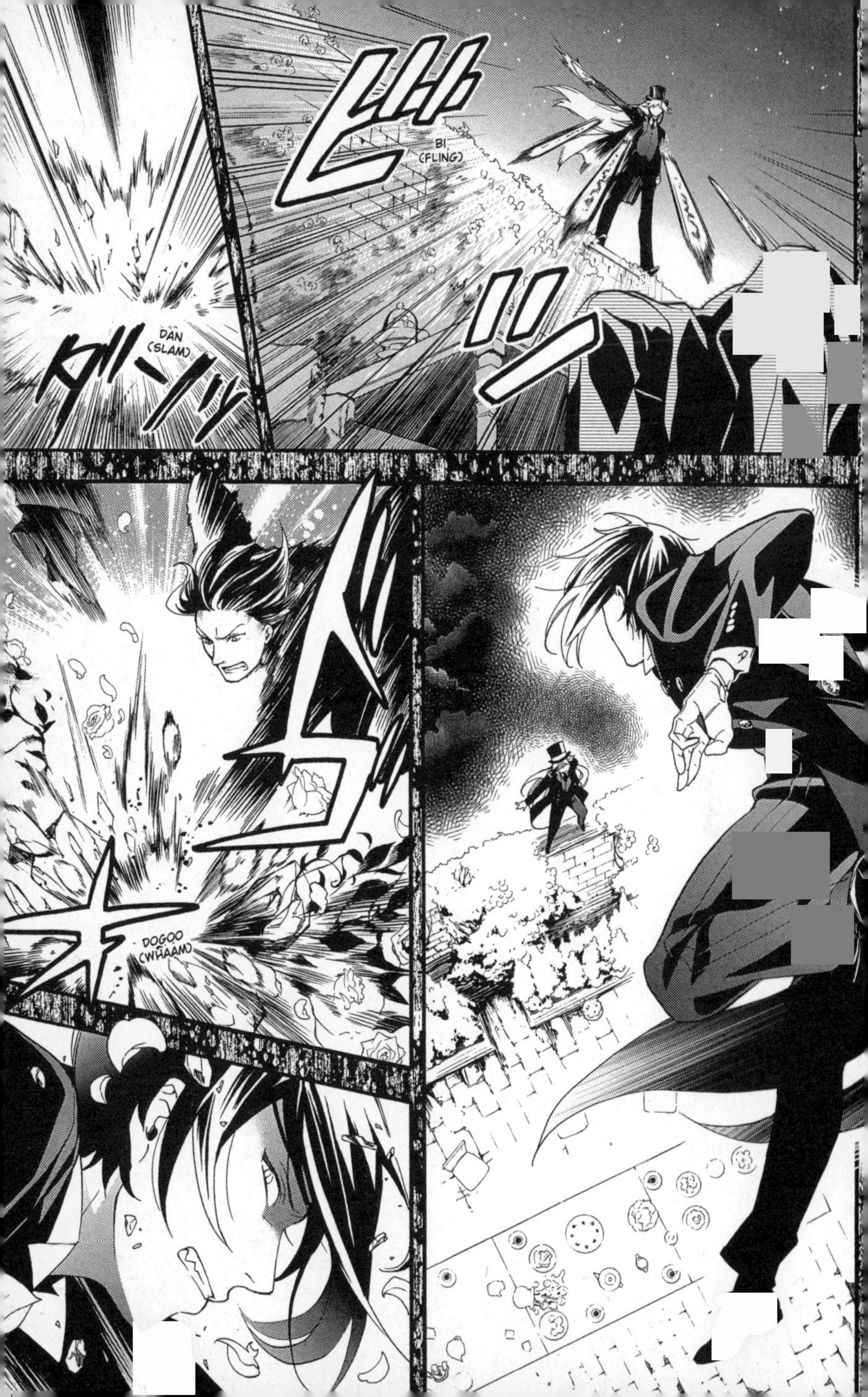
BI (FLING)
DAN (SLAM)
DOGOO (WHAAM)

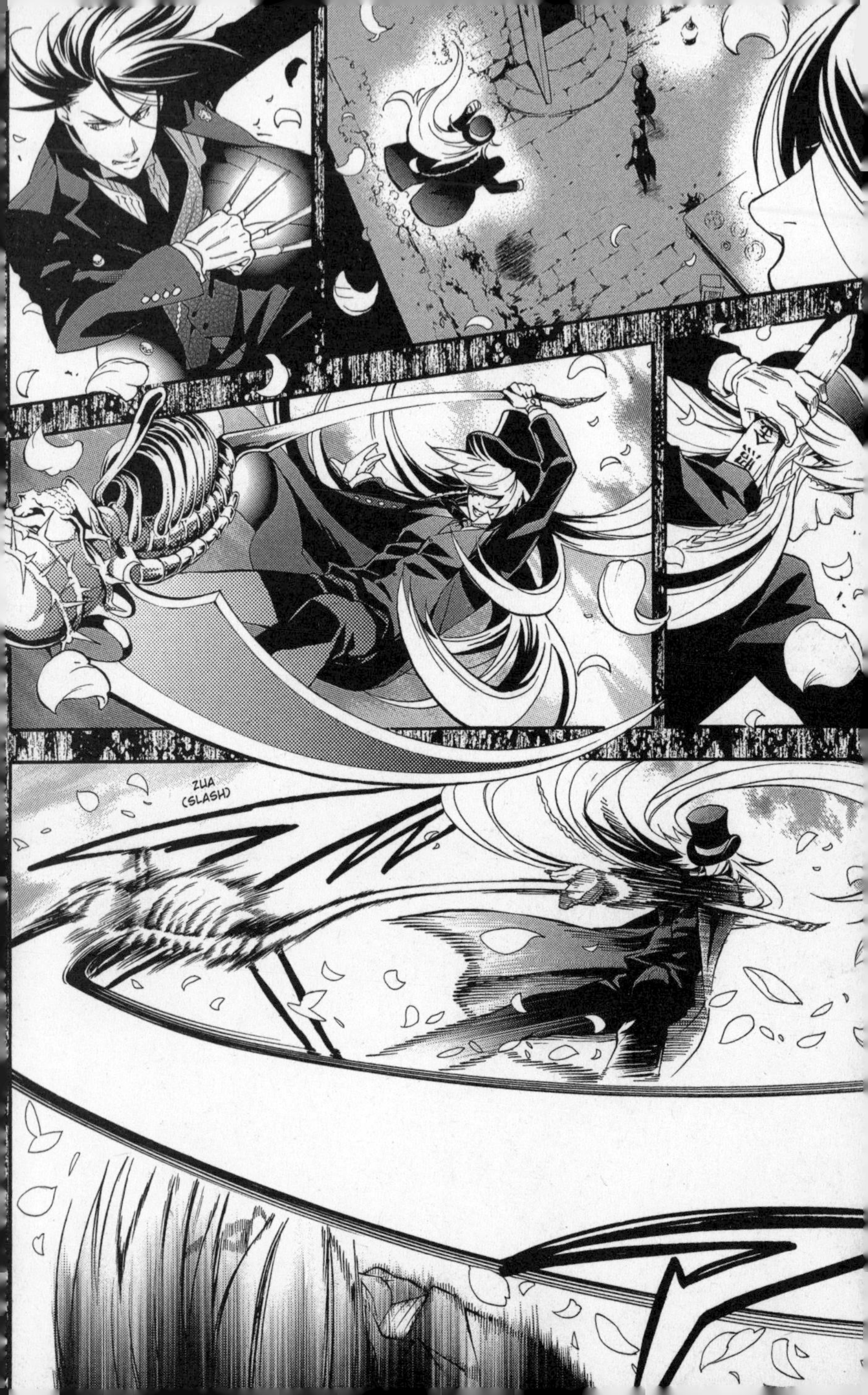
ZUA
(SLASH)

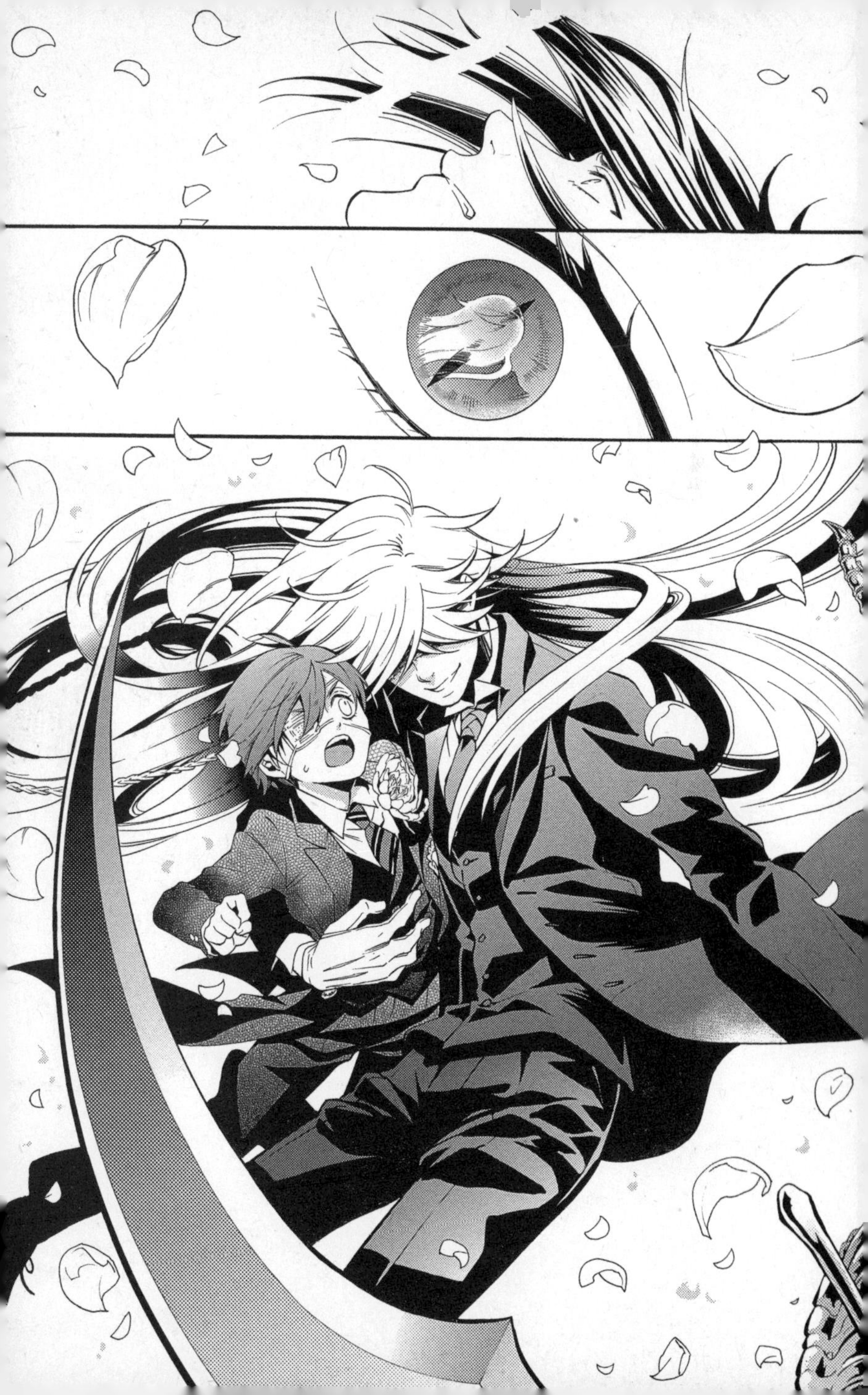

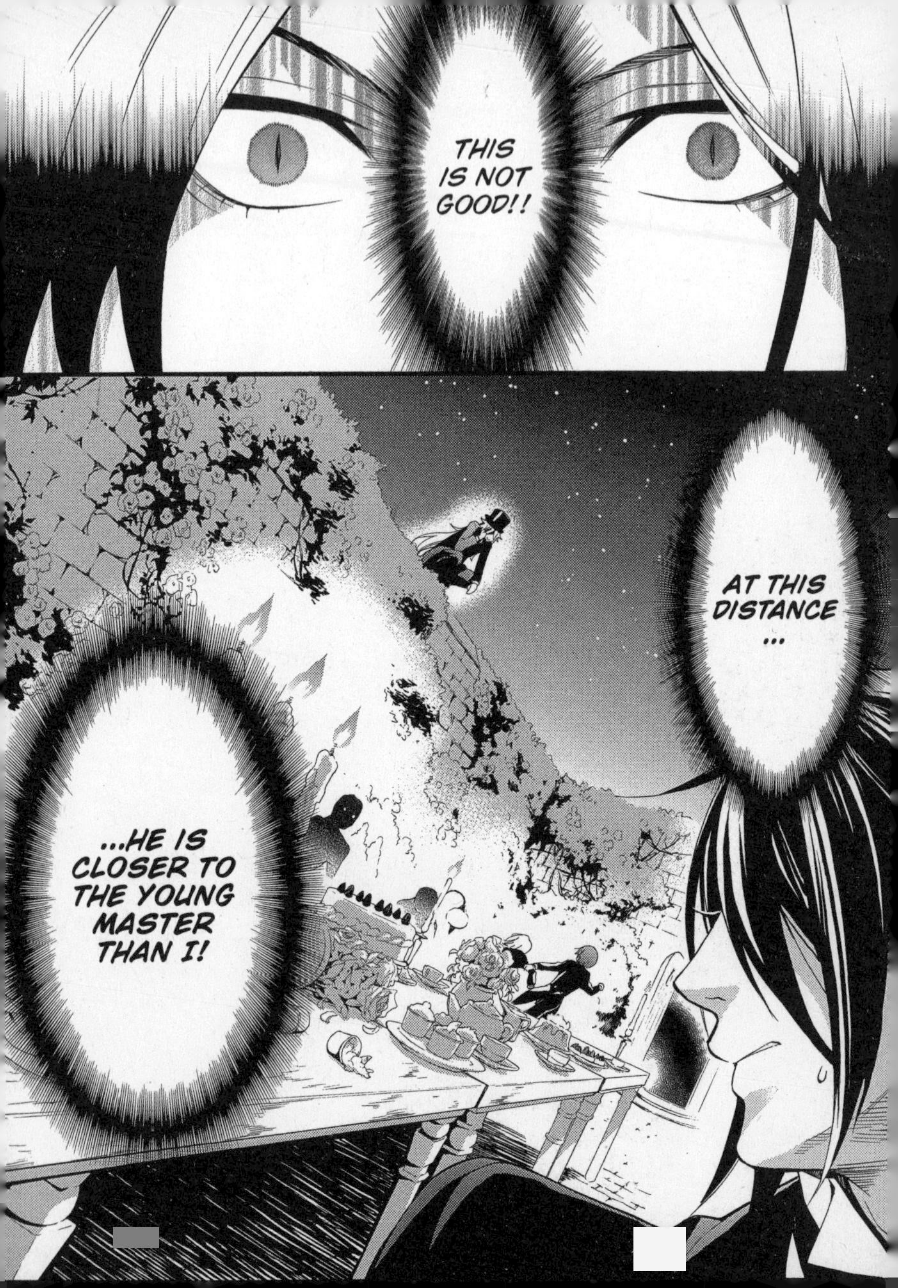
THIS IS NOT GOOD!!
AT THIS DISTANCE ...
...HE IS CLOSER TO THE YOUNG MASTER THAN I!

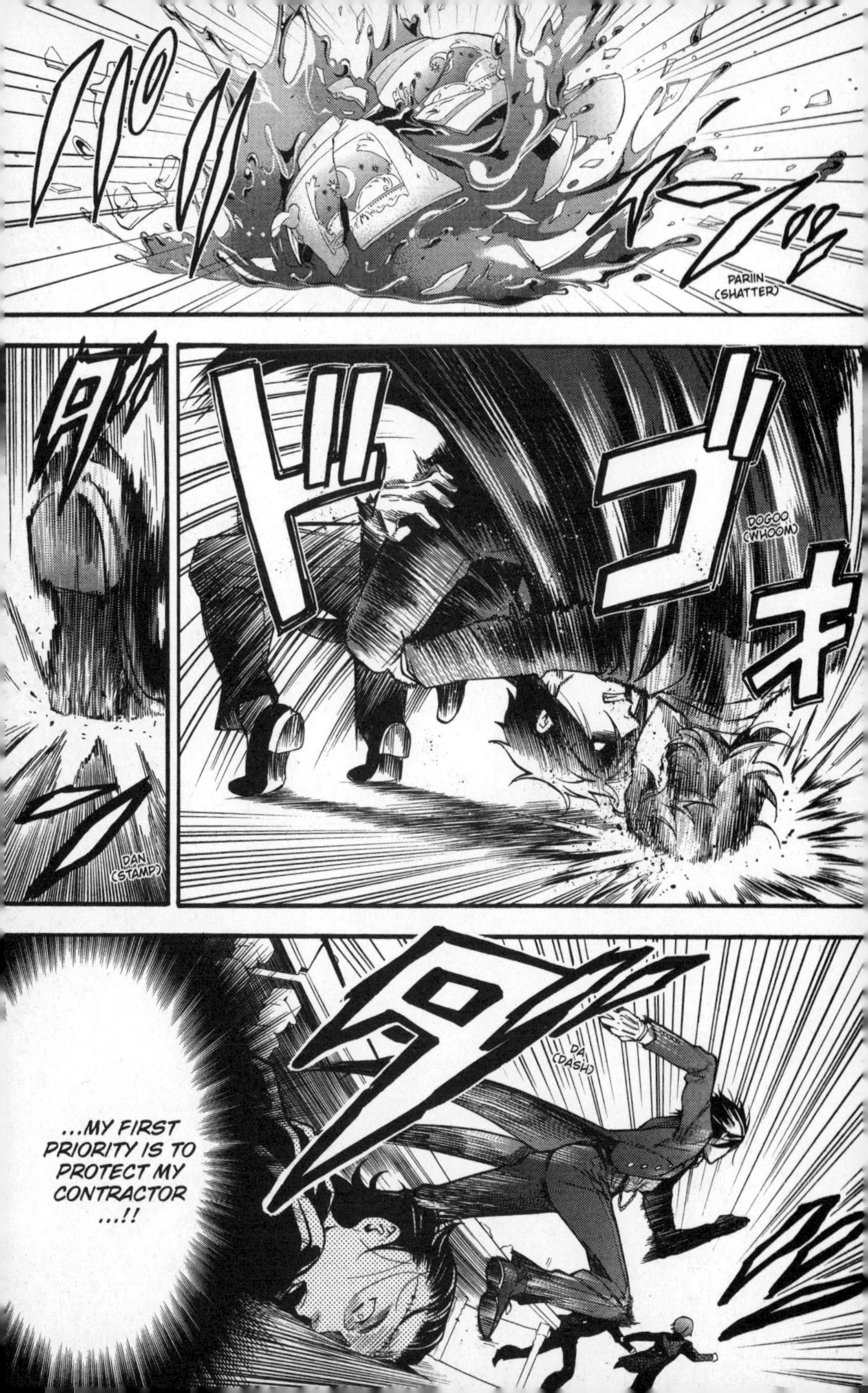
PARIIN (SHATTER)
DOGOO (WHOOM)
DAN (STAMP)
DA (DASH)
...MY FIRST PRIORITY IS TO PROTECT MY CONTRACTOR ...!!

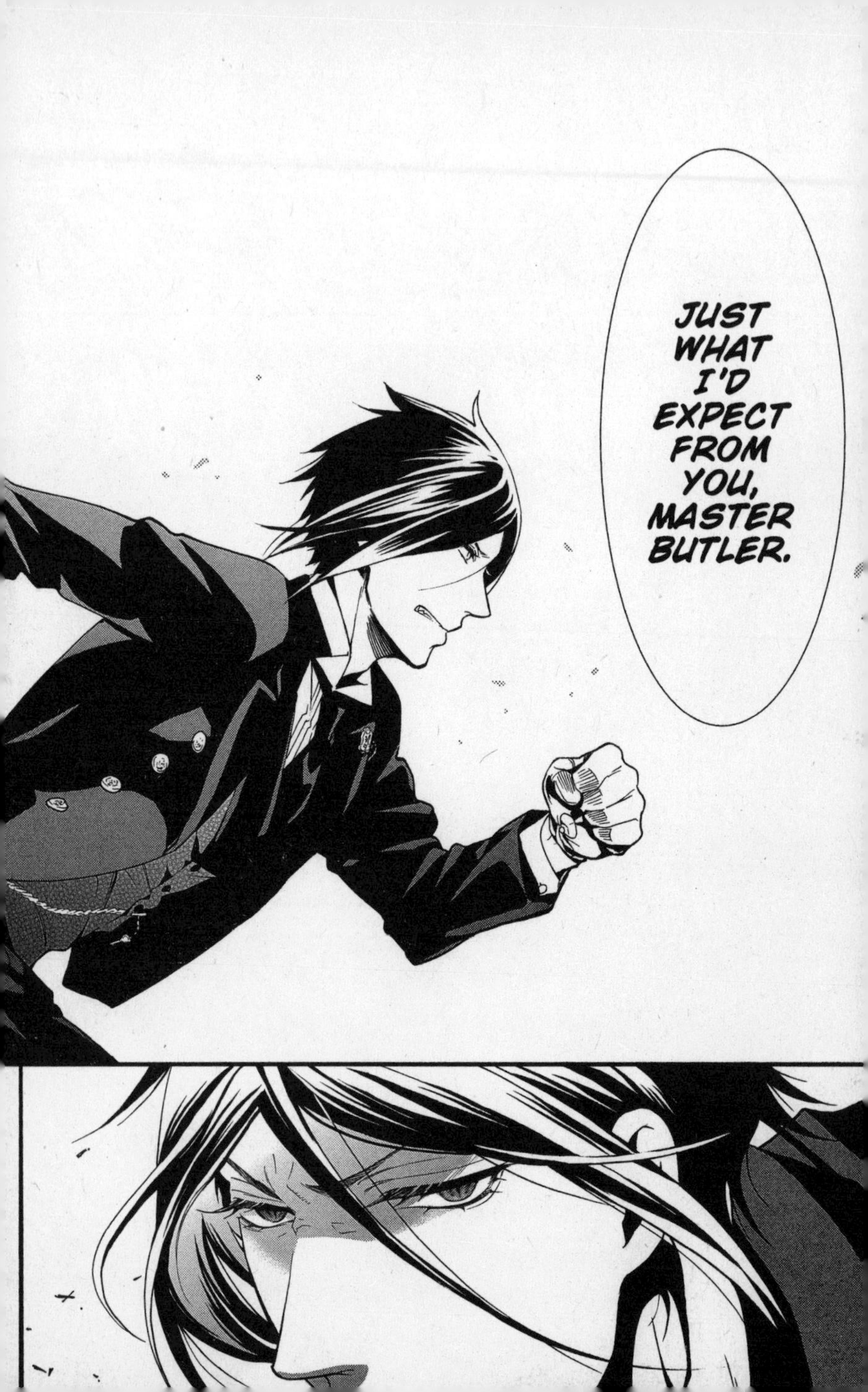
JUST WHAT I'D EXPECT FROM YOU, MASTER BUTLER.

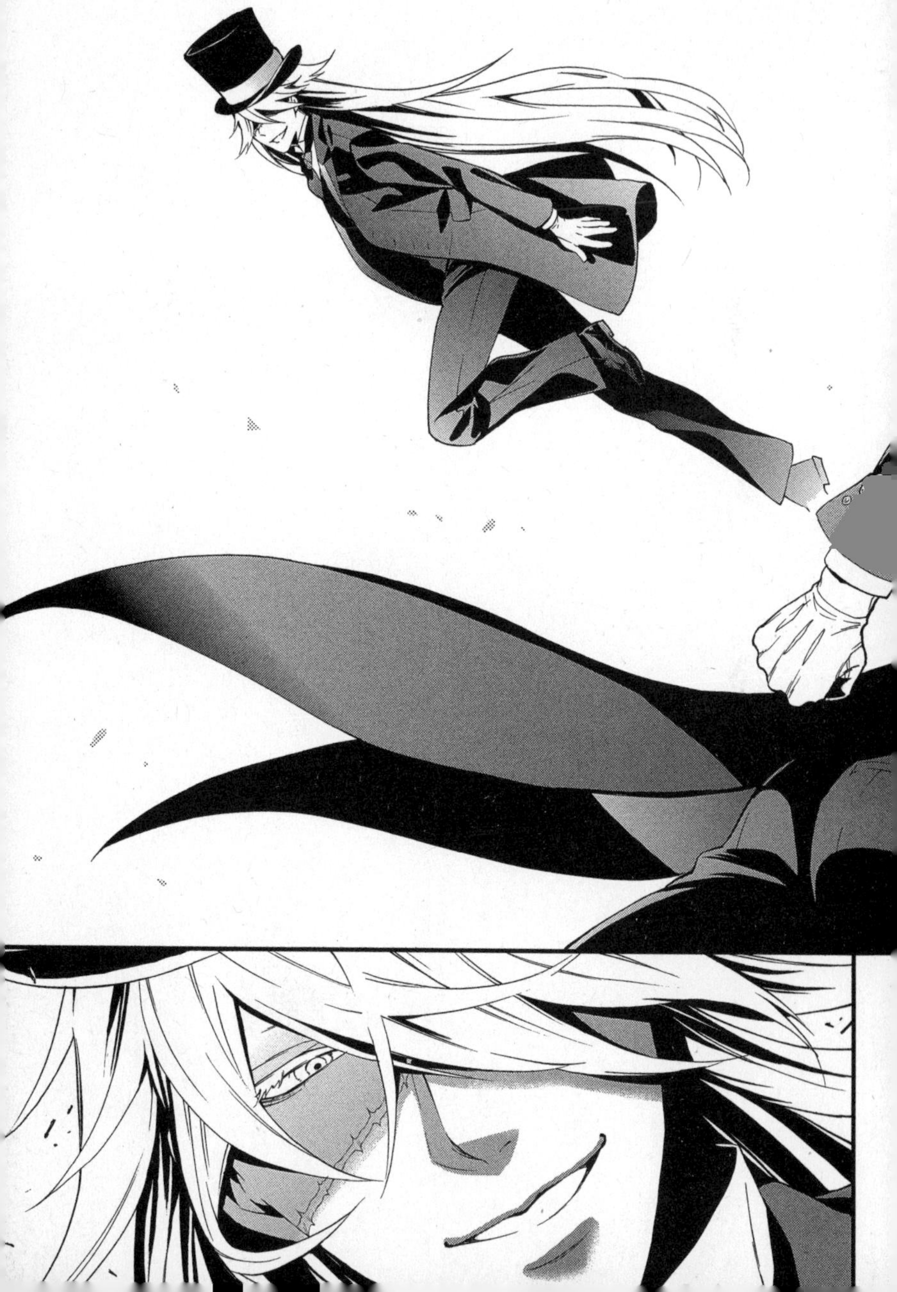

SUTO
(TMP)

I DO HOPE YOU'LL CONTINUE TO PROTECT MILORD...

...SO LOYALLY.

!?

SEBAS-TIAN!?

ZAZA
(SKSHH)

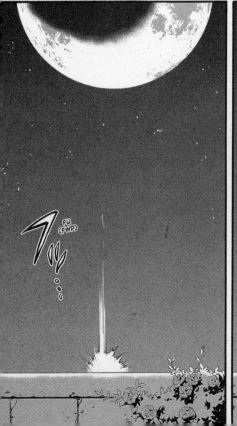

FU
(FWP)

HEE! HEE!

FARE! THEEE! WELL!

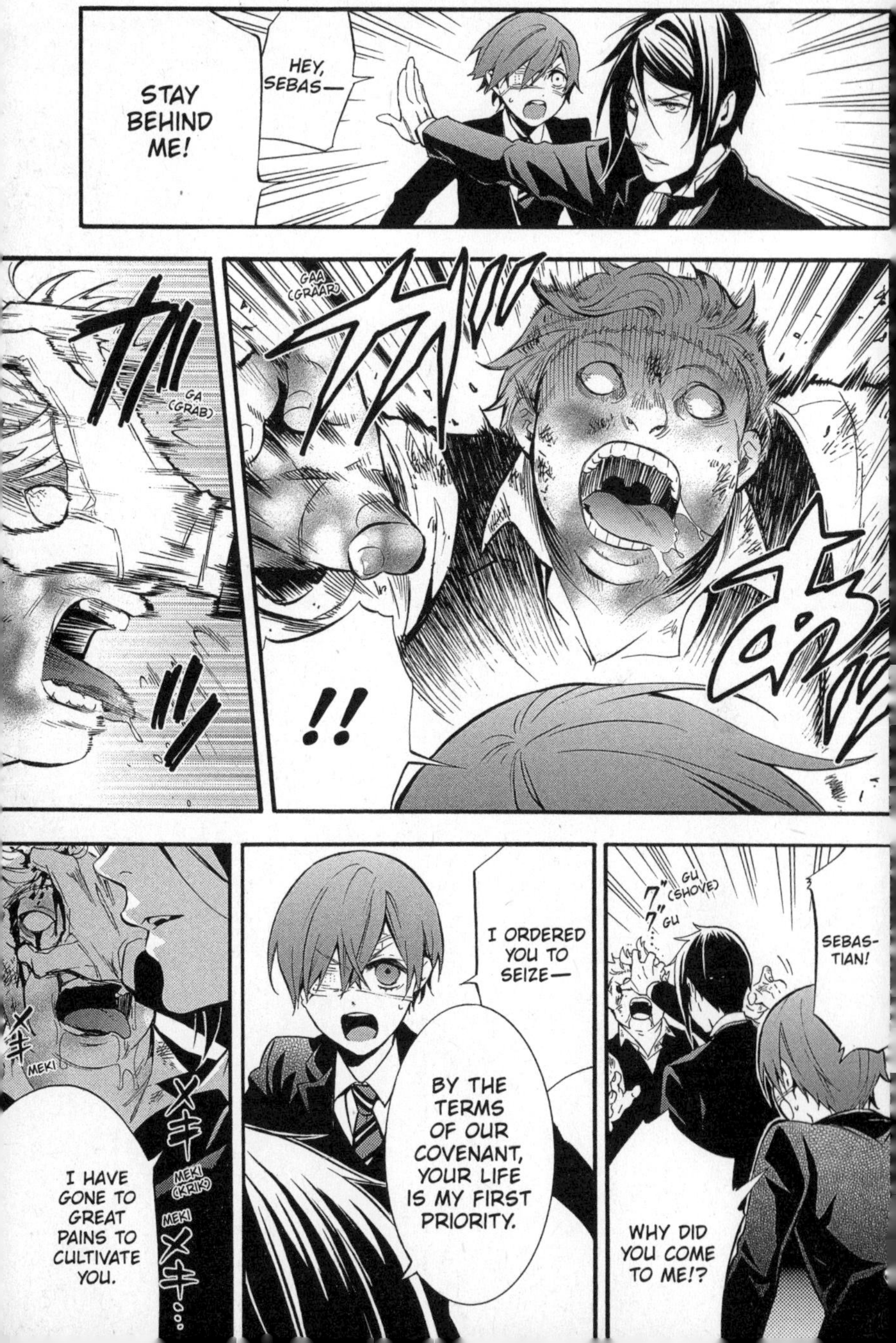
HEY, SEBAS—
STAY BEHIND ME!
GAA (GRAAR)
!!
GA (GRAB)
GU (SHOVE)
GU
SEBAS-TIAN!
WHY DID YOU COME TO ME!?
I ORDERED YOU TO SEIZE—
BY THE TERMS OF OUR COVENANT, YOUR LIFE IS MY FIRST PRIORITY.
MEKI
MEKI (KRIK)
MEKI
I HAVE GONE TO GREAT PAINS TO CULTIVATE YOU.

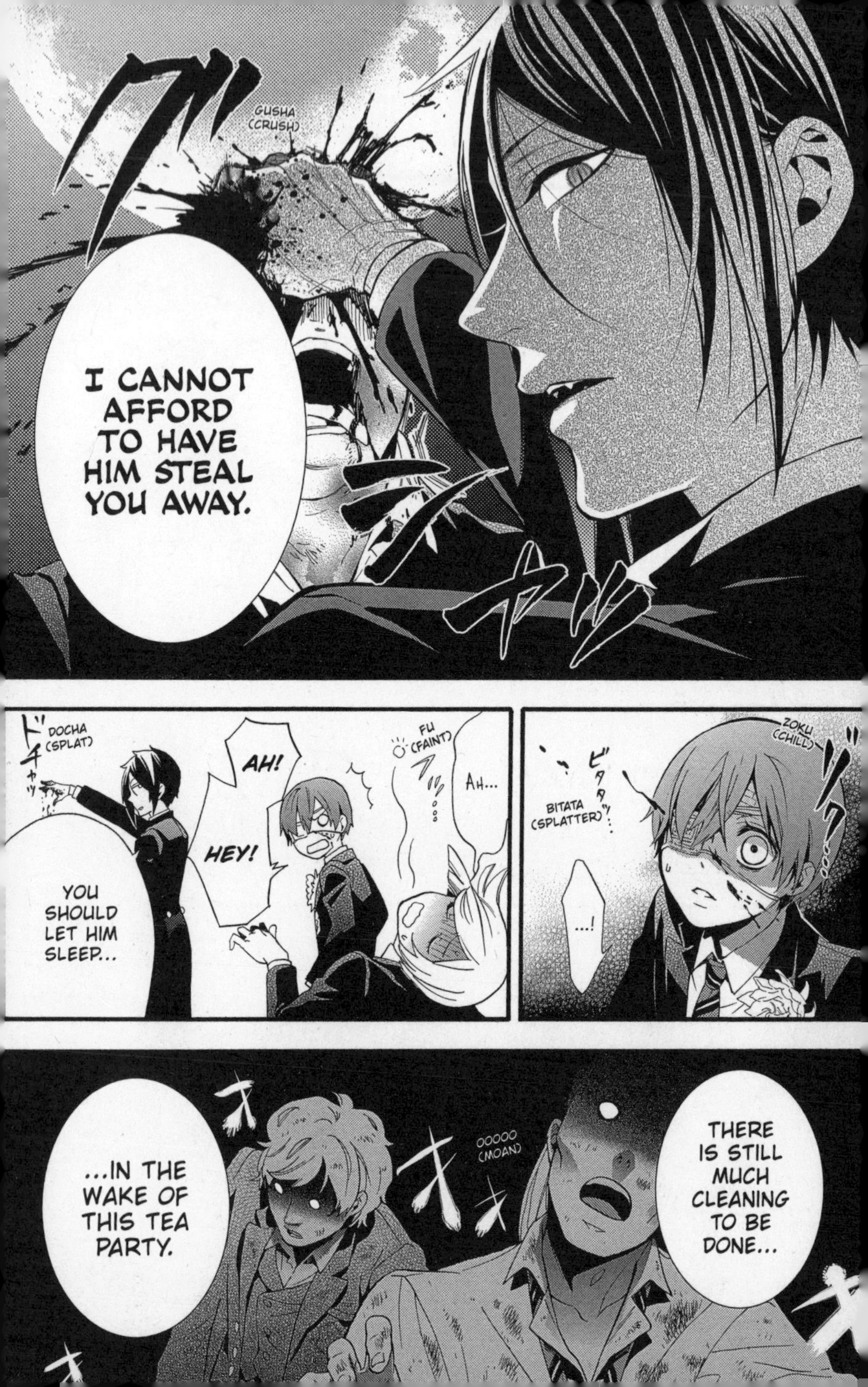
GUSHA (CRUSH)
I CANNOT AFFORD TO HAVE HIM STEAL YOU AWAY.
ZOKU (CHILL)
BITATA (SPLATTER)
...!
FU (FAINT)
AH...
AH!
HEY!
DOCHA (SPLAT)
YOU SHOULD LET HIM SLEEP...
THERE IS STILL MUCH CLEANING TO BE DONE...
OOOOO (MOAN)
...IN THE WAKE OF THIS TEA PARTY.

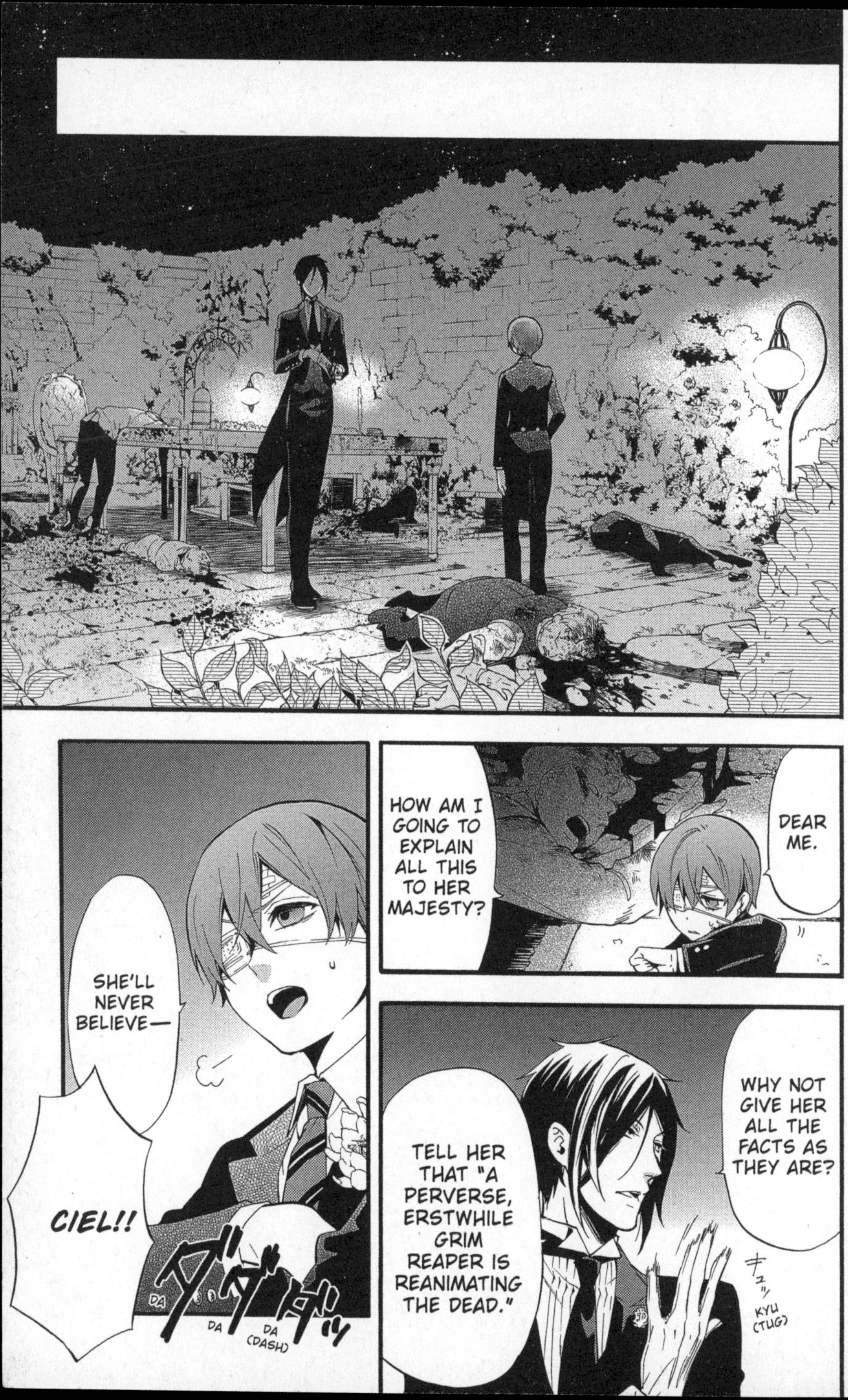
DEAR ME.
HOW AM I GOING TO EXPLAIN ALL THIS TO HER MAJESTY?
WHY NOT GIVE HER ALL THE FACTS AS THEY ARE?
TELL HER THAT "A PERVERSE, ERSTWHILE GRIM REAPER IS REANIMATING THE DEAD."
KYU (TUG)
SHE'LL NEVER BELIEVE—
CIEL!!
DA DA DA (DASH)

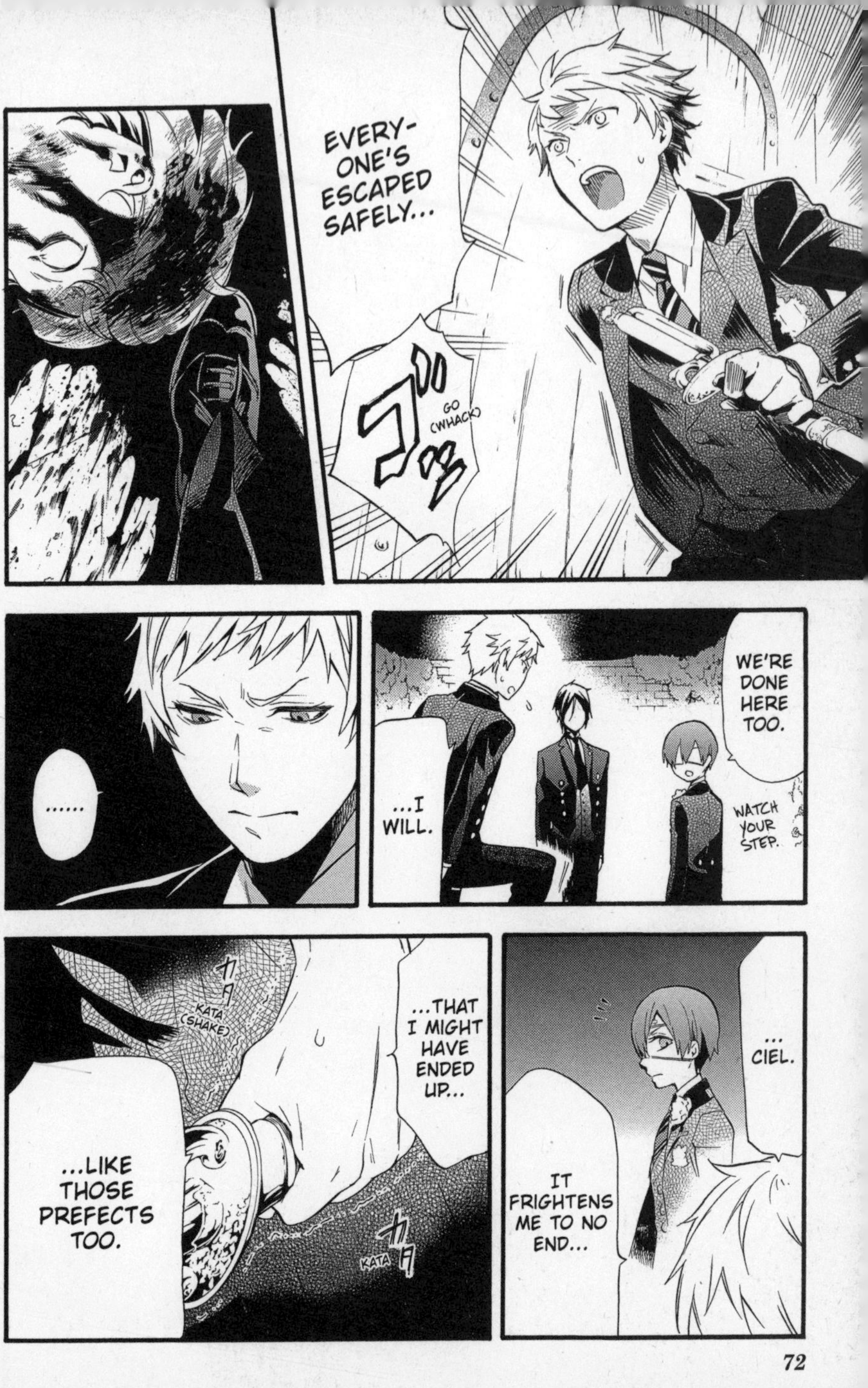
EVERY-ONE'S ESCAPED SAFELY...
GO (WHACK)
WE'RE DONE HERE TOO.
WATCH YOUR STEP.
...I WILL.
......
... CIEL.
IT FRIGHTENS ME TO NO END...
...THAT I MIGHT HAVE ENDED UP...
KATA (SHAKE)
...LIKE THOSE PREFECTS TOO.
KATA

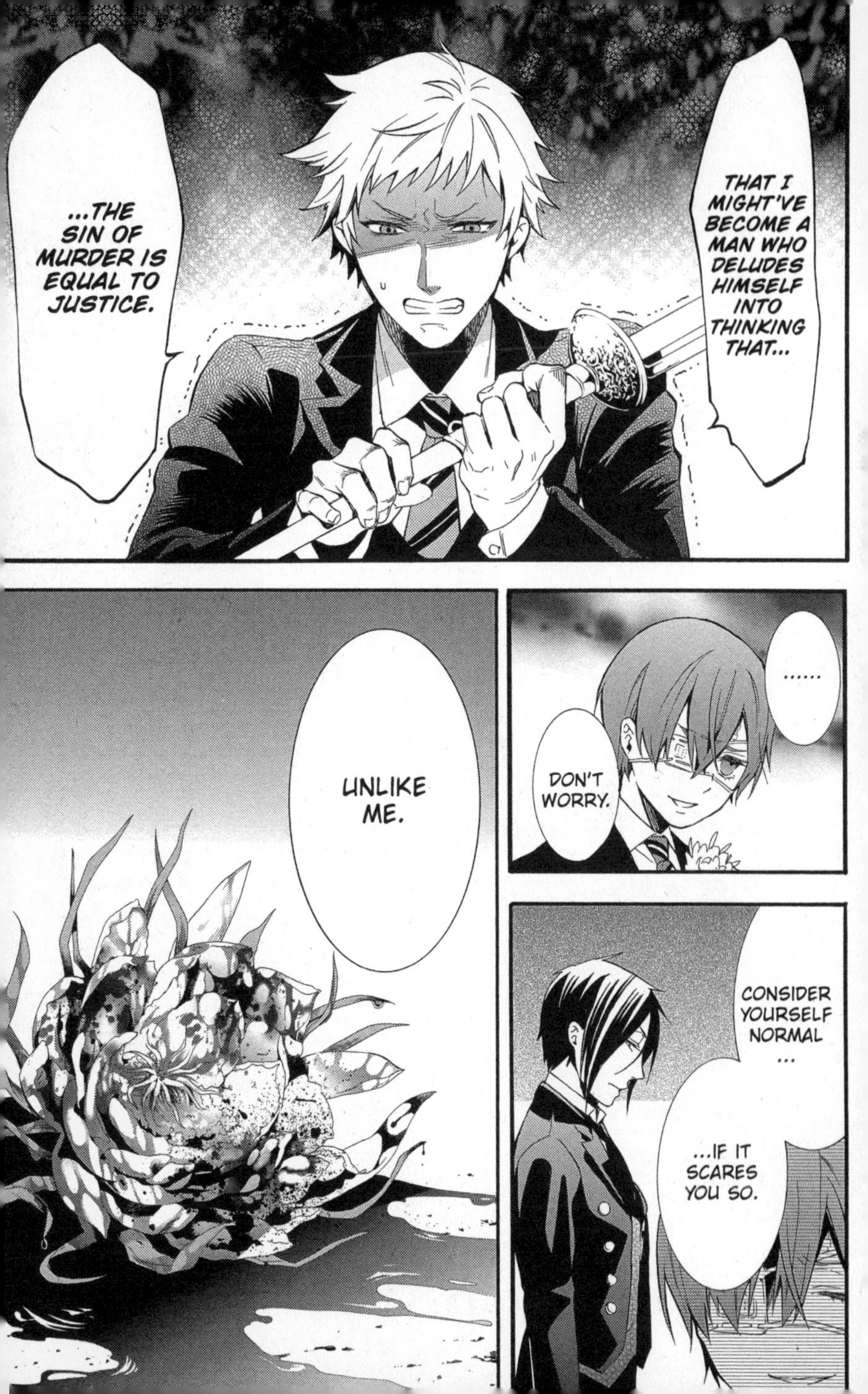
THAT I MIGHT'VE BECOME A MAN WHO DELUDES HIMSELF INTO THINKING THAT...
...THE SIN OF MURDER IS EQUAL TO JUSTICE.
......
DON'T WORRY.
CONSIDER YOURSELF NORMAL ...
...IF IT SCARES YOU SO.
UNLIKE ME.

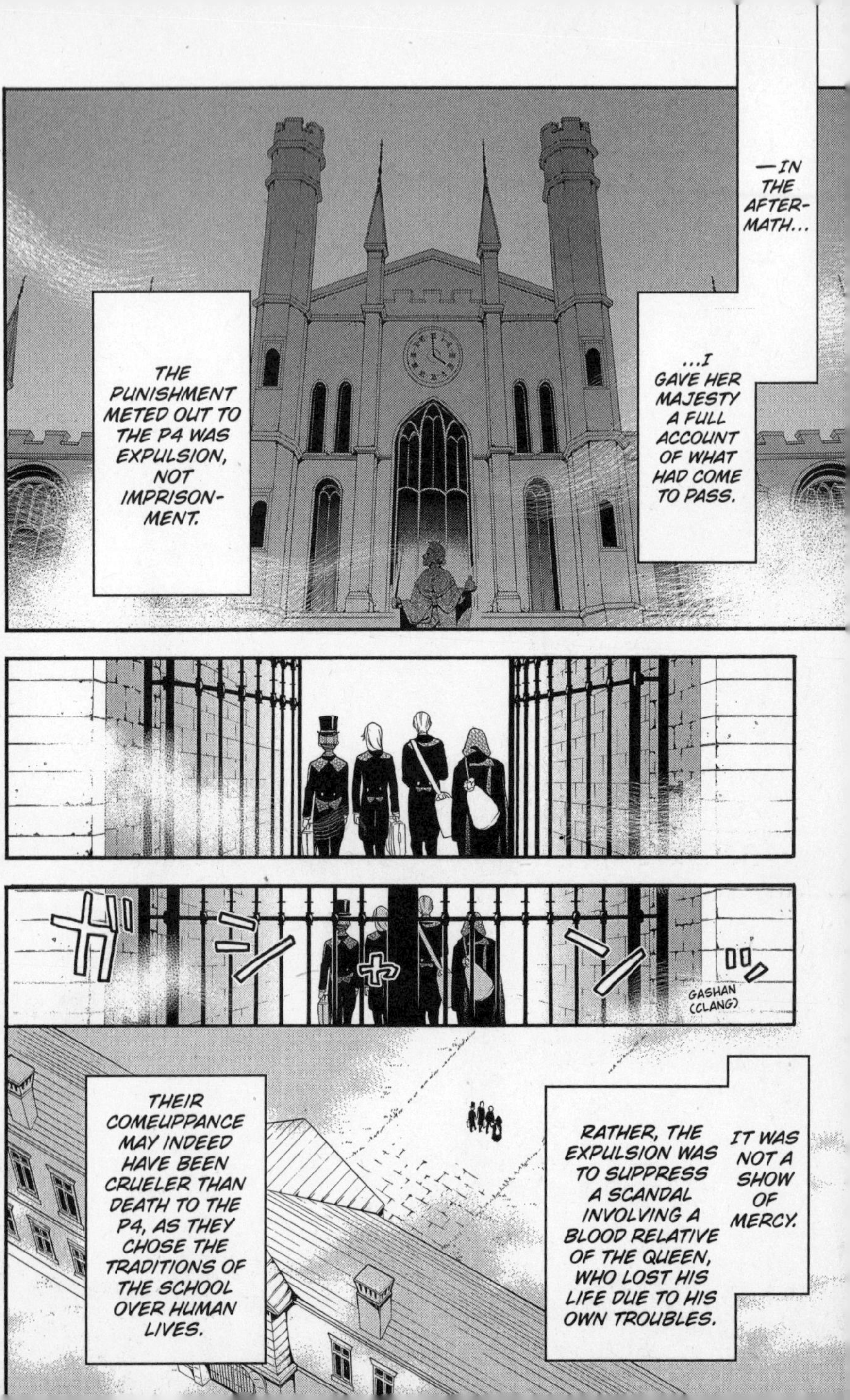
—IN THE AFTERMATH...
...I GAVE HER MAJESTY A FULL ACCOUNT OF WHAT HAD COME TO PASS.
THE PUNISHMENT METED OUT TO THE P4 WAS EXPULSION, NOT IMPRISONMENT.
GASHAN (CLANG)
IT WAS NOT A SHOW OF MERCY.
RATHER, THE EXPULSION WAS TO SUPPRESS A SCANDAL INVOLVING A BLOOD RELATIVE OF THE QUEEN, WHO LOST HIS LIFE DUE TO HIS OWN TROUBLES.
THEIR COMEUPPANCE MAY INDEED HAVE BEEN CRUELER THAN DEATH TO THE P4, AS THEY CHOSE THE TRADITIONS OF THE SCHOOL OVER HUMAN LIVES.

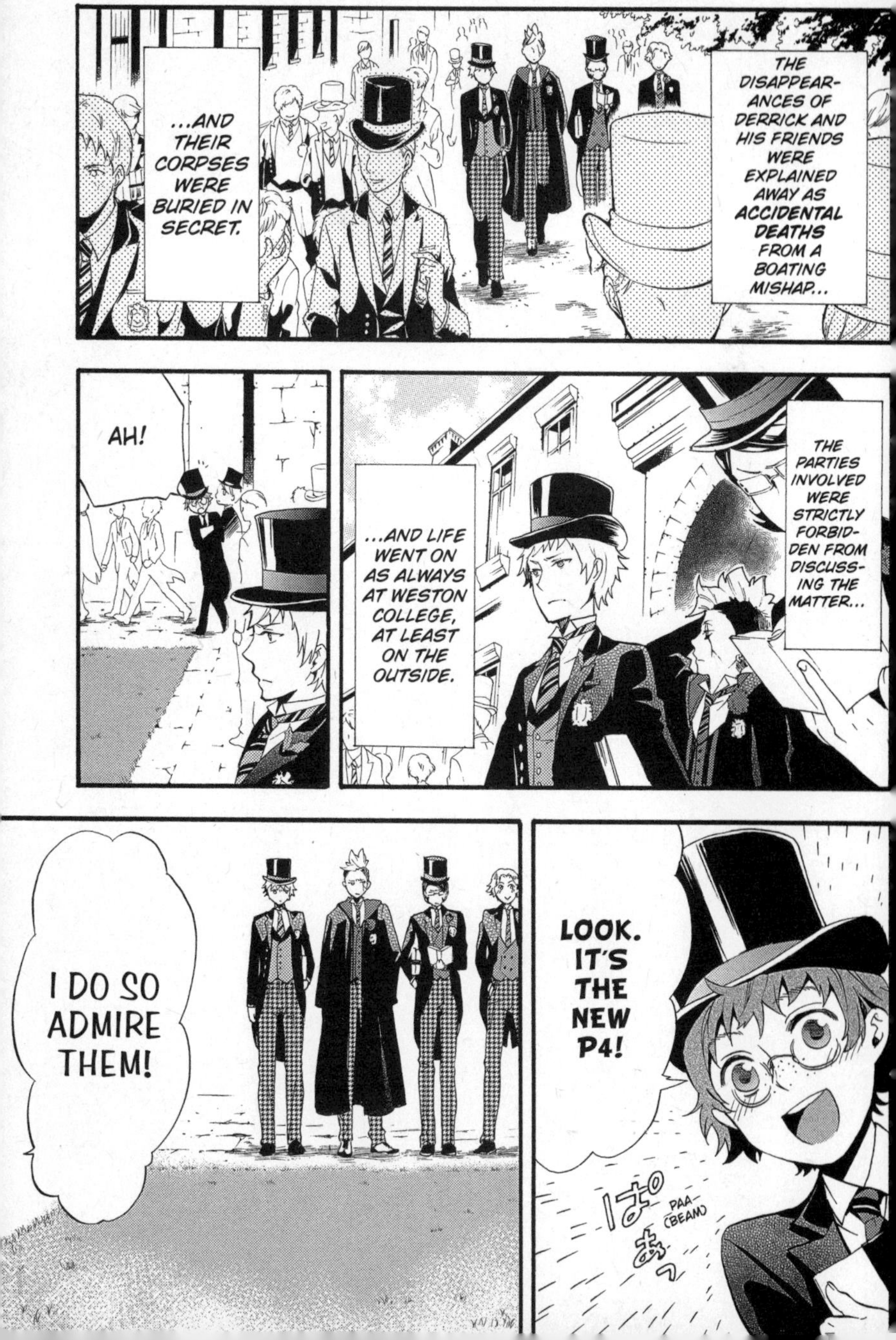
THE DISAPPEARANCES OF DERRICK AND HIS FRIENDS WERE EXPLAINED AWAY AS ACCIDENTAL DEATHS FROM A BOATING MISHAP...
...AND THEIR CORPSES WERE BURIED IN SECRET.
THE PARTIES INVOLVED WERE STRICTLY FORBIDDEN FROM DISCUSSING THE MATTER...
...AND LIFE WENT ON AS ALWAYS AT WESTON COLLEGE, AT LEAST ON THE OUTSIDE.
AH!
LOOK. IT'S THE NEW P4!
ぱあっ
PAA (BEAM)
I DO SO ADMIRE THEM!

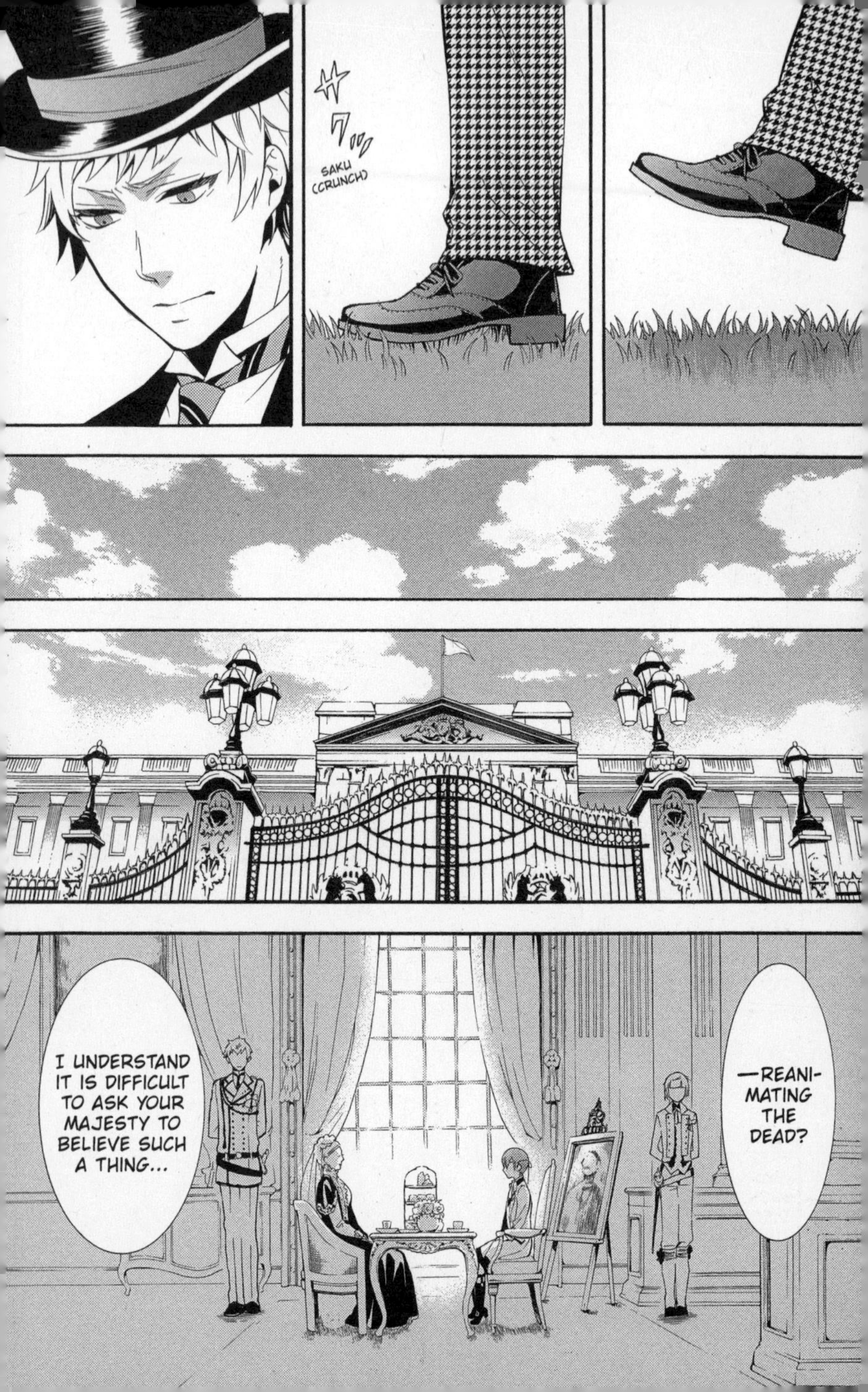
SAKU (CRUNCH)
—REANI-MATING THE DEAD?
I UNDERSTAND IT IS DIFFICULT TO ASK YOUR MAJESTY TO BELIEVE SUCH A THING...

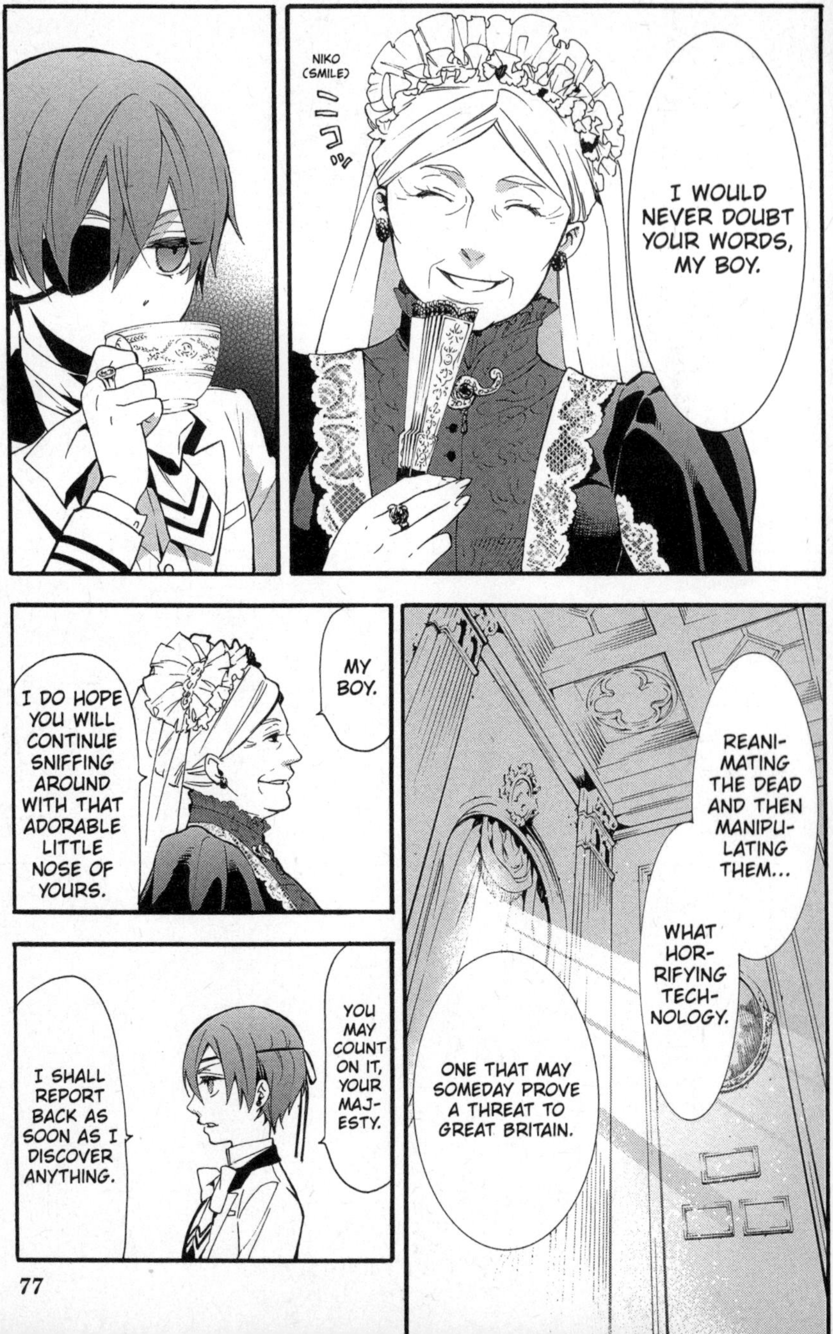
NIKO (SMILE)
I WOULD NEVER DOUBT YOUR WORDS, MY BOY.
REANIMATING THE DEAD AND THEN MANIPULATING THEM...
WHAT HORRIFYING TECHNOLOGY.
ONE THAT MAY SOMEDAY PROVE A THREAT TO GREAT BRITAIN.
MY BOY.
I DO HOPE YOU WILL CONTINUE SNIFFING AROUND WITH THAT ADORABLE LITTLE NOSE OF YOURS.
YOU MAY COUNT ON IT, YOUR MAJESTY.
I SHALL REPORT BACK AS SOON AS I DISCOVER ANYTHING.

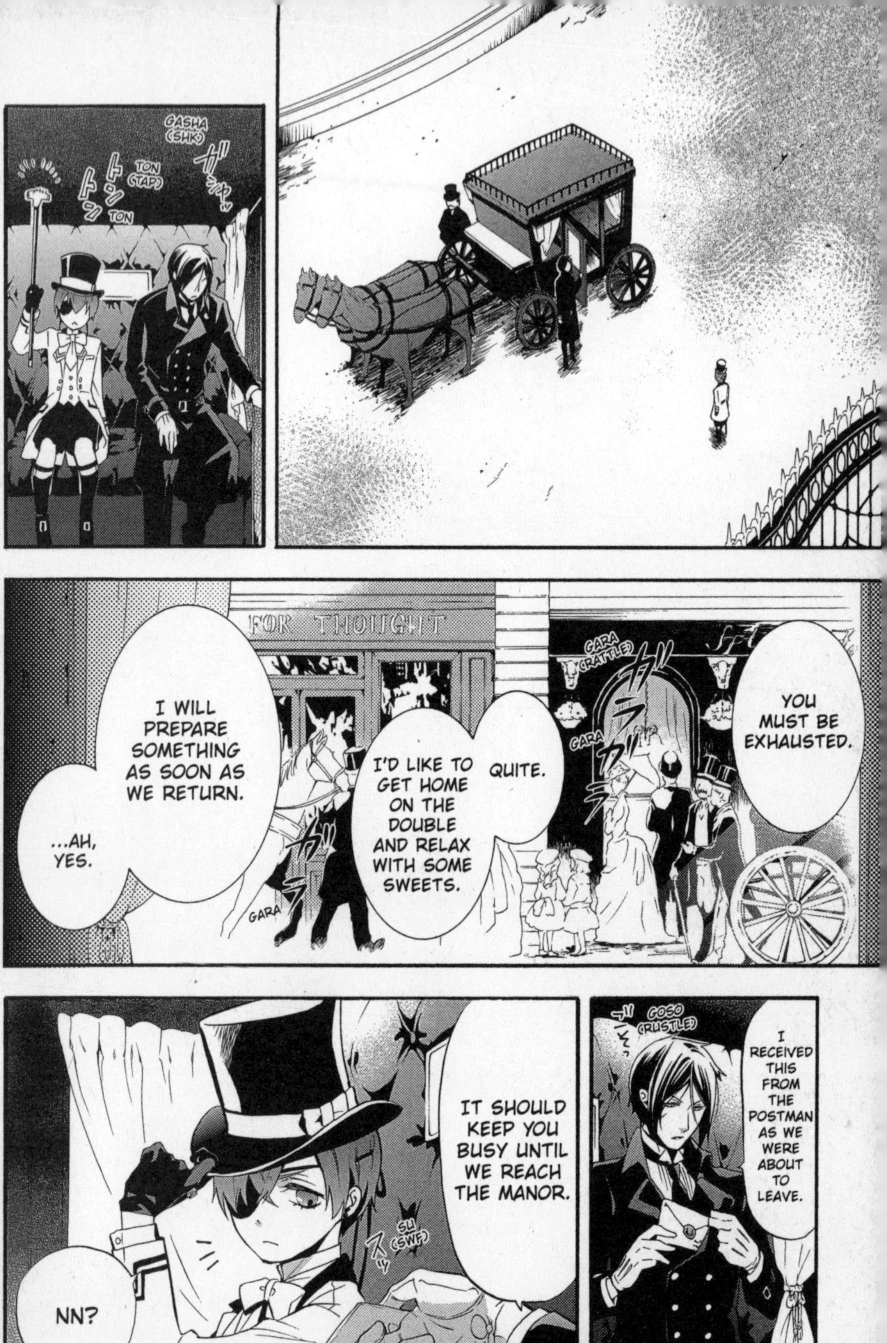
GASHA (SHK)
TON (TAP)
TON
GARA (RATTLE)
YOU MUST BE EXHAUSTED.
GARA
QUITE.
I'D LIKE TO GET HOME ON THE DOUBLE AND RELAX WITH SOME SWEETS.
I WILL PREPARE SOMETHING AS SOON AS WE RETURN.
...AH, YES.
GARA
FOR THOUGHT
GOSO (RUSTLE)
I RECEIVED THIS FROM THE POSTMAN AS WE WERE ABOUT TO LEAVE.
IT SHOULD KEEP YOU BUSY UNTIL WE REACH THE MANOR.
SU (SWF)
NN?

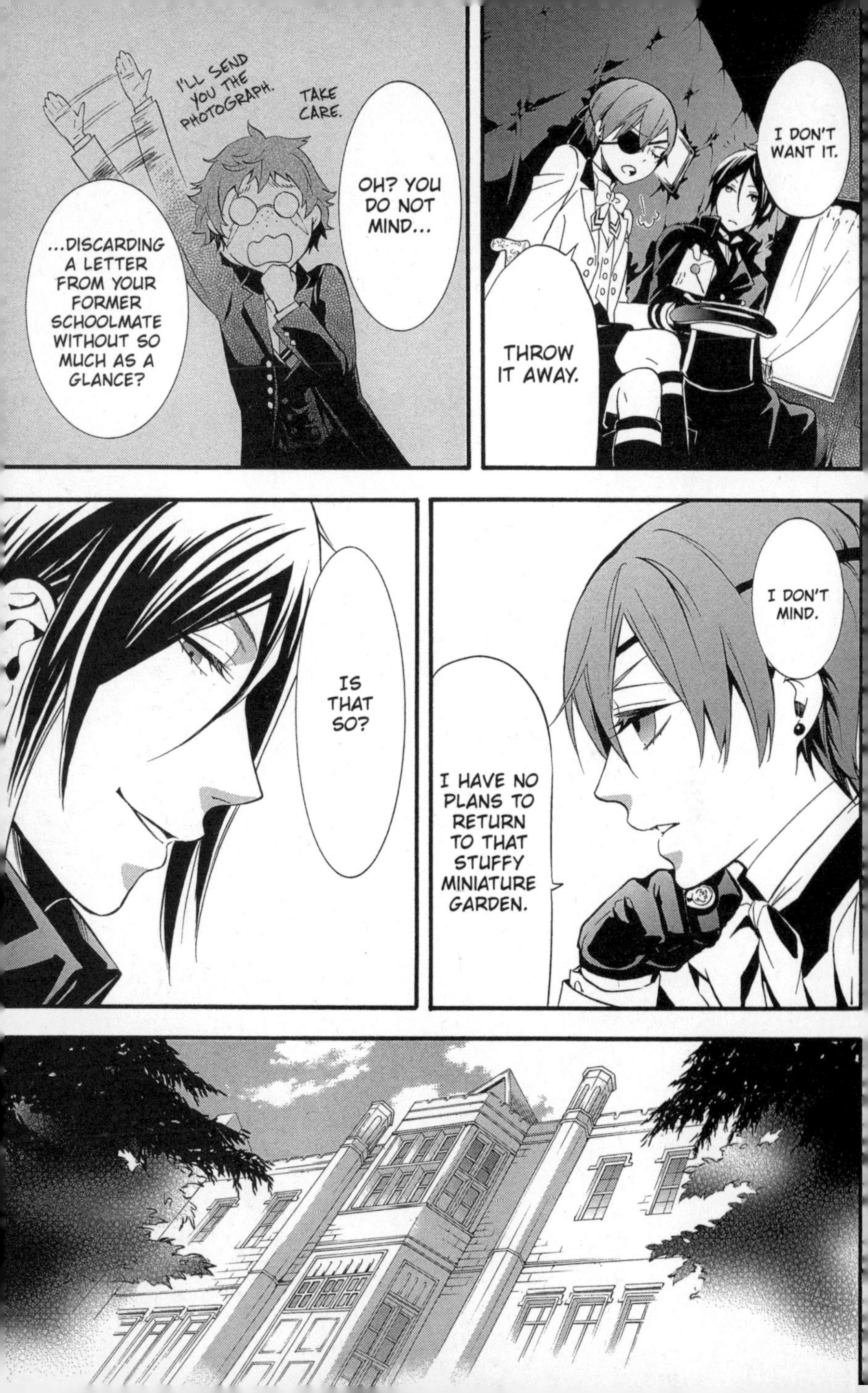
I DON'T WANT IT.
THROW IT AWAY.
TAKE CARE.
I'LL SEND YOU THE PHOTOGRAPH.
OH? YOU DO NOT MIND...
...DISCARDING A LETTER FROM YOUR FORMER SCHOOLMATE WITHOUT SO MUCH AS A GLANCE?
I DON'T MIND.
I HAVE NO PLANS TO RETURN TO THAT STUFFY MINIATURE GARDEN.
IS THAT SO?

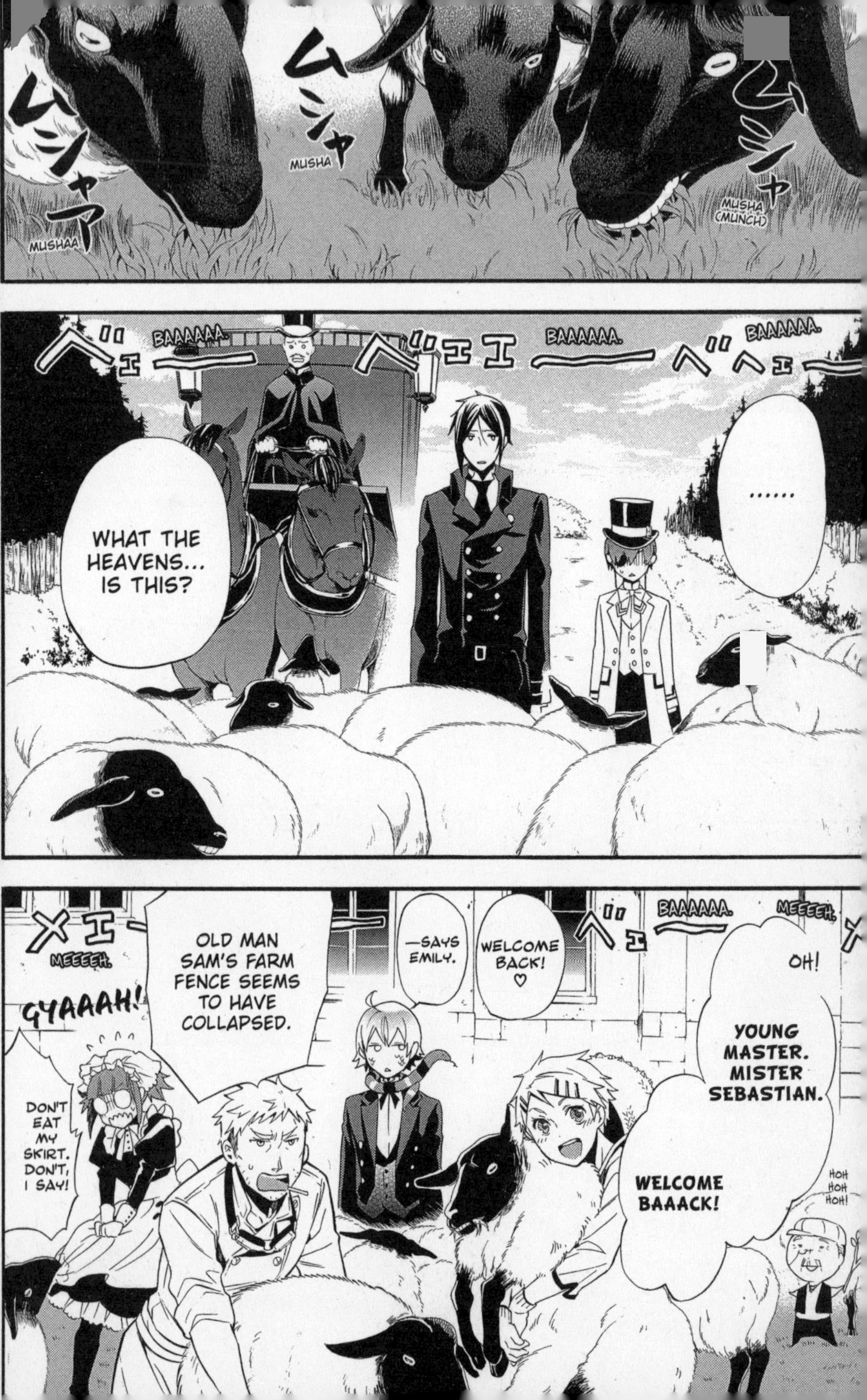
MUSHA (MUNCH)
MUSHA
MUSHAA
BAAAAAA.
BAAAAAA.
BAAAAAA.
......
WHAT THE HEAVENS... IS THIS?
MEEEEH.
BAAAAAA.
OH!
YOUNG MASTER. MISTER SEBASTIAN.
WELCOME BAAACK!
HOH HOH HOH!
WELCOME BACK! ♡
—SAYS EMILY.
OLD MAN SAM'S FARM FENCE SEEMS TO HAVE COLLAPSED.
GYAAAH!
DON'T EAT MY SKIRT. DON'T, I SAY!
MEEEEH.

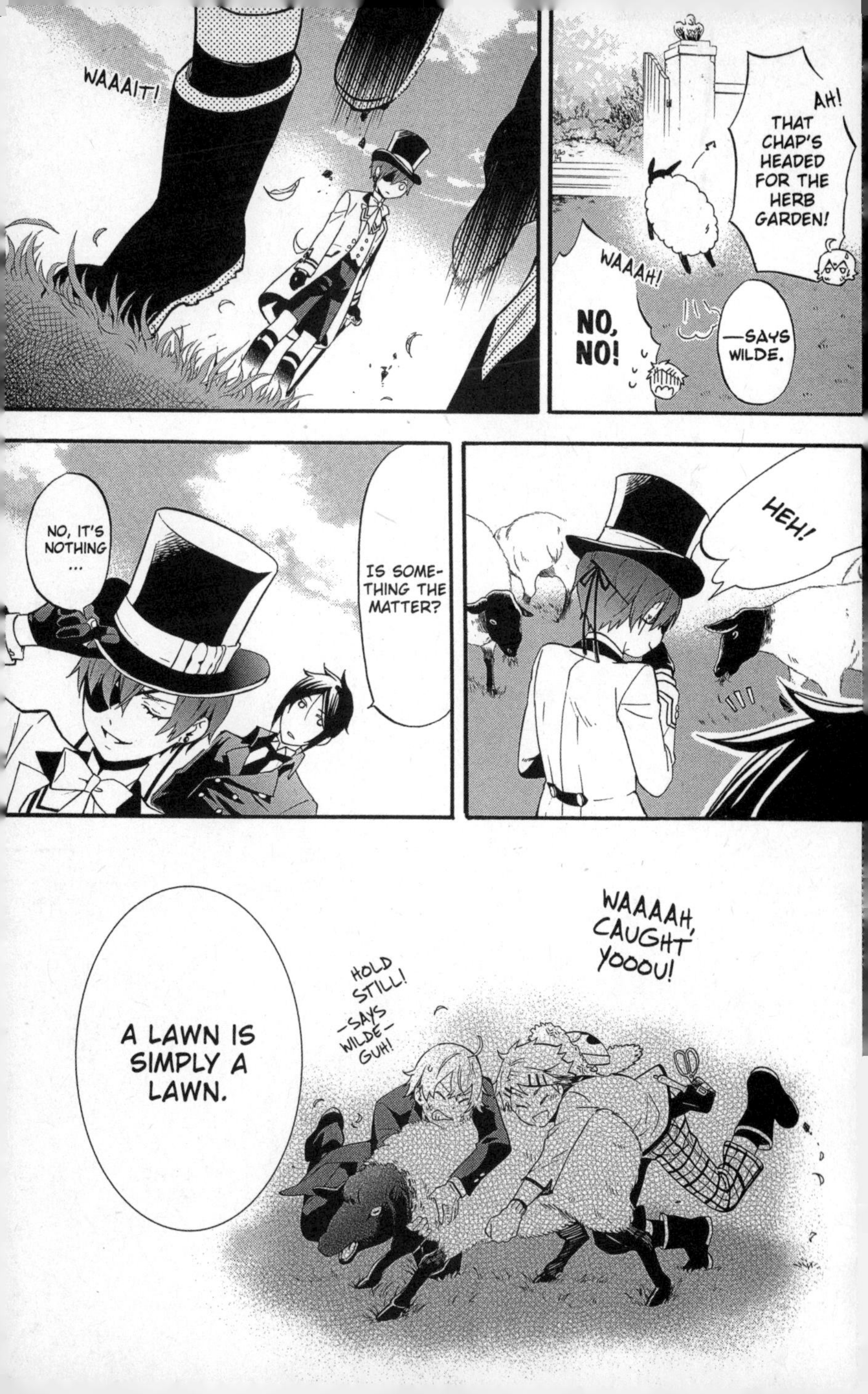
AH! THAT CHAP'S HEADED FOR THE HERB GARDEN!
—SAYS WILDE.
WAAAH!
NO, NO!
WAAAIT!
HEH!
IS SOME-THING THE MATTER?
NO, IT'S NOTHING ...
WAAAAH, CAUGHT YOOOU!
HOLD STILL!
—SAYS WILDE—
GUH!
A LAWN IS SIMPLY A LAWN.

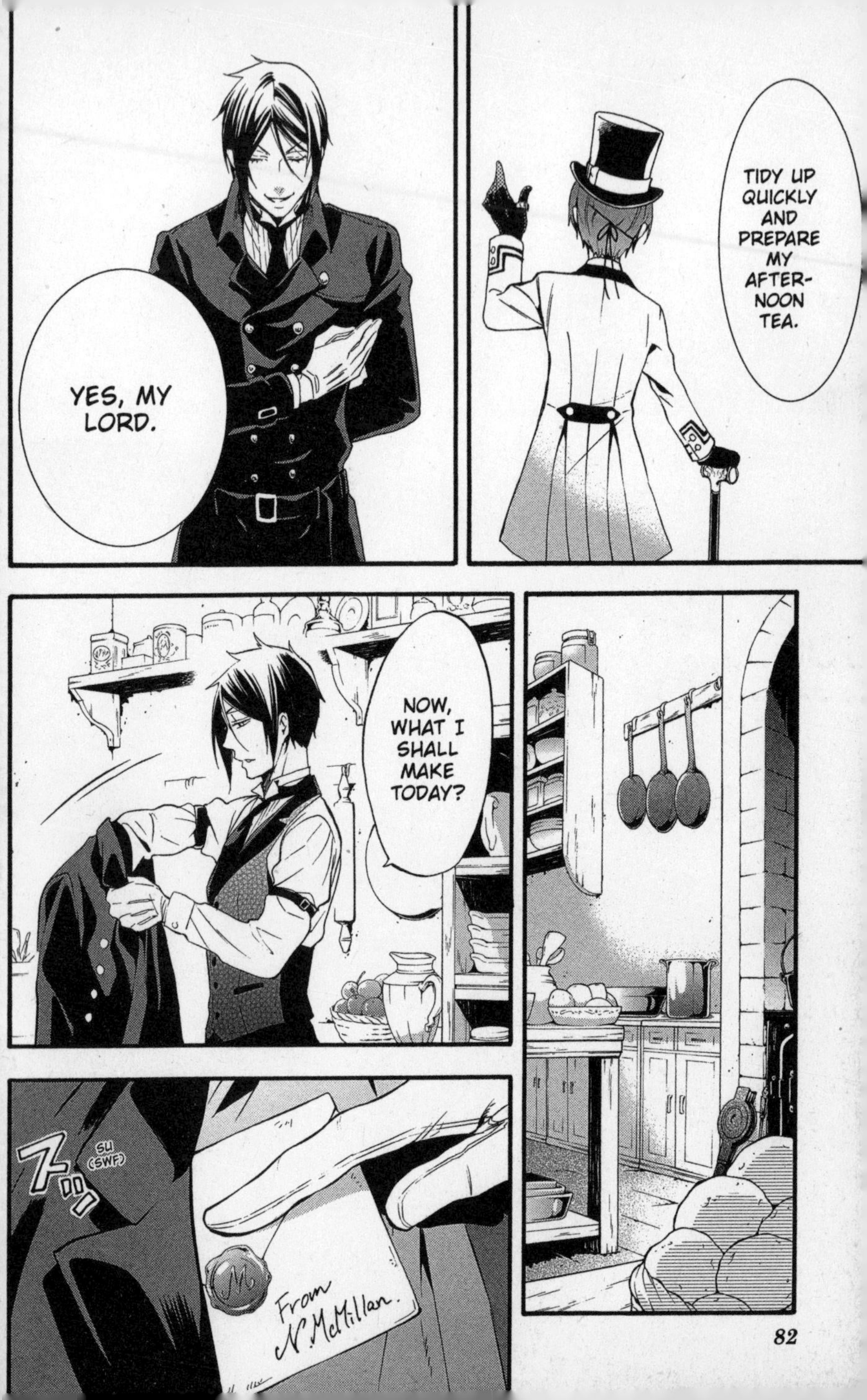
TIDY UP QUICKLY AND PREPARE MY AFTER-NOON TEA.
YES, MY LORD.
NOW, WHAT I SHALL MAKE TODAY?
SU (SWF)
From N.McMillan.

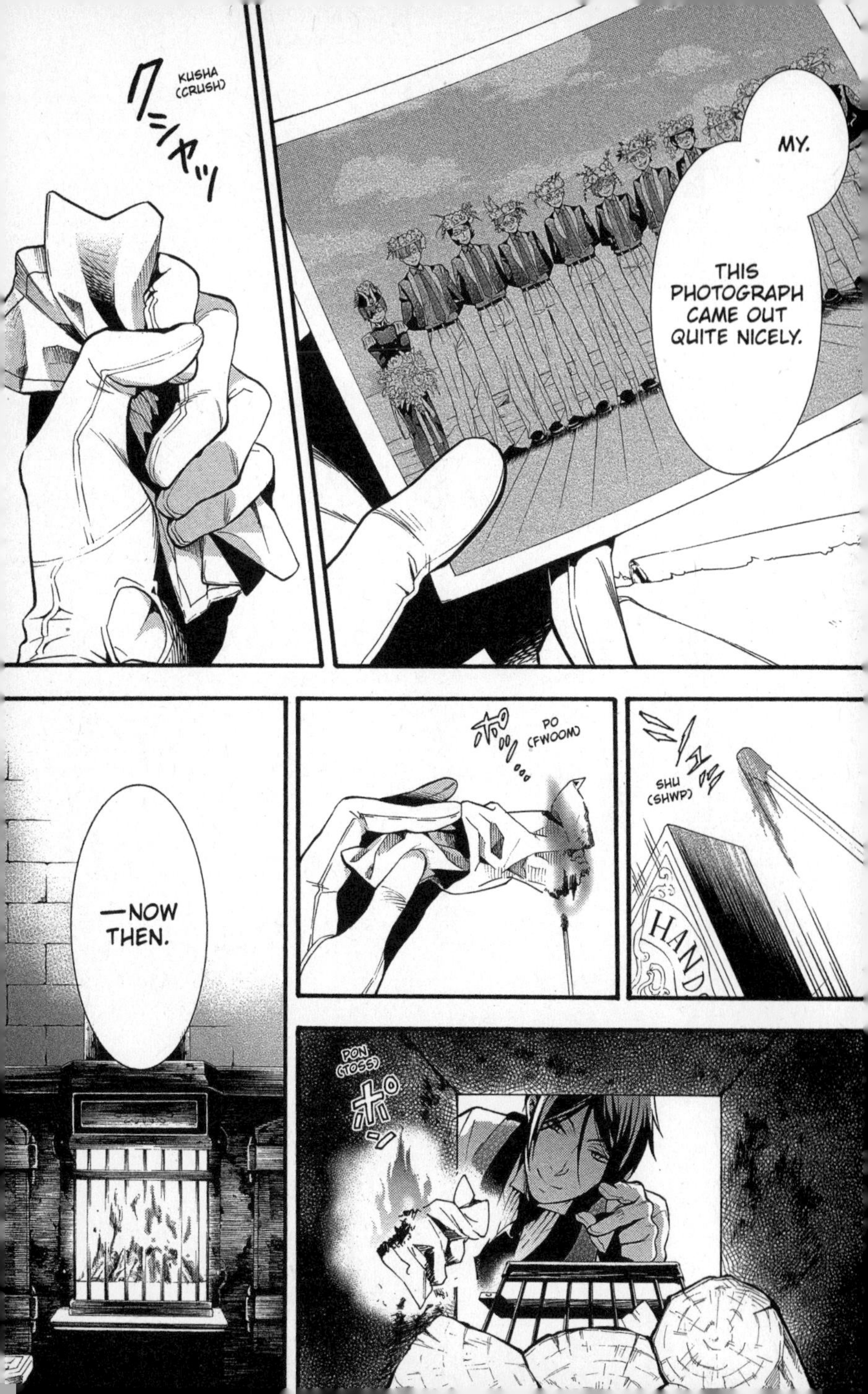
MY.
THIS PHOTOGRAPH CAME OUT QUITE NICELY.
クシャッ
KUSHA (CRUSH)
シュッ
SHU (SHWP)
HAND
ポッ
PO (FWOOM)
ポーン
PON (TOSS)
—NOW THEN.

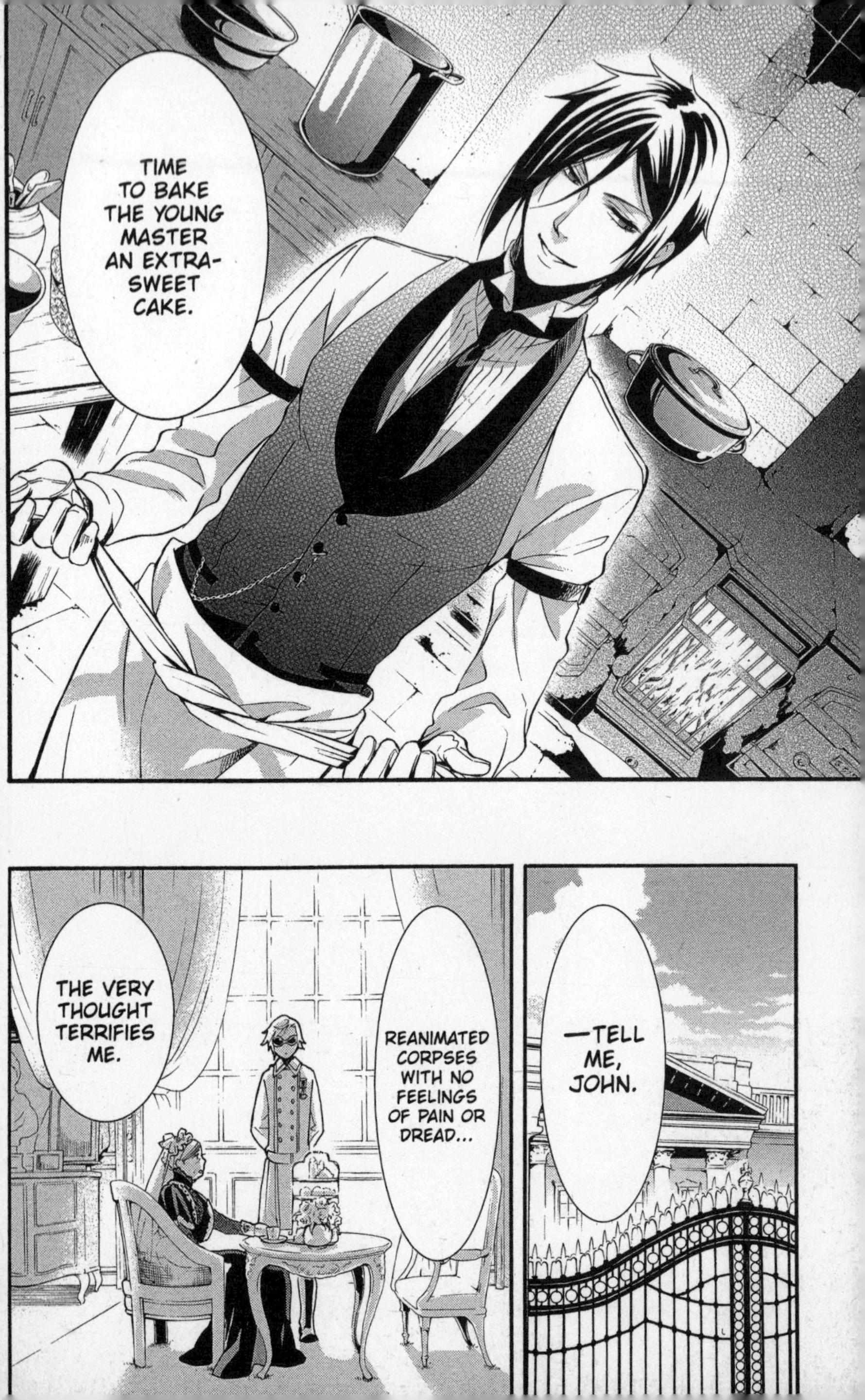
TIME TO BAKE THE YOUNG MASTER AN EXTRA-SWEET CAKE.
—TELL ME, JOHN.
REANIMATED CORPSES WITH NO FEELINGS OF PAIN OR DREAD...
THE VERY THOUGHT TERRIFIES ME.

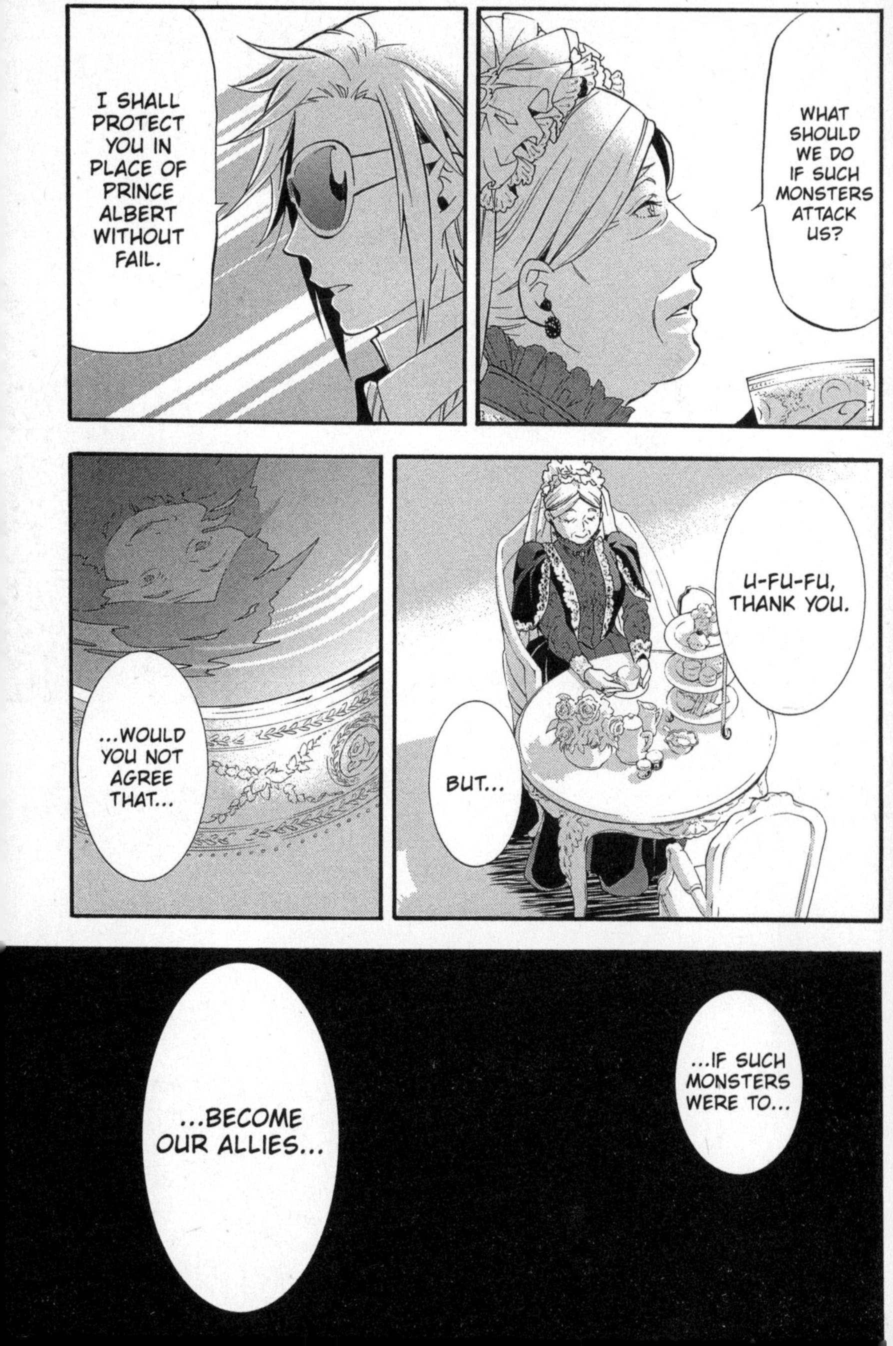
WHAT SHOULD WE DO IF SUCH MONSTERS ATTACK US?
I SHALL PROTECT YOU IN PLACE OF PRINCE ALBERT WITHOUT FAIL.
U-FU-FU, THANK YOU.
BUT...
...WOULD YOU NOT AGREE THAT...
...IF SUCH MONSTERS WERE TO...
...BECOME OUR ALLIES...

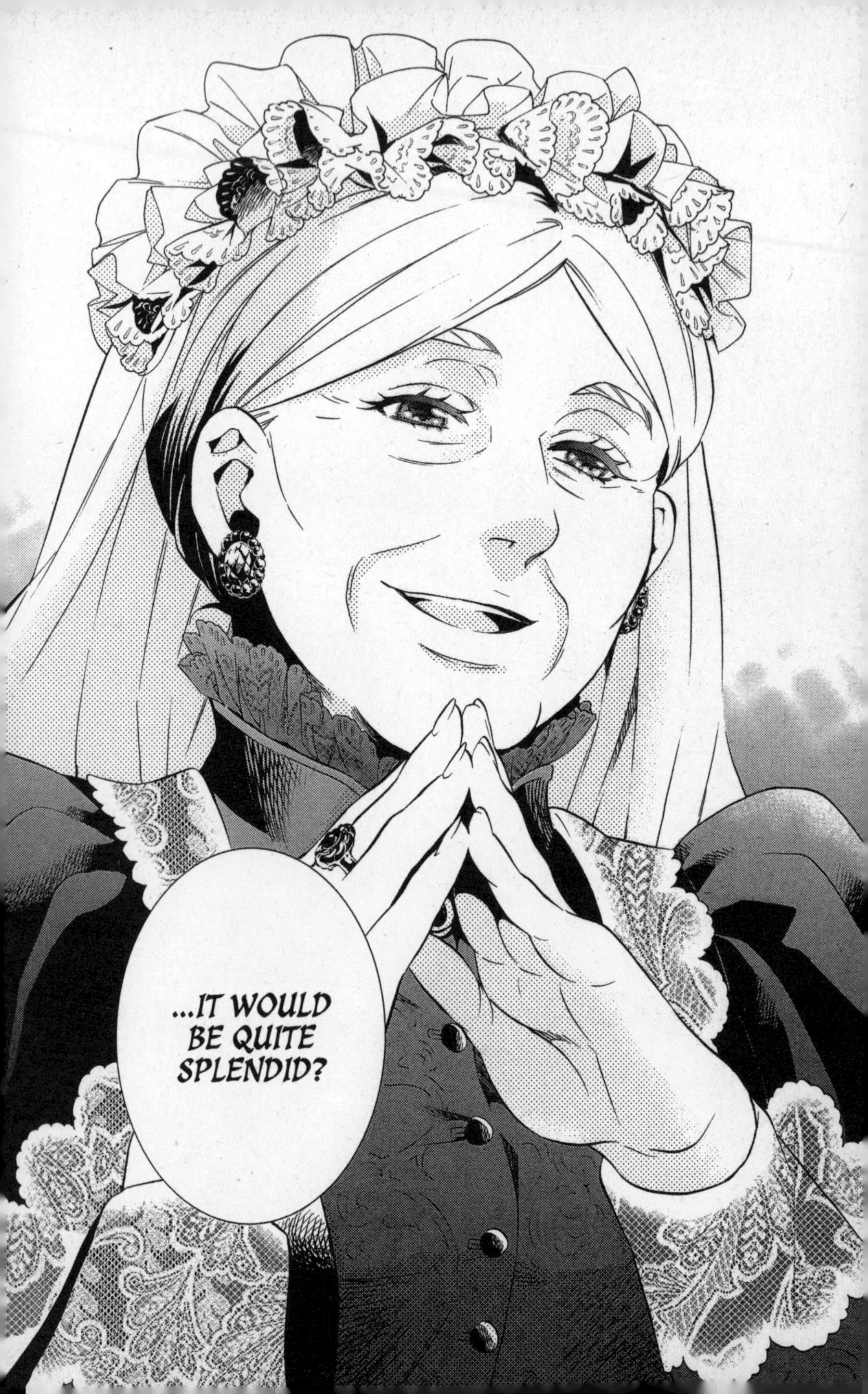
...IT WOULD BE QUITE SPLENDID?

Book Store

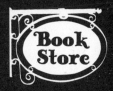

Black Butler

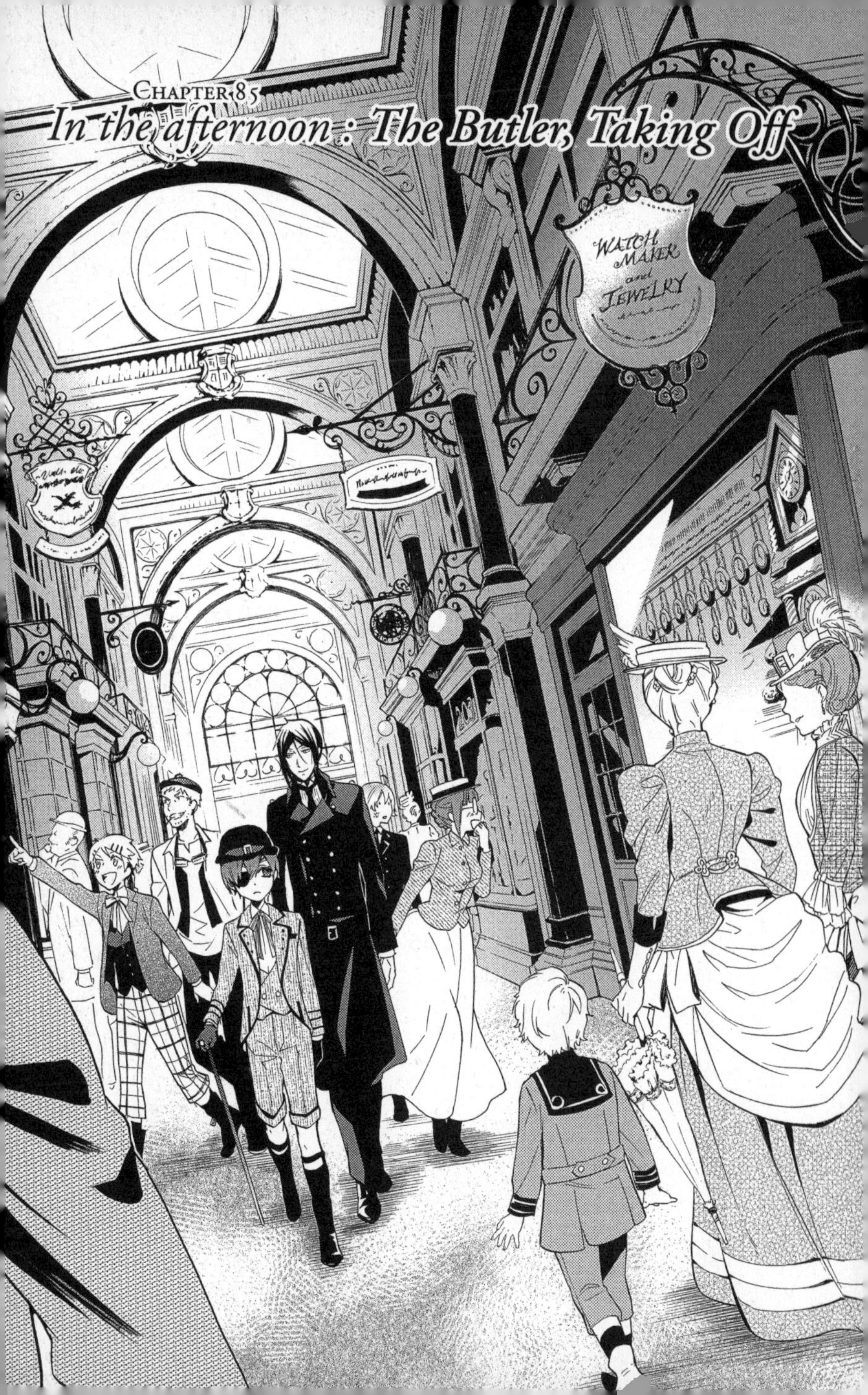
Chapter 85
In the afternoon : The Butler, Taking Off
WATCH MAKER and JEWELRY

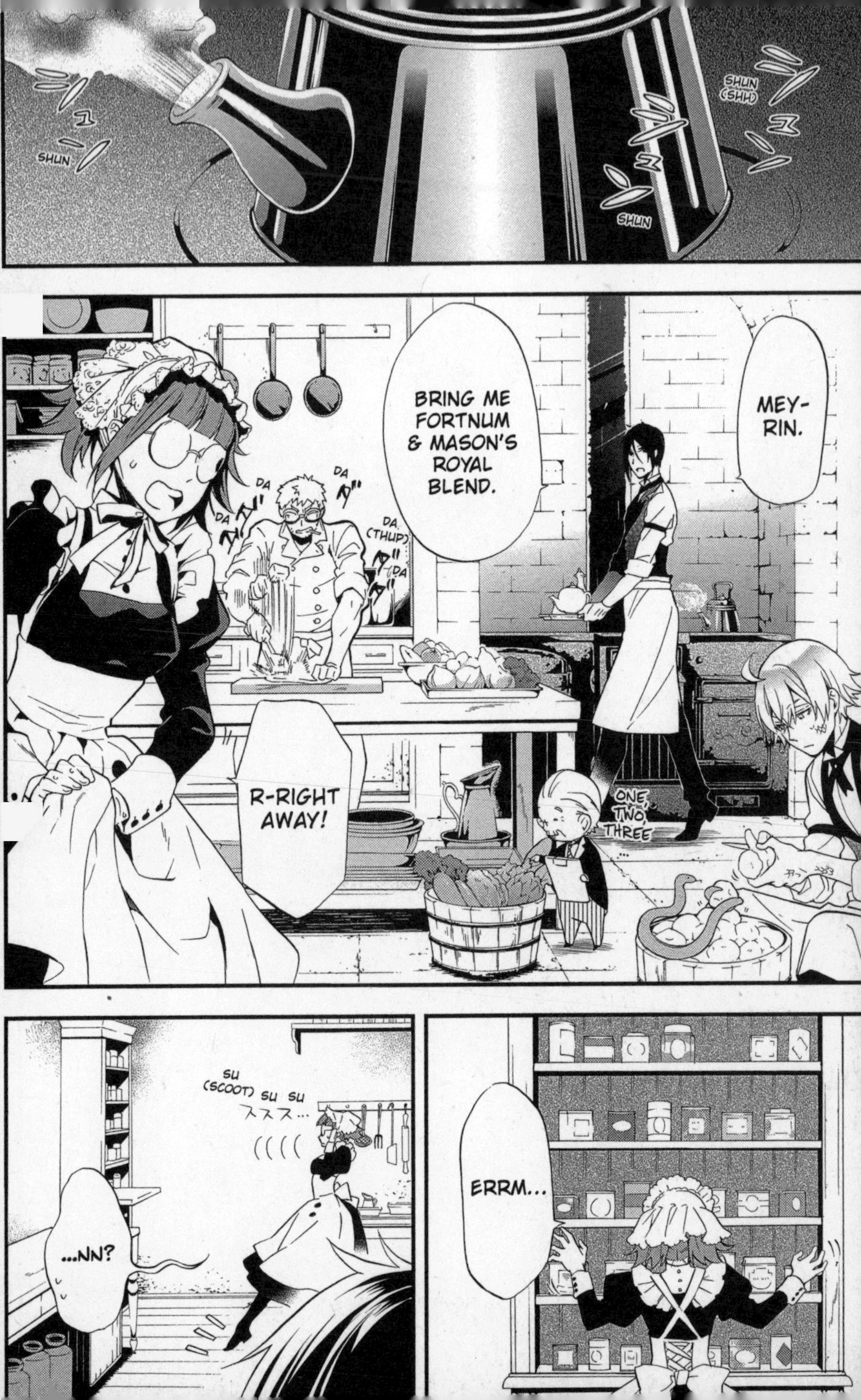
SHUN (SHH)
SHUN
SHUN
MEY-RIN.
BRING ME FORTNUM & MASON'S ROYAL BLEND.
ONE, TWO, THREE ...
DA (THUP) DA
DA
DA
R-RIGHT AWAY!
ERRM...
SU (SCOOT) SU SU
...NN?

HMM...

NOW
WASH
THEM.

MISTER
SEBAS-
TIAAAN,
I'VE
PICKED
THE
HERBS!

'KAYYY!

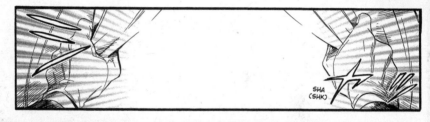

SHA
(SHK)

IT IS
TIME TO
RISE.

YOUNG
MASTER.

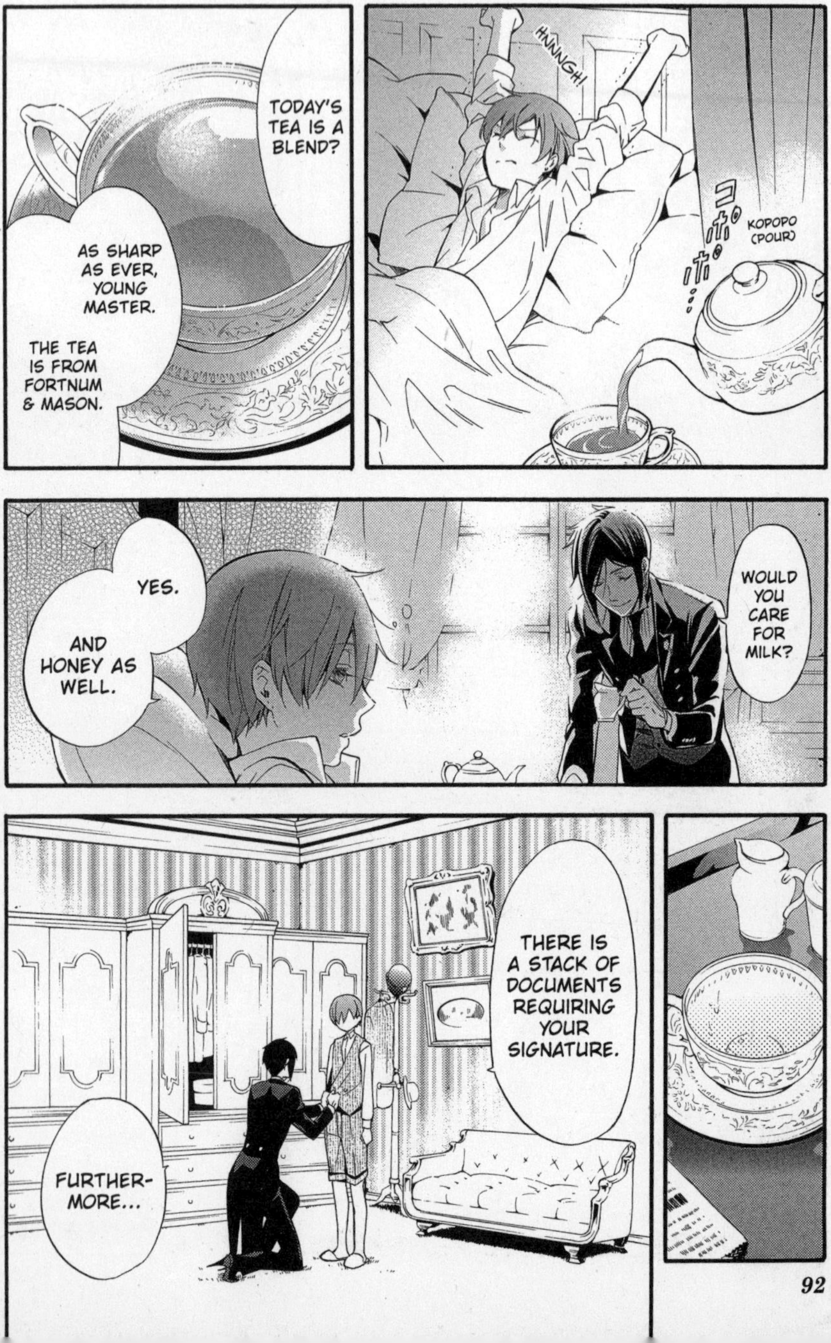
HNNNGH!
KOPOPO (POUR)
TODAY'S TEA IS A BLEND?
AS SHARP AS EVER, YOUNG MASTER.
THE TEA IS FROM FORTNUM & MASON.
WOULD YOU CARE FOR MILK?
YES.
AND HONEY AS WELL.
THERE IS A STACK OF DOCUMENTS REQUIRING YOUR SIGNATURE.
FURTHER-MORE...

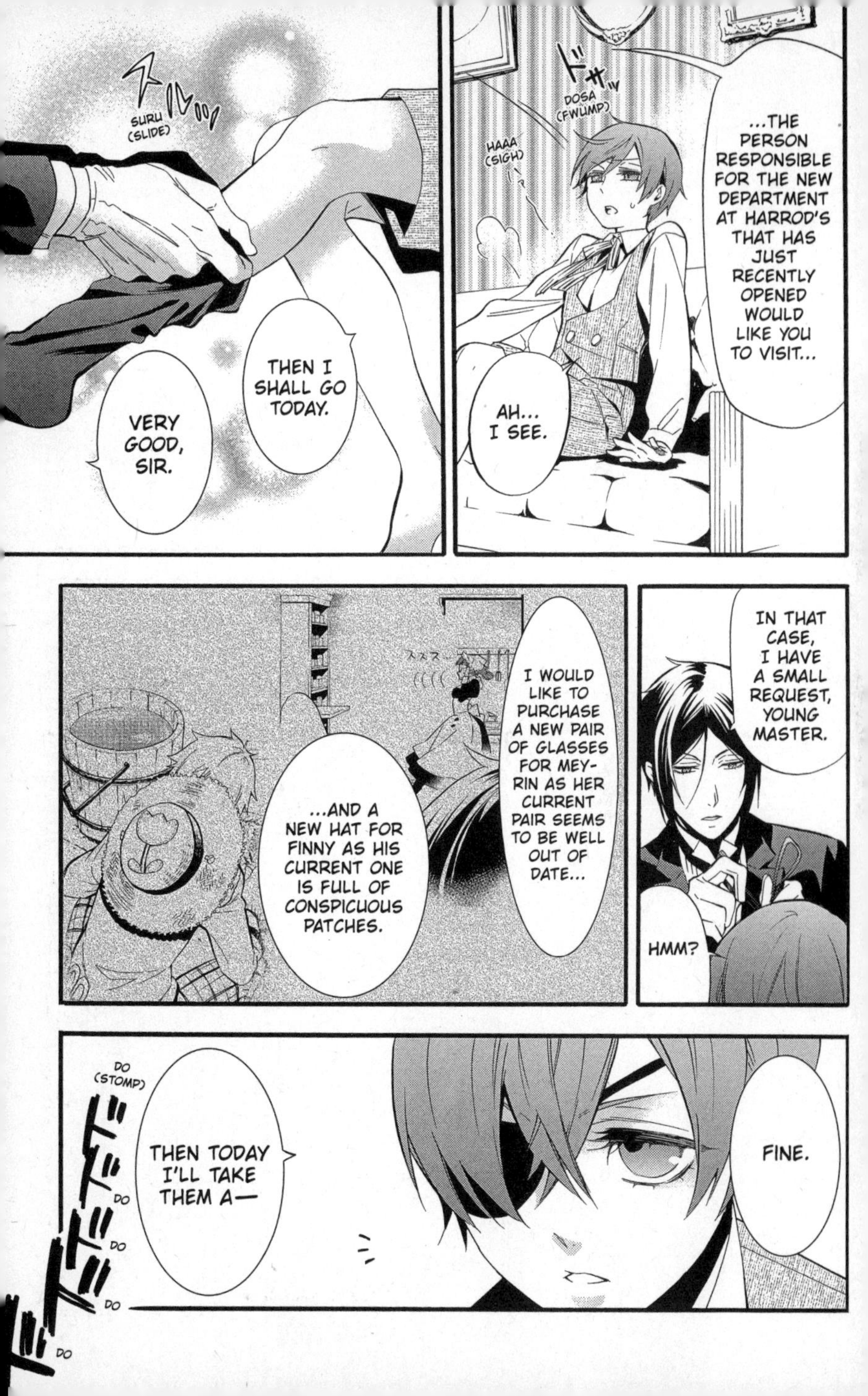
DOSA (FWUMP)
...THE PERSON RESPONSIBLE FOR THE NEW DEPARTMENT AT HARROD'S THAT HAS JUST RECENTLY OPENED WOULD LIKE YOU TO VISIT...
HAAA (SIGH)
AH... I SEE.
SURU (SLIDE)
THEN I SHALL GO TODAY.
VERY GOOD, SIR.
IN THAT CASE, I HAVE A SMALL REQUEST, YOUNG MASTER.
HMM?
I WOULD LIKE TO PURCHASE A NEW PAIR OF GLASSES FOR MEY-RIN AS HER CURRENT PAIR SEEMS TO BE WELL OUT OF DATE...
...AND A NEW HAT FOR FINNY AS HIS CURRENT ONE IS FULL OF CONSPICUOUS PATCHES.
FINE.
THEN TODAY I'LL TAKE THEM A—
DO (STOMP)
DO
DO
DO
DO

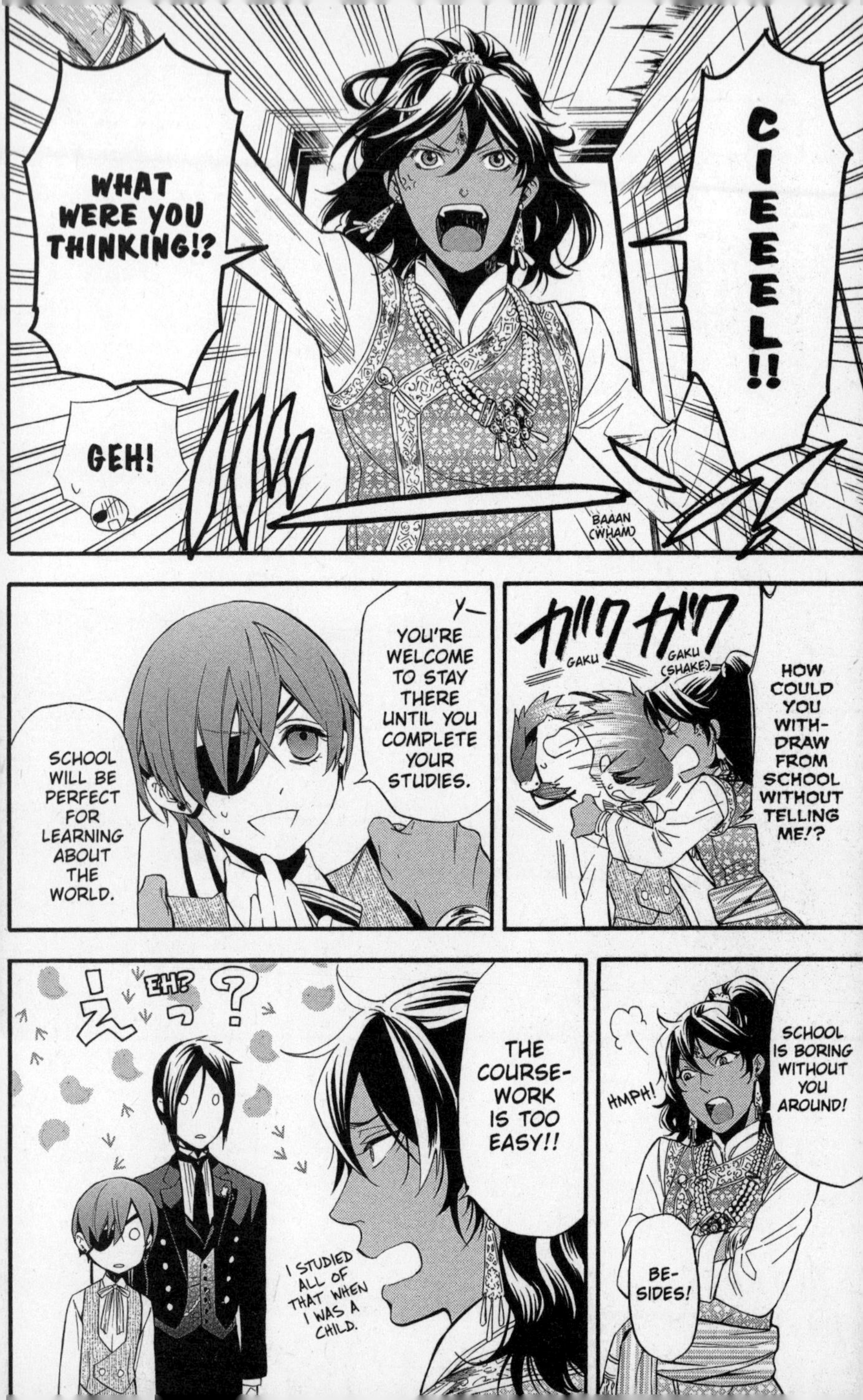
CIEEEL!!
WHAT WERE YOU THINKING!?
BAAAN (WHAM)
GEH!
ガクガク
GAKU GAKU (SHAKE)
HOW COULD YOU WITH-DRAW FROM SCHOOL WITHOUT TELLING ME!?
Y—
YOU'RE WELCOME TO STAY THERE UNTIL YOU COMPLETE YOUR STUDIES.
SCHOOL WILL BE PERFECT FOR LEARNING ABOUT THE WORLD.
SCHOOL IS BORING WITHOUT YOU AROUND!
HMPH!
BE-SIDES!
THE COURSE-WORK IS TOO EASY!!
I STUDIED ALL OF THAT WHEN I WAS A CHILD.
えっ
EH?
?

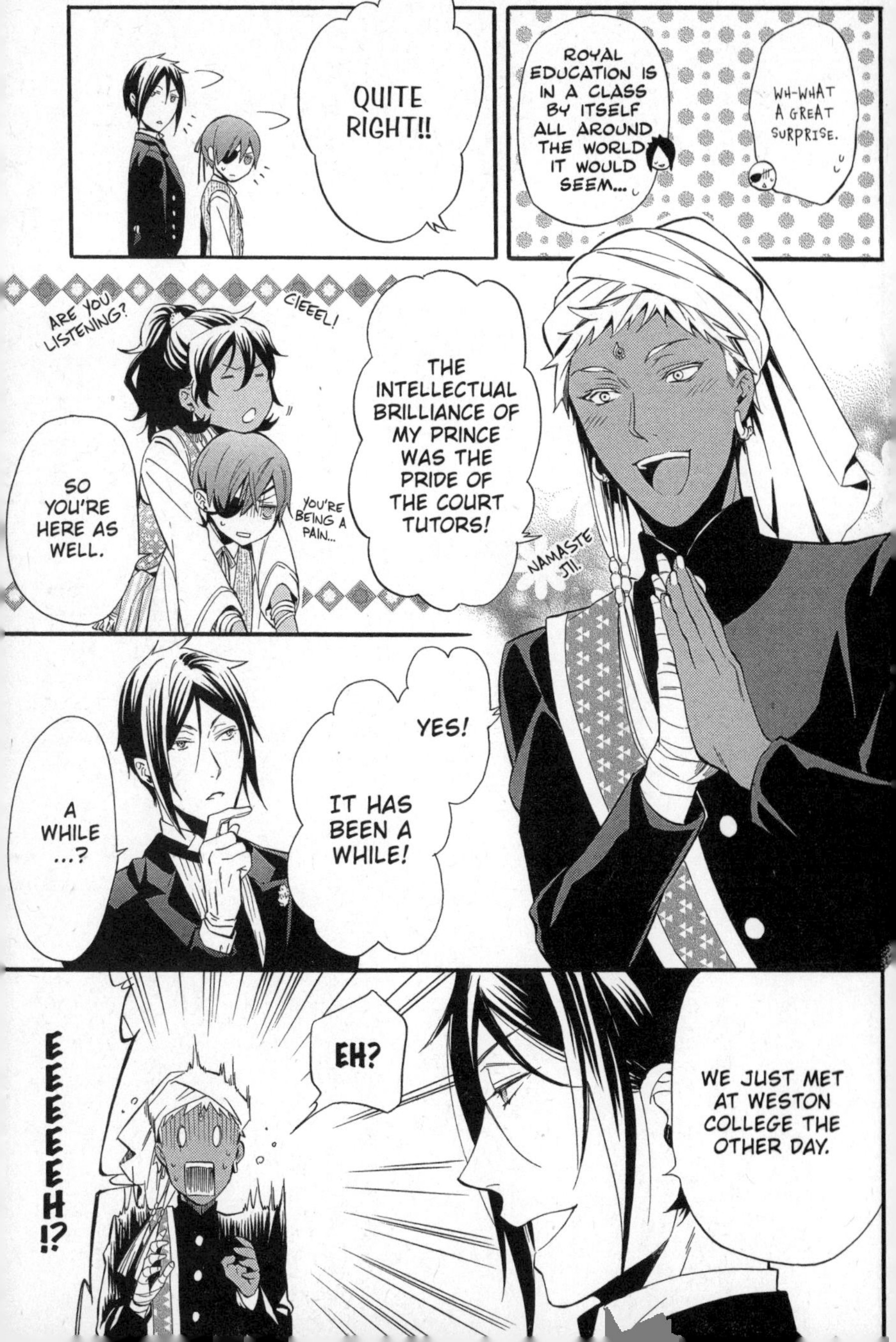

WH-WHAT A GREAT SURPRISE.
ROYAL EDUCATION IS IN A CLASS BY ITSELF ALL AROUND THE WORLD IT WOULD SEEM...
QUITE RIGHT!!
NAMASTE JI!
THE INTELLECTUAL BRILLIANCE OF MY PRINCE WAS THE PRIDE OF THE COURT TUTORS!
CIEEEL!
ARE YOU LISTENING?
YOU'RE BEING A PAIN...
SO YOU'RE HERE AS WELL.
YES!
IT HAS BEEN A WHILE!
A WHILE ...?
WE JUST MET AT WESTON COLLEGE THE OTHER DAY.
EH?
EEEEEEEH!?

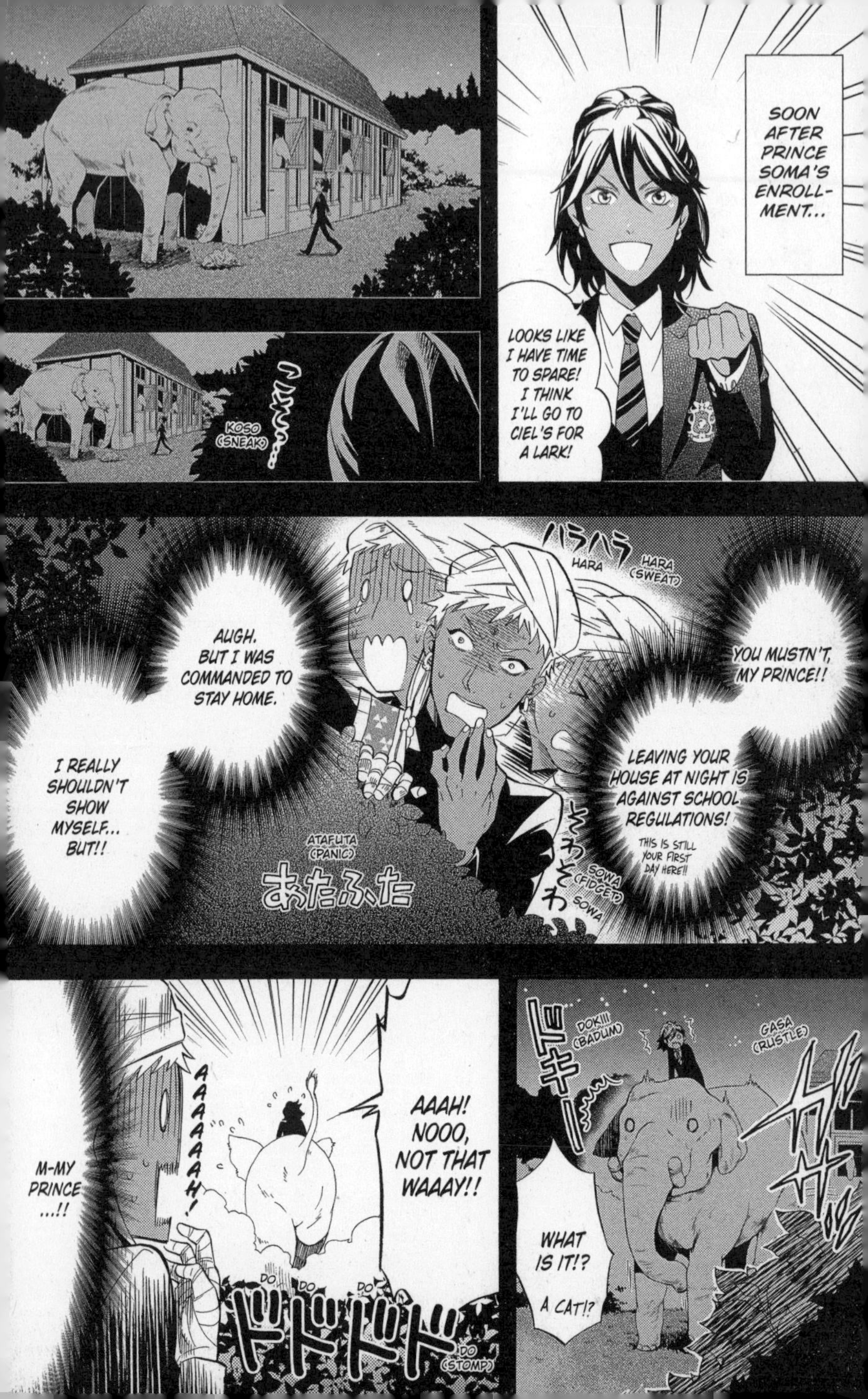
SOON AFTER PRINCE SOMA'S ENROLL-MENT...
LOOKS LIKE I HAVE TIME TO SPARE! I THINK I'LL GO TO CIEL'S FOR A LARK!
KOSO (SNEAK)
ハラハラ
HARA HARA (SWEAT)
YOU MUSTN'T, MY PRINCE!!
LEAVING YOUR HOUSE AT NIGHT IS AGAINST SCHOOL REGULATIONS!
THIS IS STILL YOUR FIRST DAY HERE!!
そわそわ
SOWA (FIDGET) SOWA
AUGH. BUT I WAS COMMANDED TO STAY HOME.
I REALLY SHOULDN'T SHOW MYSELF... BUT!!
ATAFUTA (PANIC)
あたふた
DOKIII (BADUM)
GASA (RUSTLE)
WHAT IS IT!?
A CAT!?
AAAH! NOOO, NOT THAT WAAAY!!
AAAAAAAH!
M-MY PRINCE ...!!
DO DO DO DO (STOMP)

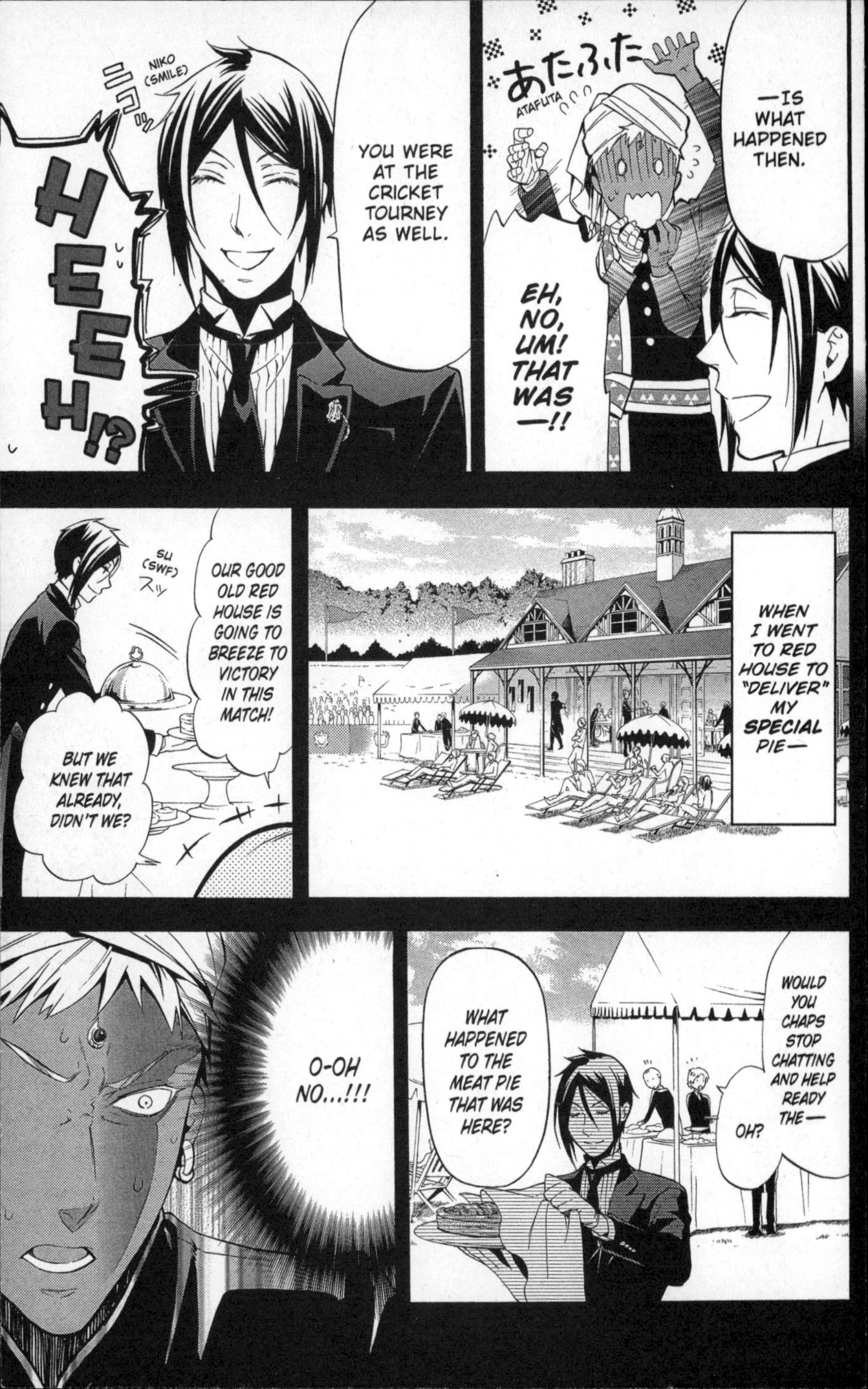
—IS WHAT HAPPENED THEN.
あたふた
ATAFUTA
EH, NO, UM! THAT WAS—!!
YOU WERE AT THE CRICKET TOURNEY AS WELL.
ニコッ
NIKO (SMILE)
HEEEH!?
WHEN I WENT TO RED HOUSE TO "DELIVER" MY SPECIAL PIE—
OUR GOOD OLD RED HOUSE IS GOING TO BREEZE TO VICTORY IN THIS MATCH!
BUT WE KNEW THAT ALREADY, DIDN'T WE?
スッ
SU (SWF)
WOULD YOU CHAPS STOP CHATTING AND HELP READY THE—
OH?
WHAT HAPPENED TO THE MEAT PIE THAT WAS HERE?
O-OH NO...!!!

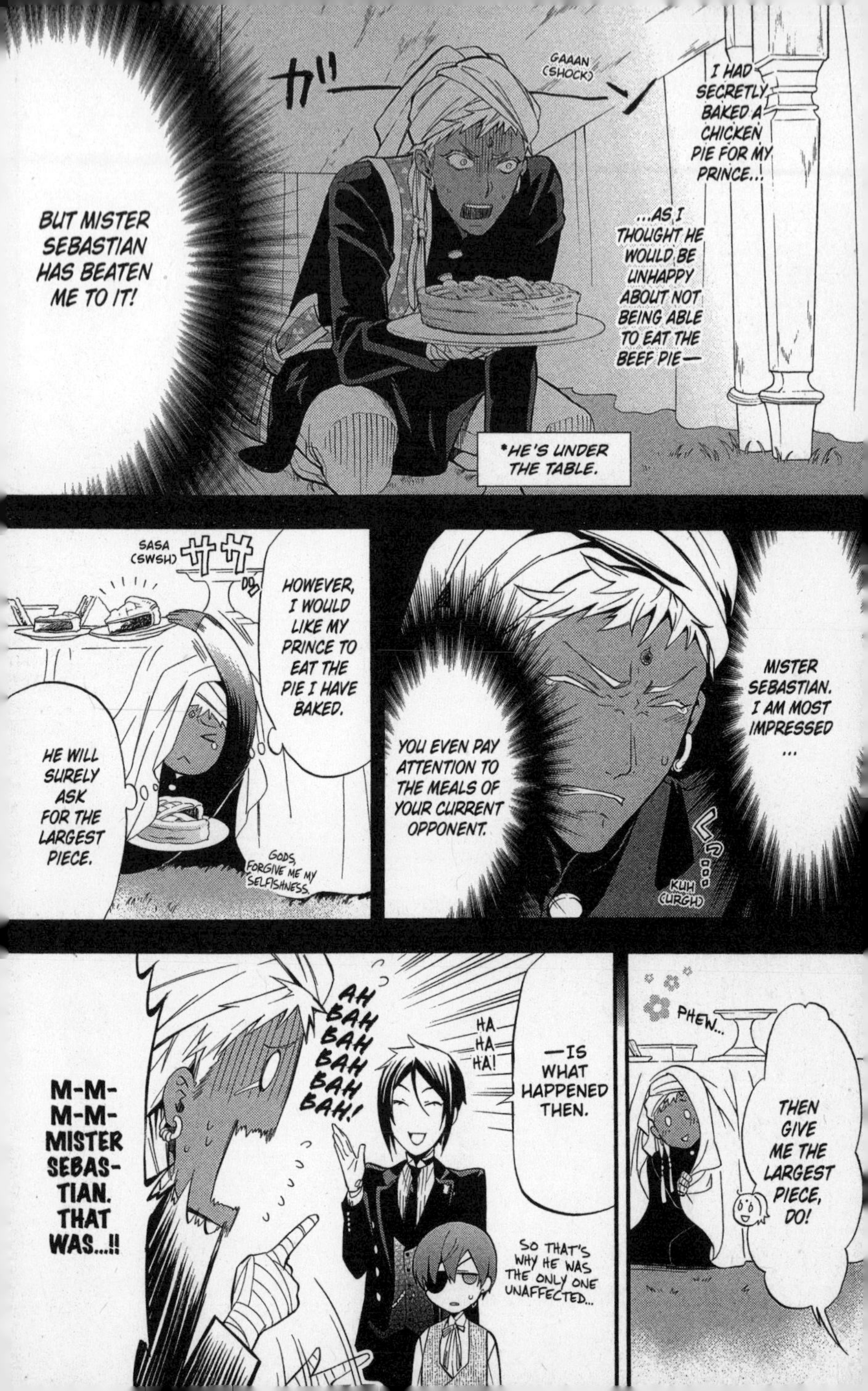
GAAAN (SHOCK)
I HAD SECRETLY BAKED A CHICKEN PIE FOR MY PRINCE...
...AS I THOUGHT HE WOULD BE UNHAPPY ABOUT NOT BEING ABLE TO EAT THE BEEF PIE—
BUT MISTER SEBASTIAN HAS BEATEN ME TO IT!
*HE'S UNDER THE TABLE.
MISTER SEBASTIAN. I AM MOST IMPRESSED ...
YOU EVEN PAY ATTENTION TO THE MEALS OF YOUR CURRENT OPPONENT.
KUH (URGH)
SASA (SWSH)
HOWEVER, I WOULD LIKE MY PRINCE TO EAT THE PIE I HAVE BAKED.
HE WILL SURELY ASK FOR THE LARGEST PIECE.
GODS, FORGIVE ME MY SELFISHNESS.
PHEW...
THEN GIVE ME THE LARGEST PIECE, DO!
—IS WHAT HAPPENED THEN.
HA HA HA!
AH BAH BAH BAH BAH BAH!
M-M-M-M-MISTER SEBASTIAN. THAT WAS...!!
SO THAT'S WHY HE WAS THE ONLY ONE UNAFFECTED...

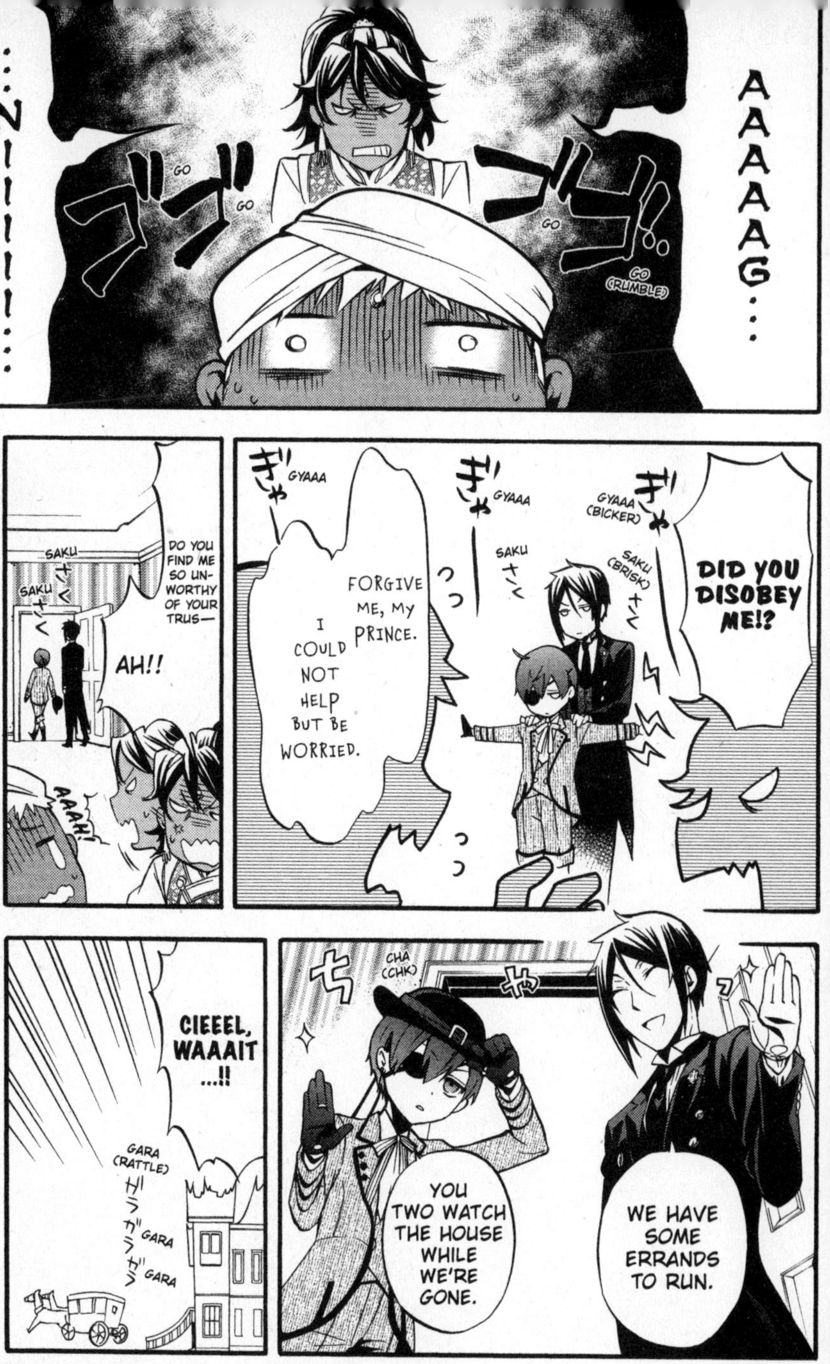
AAAAAG...
ゴゴ!!
GO
GO (RUMBLE)
ゴゴ
GO
GO
...NIIIIII...
ぎゃー
GYAAA (BICKER)
DID YOU DISOBEY ME!?
さく
SAKU (BRISK)
さく
SAKU
ぎゃー
GYAAA
FORGIVE ME, MY PRINCE.
I COULD NOT HELP BUT BE WORRIED.
ぎゃー
GYAAA
DO YOU FIND ME SO UNWORTHY OF YOUR TRUS—
さく
SAKU
さく
SAKU
AH!!
AAAH!
WE HAVE SOME ERRANDS TO RUN.
ちゃ
CHA (CHK)
YOU TWO WATCH THE HOUSE WHILE WE'RE GONE.
CIEEEL, WAAAIT ...!!
ガラ
GARA (RATTLE)
ガラ
GARA
ガラ
GARA

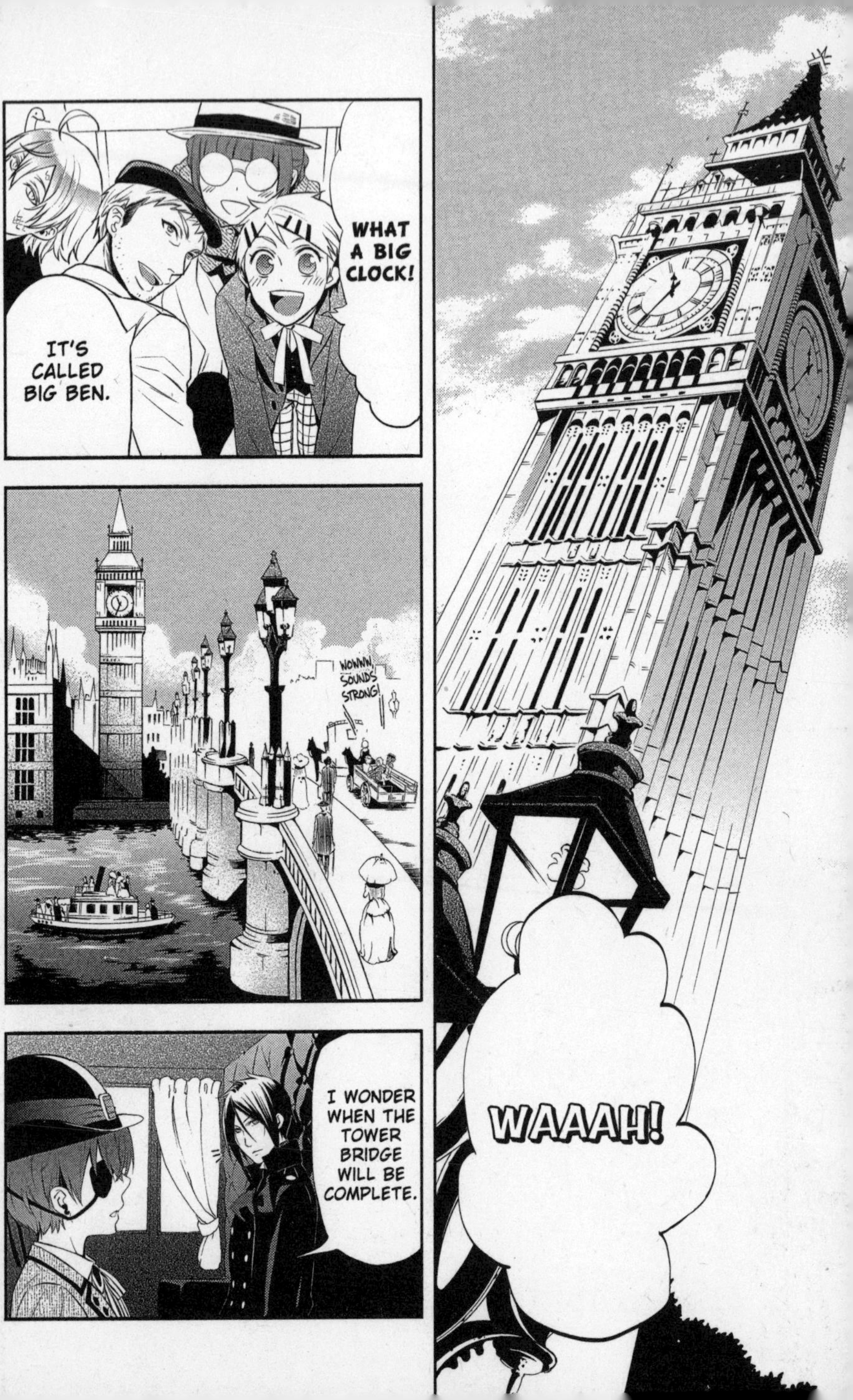
WAAAH!
WHAT A BIG CLOCK!
IT'S CALLED BIG BEN.
WOWWW, SOUNDS STRONG!
I WONDER WHEN THE TOWER BRIDGE WILL BE COMPLETE.

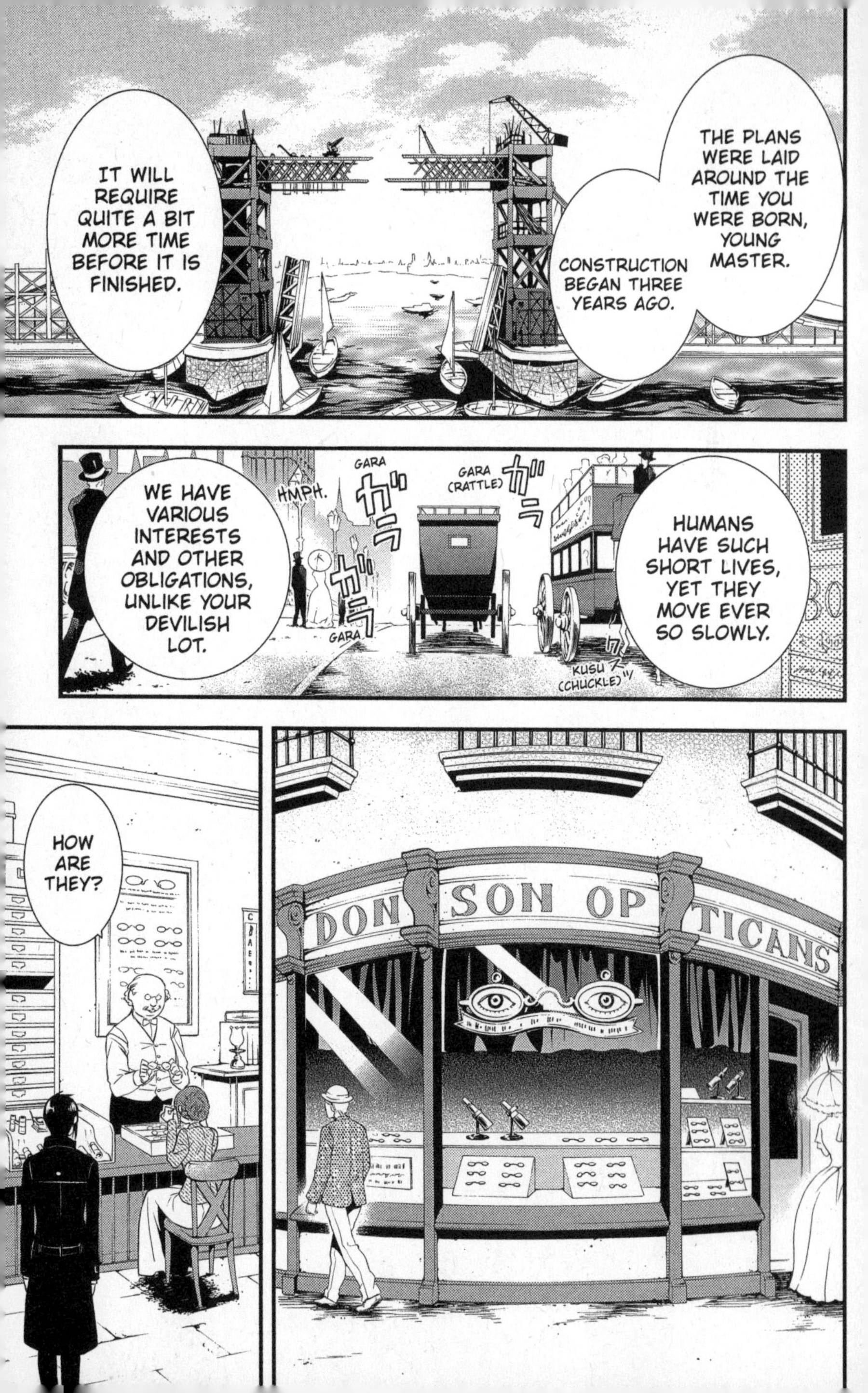
THE PLANS WERE LAID AROUND THE TIME YOU WERE BORN, YOUNG MASTER.
CONSTRUCTION BEGAN THREE YEARS AGO.
IT WILL REQUIRE QUITE A BIT MORE TIME BEFORE IT IS FINISHED.
HUMANS HAVE SUCH SHORT LIVES, YET THEY MOVE EVER SO SLOWLY.
KUSU (CHUCKLE)
GARA (RATTLE)
GARA
GARA
HMPH.
WE HAVE VARIOUS INTERESTS AND OTHER OBLIGATIONS, UNLIKE YOUR DEVILISH LOT.
DON SON OP TICANS
HOW ARE THEY?

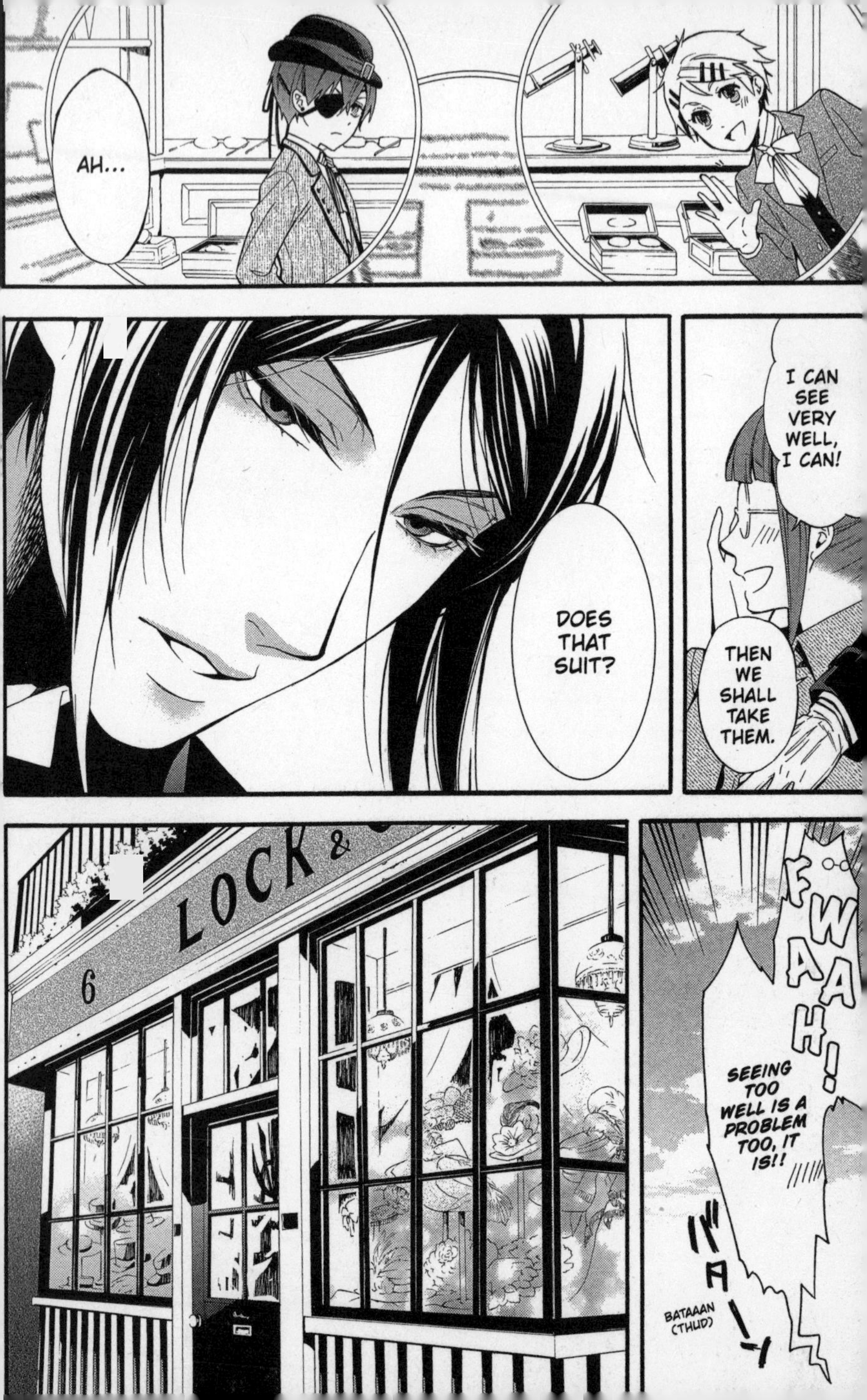
AH...
I CAN SEE VERY WELL, I CAN!
THEN WE SHALL TAKE THEM.
DOES THAT SUIT?
FWAAH!
SEEING TOO WELL IS A PROBLEM TOO, IT IS!!
BATAAAN (THUD)
LOCK &
6

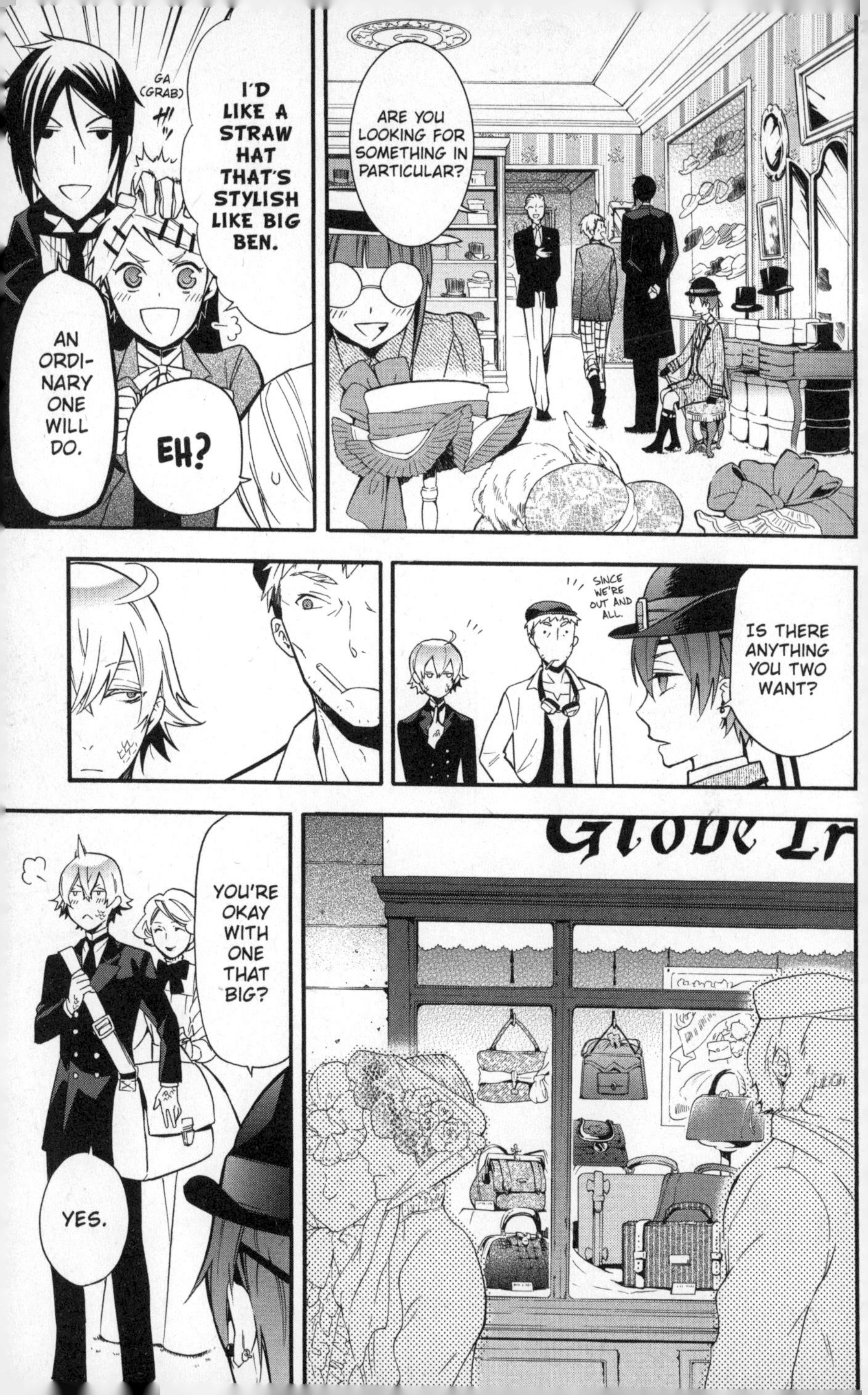
ARE YOU LOOKING FOR SOMETHING IN PARTICULAR?
I'D LIKE A STRAW HAT THAT'S STYLISH LIKE BIG BEN.
GA (GRAB)
AN ORDINARY ONE WILL DO.
EH?
SINCE WE'RE OUT AND ALL.
IS THERE ANYTHING YOU TWO WANT?
Globe
YOU'RE OKAY WITH ONE THAT BIG?
YES.

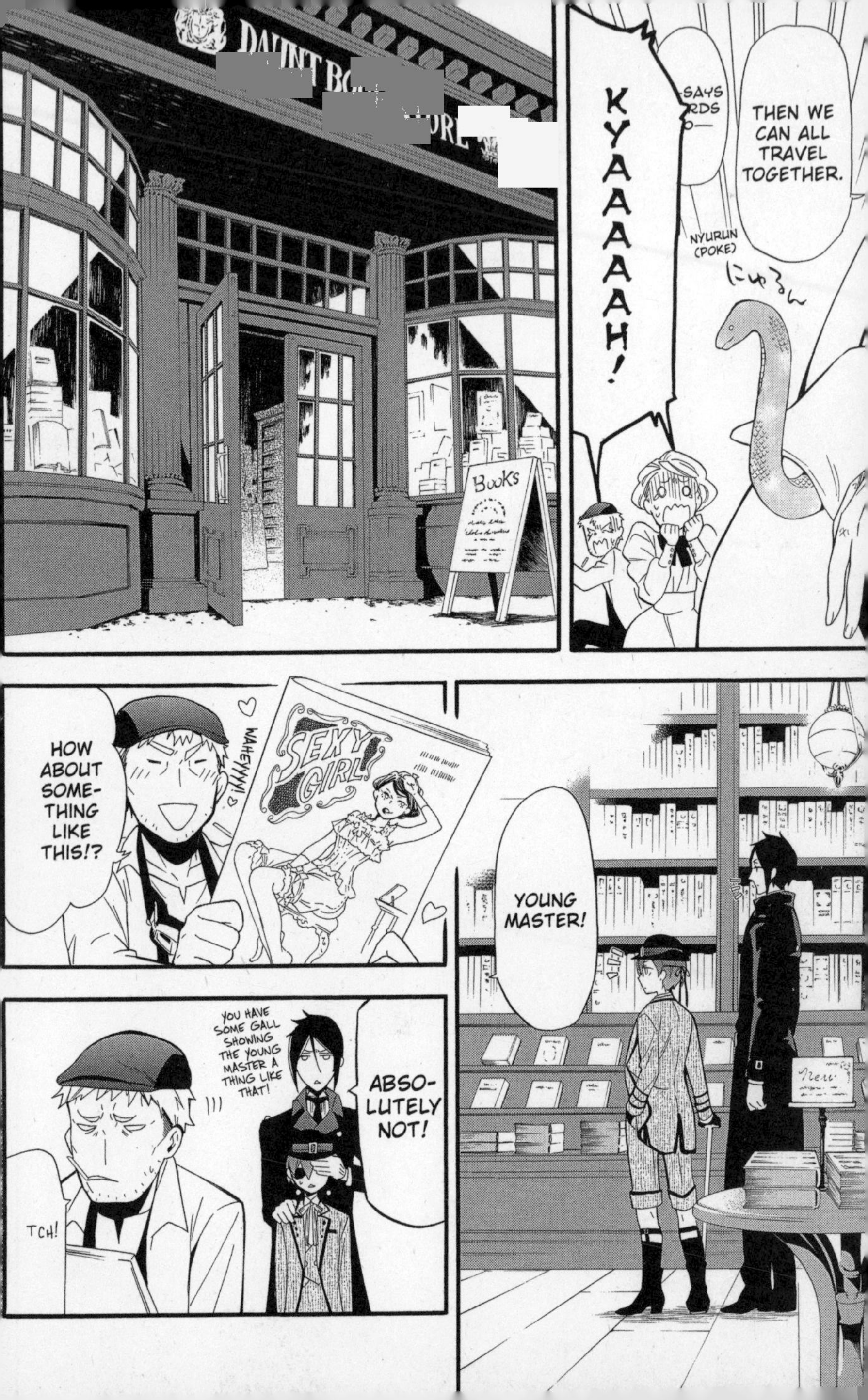
THEN WE CAN ALL TRAVEL TOGETHER.
NYURUN (POKE)
にゅるん
KYAAAAAH!
Books
YOUNG MASTER!
HOW ABOUT SOMETHING LIKE THIS!?
WAHEYYY!
SEXY GIRL
ABSOLUTELY NOT!
YOU HAVE SOME GALL SHOWING THE YOUNG MASTER A THING LIKE THAT!
TCH!

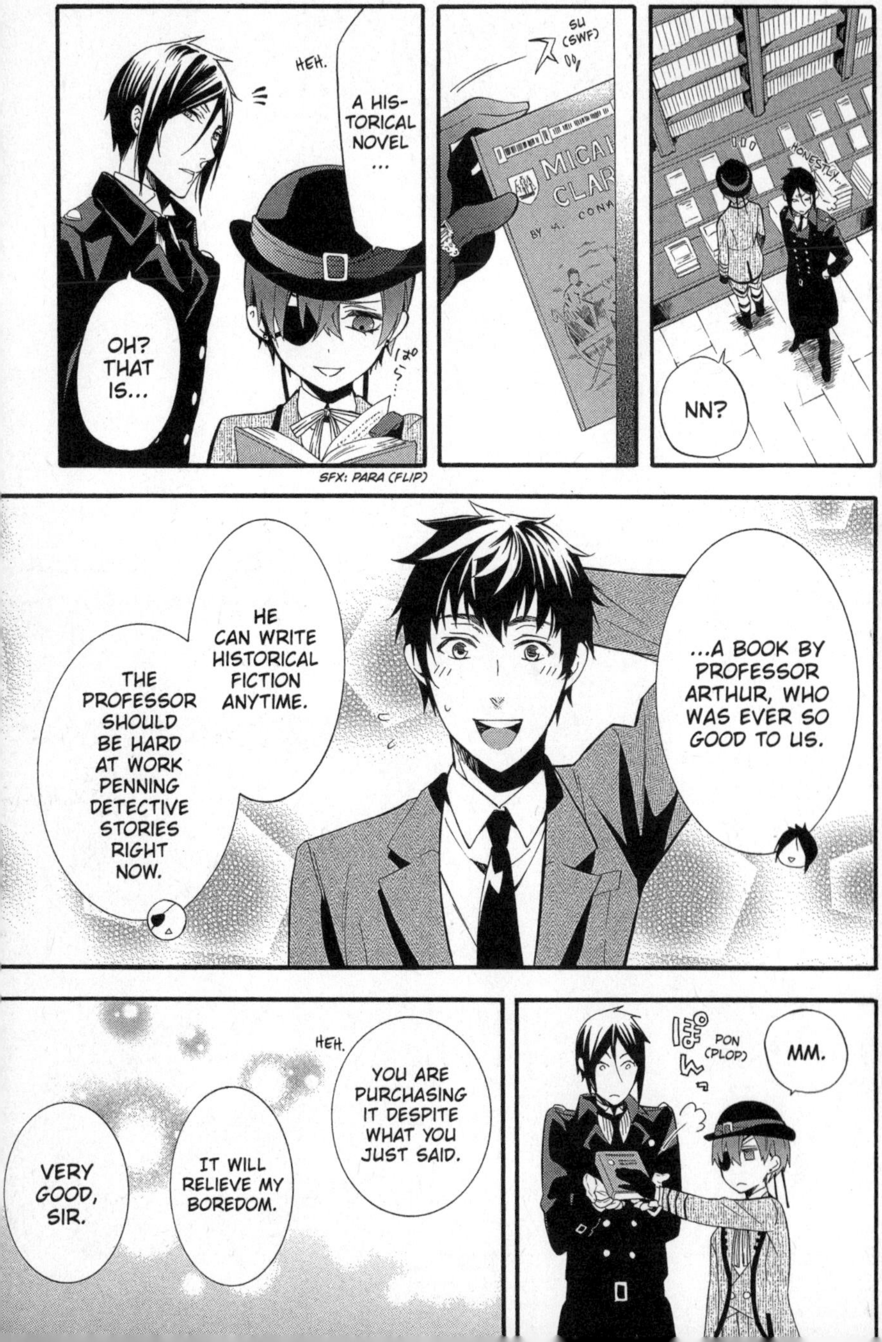
HONESTLY
NN?
SU (SWF)
HEH.
A HIS-TORICAL NOVEL ...
OH? THAT IS...
SFX: PARA (FLIP)
...A BOOK BY PROFESSOR ARTHUR, WHO WAS EVER SO GOOD TO US.
HE CAN WRITE HISTORICAL FICTION ANYTIME.
THE PROFESSOR SHOULD BE HARD AT WORK PENNING DETECTIVE STORIES RIGHT NOW.
MM.
PON (PLOP)
HEH.
YOU ARE PURCHASING IT DESPITE WHAT YOU JUST SAID.
IT WILL RELIEVE MY BOREDOM.
VERY GOOD, SIR.

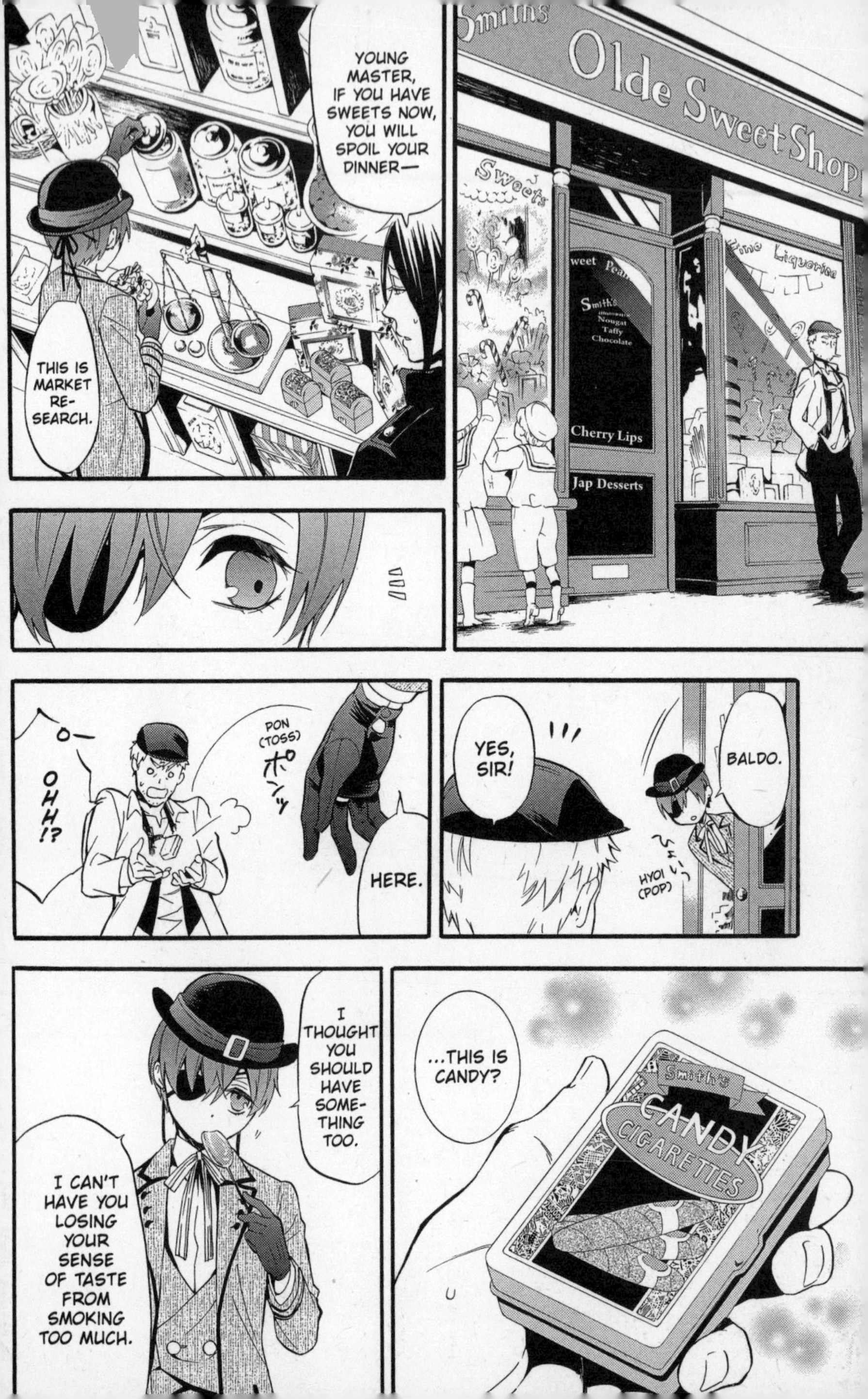
Smith's
Olde Sweet Shop
Sweets
Smith's
Nougat
Taffy
Chocolate
Fine Liquorice
Cherry Lips
Jap Desserts
YOUNG MASTER, IF YOU HAVE SWEETS NOW, YOU WILL SPOIL YOUR DINNER—
THIS IS MARKET RE-SEARCH.
BALDO.
HYOI (POP)
YES, SIR!
HERE.
PON (TOSS)
O— OHH!?
...THIS IS CANDY?
Smith's
CANDY CIGARETTES
I THOUGHT YOU SHOULD HAVE SOME-THING TOO.
I CAN'T HAVE YOU LOSING YOUR SENSE OF TASTE FROM SMOKING TOO MUCH.

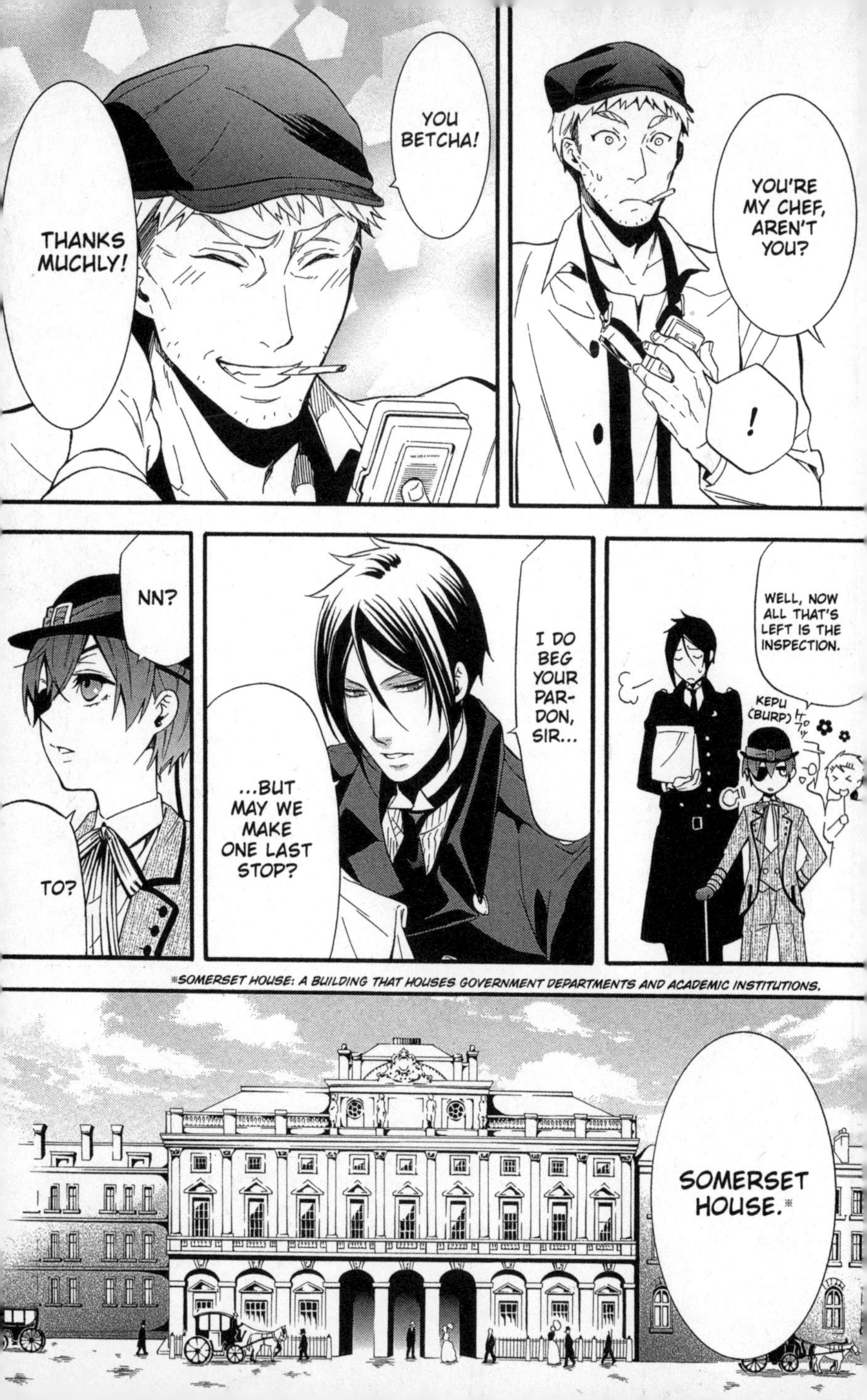
YOU'RE MY CHEF, AREN'T YOU?
!
YOU BETCHA!
THANKS MUCHLY!
WELL, NOW ALL THAT'S LEFT IS THE INSPECTION.
KEPU (BURP)
I DO BEG YOUR PAR-DON, SIR...
...BUT MAY WE MAKE ONE LAST STOP?
NN?
TO?
SOMERSET HOUSE.※

※SOMERSET HOUSE: A BUILDING THAT HOUSES GOVERNMENT DEPARTMENTS AND ACADEMIC INSTITUTIONS.

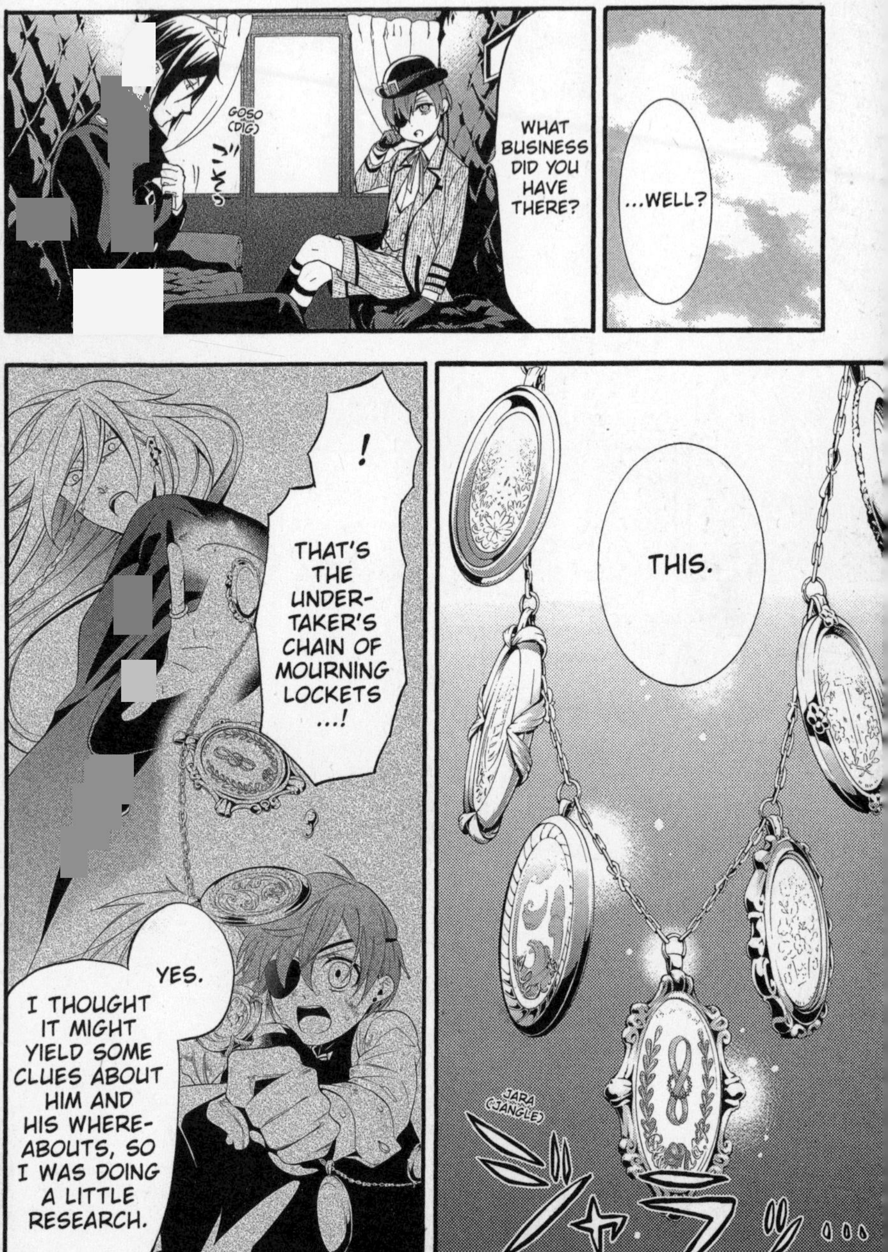
...WELL?
WHAT BUSINESS DID YOU HAVE THERE?
GOSO (DIG)
THIS.
JARA (JANGLE)
!
THAT'S THE UNDER-TAKER'S CHAIN OF MOURNING LOCKETS ...!
YES.
I THOUGHT IT MIGHT YIELD SOME CLUES ABOUT HIM AND HIS WHERE-ABOUTS, SO I WAS DOING A LITTLE RESEARCH.

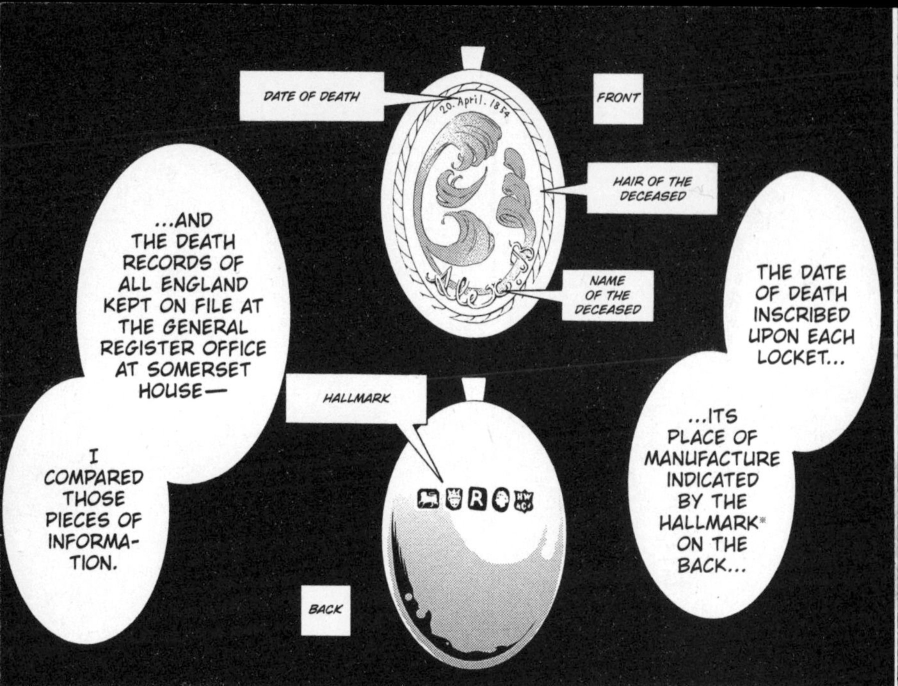
FRONT
DATE OF DEATH
20. April. 1854
HAIR OF THE DECEASED
NAME OF THE DECEASED
THE DATE OF DEATH INSCRIBED UPON EACH LOCKET...
...ITS PLACE OF MANUFACTURE INDICATED BY THE HALLMARK※ ON THE BACK...
...AND THE DEATH RECORDS OF ALL ENGLAND KEPT ON FILE AT THE GENERAL REGISTER OFFICE AT SOMERSET HOUSE—
HALLMARK
I COMPARED THOSE PIECES OF INFORMATION.
BACK

※HALLMARK: A SERIES OF OFFICIAL MARKS THAT GUARANTEE THE QUALITY OF THE SILVER. SILVER PURITY AND PLACE OF MANUFACTURE CAN BE DETERMINED FROM THE HALLMARK.

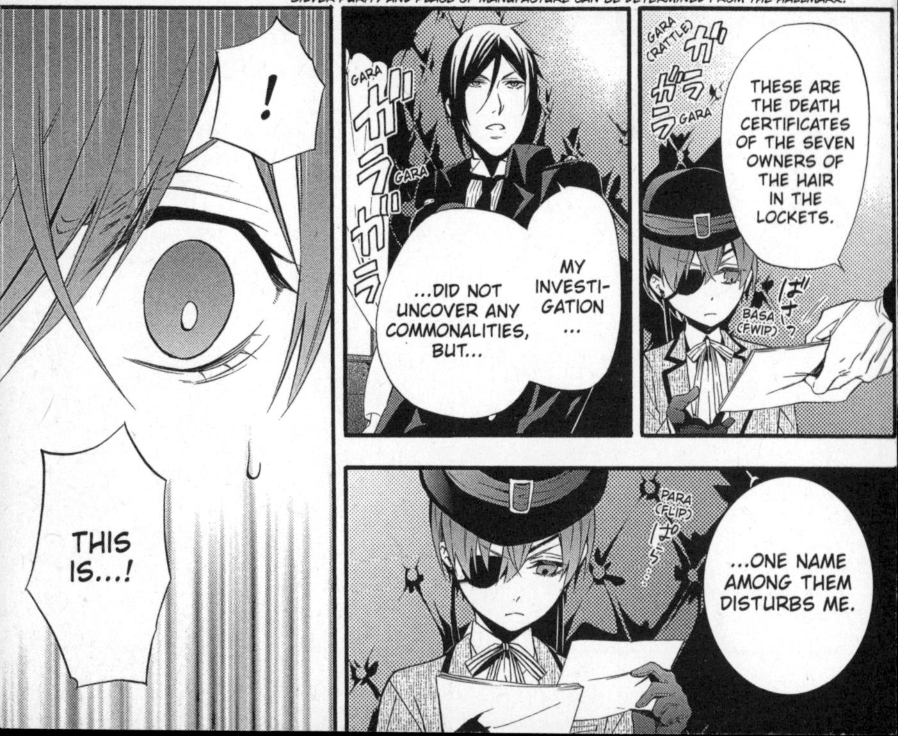
GARA (RATTLE)
GARA
THESE ARE THE DEATH CERTIFICATES OF THE SEVEN OWNERS OF THE HAIR IN THE LOCKETS.
BASA (FWIP)
GARA
GARA
MY INVESTIGATION...
...DID NOT UNCOVER ANY COMMONALITIES, BUT...
PARA (FLIP)
...ONE NAME AMONG THEM DISTURBS ME.
!
THIS IS...!

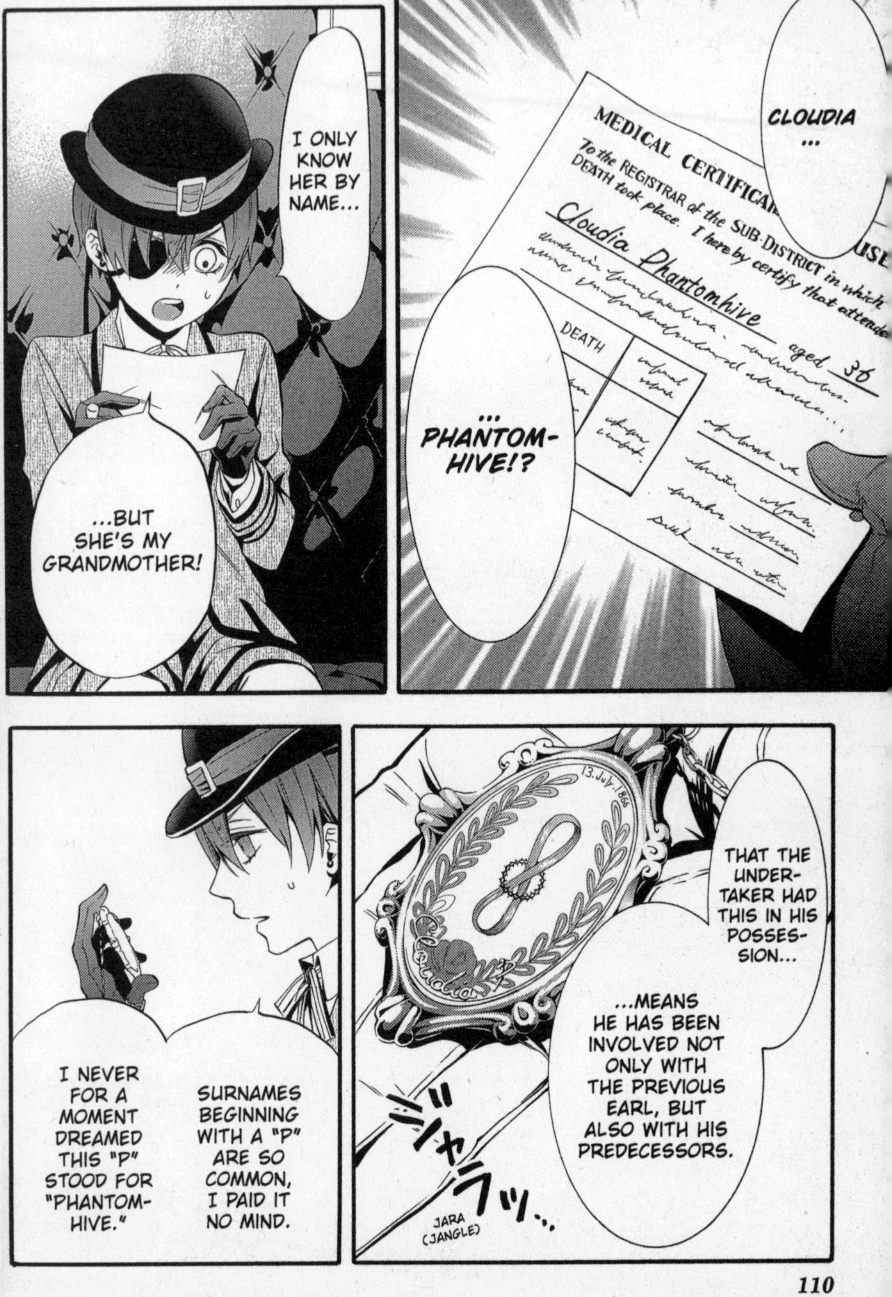
CLOUDIA ...
MEDICAL CERTIFICA
To the REGISTRAR of the SUB-DISTRICT in which DEATH took place. I here by certify that attende
Cloudia Phantomhive
aged 36
DEATH
... PHANTOM-HIVE!?
I ONLY KNOW HER BY NAME...
...BUT SHE'S MY GRANDMOTHER!
13. July. 1866
Cloudia
THAT THE UNDER-TAKER HAD THIS IN HIS POSSES-SION...
...MEANS HE HAS BEEN INVOLVED NOT ONLY WITH THE PREVIOUS EARL, BUT ALSO WITH HIS PREDECESSORS.
JARA (JANGLE)
SURNAMES BEGINNING WITH A "P" ARE SO COMMON, I PAID IT NO MIND.
I NEVER FOR A MOMENT DREAMED THIS "P" STOOD FOR "PHANTOM-HIVE."

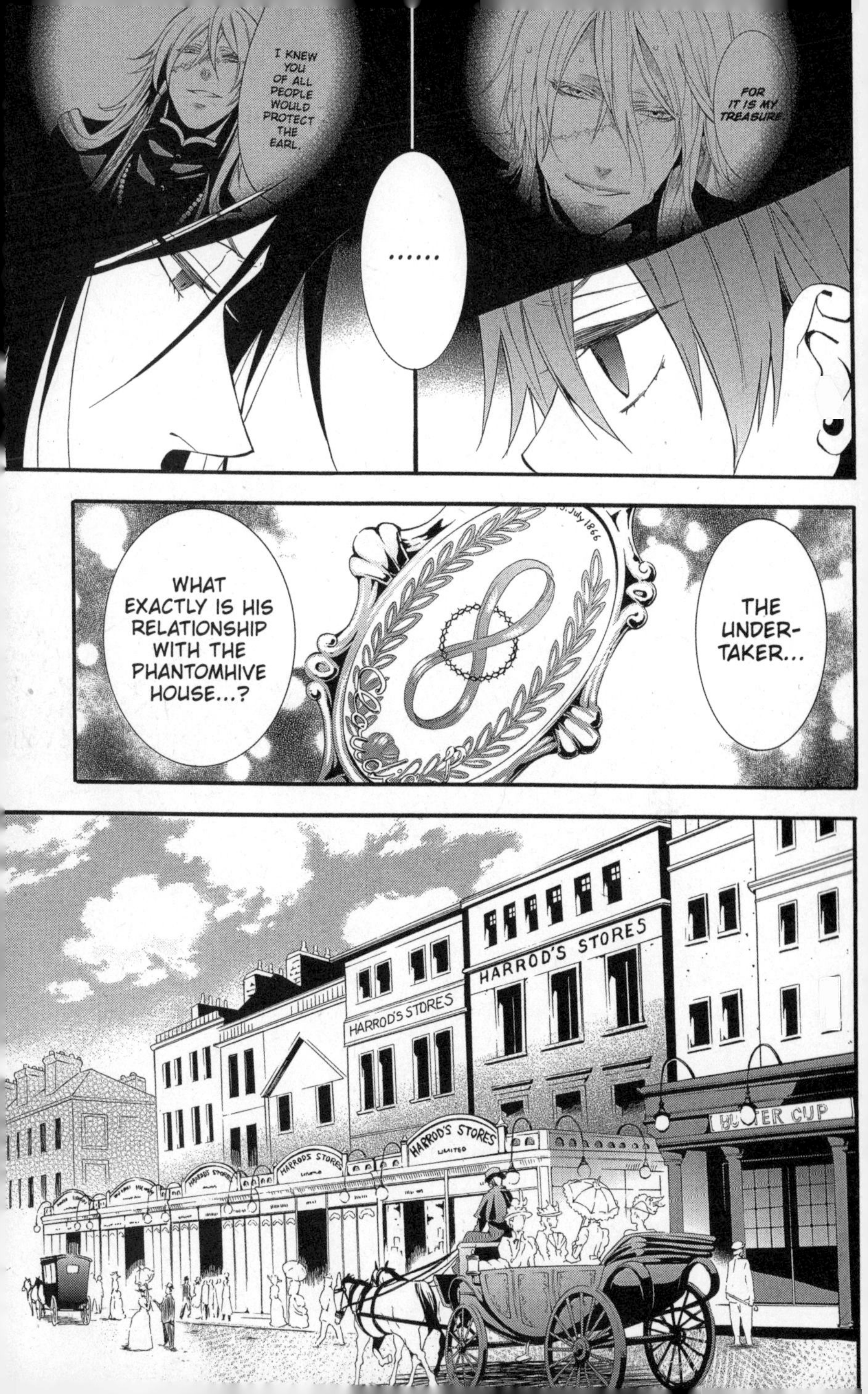
FOR IT IS MY TREASURE.
I KNEW YOU OF ALL PEOPLE WOULD PROTECT THE EARL.
......
THE UNDER-TAKER...
WHAT EXACTLY IS HIS RELATIONSHIP WITH THE PHANTOMHIVE HOUSE...?
July 1866
HARROD'S STORES
HARROD'S STORES
HARROD'S STORES LIMITED
HARROD'S STORES
HARROD'S STORES

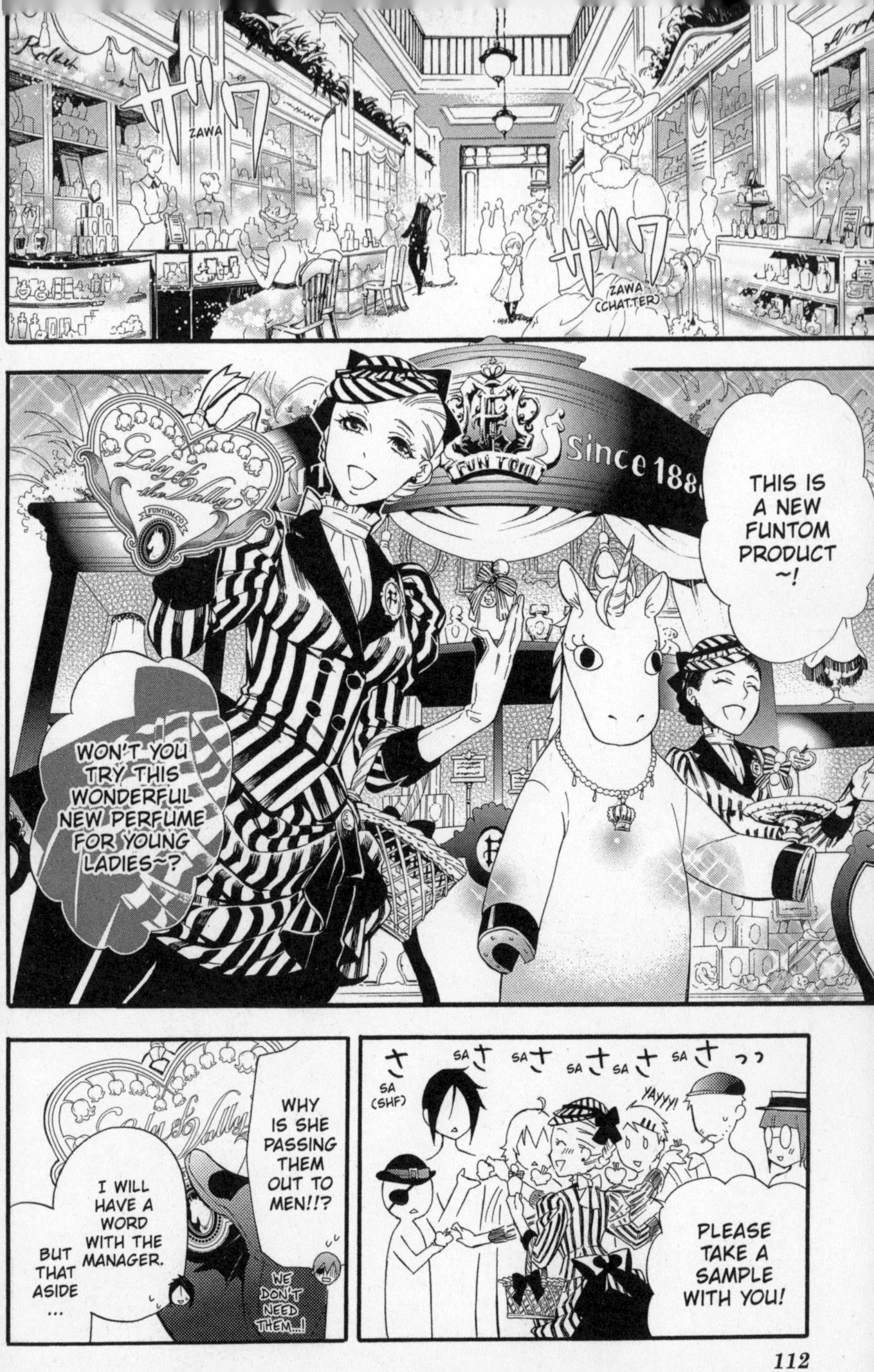

ザワ
ZAWA (CHATTER)
ザワ
ZAWA
since 188
FUNTOM
Lily of the Valley
FUNTOM CO.
THIS IS A NEW FUNTOM PRODUCT ~!
WON'T YOU TRY THIS WONDERFUL NEW PERFUME FOR YOUNG LADIES~?
さっ SA さ SA さ SA さ SA さ SA さ
SA (SHF)
YAYYY!
PLEASE TAKE A SAMPLE WITH YOU!
WHY IS SHE PASSING THEM OUT TO MEN!!?
WE DON'T NEED THEM...!
I WILL HAVE A WORD WITH THE MANAGER.
BUT THAT ASIDE ...

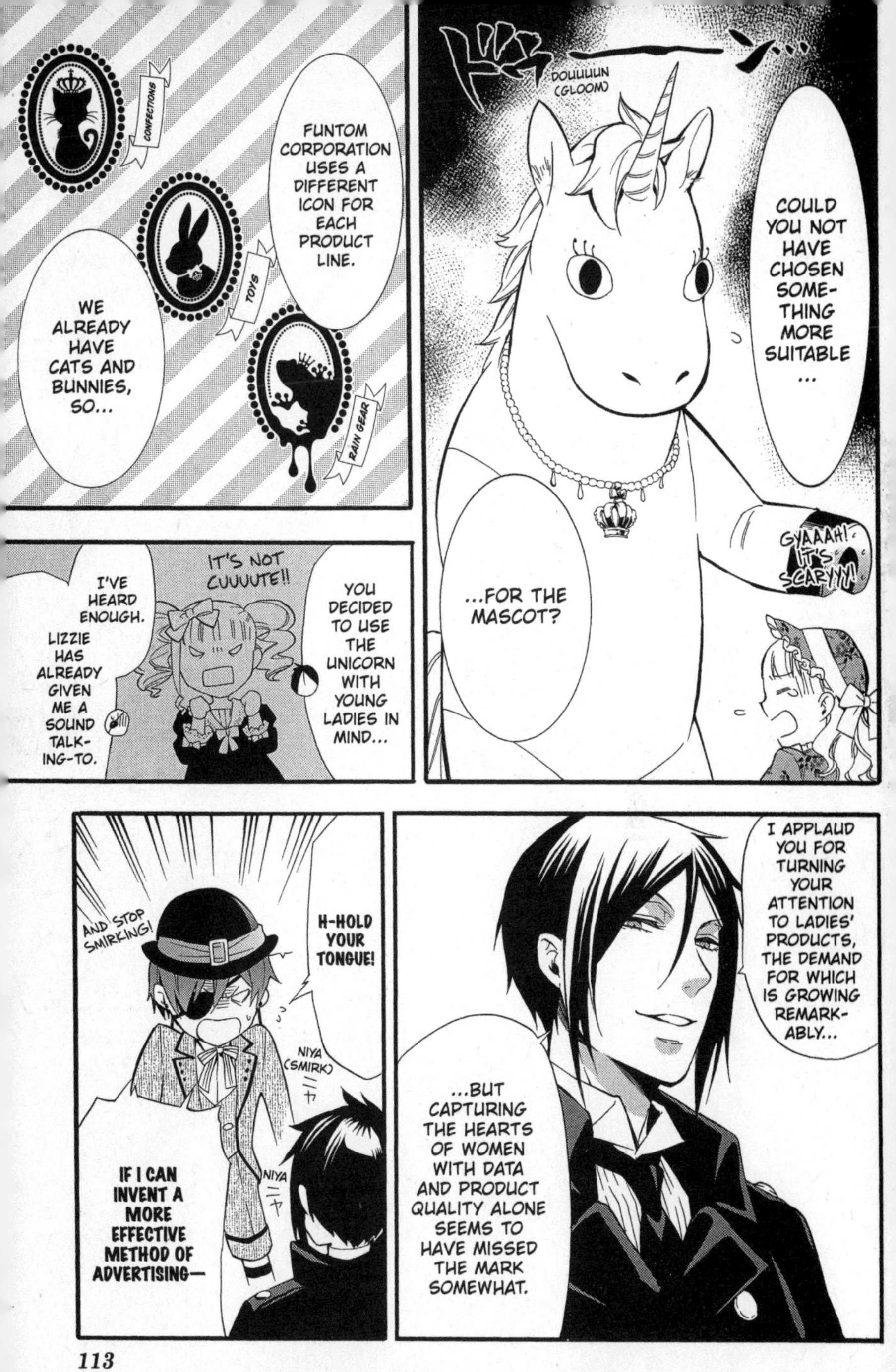
DOUUUUN (GLOOM)
COULD YOU NOT HAVE CHOSEN SOME-THING MORE SUITABLE...
...FOR THE MASCOT?
GYAAAH! IT'S SCARYYY!
FUNTOM CORPORATION USES A DIFFERENT ICON FOR EACH PRODUCT LINE.
CONFECTIONS
TOYS
RAIN GEAR
WE ALREADY HAVE CATS AND BUNNIES, SO...
YOU DECIDED TO USE THE UNICORN WITH YOUNG LADIES IN MIND...
IT'S NOT CUUUUTE!!
I'VE HEARD ENOUGH.
LIZZIE HAS ALREADY GIVEN ME A SOUND TALK-ING-TO.
I APPLAUD YOU FOR TURNING YOUR ATTENTION TO LADIES' PRODUCTS, THE DEMAND FOR WHICH IS GROWING REMARK-ABLY...
...BUT CAPTURING THE HEARTS OF WOMEN WITH DATA AND PRODUCT QUALITY ALONE SEEMS TO HAVE MISSED THE MARK SOMEWHAT.
H-HOLD YOUR TONGUE!
AND STOP SMIRKING!
NIYA (SMIRK)
NIYA
IF I CAN INVENT A MORE EFFECTIVE METHOD OF ADVERTISING—

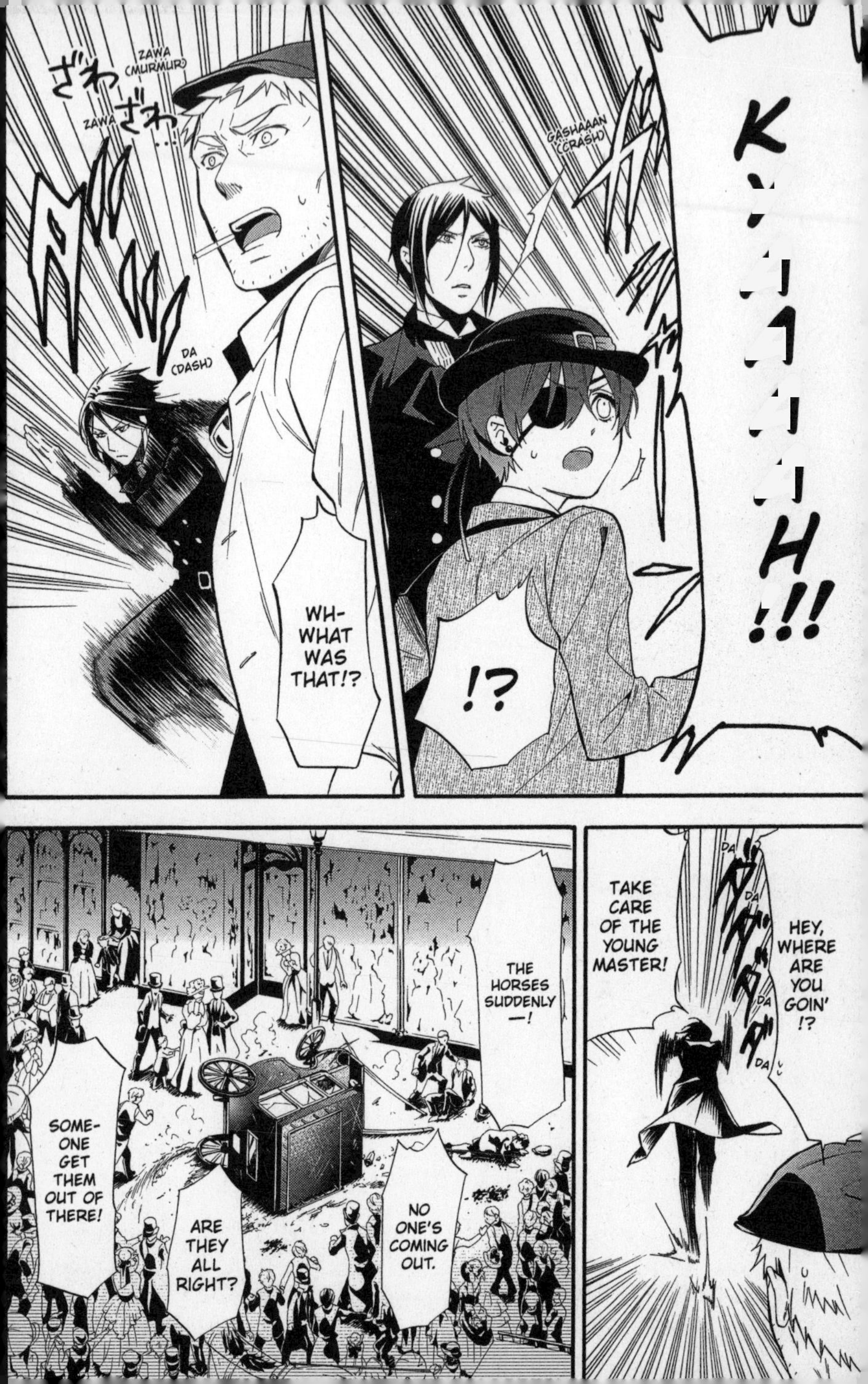
GASHAAAN (CRASH)
!?
ざわ ざわ
ZAWA (MURMUR)
ZAWA
DA (DASH)
WH-WHAT WAS THAT!?
TAKE CARE OF THE YOUNG MASTER!
DA DA DA DA
HEY, WHERE ARE YOU GOIN'!?
THE HORSES SUDDENLY—!
NO ONE'S COMING OUT.
ARE THEY ALL RIGHT?
SOME-ONE GET THEM OUT OF THERE!

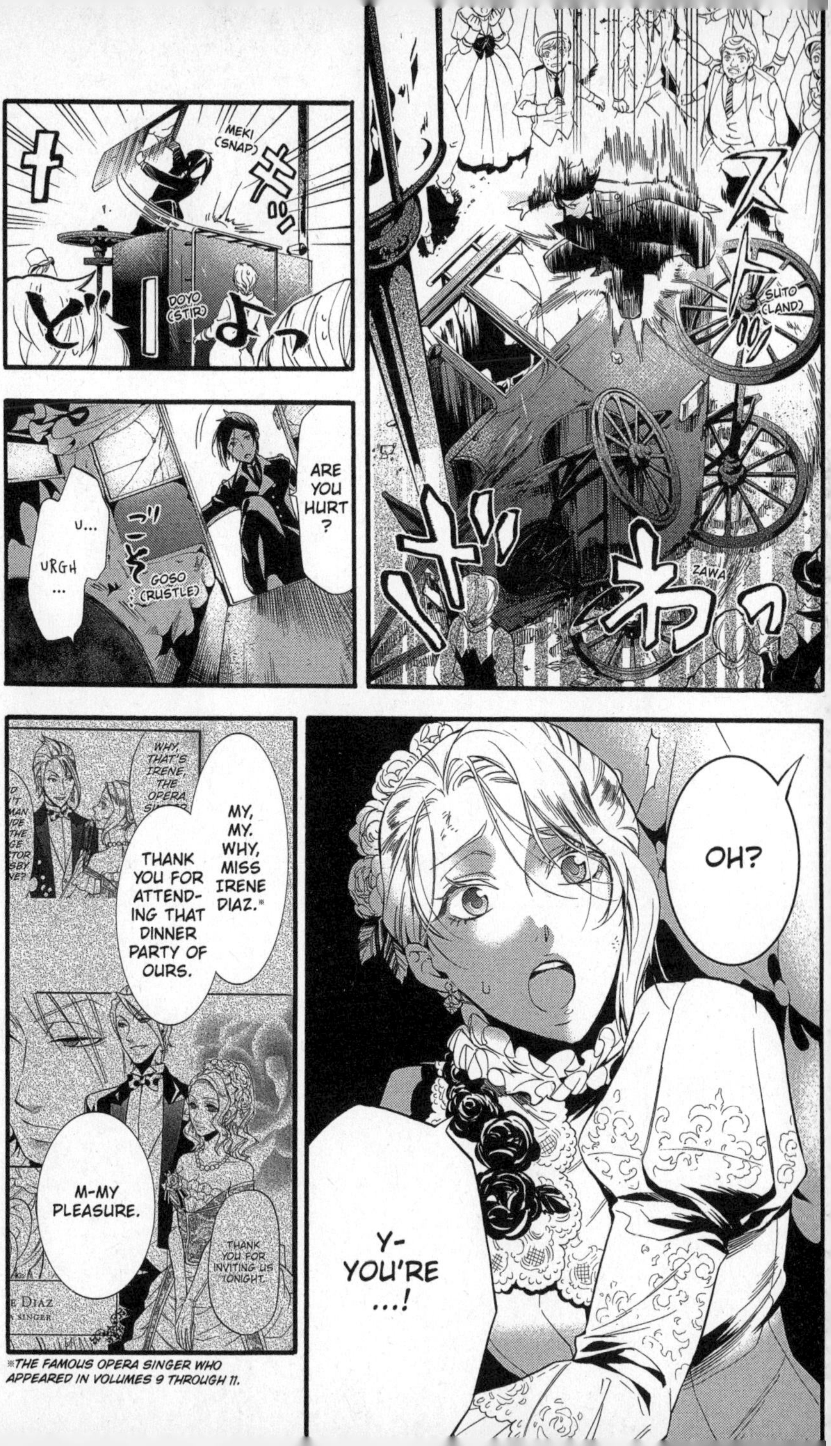
SUTO (LAND)
ZAWA
MEKI (SNAP)
DOYO (STIR)
ARE YOU HURT?
U...
URGH...
GOSO (RUSTLE)
OH?
Y- YOU'RE ...!
WHY, THAT'S IRENE, THE OPERA
MY, MY. WHY, MISS IRENE DIAZ.※
THANK YOU FOR ATTENDING THAT DINNER PARTY OF OURS.
M-MY PLEASURE.
THANK YOU FOR INVITING US TONIGHT.

※THE FAMOUS OPERA SINGER WHO APPEARED IN VOLUMES 9 THROUGH 11.

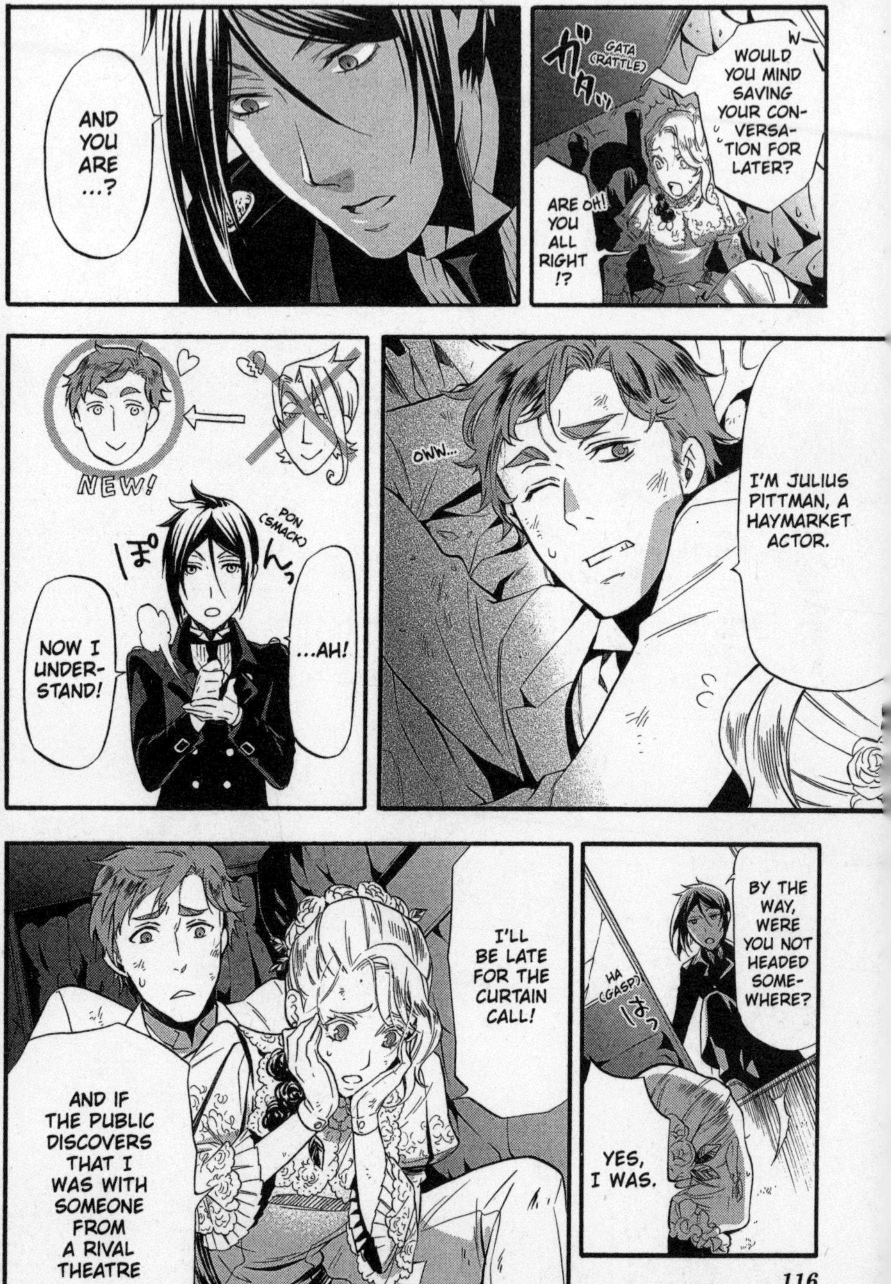
GATA (RATTLE)
W- WOULD YOU MIND SAVING YOUR CONVERSATION FOR LATER?
OH!
ARE YOU ALL RIGHT!?
AND YOU ARE ...?
OWW...
I'M JULIUS PITTMAN, A HAYMARKET ACTOR.
NEW!
PON (SMACK)
...AH!
NOW I UNDERSTAND!
BY THE WAY, WERE YOU NOT HEADED SOMEWHERE?
HA (GASP)
YES, I WAS.
I'LL BE LATE FOR THE CURTAIN CALL!
AND IF THE PUBLIC DISCOVERS THAT I WAS WITH SOMEONE FROM A RIVAL THEATRE ......

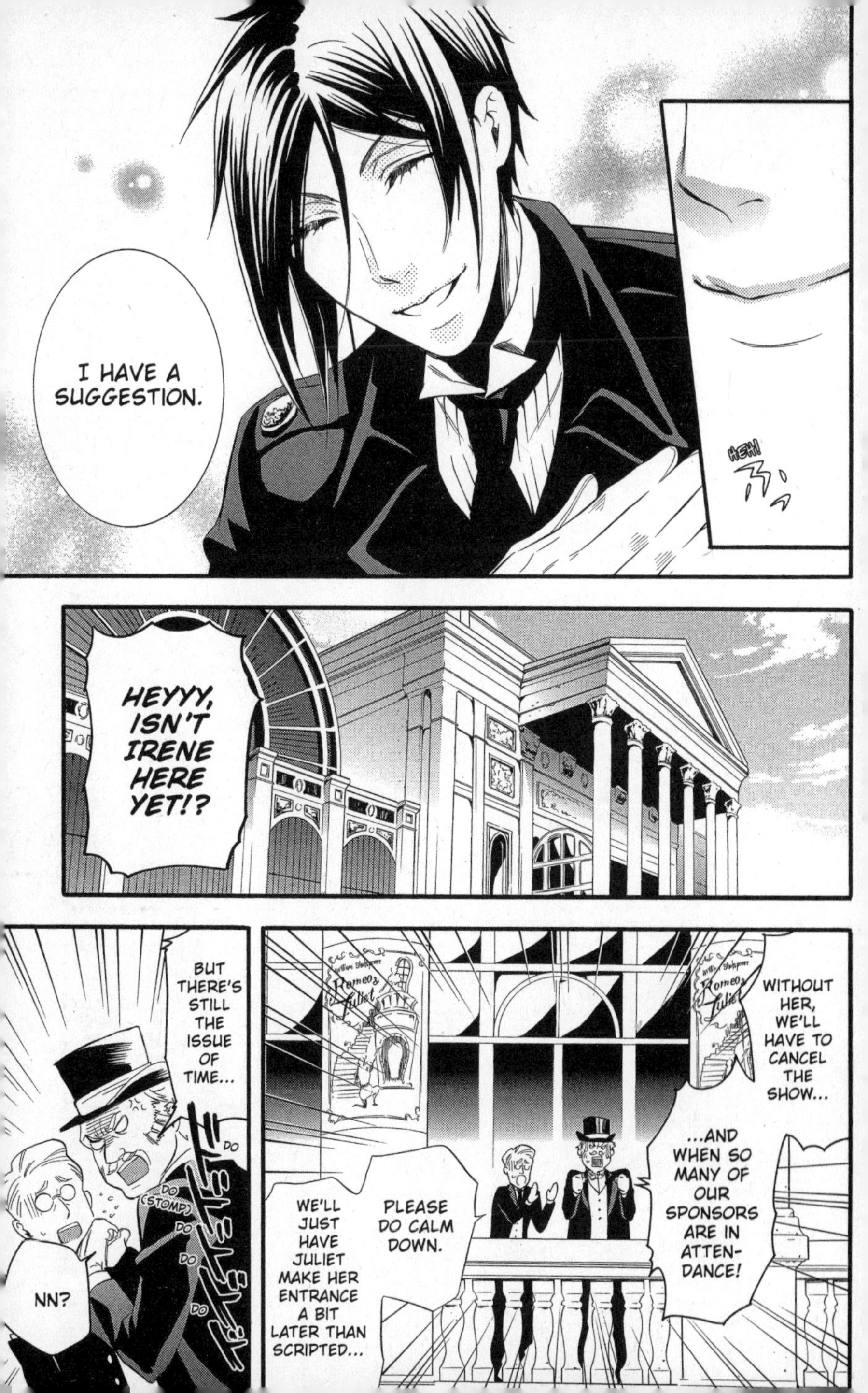
HEH!
I HAVE A SUGGESTION.
HEYYY, ISN'T IRENE HERE YET!?
WITHOUT HER, WE'LL HAVE TO CANCEL THE SHOW...
...AND WHEN SO MANY OF OUR SPONSORS ARE IN ATTENDANCE!
PLEASE DO CALM DOWN.
WE'LL JUST HAVE JULIET MAKE HER ENTRANCE A BIT LATER THAN SCRIPTED...
BUT THERE'S STILL THE ISSUE OF TIME...
DO DO (STOMP) DO DO DO
NN?

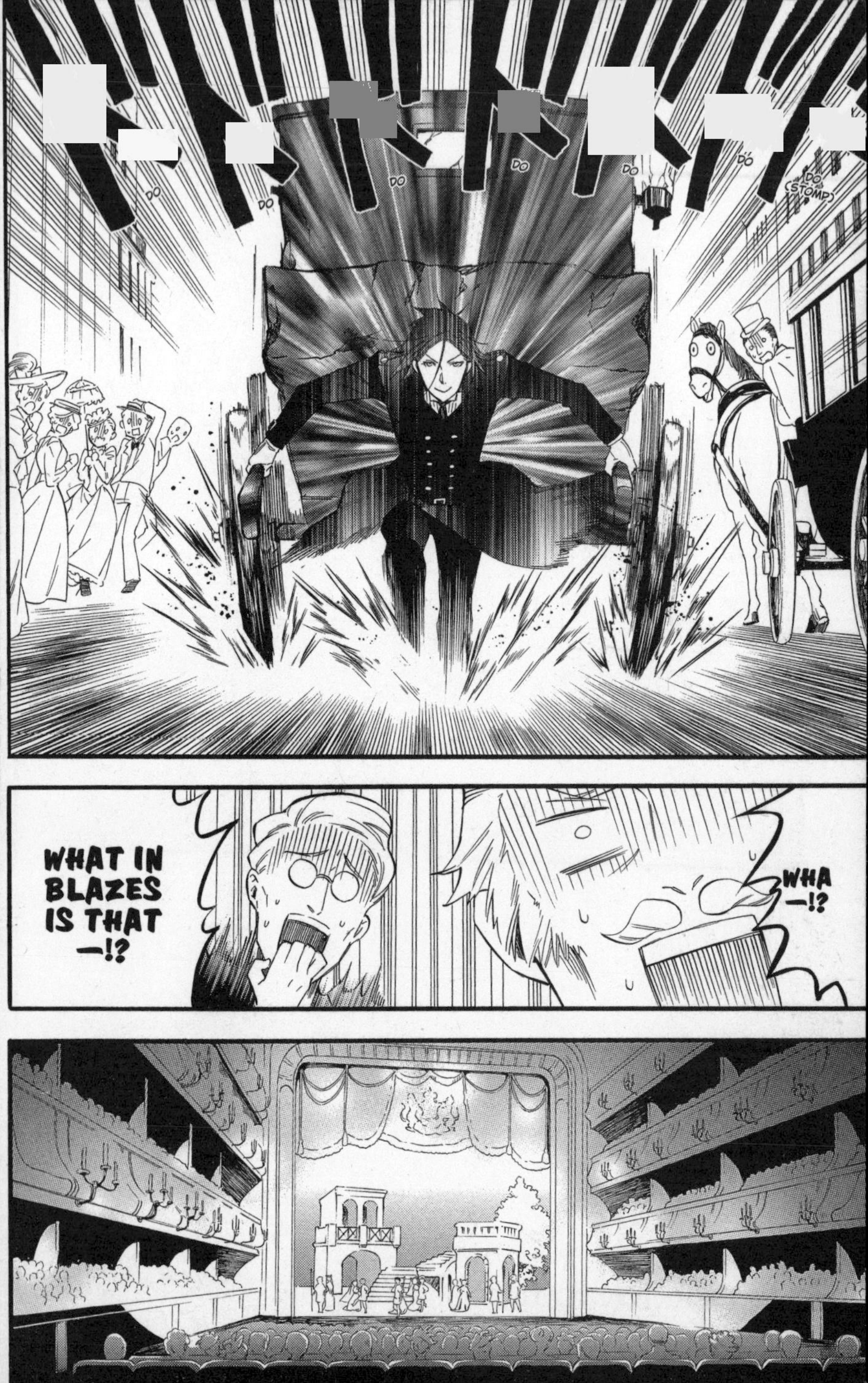
DO (STOMP)
DO
DO
DO
DO
DO
DO
WHA—!?
WHAT IN BLAZES IS THAT—!?

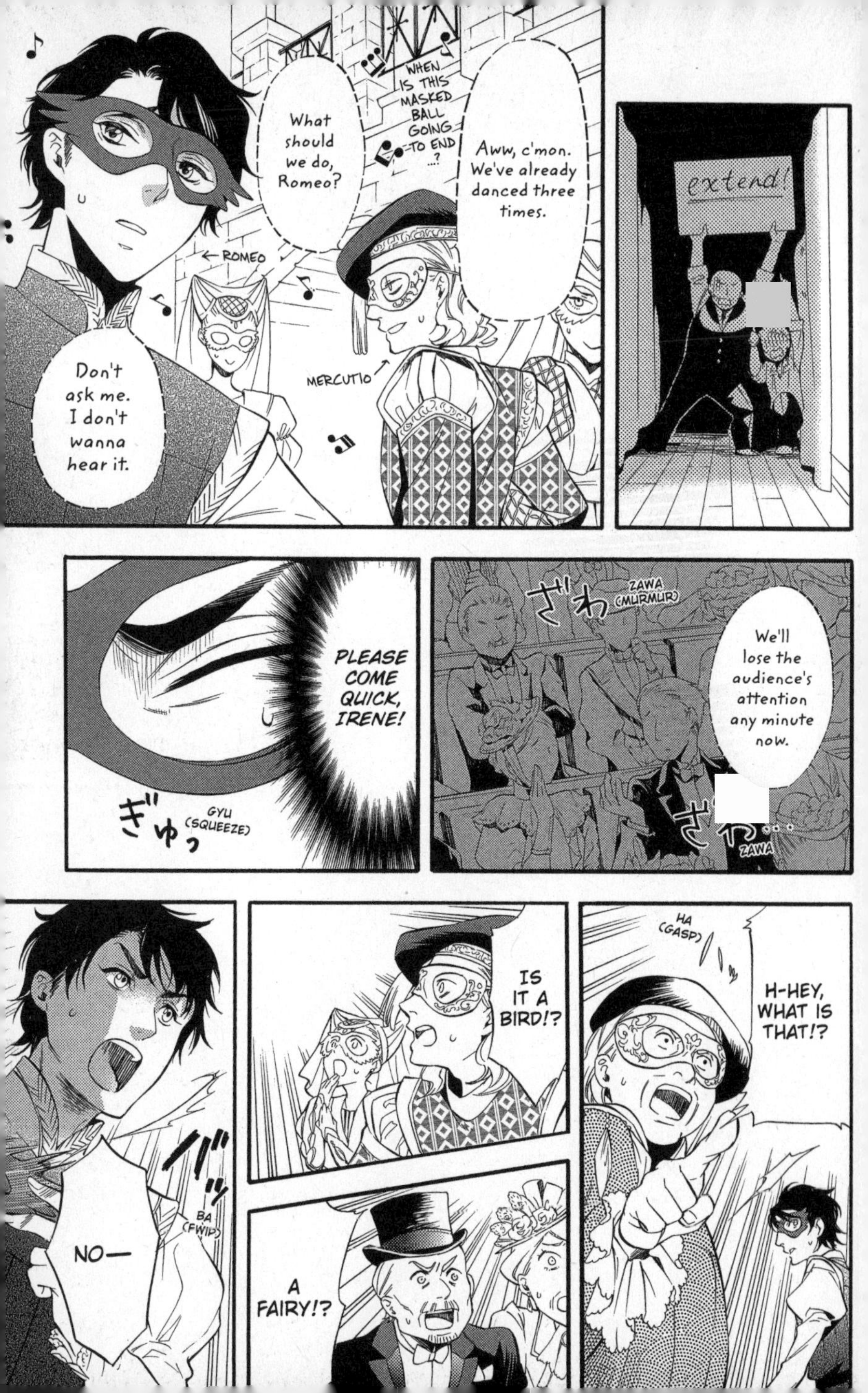

extend!
Aww, c'mon. We've already danced three times.
WHEN IS THIS MASKED BALL GOING TO END ...?
What should we do, Romeo?
← ROMEO
MERCUTIO
Don't ask me. I don't wanna hear it.
ざわ ZAWA (MURMUR)
We'll lose the audience's attention any minute now.
ざわ... ZAWA
PLEASE COME QUICK, IRENE!
ぎゅっ GYU (SQUEEZE)
HA (GASP)
H-HEY, WHAT IS THAT!?
IS IT A BIRD!?
A FAIRY!?
NO—
BA (FWIP)

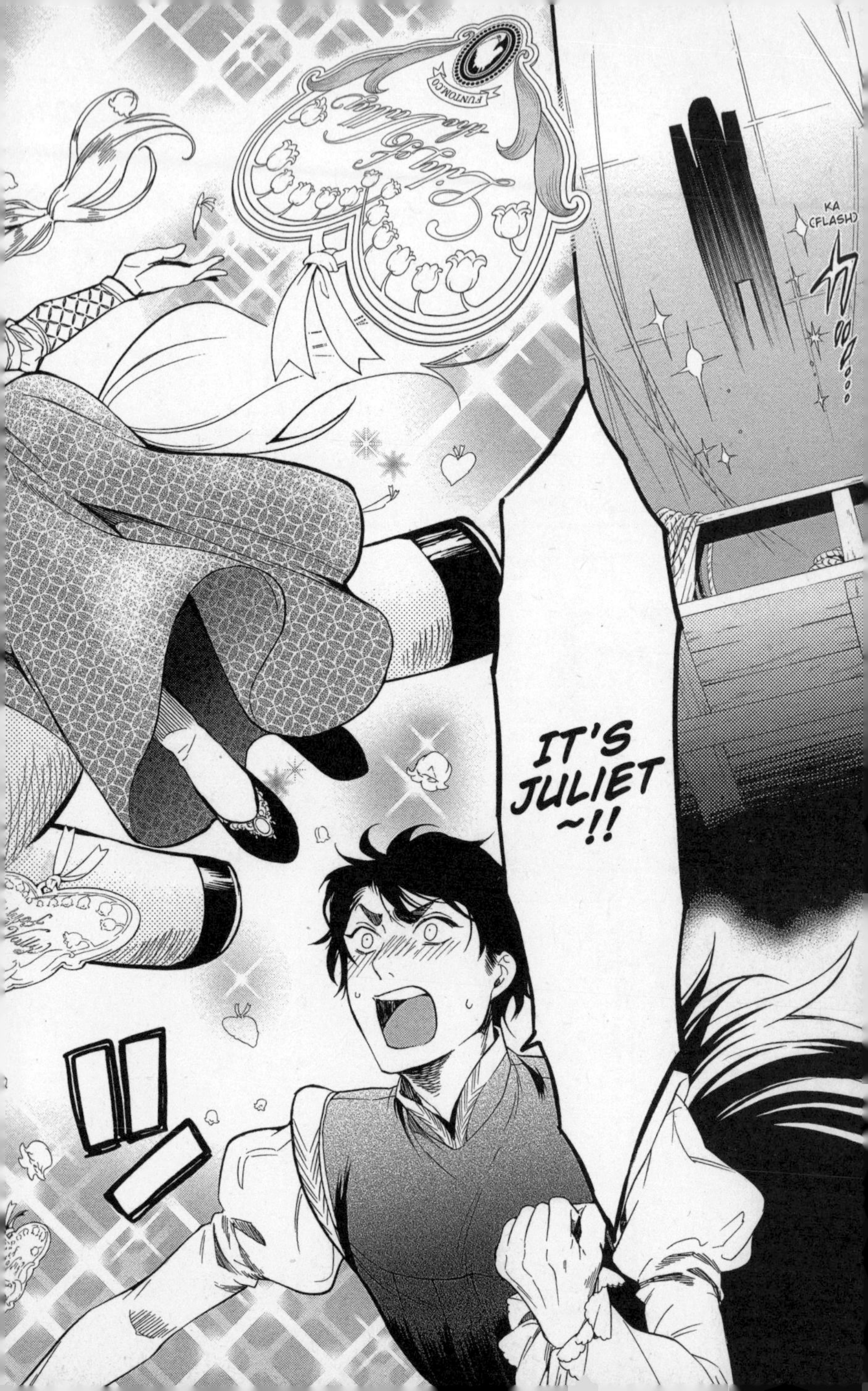
KA (FLASH)
IT'S JULIET ~!!

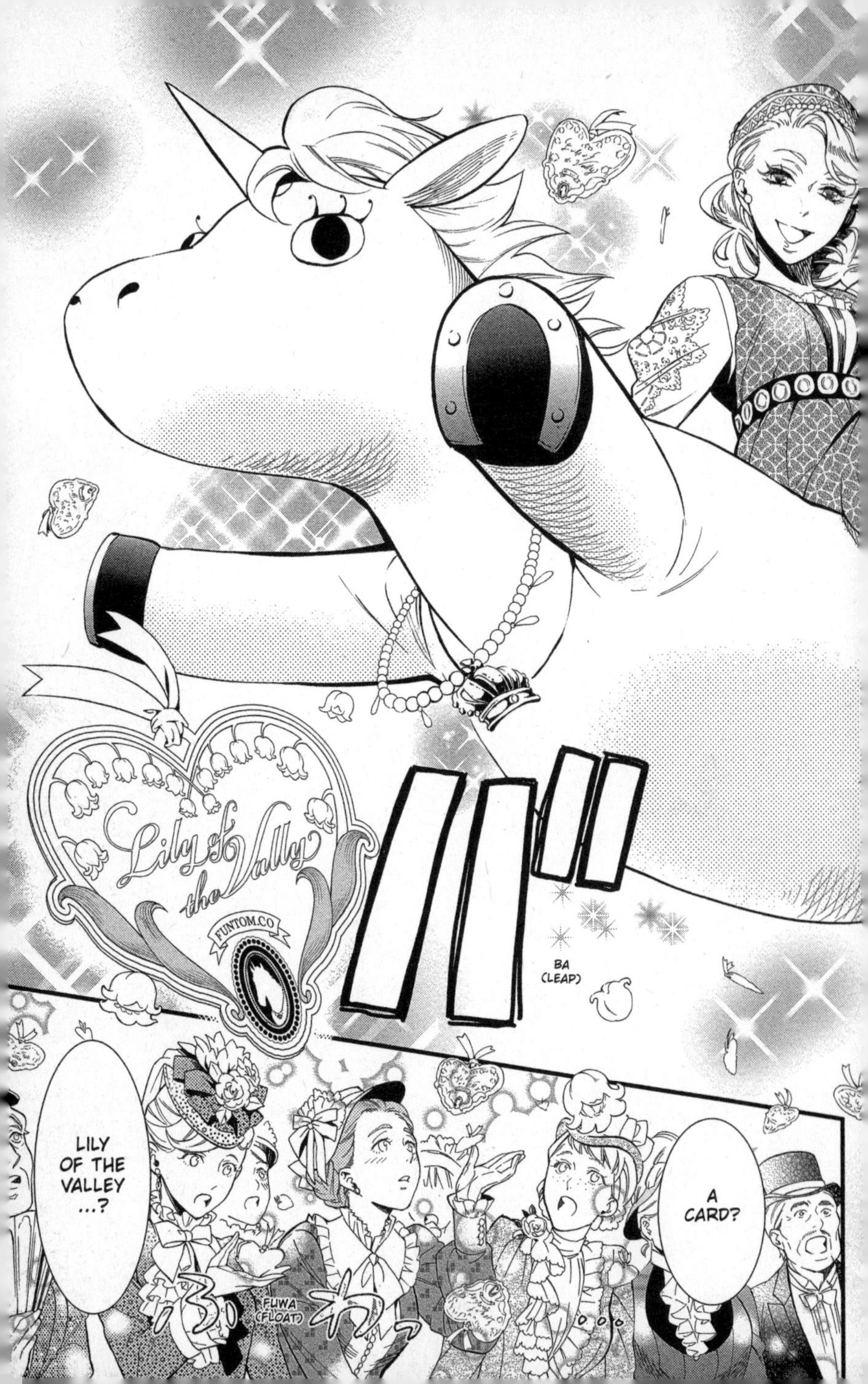
Lily of the Vally
FUNTOM.CO
BA (LEAP)
A CARD?
FUWA (FLOAT)
LILY OF THE VALLEY ...?

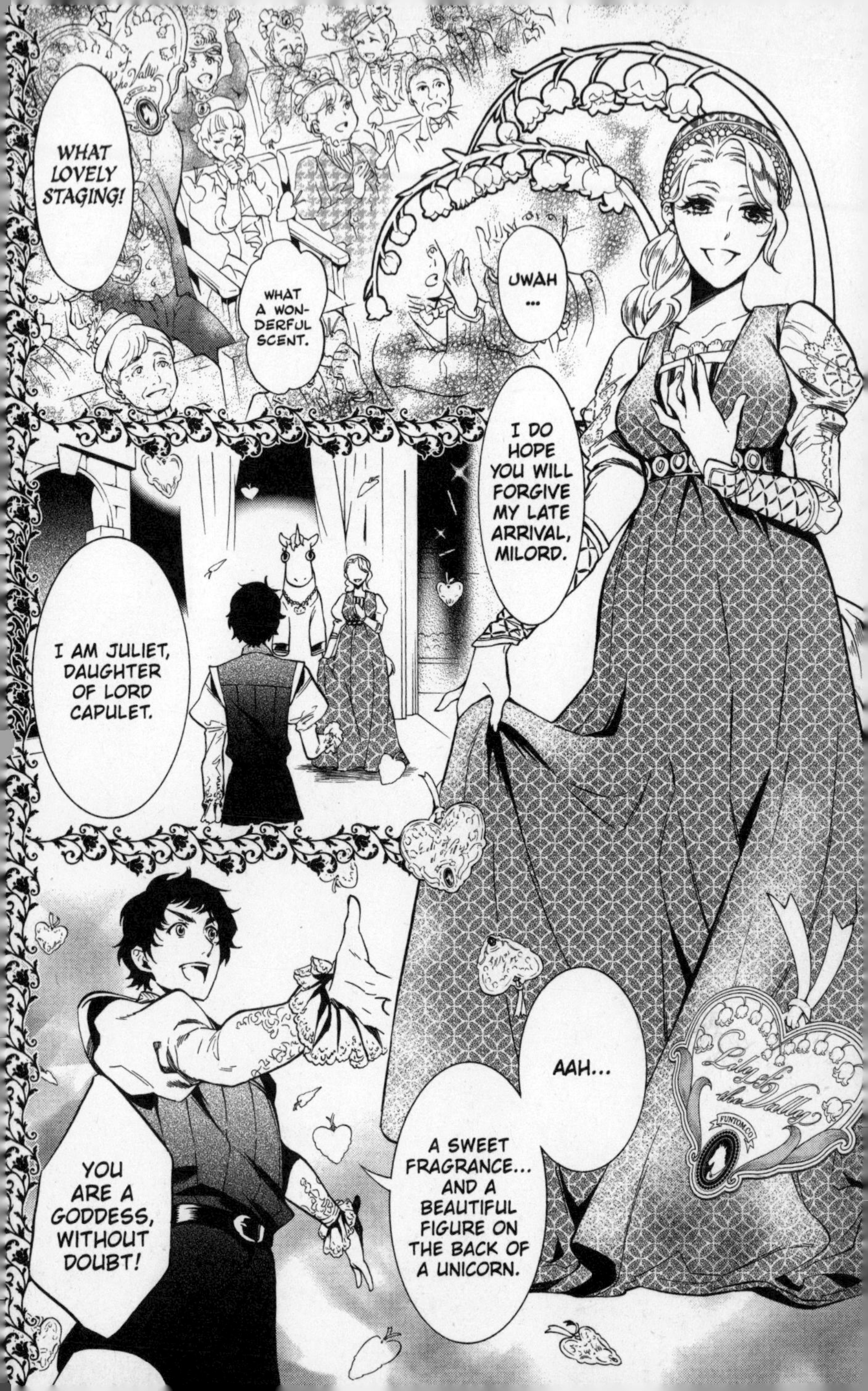
UWAH...
WHAT A WONDERFUL SCENT.
WHAT LOVELY STAGING!
I DO HOPE YOU WILL FORGIVE MY LATE ARRIVAL, MILORD.
I AM JULIET, DAUGHTER OF LORD CAPULET.
AAH...
A SWEET FRAGRANCE... AND A BEAUTIFUL FIGURE ON THE BACK OF A UNICORN.
YOU ARE A GODDESS, WITHOUT DOUBT!
Lily of the Valley
FUNTOM.CO

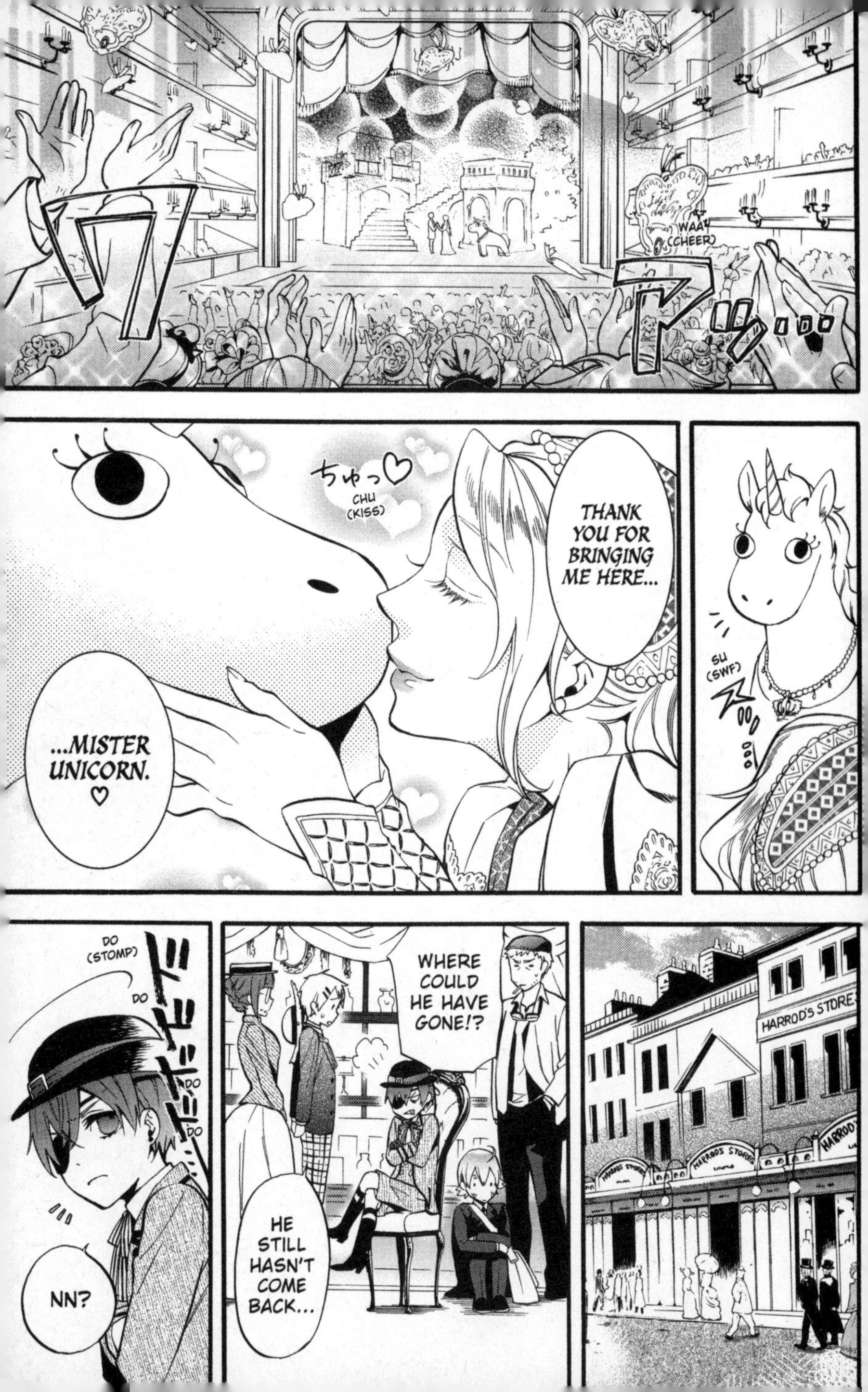
ワァッ
WAA (CHEER)
ス
SU (SWF)
ちゅっ♡
CHU (KISS)
THANK YOU FOR BRINGING ME HERE...
...MISTER UNICORN. ♡
HARROD'S STORES
WHERE COULD HE HAVE GONE!?
HE STILL HASN'T COME BACK...
DO (STOMP)
DO
DO
DO
NN?

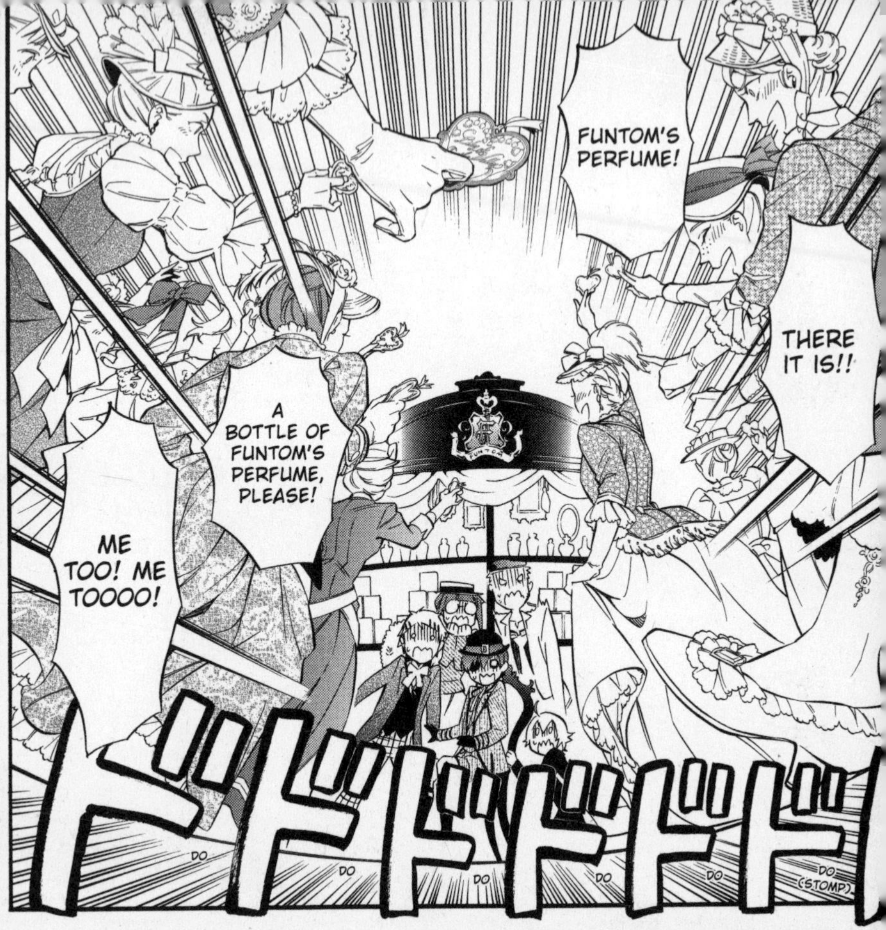
FUNTOM'S PERFUME!
THERE IT IS!!
A BOTTLE OF FUNTOM'S PERFUME, PLEASE!
ME TOO! ME TOOOO!
ドドドドドド
DO DO DO DO DO DO (STOMP)
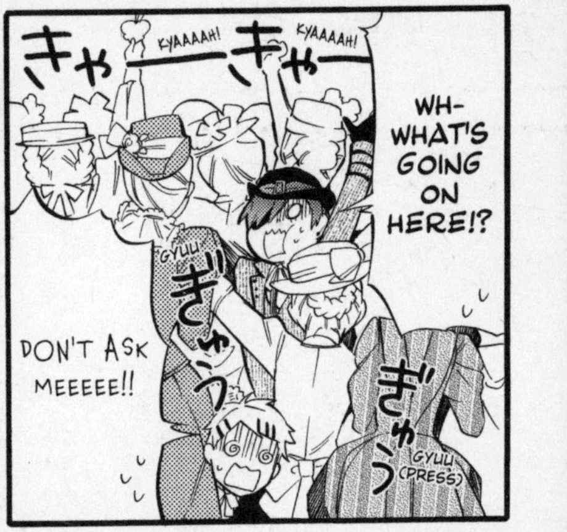
きゃーきゃー
KYAAAAH! KYAAAAH!
WH-WHAT'S GOING ON HERE!?
ぎゅう
GYUU
DON'T ASK MEEEEE!!
ぎゅう
GYUU (PRESS)
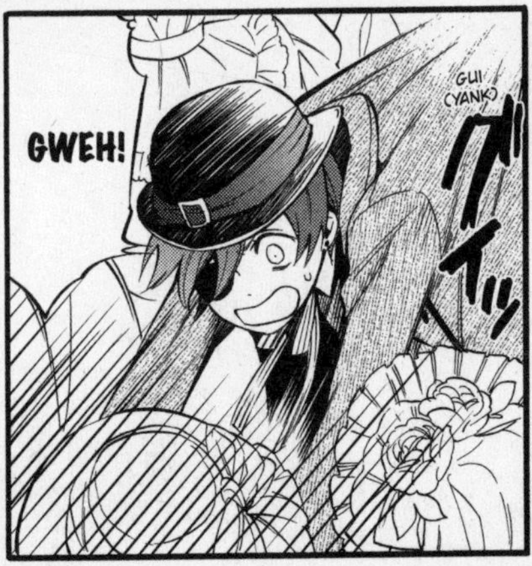
グイッ
GUI (YANK)
GWEH!

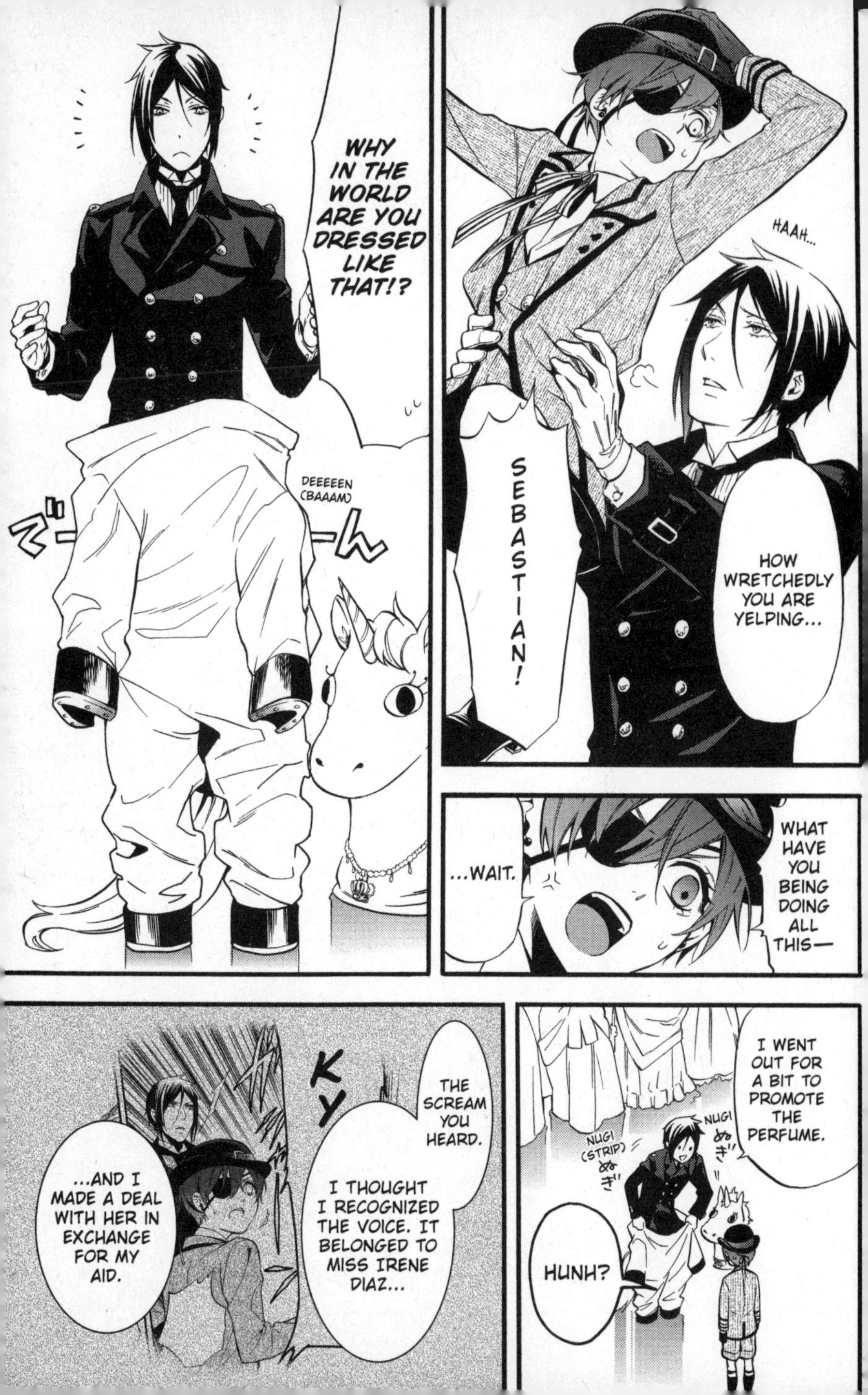
HAAH...
SEBASTIAN!
HOW WRETCHEDLY YOU ARE YELPING...
WHAT HAVE YOU BEING DOING ALL THIS—
...WAIT.
WHY IN THE WORLD ARE YOU DRESSED LIKE THAT!?
DEEEEEN (BAAAM)
I WENT OUT FOR A BIT TO PROMOTE THE PERFUME.
NUGI ぬぎ
NUGI (STRIP) ぬぎ
HUNH?
THE SCREAM YOU HEARD.
KY
I THOUGHT I RECOGNIZED THE VOICE. IT BELONGED TO MISS IRENE DIAZ...
...AND I MADE A DEAL WITH HER IN EXCHANGE FOR MY AID.

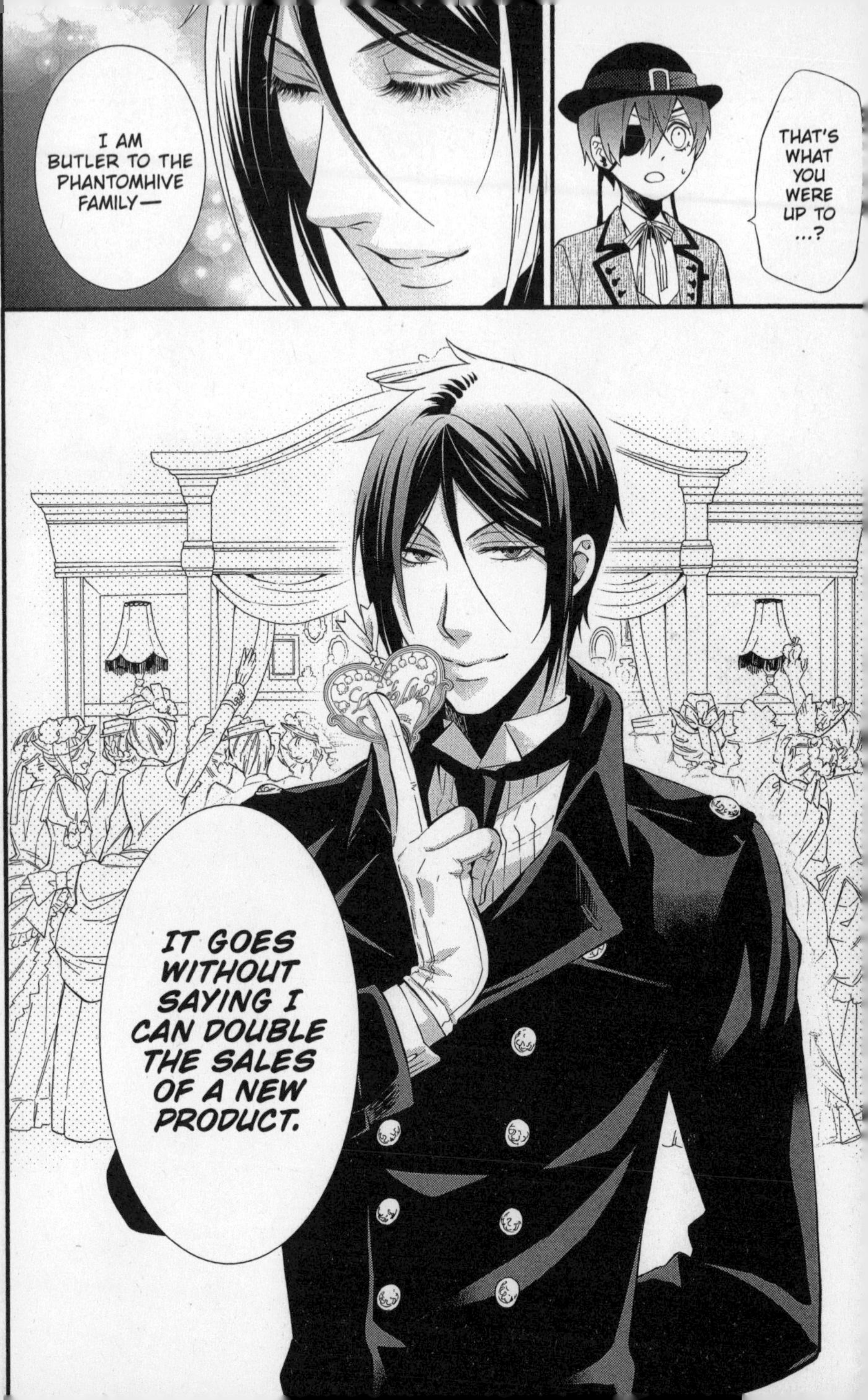
THAT'S WHAT YOU WERE UP TO ...?
I AM BUTLER TO THE PHANTOMHIVE FAMILY—
IT GOES WITHOUT SAYING I CAN DOUBLE THE SALES OF A NEW PRODUCT.

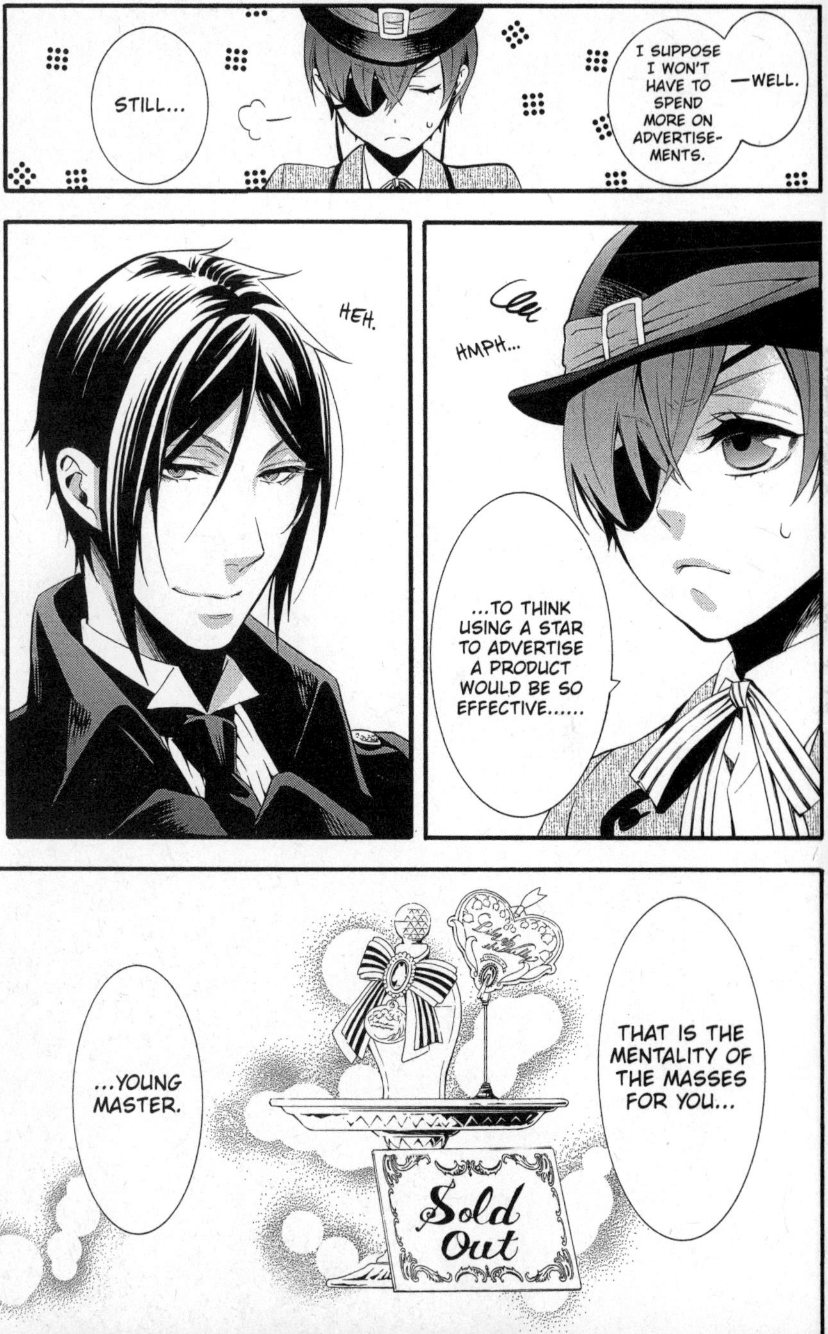
—WELL.
I SUPPOSE I WON'T HAVE TO SPEND MORE ON ADVERTISE-MENTS.
STILL...
HMPH...
...TO THINK USING A STAR TO ADVERTISE A PRODUCT WOULD BE SO EFFECTIVE......
HEH.
THAT IS THE MENTALITY OF THE MASSES FOR YOU...
...YOUNG MASTER.
Sold Out

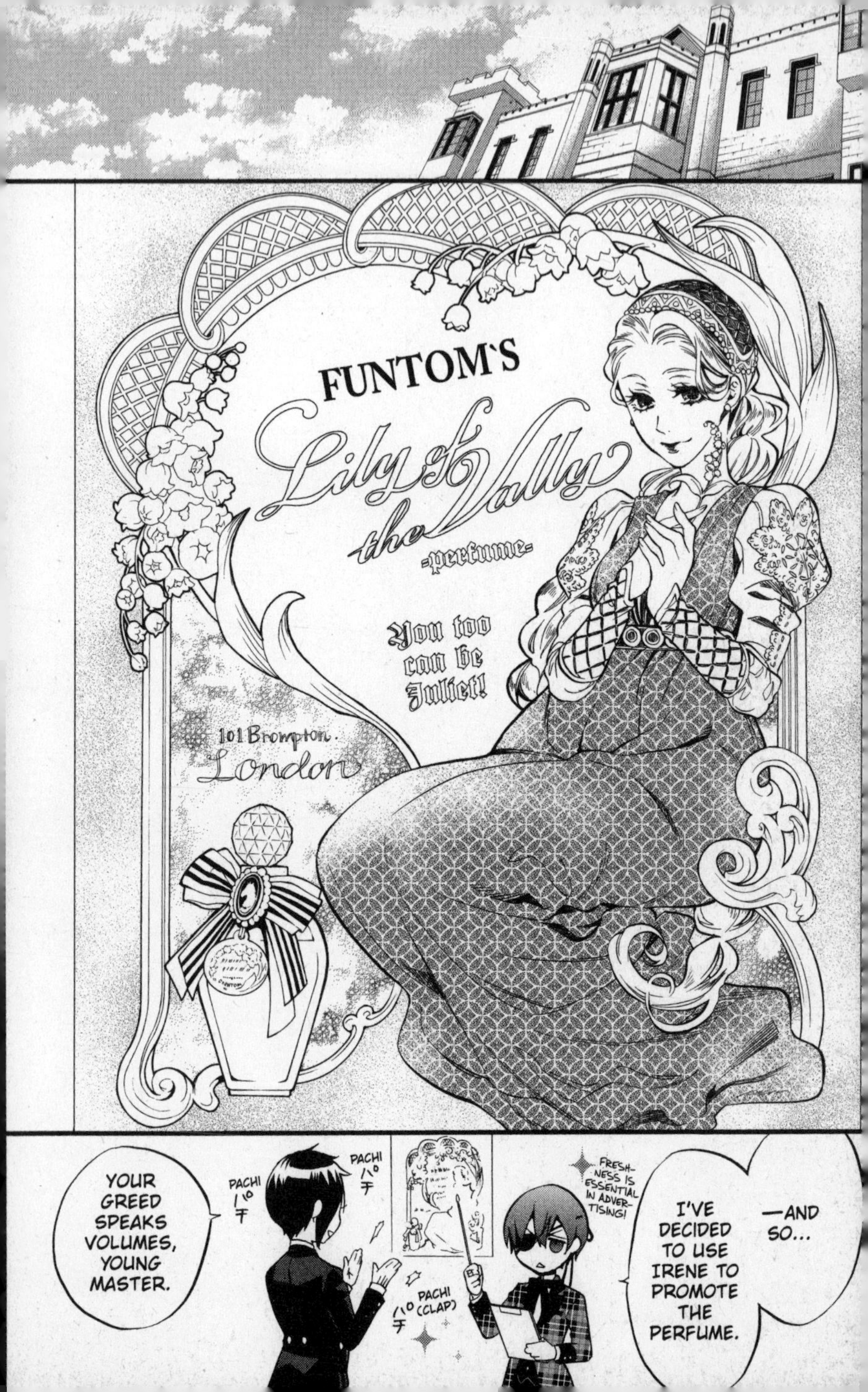
FUNTOM'S
Lily of the Valley
-perfume-
You too can be Juliet!
101 Brompton. London
—AND SO...
I'VE DECIDED TO USE IRENE TO PROMOTE THE PERFUME.
FRESH-NESS IS ESSENTIAL IN ADVER-TISING!
PACHI パチ
PACHI パチ (CLAP)
PACHI パチ
YOUR GREED SPEAKS VOLUMES, YOUNG MASTER.

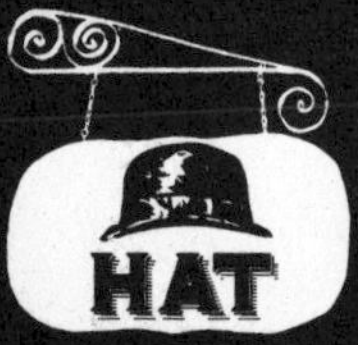
HAT

Black Butler

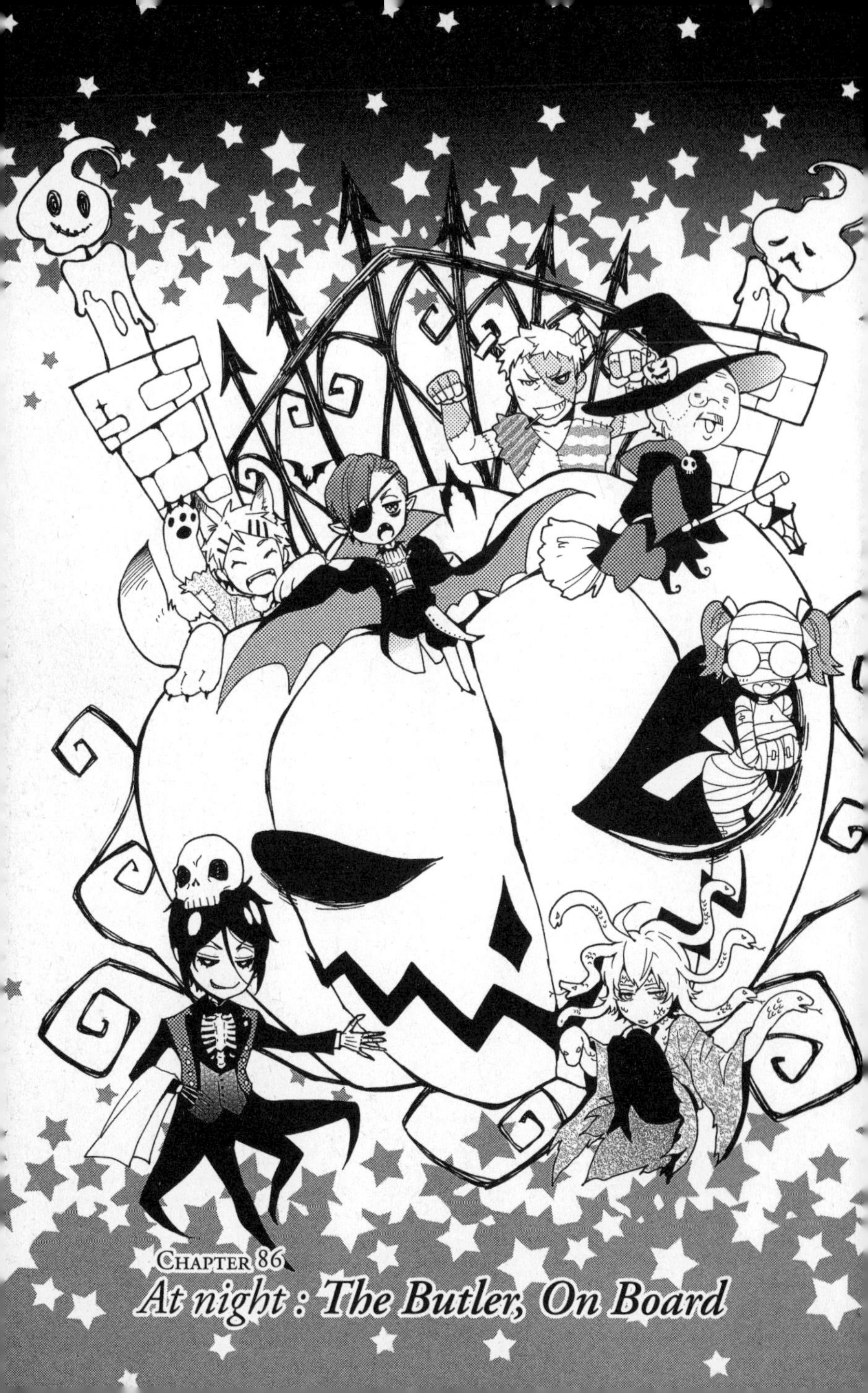

Chapter 86

At night : The Butler, On Board

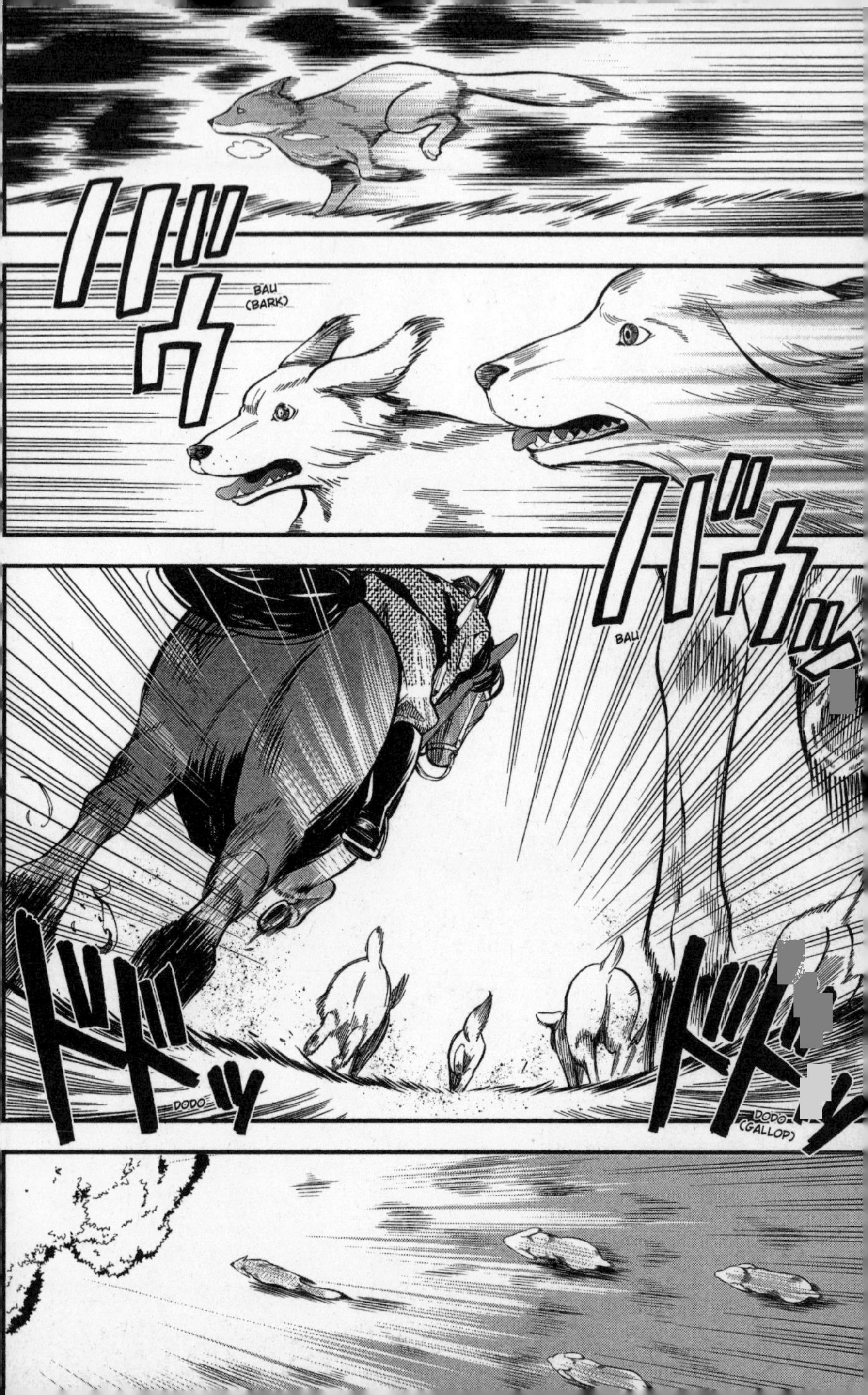
バウ
BAU (BARK)
バウッ
BAU
ドドッ
DODO (GALLOP)
ドドッ
DODO

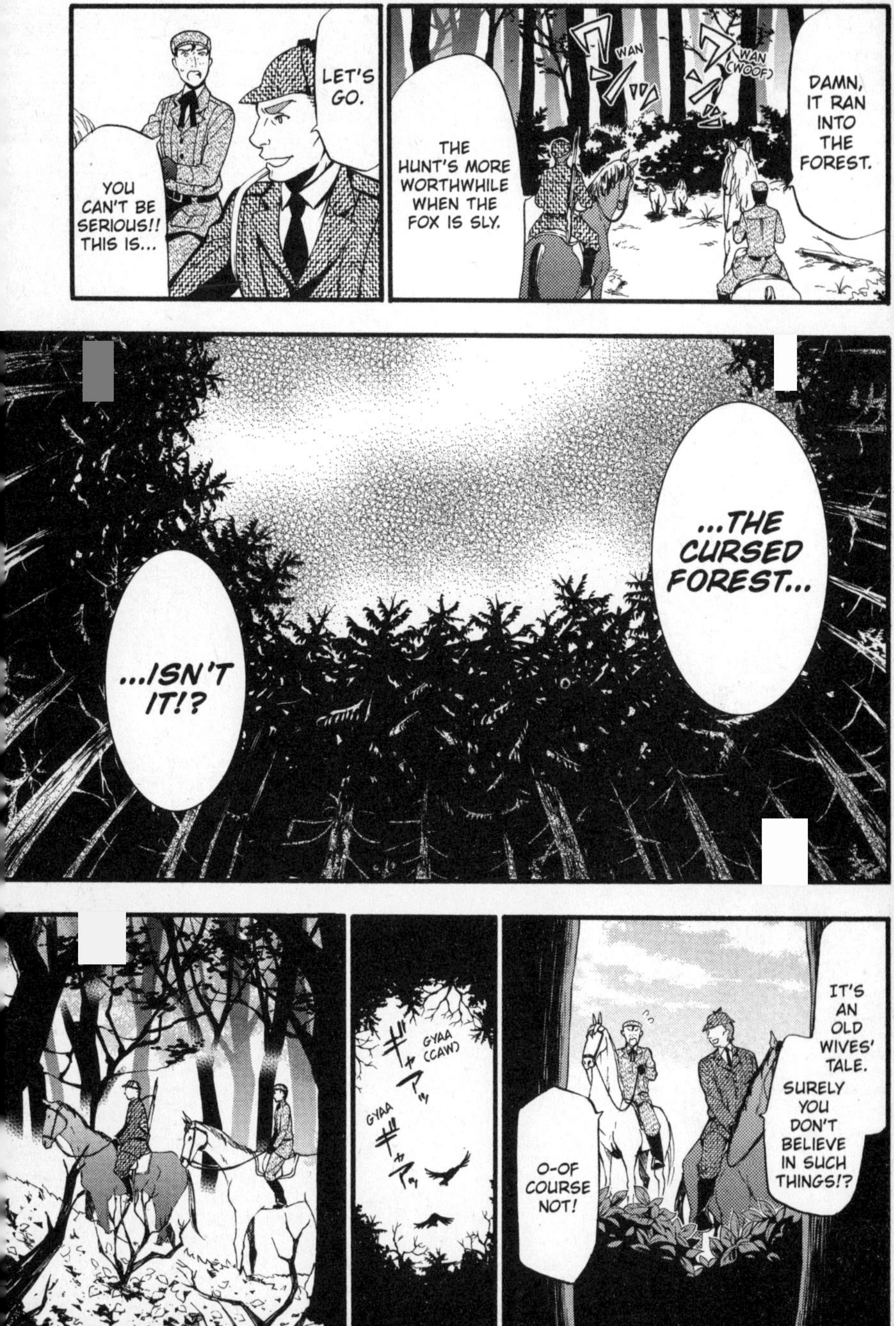
DAMN, IT RAN INTO THE FOREST.
WAN
WAN (WOOF)
THE HUNT'S MORE WORTHWHILE WHEN THE FOX IS SLY.
LET'S GO.
YOU CAN'T BE SERIOUS!! THIS IS...
...THE CURSED FOREST...
...ISN'T IT!?
IT'S AN OLD WIVES' TALE. SURELY YOU DON'T BELIEVE IN SUCH THINGS!?
O-OF COURSE NOT!
GYAA (CAW)
GYAA

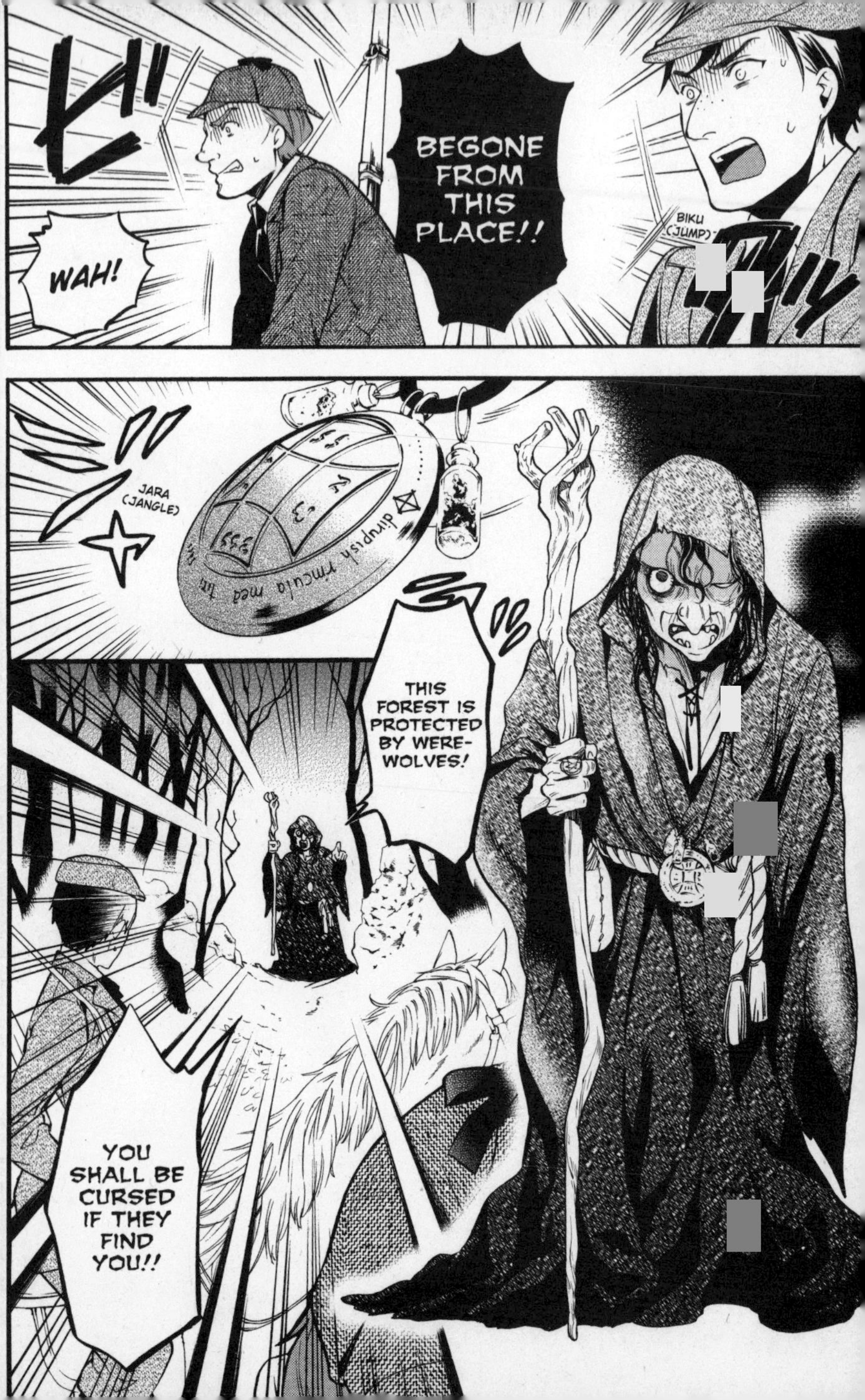
BEGONE FROM THIS PLACE!!
BIKU (JUMP)
WAH!
JARA (JANGLE)
THIS FOREST IS PROTECTED BY WERE-WOLVES!
YOU SHALL BE CURSED IF THEY FIND YOU!!

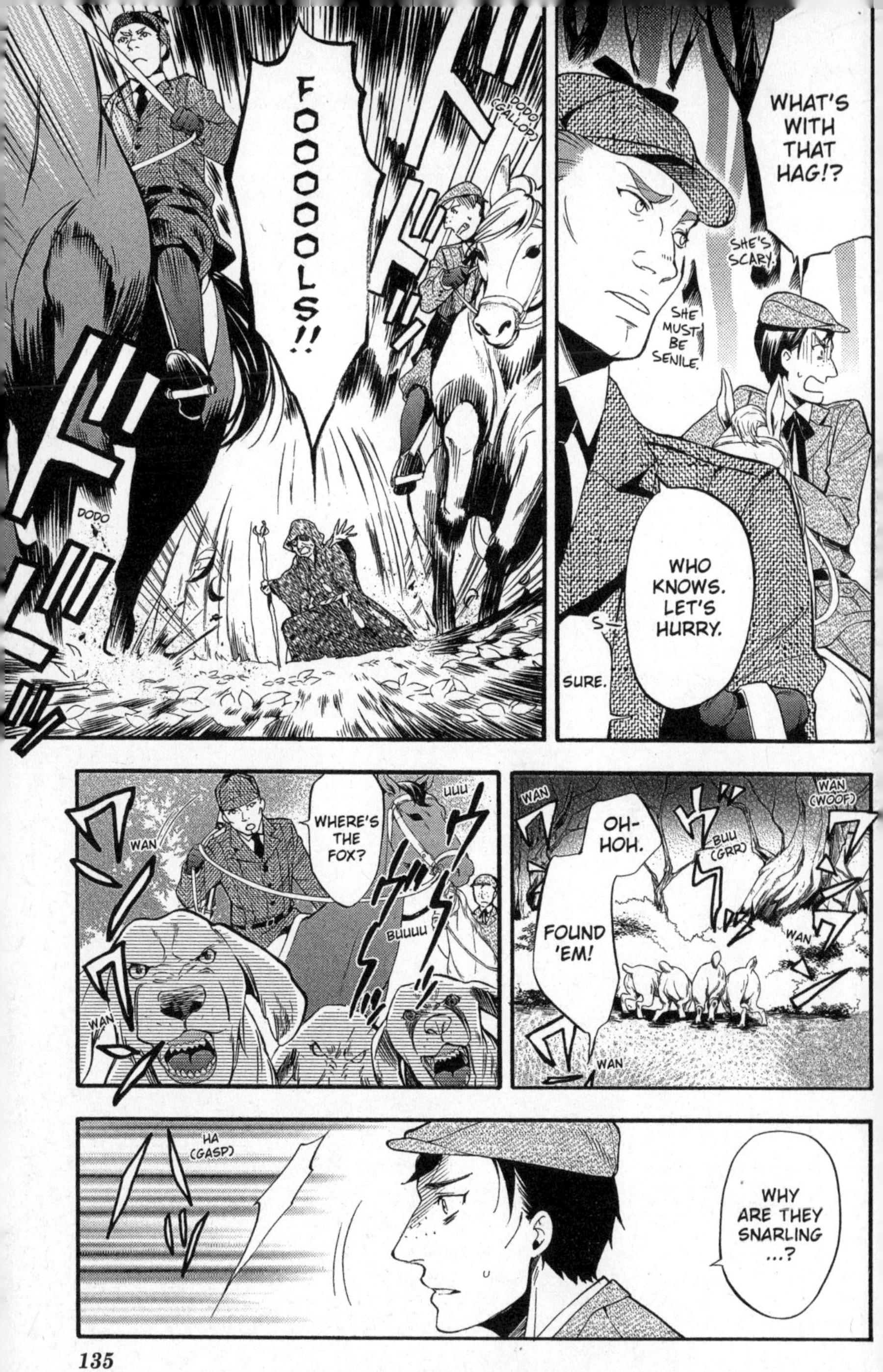
DODO (GALLOP)
FOOOOOOOLS!!
DODO
WHAT'S WITH THAT HAG!?
SHE'S SCARY.
SHE MUST BE SENILE.
WHO KNOWS. LET'S HURRY.
S- SURE.
WAN
UUU
WHERE'S THE FOX?
BUUUU
WAN
WAN
WAN (WOOF)
OH-HOH.
BUU (GRR)
FOUND 'EM!
WAN
WAN
HA (GASP)
WHY ARE THEY SNARLING ...?

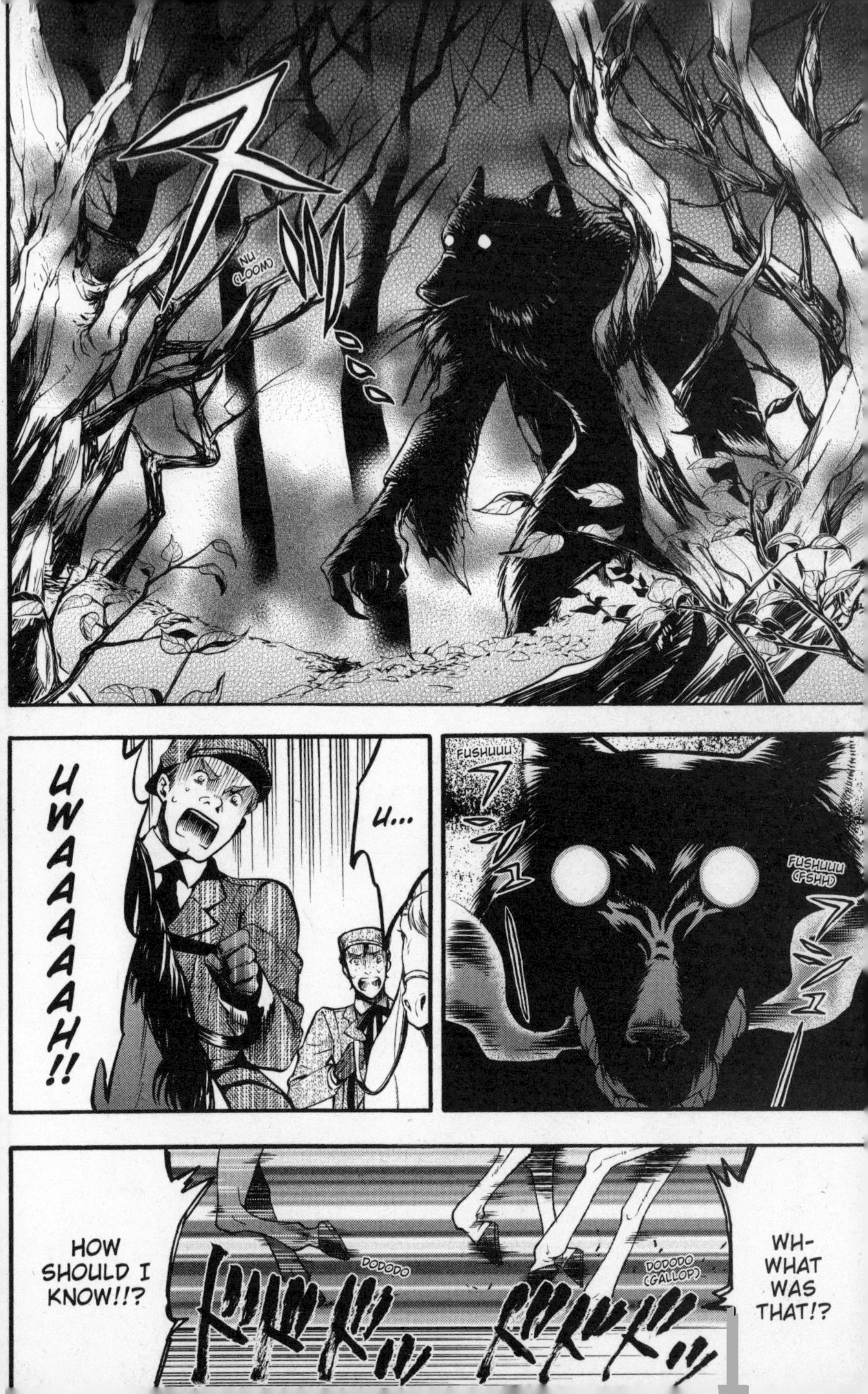
NU
(LOOM)
FUSHUUU
(FSHH)
FUSHUUU
U...
UWAAAAAAAH!!
WH-
WHAT
WAS
THAT!?
DODODO
(GALLOP)
DODODO
HOW
SHOULD I
KNOW!!?

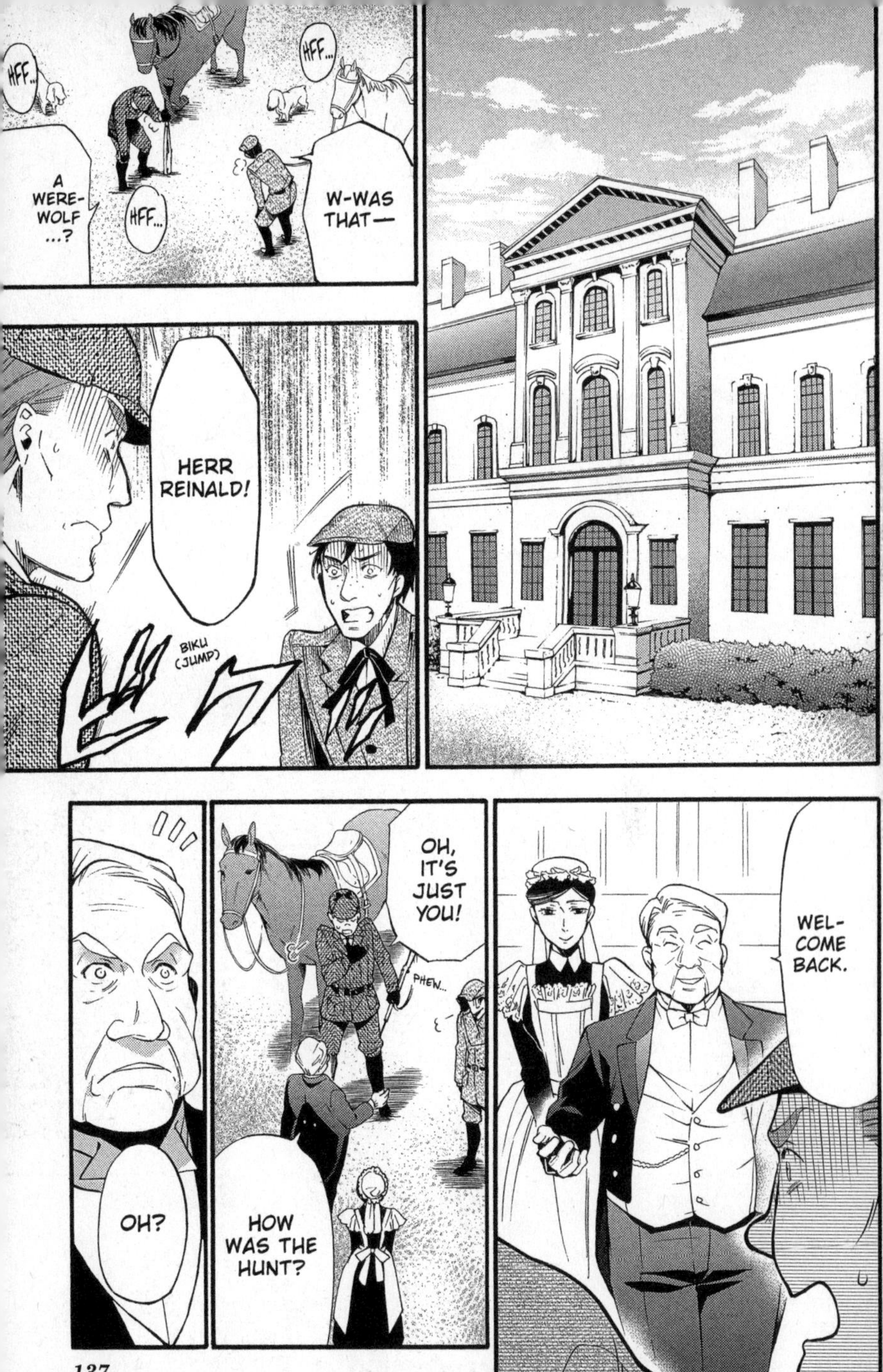
HFF...
W-WAS THAT—
HFF...
A WERE-WOLF ...?
HFF...
HERR REINALD!
BIKU (JUMP)
WEL-COME BACK.
OH, IT'S JUST YOU!
PHEW...
HOW WAS THE HUNT?
OH?

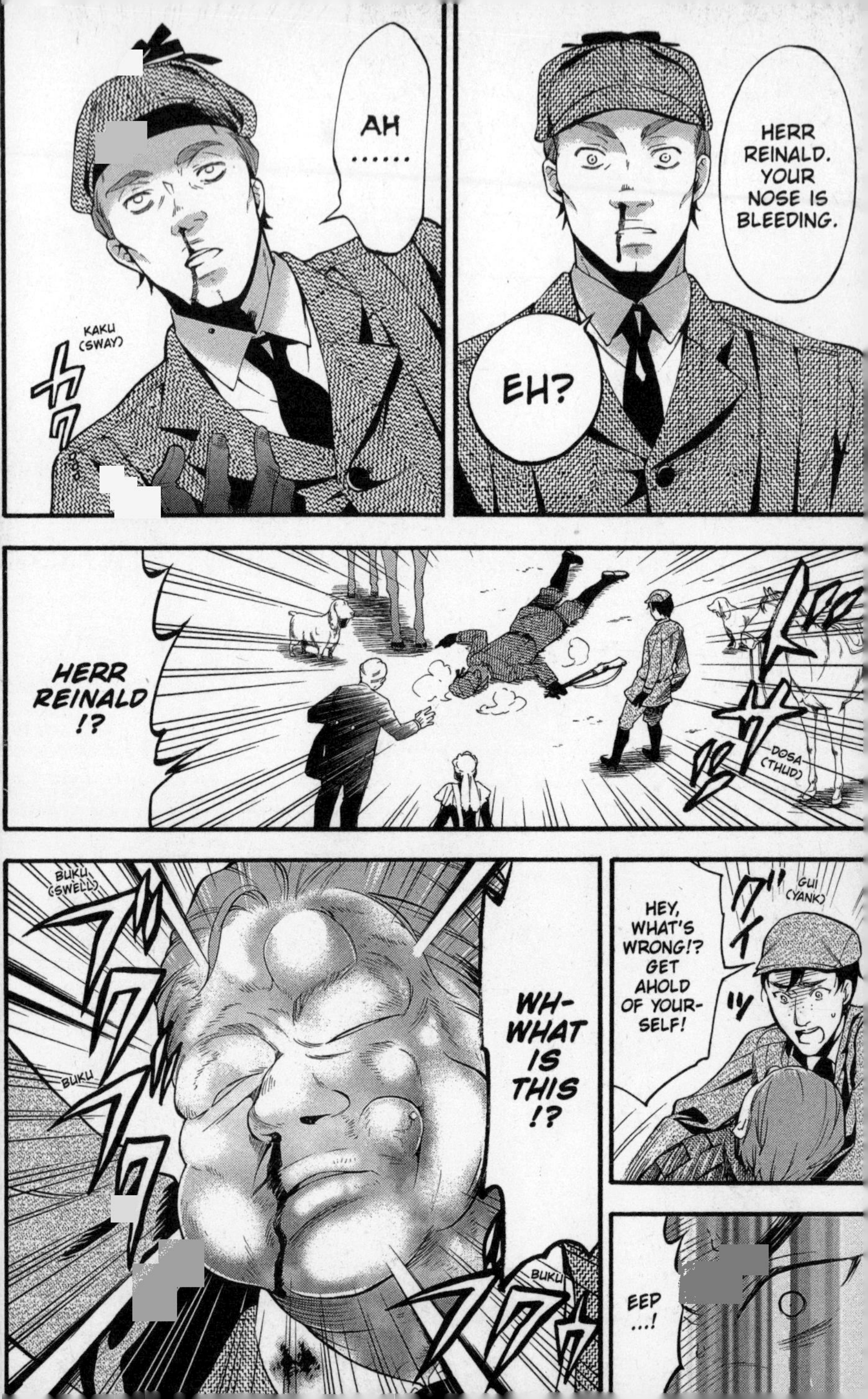
HERR REINALD. YOUR NOSE IS BLEEDING.
EH?
AH ......
KAKU (SWAY)
DOSA (THUD)
HERR REINALD !?
GUI (YANK)
HEY, WHAT'S WRONG!? GET AHOLD OF YOURSELF!
EEP ...!
BUKU (SWELL)
WH-WHAT IS THIS !?
BUKU
BUKU

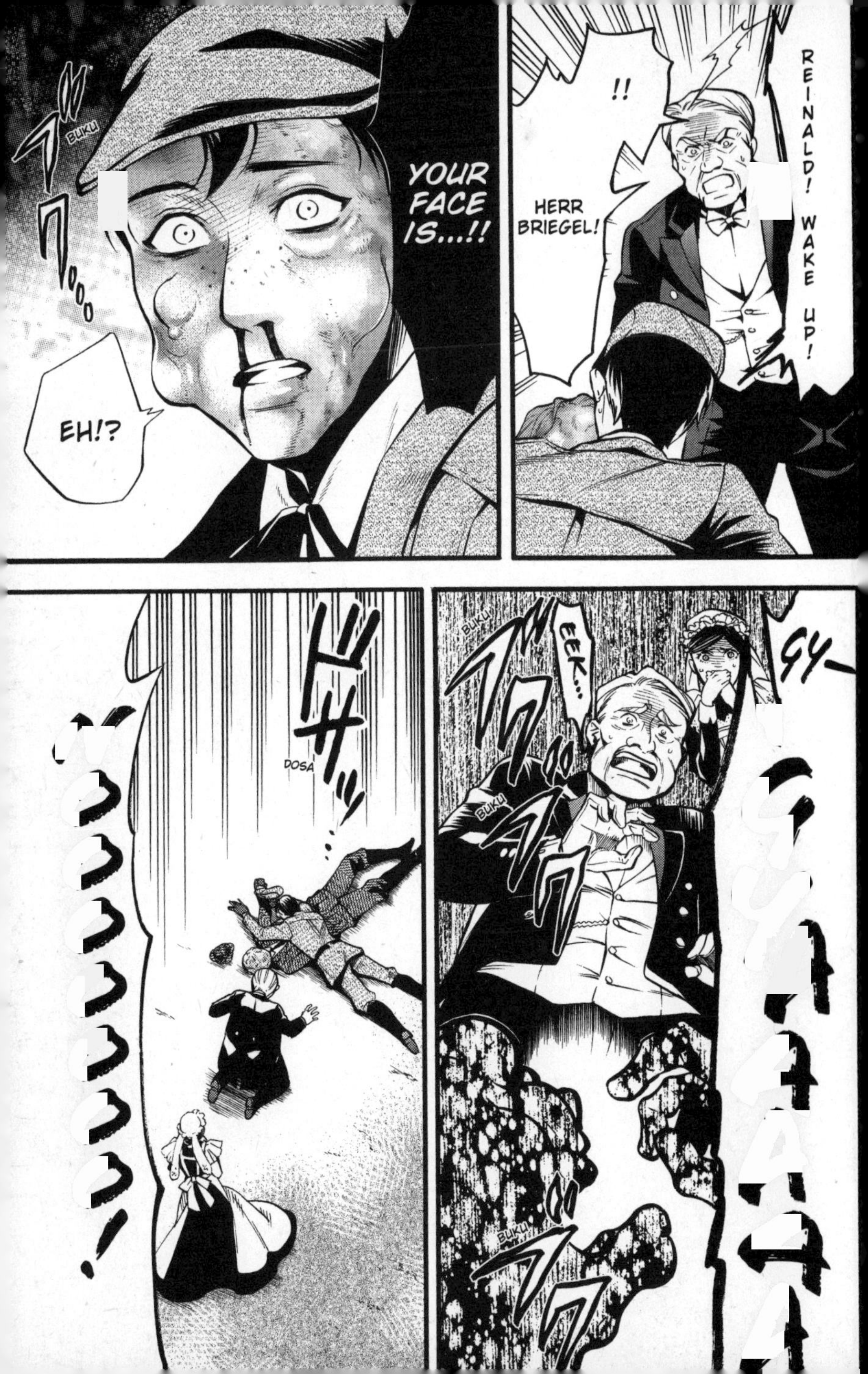
REINALD! WAKE UP!
!!
HERR BRIEGEL!
YOUR FACE IS...!!
BUKU
EH!?
GY-
EEK...
BUKU
BUKU
BUKU
DOSA

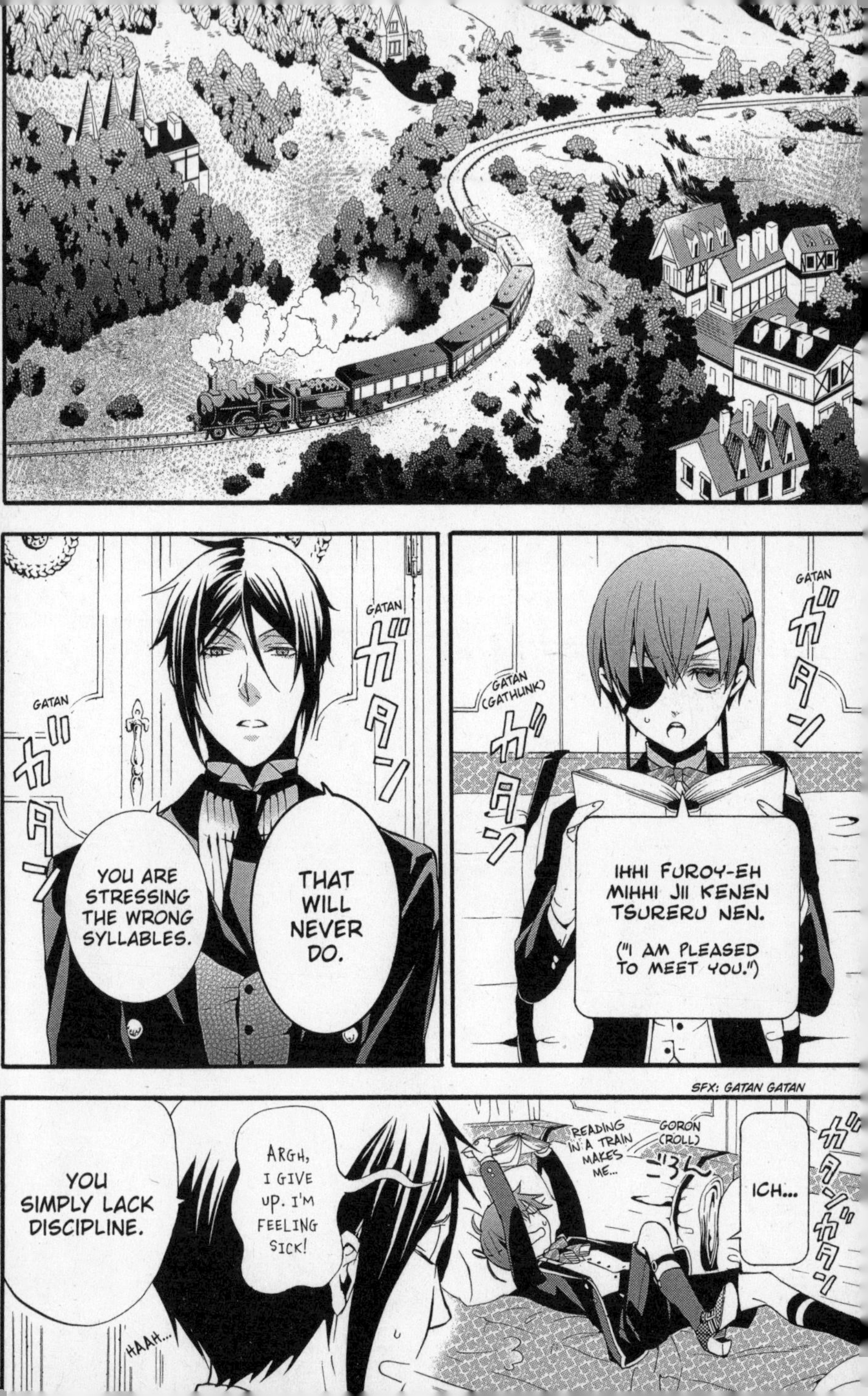
GATAN
GATAN (GATHUNK)
IHHI FUROY-EH MIHHI JII KENEN TSURERU NEN.
("I AM PLEASED TO MEET YOU.")
GATAN
THAT WILL NEVER DO.
YOU ARE STRESSING THE WRONG SYLLABLES.
GATAN
SFX: GATAN GATAN
ICH...
GORON (ROLL)
READING IN A TRAIN MAKES ME...
ARGH, I GIVE UP. I'M FEELING SICK!
YOU SIMPLY LACK DISCIPLINE.
HAAH...

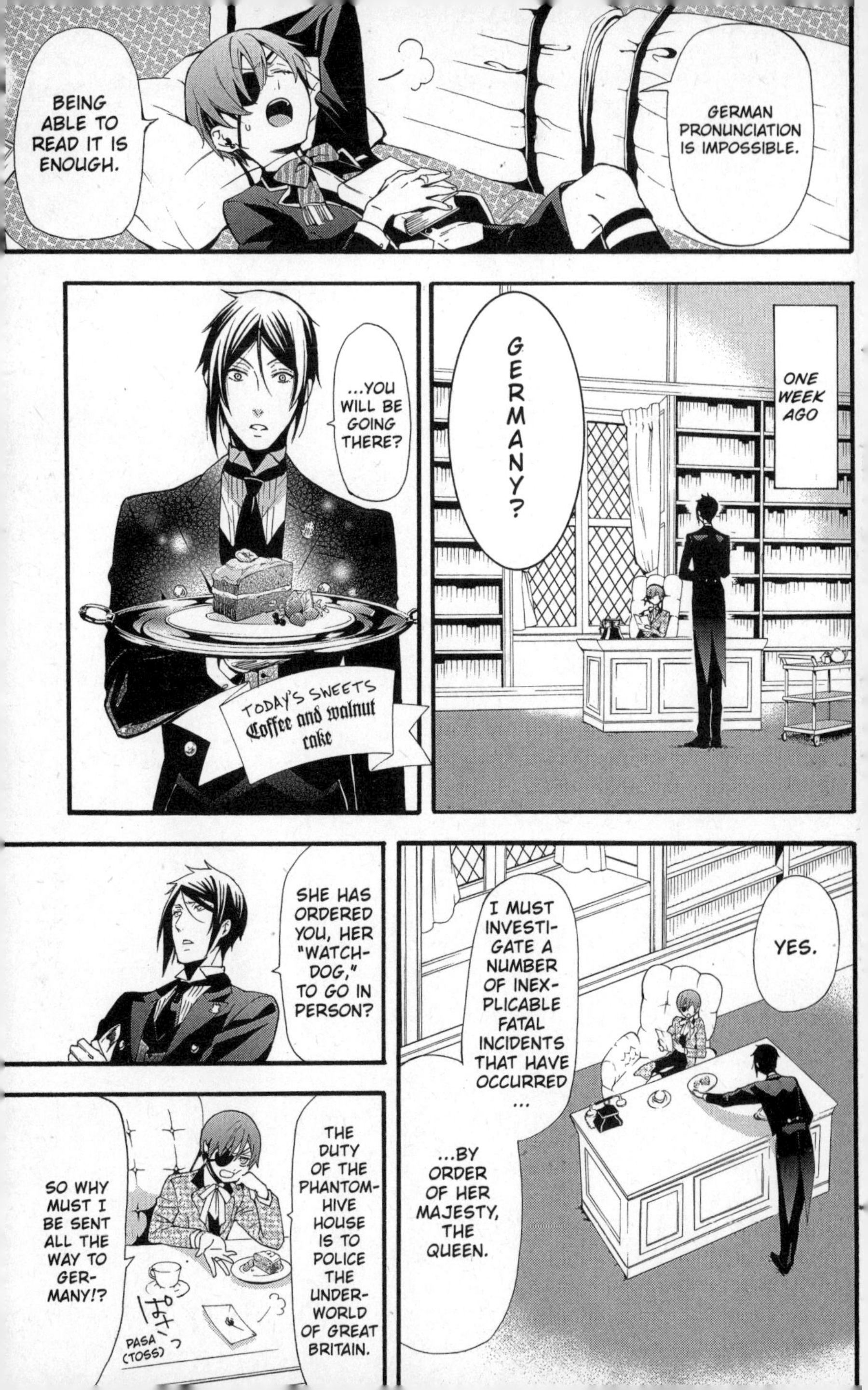
GERMAN PRONUNCIATION IS IMPOSSIBLE.
BEING ABLE TO READ IT IS ENOUGH.
ONE WEEK AGO
GERMANY?
...YOU WILL BE GOING THERE?
TODAY'S SWEETS Coffee and walnut cake
YES.
I MUST INVESTIGATE A NUMBER OF INEXPLICABLE FATAL INCIDENTS THAT HAVE OCCURRED ...
...BY ORDER OF HER MAJESTY, THE QUEEN.
SHE HAS ORDERED YOU, HER "WATCHDOG," TO GO IN PERSON?
THE DUTY OF THE PHANTOMHIVE HOUSE IS TO POLICE THE UNDERWORLD OF GREAT BRITAIN.
SO WHY MUST I BE SENT ALL THE WAY TO GERMANY!?
PASA (TOSS)

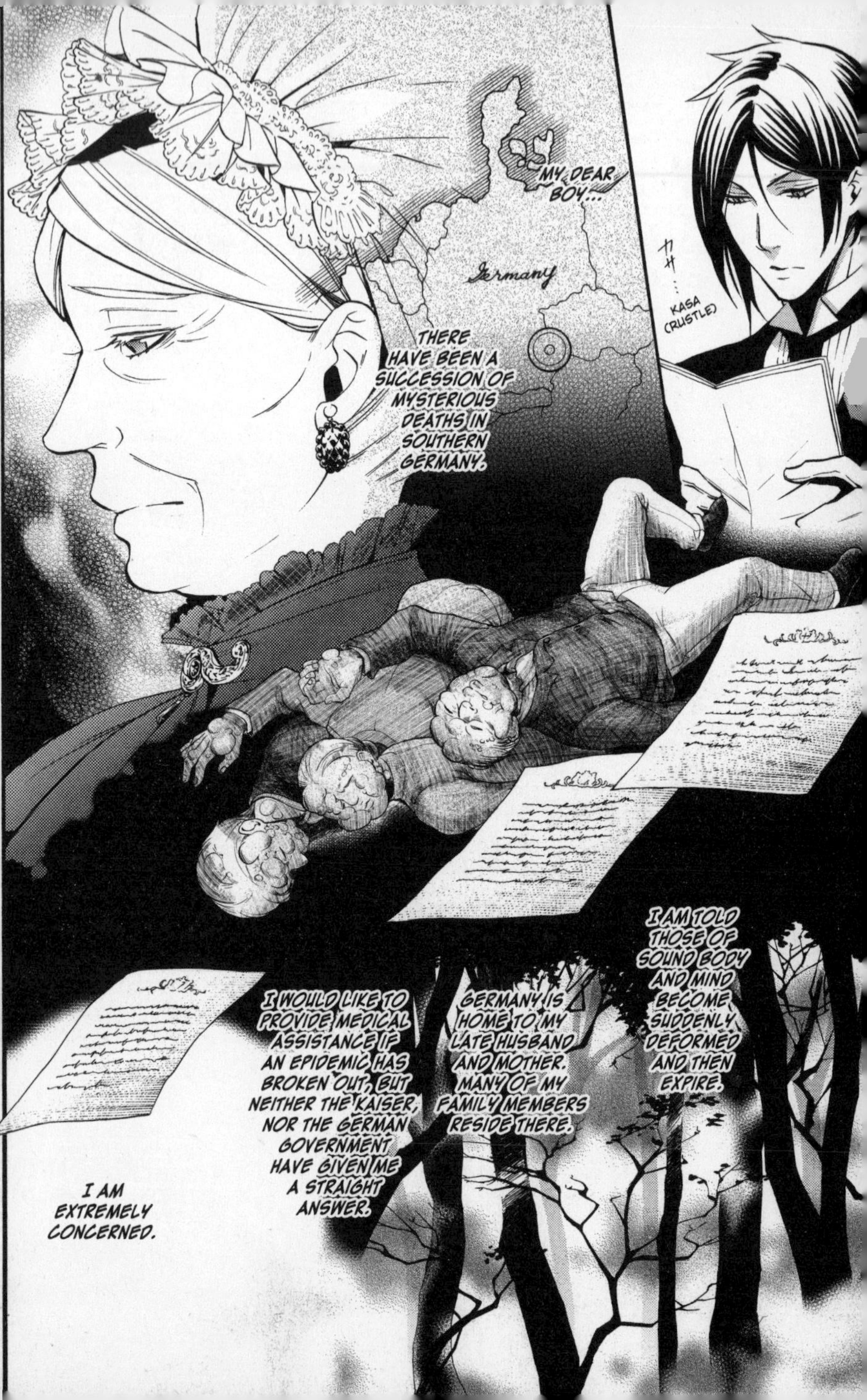

カサ…
KASA (RUSTLE)
MY DEAR BOY...
Germany
THERE HAVE BEEN A SUCCESSION OF MYSTERIOUS DEATHS IN SOUTHERN GERMANY.
I AM TOLD THOSE OF SOUND BODY AND MIND BECOME SUDDENLY DEFORMED AND THEN EXPIRE.
GERMANY IS HOME TO MY LATE HUSBAND AND MOTHER. MANY OF MY FAMILY MEMBERS RESIDE THERE.
I WOULD LIKE TO PROVIDE MEDICAL ASSISTANCE IF AN EPIDEMIC HAS BROKEN OUT, BUT NEITHER THE KAISER, NOR THE GERMAN GOVERNMENT HAVE GIVEN ME A STRAIGHT ANSWER.
I AM EXTREMELY CONCERNED.

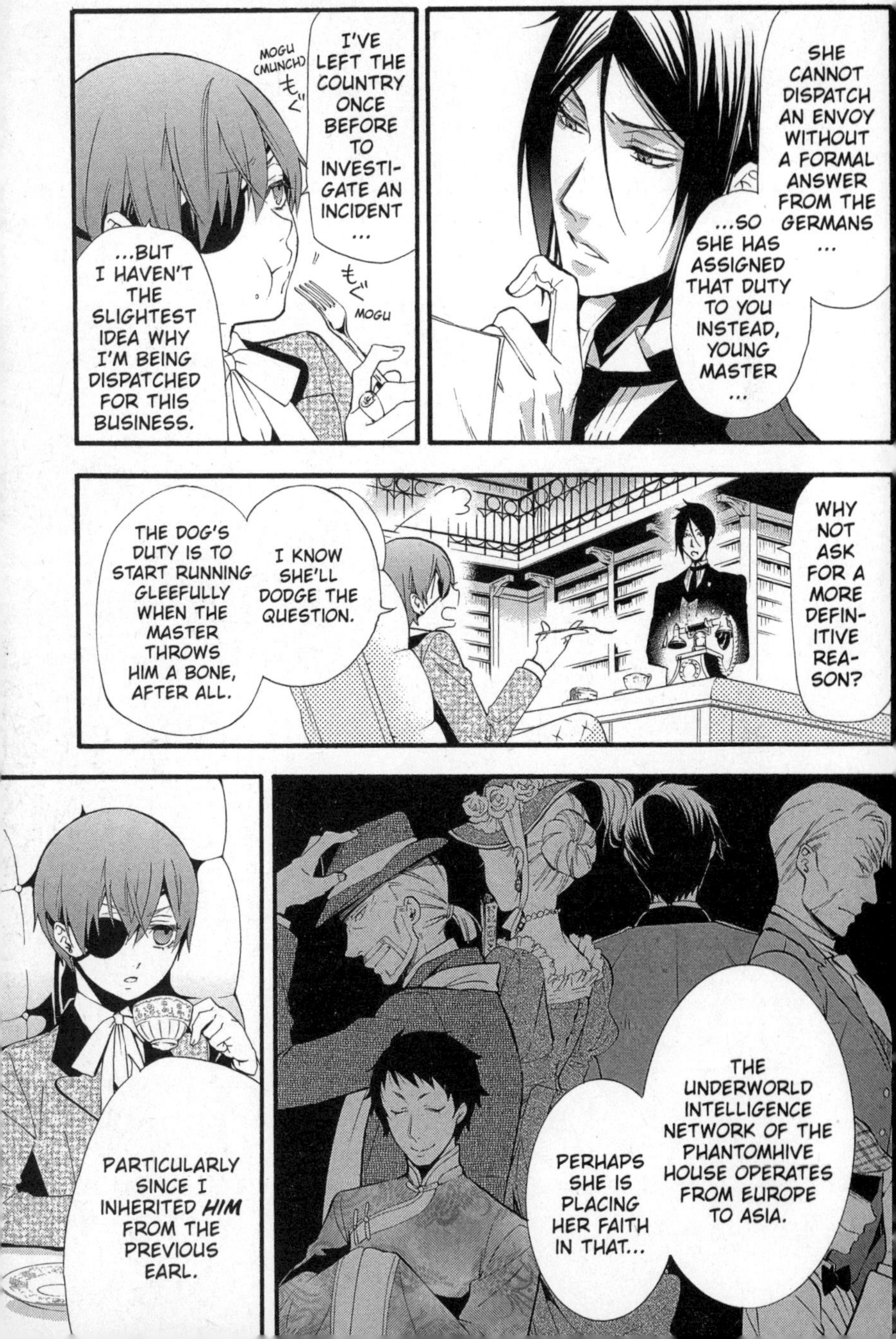
SHE CANNOT DISPATCH AN ENVOY WITHOUT A FORMAL ANSWER FROM THE GERMANS ...
...SO SHE HAS ASSIGNED THAT DUTY TO YOU INSTEAD, YOUNG MASTER ...
I'VE LEFT THE COUNTRY ONCE BEFORE TO INVESTIGATE AN INCIDENT ...
MOGU (MUNCH)
もぐ
...BUT I HAVEN'T THE SLIGHTEST IDEA WHY I'M BEING DISPATCHED FOR THIS BUSINESS.
もぐ
MOGU
WHY NOT ASK FOR A MORE DEFINITIVE REASON?
I KNOW SHE'LL DODGE THE QUESTION.
THE DOG'S DUTY IS TO START RUNNING GLEEFULLY WHEN THE MASTER THROWS HIM A BONE, AFTER ALL.
THE UNDERWORLD INTELLIGENCE NETWORK OF THE PHANTOMHIVE HOUSE OPERATES FROM EUROPE TO ASIA.
PERHAPS SHE IS PLACING HER FAITH IN THAT...
PARTICULARLY SINCE I INHERITED *HIM* FROM THE PREVIOUS EARL.

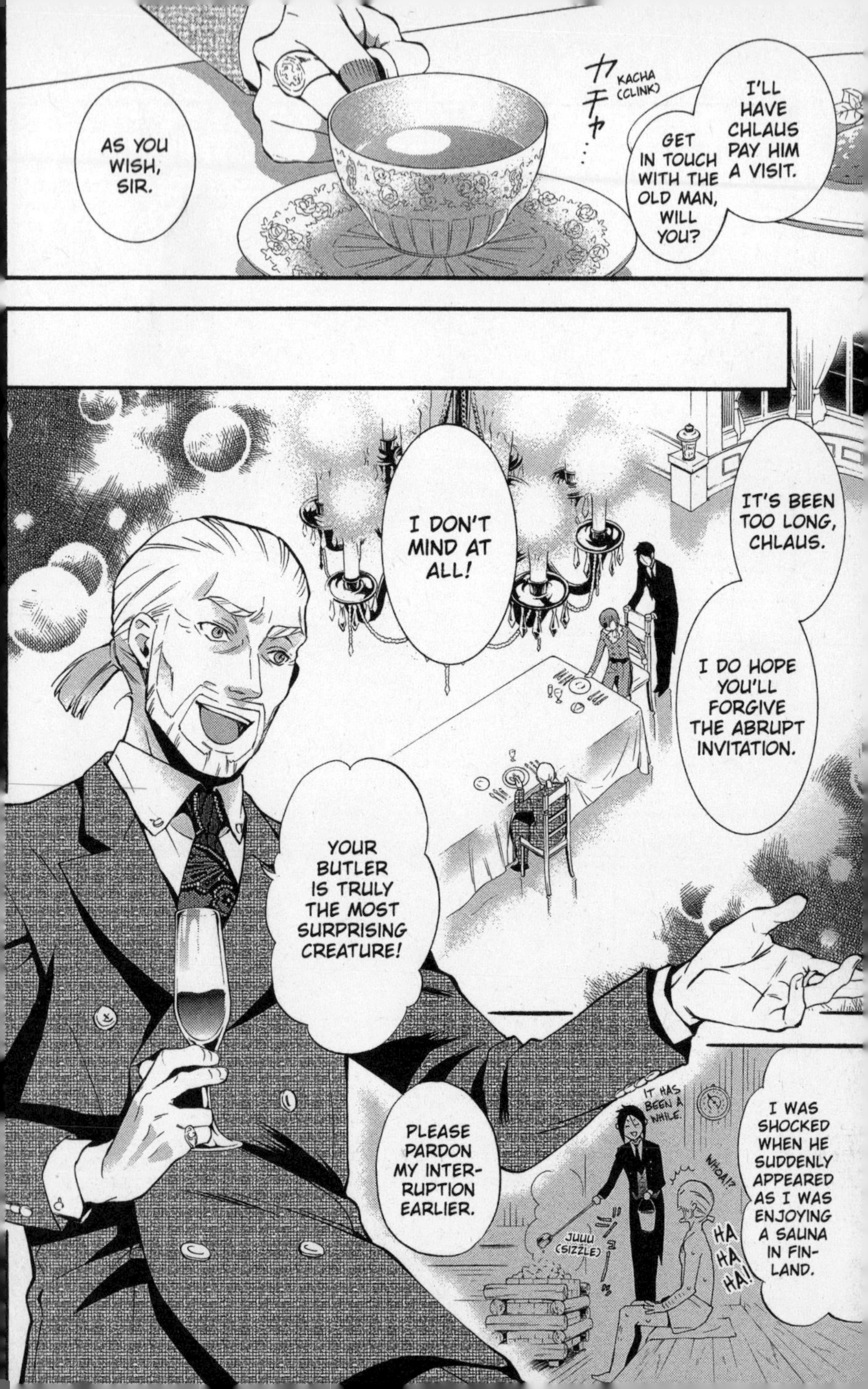
I'LL HAVE CHLAUS PAY HIM A VISIT.
GET IN TOUCH WITH THE OLD MAN, WILL YOU?
KACHA (CLINK)
AS YOU WISH, SIR.
IT'S BEEN TOO LONG, CHLAUS.
I DO HOPE YOU'LL FORGIVE THE ABRUPT INVITATION.
I DON'T MIND AT ALL!
YOUR BUTLER IS TRULY THE MOST SURPRISING CREATURE!
I WAS SHOCKED WHEN HE SUDDENLY APPEARED AS I WAS ENJOYING A SAUNA IN FIN-LAND.
HA HA HA!
WHOA!?
IT HAS BEEN A WHILE.
JUUU (SIZZLE)
PLEASE PARDON MY INTER-RUPTION EARLIER.

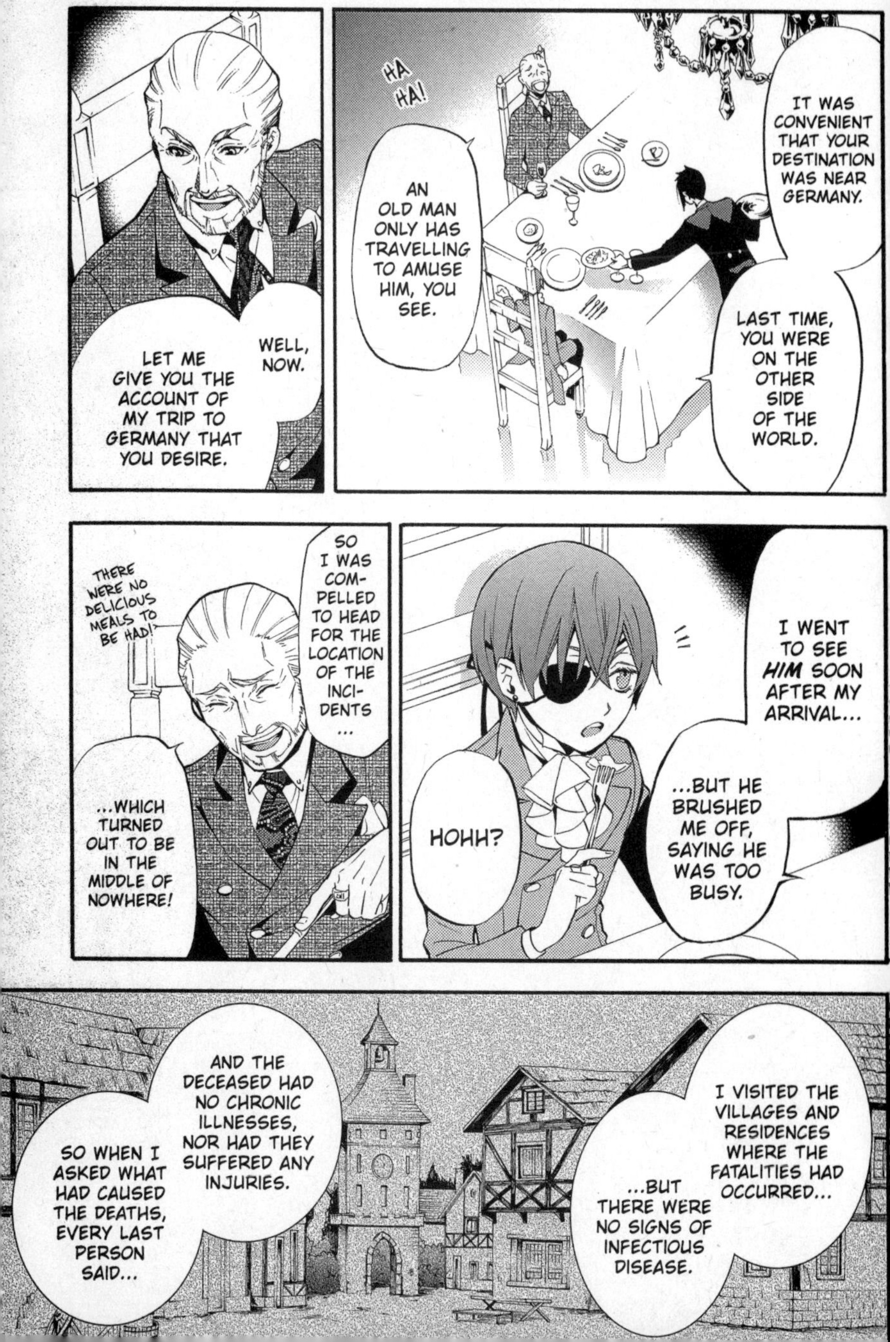
IT WAS CONVENIENT THAT YOUR DESTINATION WAS NEAR GERMANY.
LAST TIME, YOU WERE ON THE OTHER SIDE OF THE WORLD.
HA HA!
AN OLD MAN ONLY HAS TRAVELLING TO AMUSE HIM, YOU SEE.
WELL, NOW.
LET ME GIVE YOU THE ACCOUNT OF MY TRIP TO GERMANY THAT YOU DESIRE.
I WENT TO SEE *HIM* SOON AFTER MY ARRIVAL...
...BUT HE BRUSHED ME OFF, SAYING HE WAS TOO BUSY.
HOHH?
SO I WAS COM-PELLED TO HEAD FOR THE LOCATION OF THE INCI-DENTS...
THERE WERE NO DELICIOUS MEALS TO BE HAD!
...WHICH TURNED OUT TO BE IN THE MIDDLE OF NOWHERE!
I VISITED THE VILLAGES AND RESIDENCES WHERE THE FATALITIES HAD OCCURRED...
...BUT THERE WERE NO SIGNS OF INFECTIOUS DISEASE.
AND THE DECEASED HAD NO CHRONIC ILLNESSES, NOR HAD THEY SUFFERED ANY INJURIES.
SO WHEN I ASKED WHAT HAD CAUSED THE DEATHS, EVERY LAST PERSON SAID...

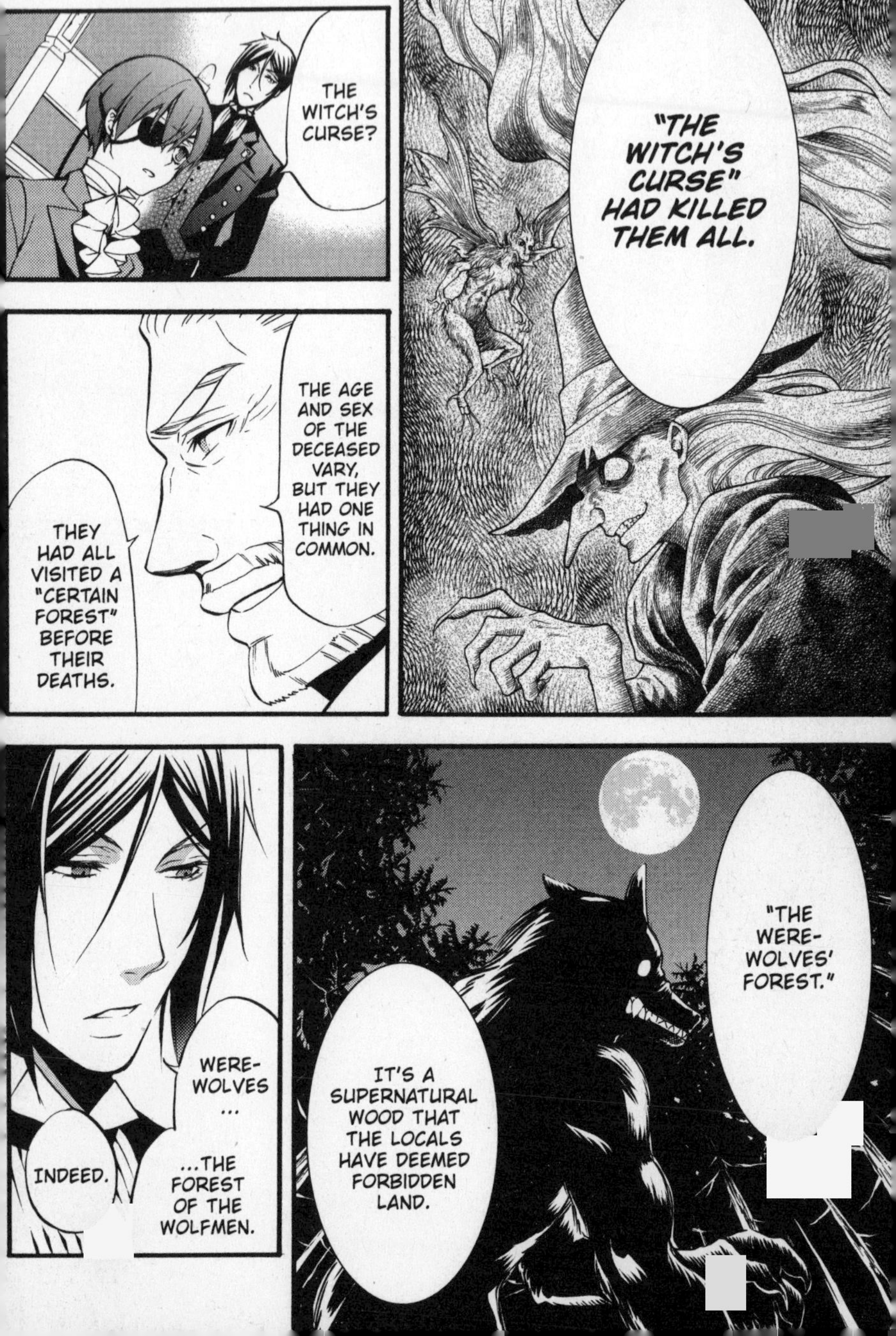
"THE WITCH'S CURSE" HAD KILLED THEM ALL.
THE WITCH'S CURSE?
THE AGE AND SEX OF THE DECEASED VARY, BUT THEY HAD ONE THING IN COMMON.
THEY HAD ALL VISITED A "CERTAIN FOREST" BEFORE THEIR DEATHS.
"THE WERE-WOLVES' FOREST."
IT'S A SUPERNATURAL WOOD THAT THE LOCALS HAVE DEEMED FORBIDDEN LAND.
WERE-WOLVES ...
...THE FOREST OF THE WOLFMEN.
INDEED.

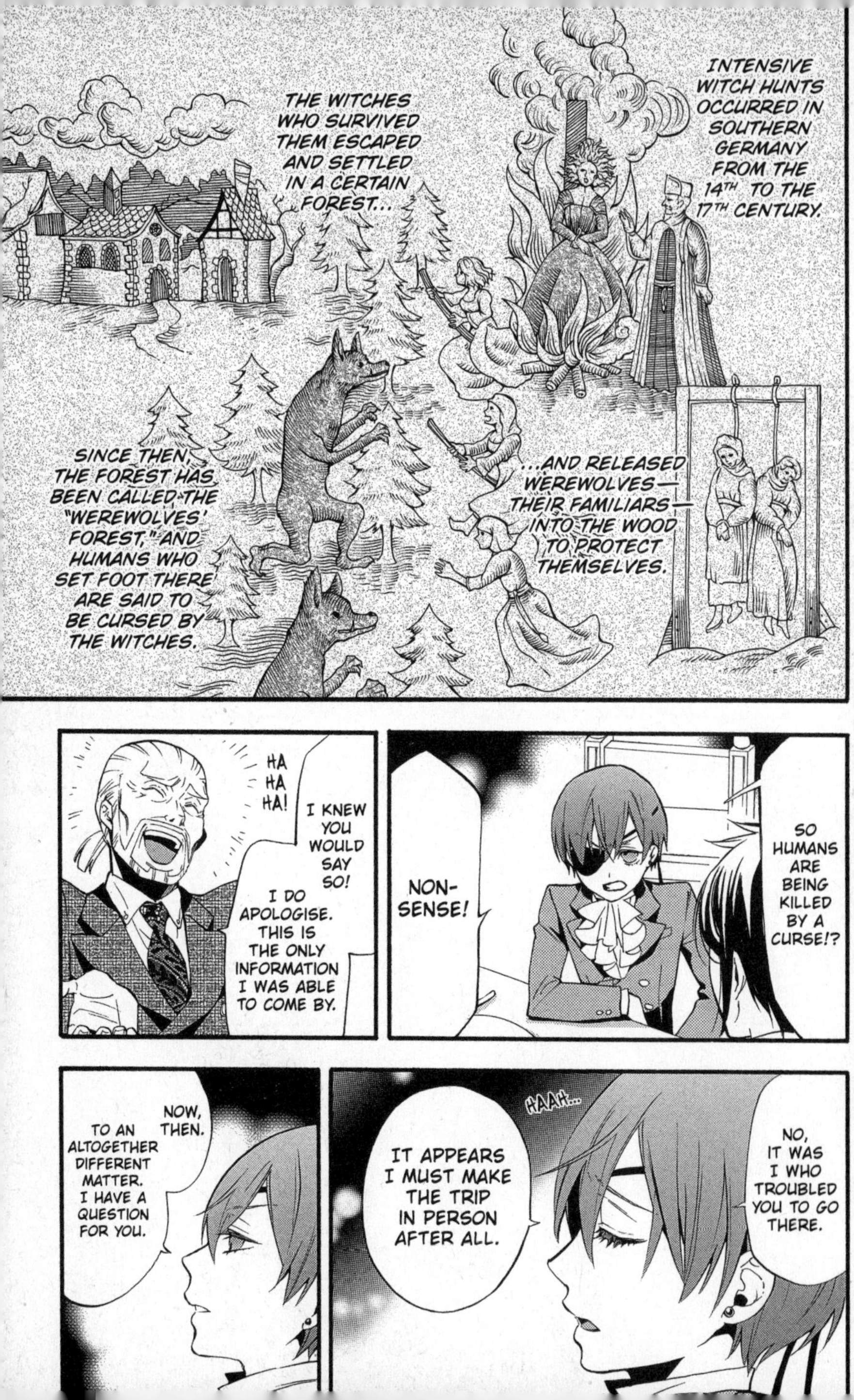
INTENSIVE WITCH HUNTS OCCURRED IN SOUTHERN GERMANY FROM THE 14TH TO THE 17TH CENTURY.
THE WITCHES WHO SURVIVED THEM ESCAPED AND SETTLED IN A CERTAIN FOREST...
...AND RELEASED WEREWOLVES—THEIR FAMILIARS—INTO THE WOOD TO PROTECT THEMSELVES.
SINCE THEN, THE FOREST HAS BEEN CALLED THE "WEREWOLVES' FOREST," AND HUMANS WHO SET FOOT THERE ARE SAID TO BE CURSED BY THE WITCHES.
SO HUMANS ARE BEING KILLED BY A CURSE!?
NON-SENSE!
HA HA HA!
I KNEW YOU WOULD SAY SO!
I DO APOLOGISE. THIS IS THE ONLY INFORMATION I WAS ABLE TO COME BY.
NO, IT WAS I WHO TROUBLED YOU TO GO THERE.
HAAH...
IT APPEARS I MUST MAKE THE TRIP IN PERSON AFTER ALL.
NOW, THEN.
TO AN ALTOGETHER DIFFERENT MATTER. I HAVE A QUESTION FOR YOU.

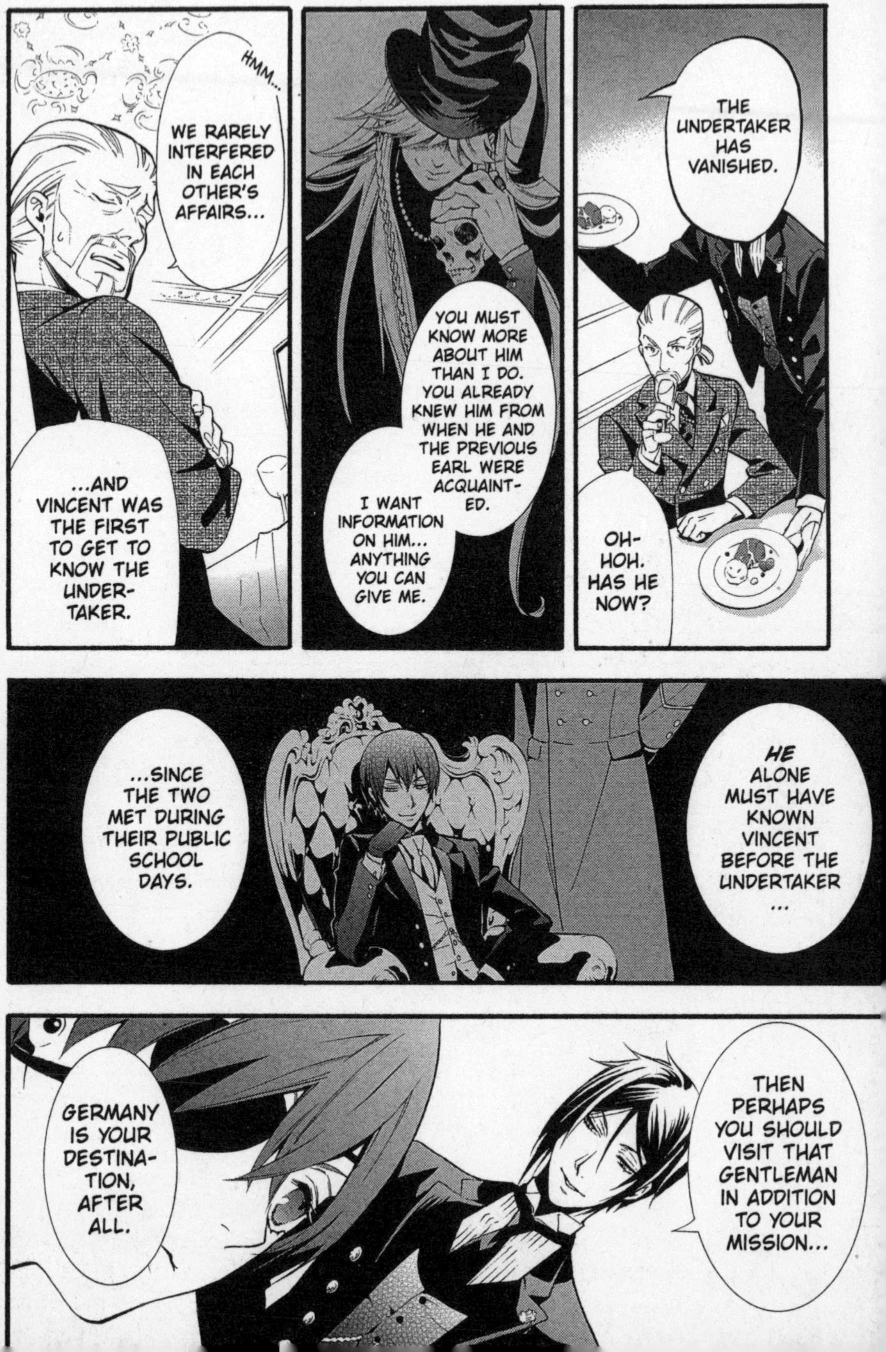
THE UNDERTAKER HAS VANISHED.
OH-HOH. HAS HE NOW?
YOU MUST KNOW MORE ABOUT HIM THAN I DO. YOU ALREADY KNEW HIM FROM WHEN HE AND THE PREVIOUS EARL WERE ACQUAINT-ED.
I WANT INFORMATION ON HIM... ANYTHING YOU CAN GIVE ME.
HMM...
WE RARELY INTERFERED IN EACH OTHER'S AFFAIRS...
...AND VINCENT WAS THE FIRST TO GET TO KNOW THE UNDER-TAKER.
HE ALONE MUST HAVE KNOWN VINCENT BEFORE THE UNDERTAKER ...
...SINCE THE TWO MET DURING THEIR PUBLIC SCHOOL DAYS.
THEN PERHAPS YOU SHOULD VISIT THAT GENTLEMAN IN ADDITION TO YOUR MISSION...
GERMANY IS YOUR DESTINA-TION, AFTER ALL.

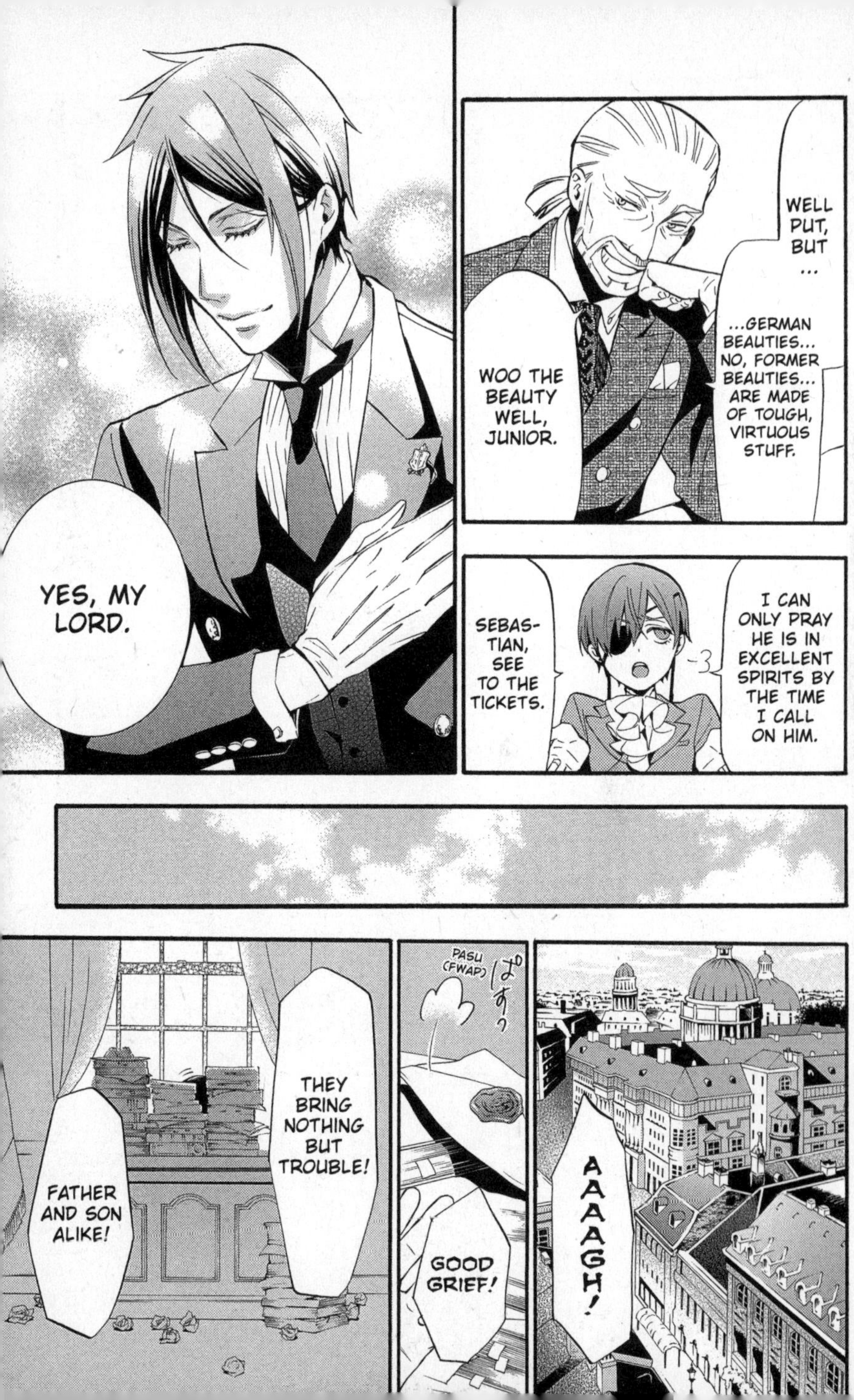
WELL PUT, BUT ...
...GERMAN BEAUTIES... NO, FORMER BEAUTIES... ARE MADE OF TOUGH, VIRTUOUS STUFF.
WOO THE BEAUTY WELL, JUNIOR.
I CAN ONLY PRAY HE IS IN EXCELLENT SPIRITS BY THE TIME I CALL ON HIM.
SEBAS-TIAN, SEE TO THE TICKETS.
YES, MY LORD.
AAAAGH!
ぱすっ
PASU (FWAP)
GOOD GRIEF!
THEY BRING NOTHING BUT TROUBLE!
FATHER AND SON ALIKE!

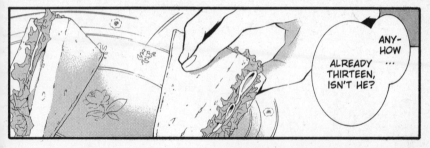

ANY-
HOW ...
ALREADY
THIRTEEN,
ISN'T HE?

HE MUST
BE EVEN
MORE LIKE
HIS FATHER
NOW...

MUSHA [MUNCH]

MUSHA

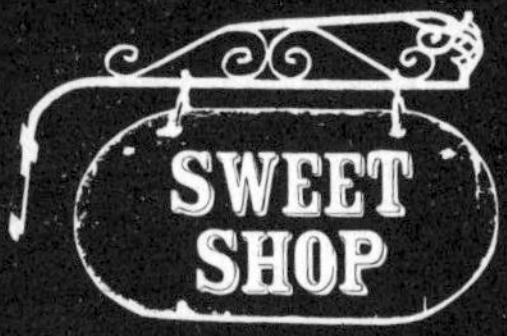
SWEET
SHOP

Black Butler

Chapter 87
At midnight : The Butler, Making Enquiries

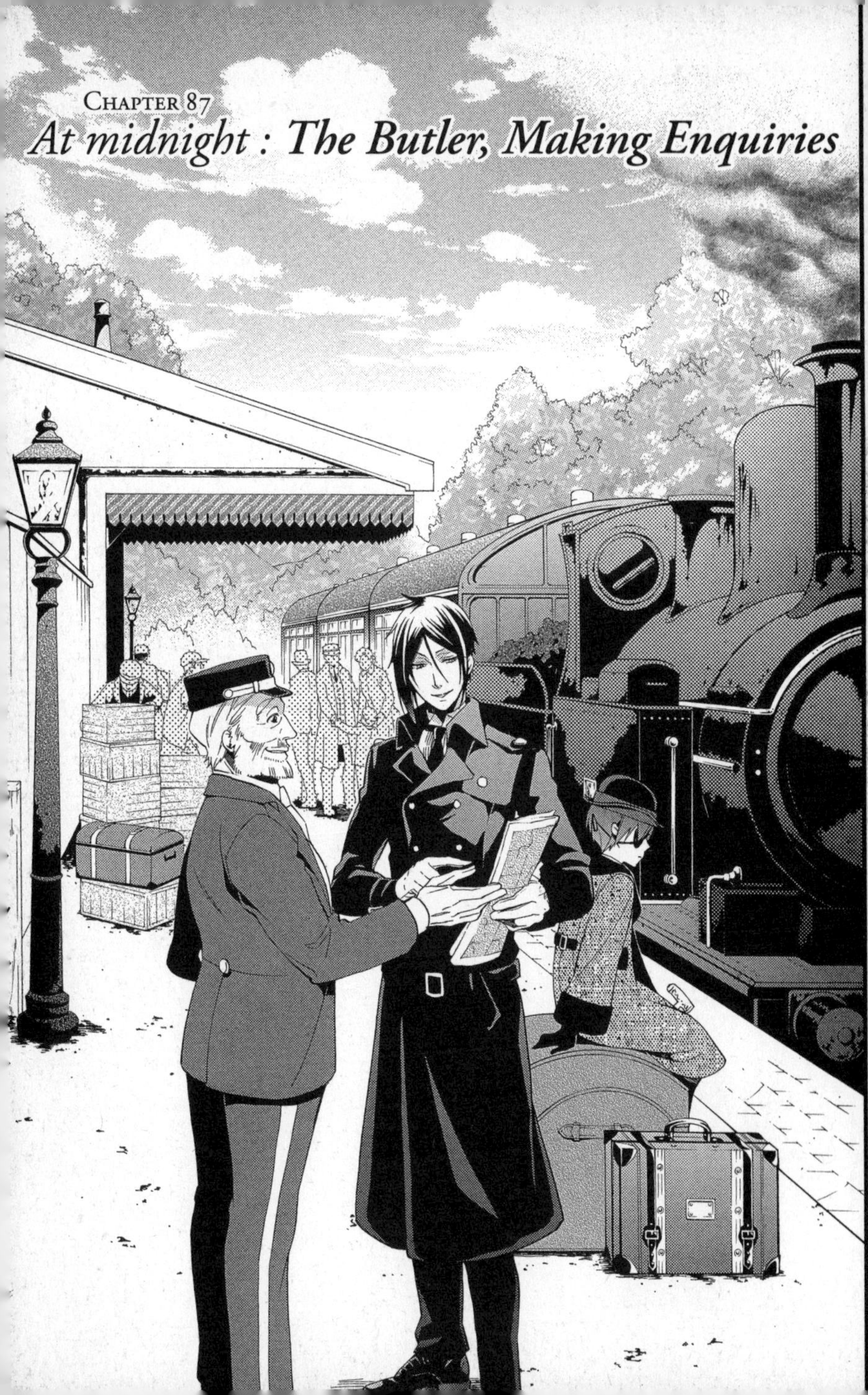

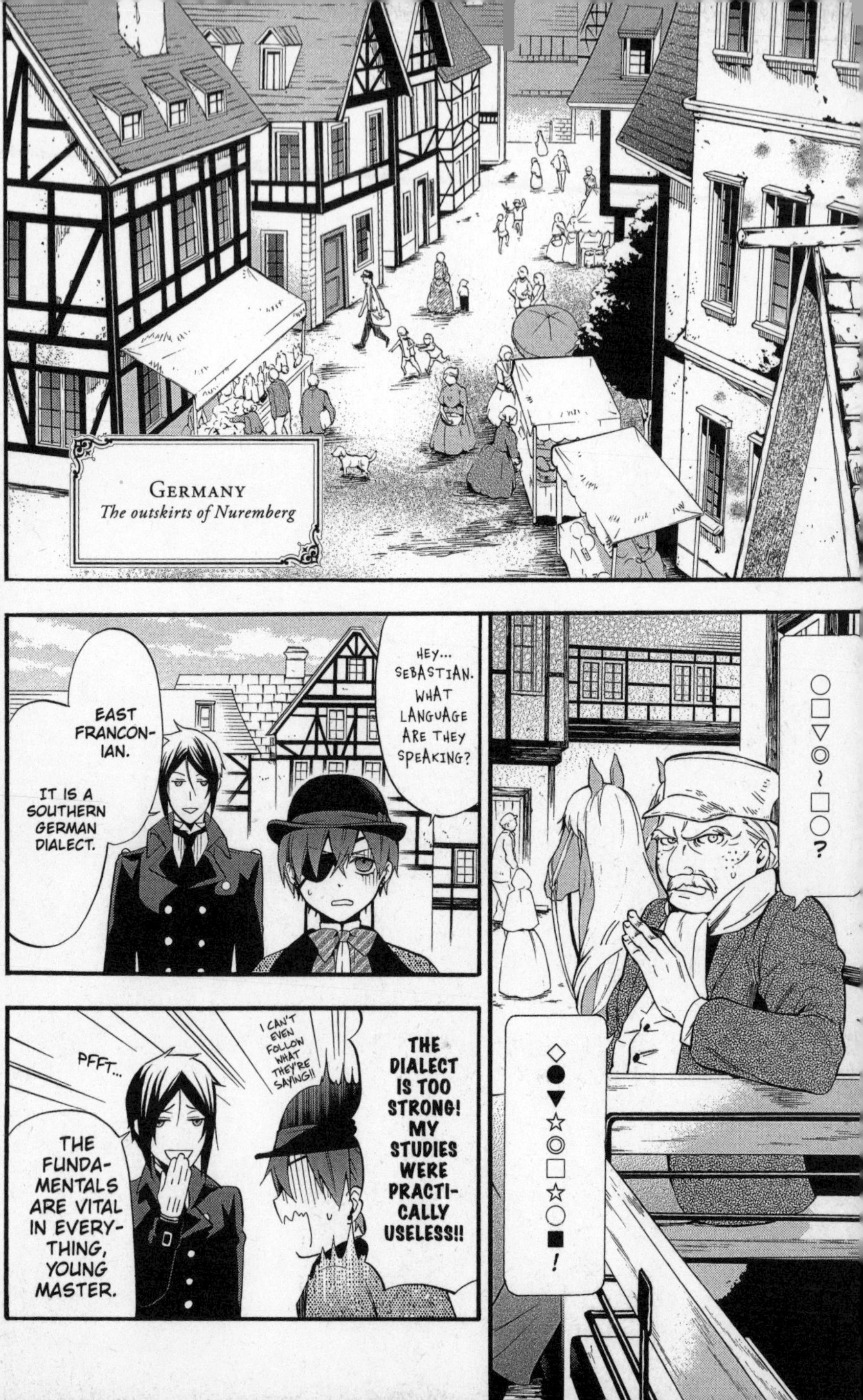
GERMANY
The outskirts of Nuremberg
○□▽◎~□○?
◇●▼☆◎□☆○■!
HEY... SEBASTIAN. WHAT LANGUAGE ARE THEY SPEAKING?
EAST FRANCONIAN.
IT IS A SOUTHERN GERMAN DIALECT.
THE DIALECT IS TOO STRONG! MY STUDIES WERE PRACTICALLY USELESS!!
I CAN'T EVEN FOLLOW WHAT THEY'RE SAYING!!
PFFT...
THE FUNDAMENTALS ARE VITAL IN EVERYTHING, YOUNG MASTER.

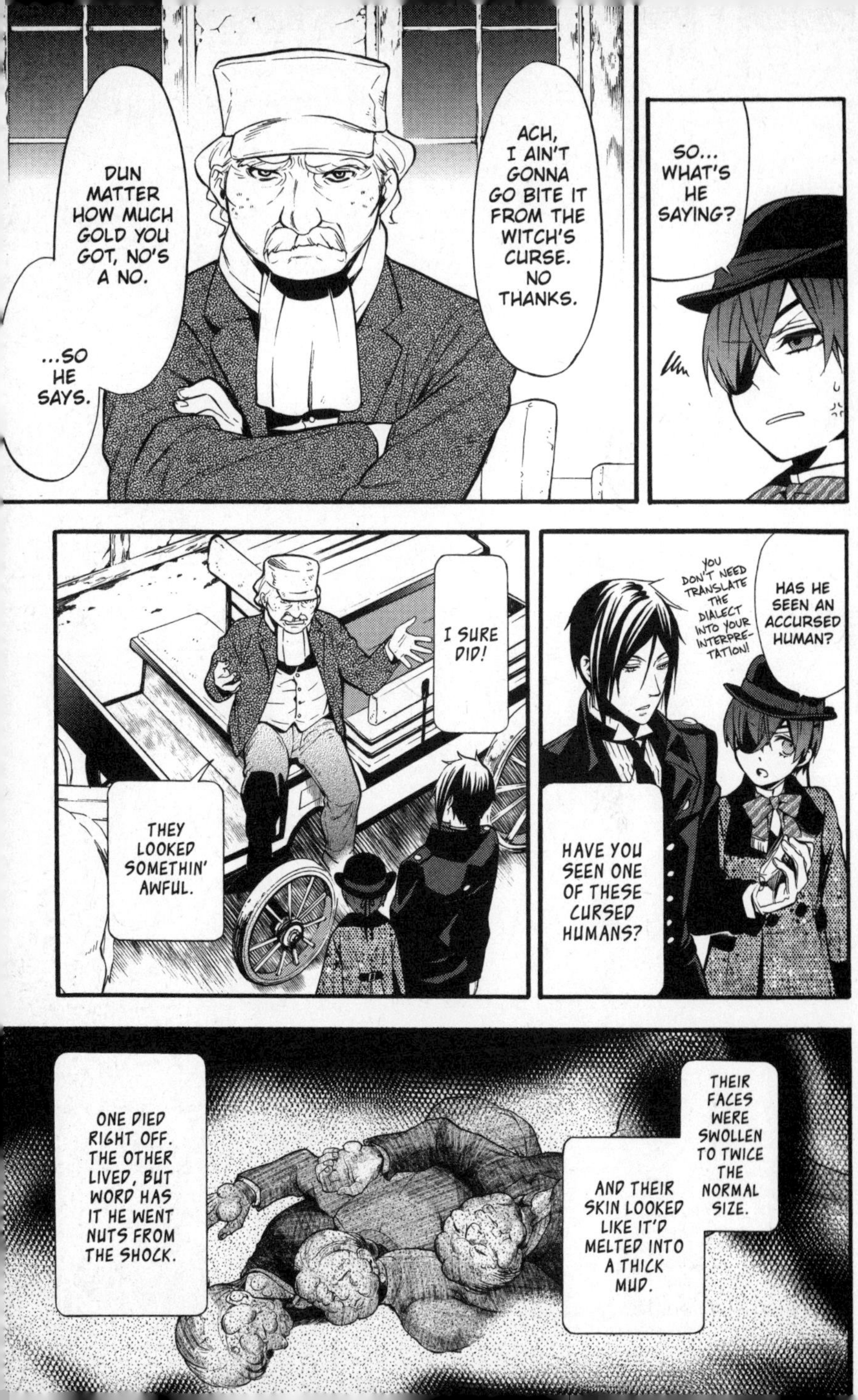
SO... WHAT'S HE SAYING?
ACH, I AIN'T GONNA GO BITE IT FROM THE WITCH'S CURSE. NO THANKS.
DUN MATTER HOW MUCH GOLD YOU GOT, NO'S A NO.
...SO HE SAYS.
HAS HE SEEN AN ACCURSED HUMAN?
YOU DON'T NEED TRANSLATE THE DIALECT INTO YOUR INTERPRETATION!
HAVE YOU SEEN ONE OF THESE CURSED HUMANS?
I SURE DID!
THEY LOOKED SOMETHIN' AWFUL.
THEIR FACES WERE SWOLLEN TO TWICE THE NORMAL SIZE.
AND THEIR SKIN LOOKED LIKE IT'D MELTED INTO A THICK MUD.
ONE DIED RIGHT OFF. THE OTHER LIVED, BUT WORD HAS IT HE WENT NUTS FROM THE SHOCK.

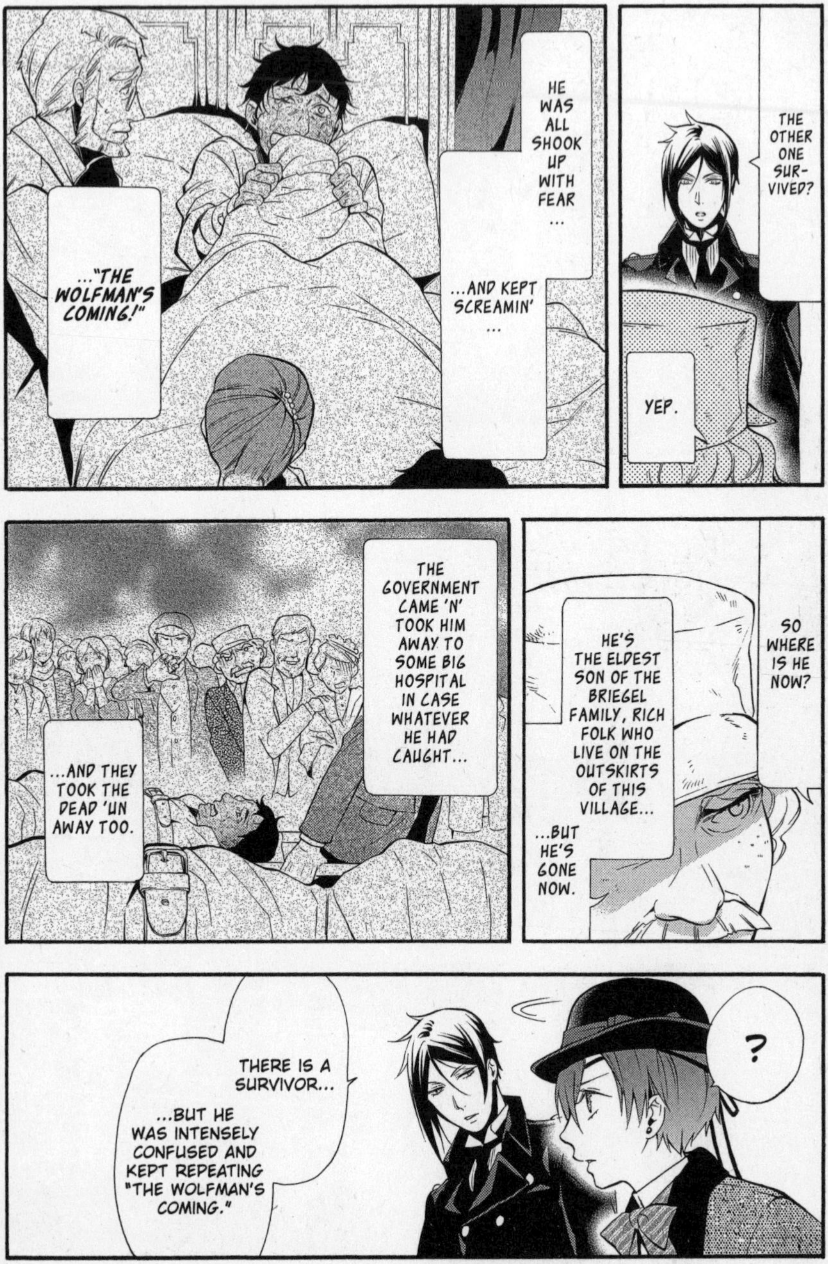
THE OTHER ONE SURVIVED?
YEP.
HE WAS ALL SHOOK UP WITH FEAR ...
...AND KEPT SCREAMIN' ...
..."THE WOLFMAN'S COMING!"
SO WHERE IS HE NOW?
HE'S THE ELDEST SON OF THE BRIEGEL FAMILY, RICH FOLK WHO LIVE ON THE OUTSKIRTS OF THIS VILLAGE...
...BUT HE'S GONE NOW.
THE GOVERNMENT CAME 'N' TOOK HIM AWAY TO SOME BIG HOSPITAL IN CASE WHATEVER HE HAD CAUGHT...
...AND THEY TOOK THE DEAD 'UN AWAY TOO.
?
THERE IS A SURVIVOR...
...BUT HE WAS INTENSELY CONFUSED AND KEPT REPEATING "THE WOLFMAN'S COMING."

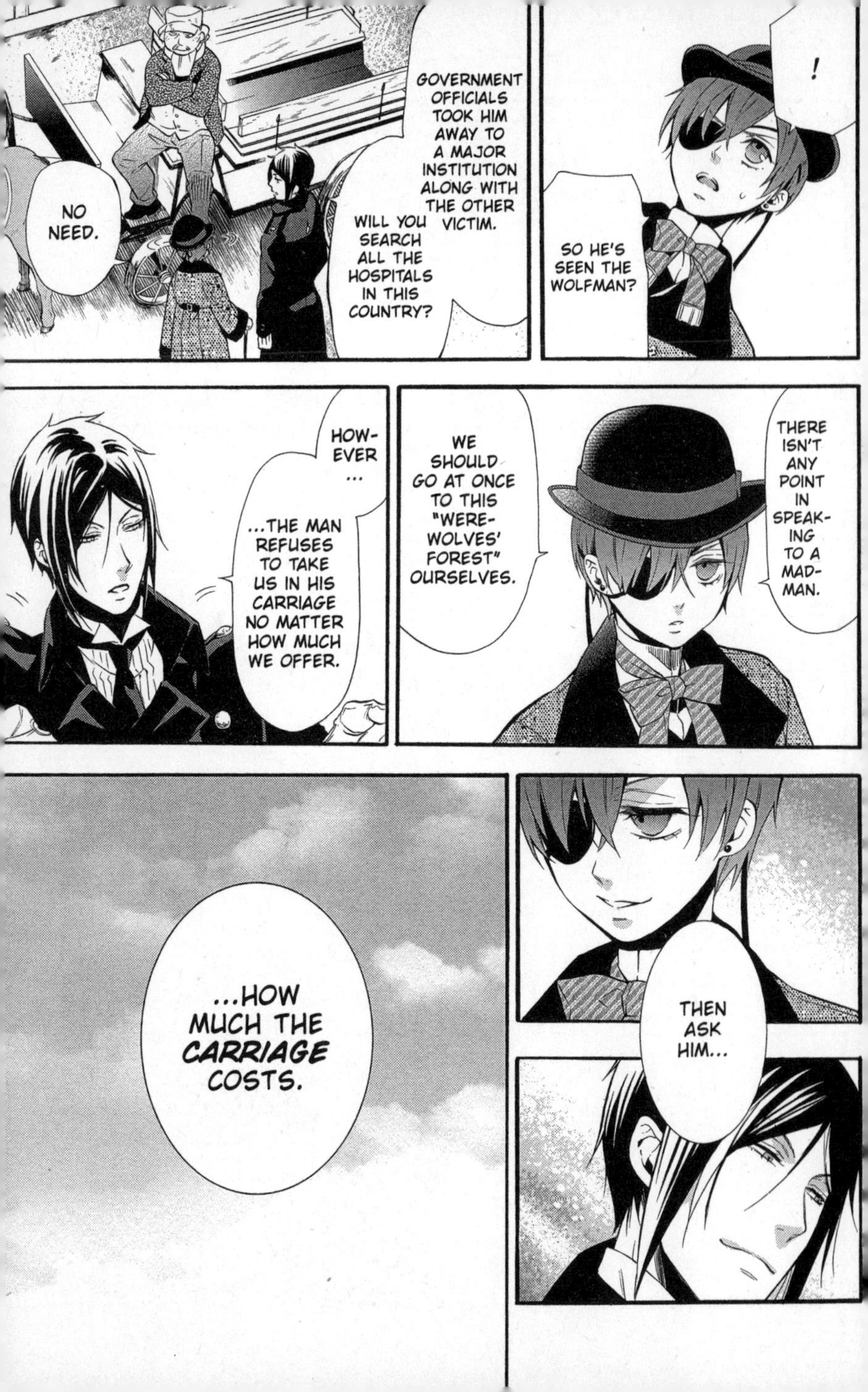
!
SO HE'S SEEN THE WOLFMAN?
GOVERNMENT OFFICIALS TOOK HIM AWAY TO A MAJOR INSTITUTION ALONG WITH THE OTHER VICTIM.
WILL YOU SEARCH ALL THE HOSPITALS IN THIS COUNTRY?
NO NEED.
THERE ISN'T ANY POINT IN SPEAKING TO A MADMAN.
WE SHOULD GO AT ONCE TO THIS "WEREWOLVES' FOREST" OURSELVES.
HOWEVER...
...THE MAN REFUSES TO TAKE US IN HIS CARRIAGE NO MATTER HOW MUCH WE OFFER.
THEN ASK HIM...
...HOW MUCH THE *CARRIAGE* COSTS.

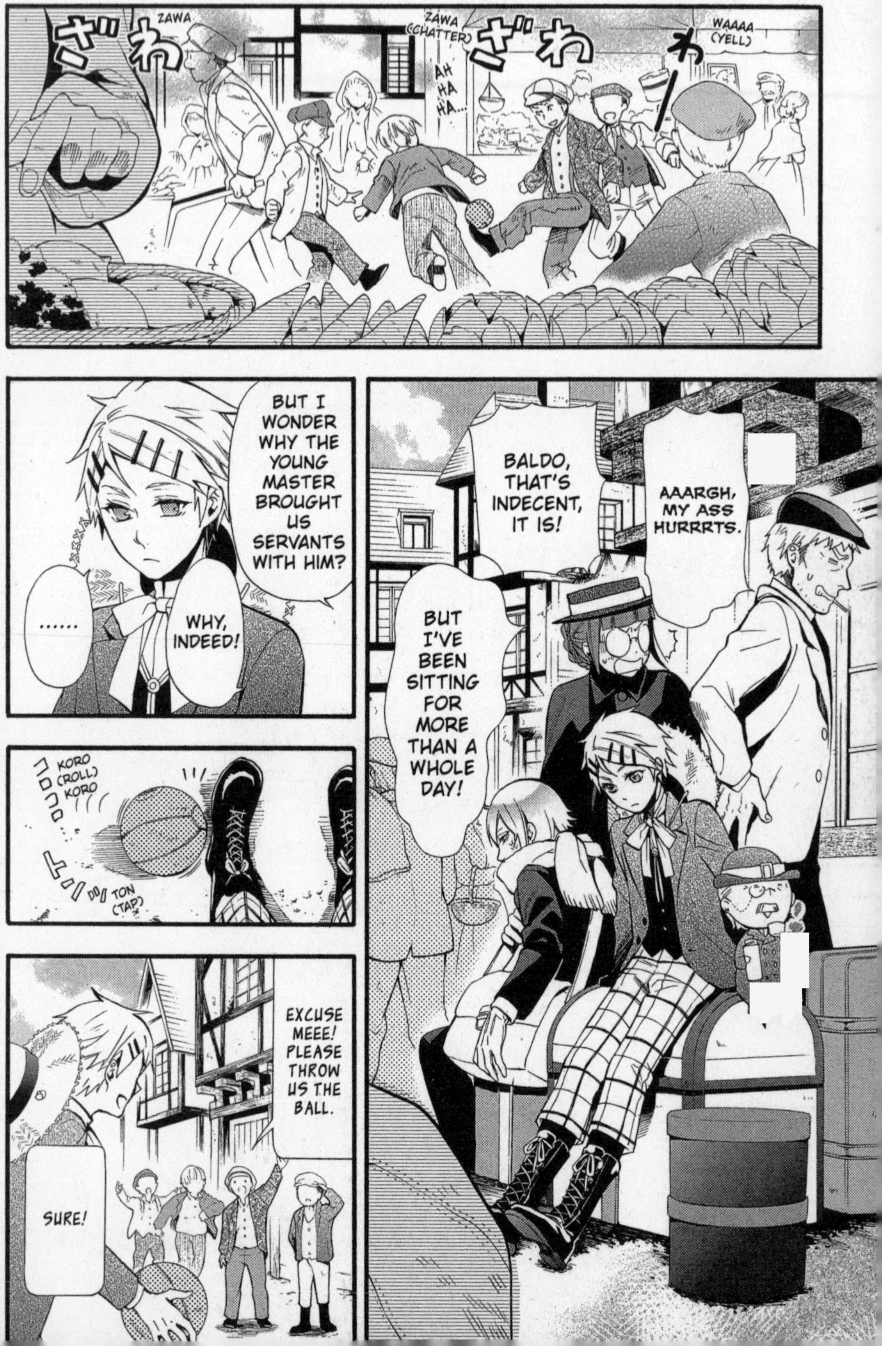

WAAAA (YELL)
わー
ざわ
ZAWA (CHATTER)
AH HA HA...
ざわ
ZAWA
AAARGH, MY ASS HURRRTS.
BALDO, THAT'S INDECENT, IT IS!
BUT I'VE BEEN SITTING FOR MORE THAN A WHOLE DAY!
BUT I WONDER WHY THE YOUNG MASTER BROUGHT US SERVANTS WITH HIM?
WHY, INDEED!
......
コロコロ
KORO (ROLL) KORO
トン
TON (TAP)
EXCUSE MEEE! PLEASE THROW US THE BALL.
SURE!

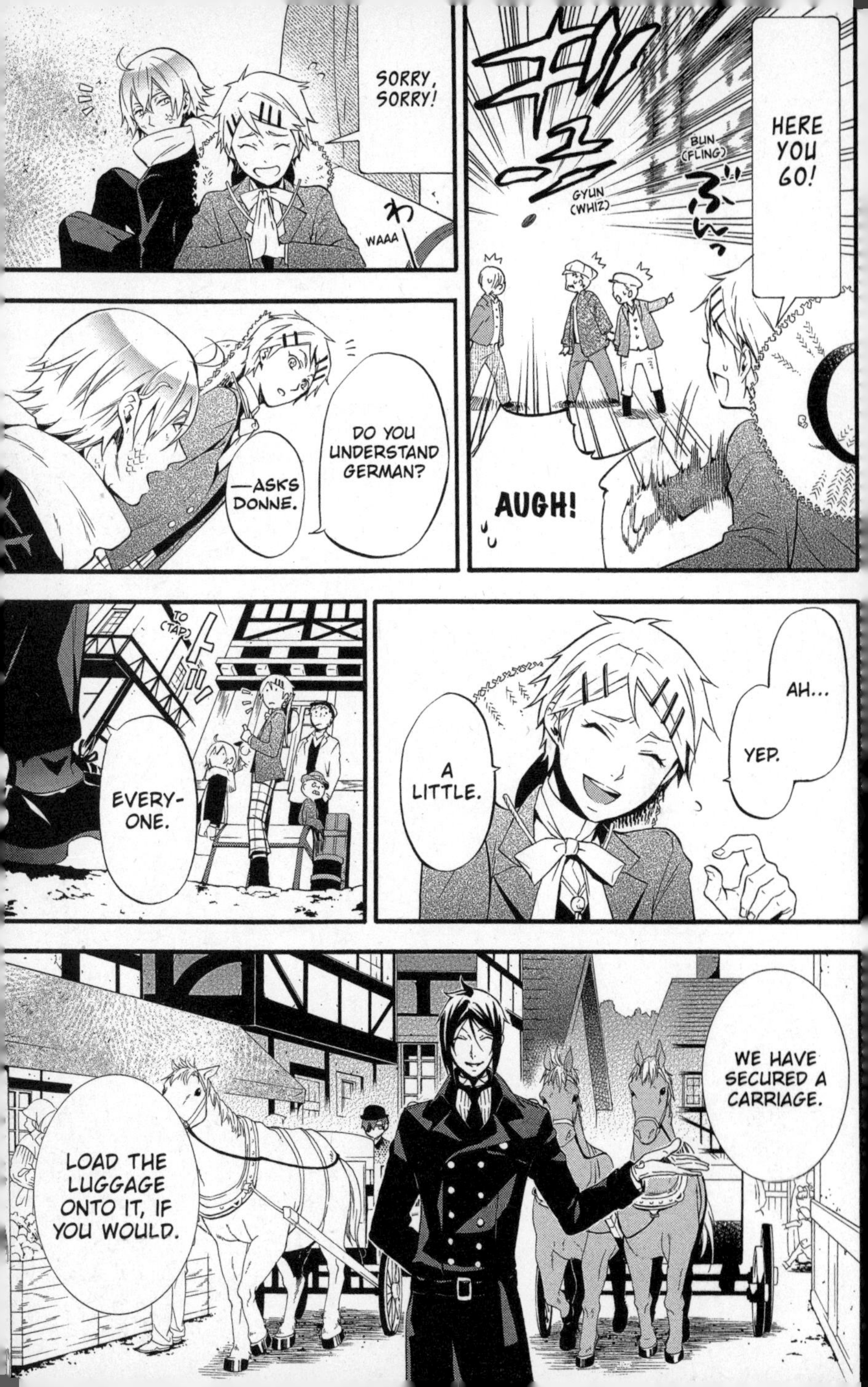
HERE YOU GO!
BUN (FLING)
GYUN (WHIZ)
AUGH!
SORRY, SORRY!
わ
WAAA
DO YOU UNDERSTAND GERMAN?
—ASKS DONNE.
AH... YEP.
A LITTLE.
TO (TAP)
ト
EVERY-ONE.
WE HAVE SECURED A CARRIAGE.
LOAD THE LUGGAGE ONTO IT, IF YOU WOULD.

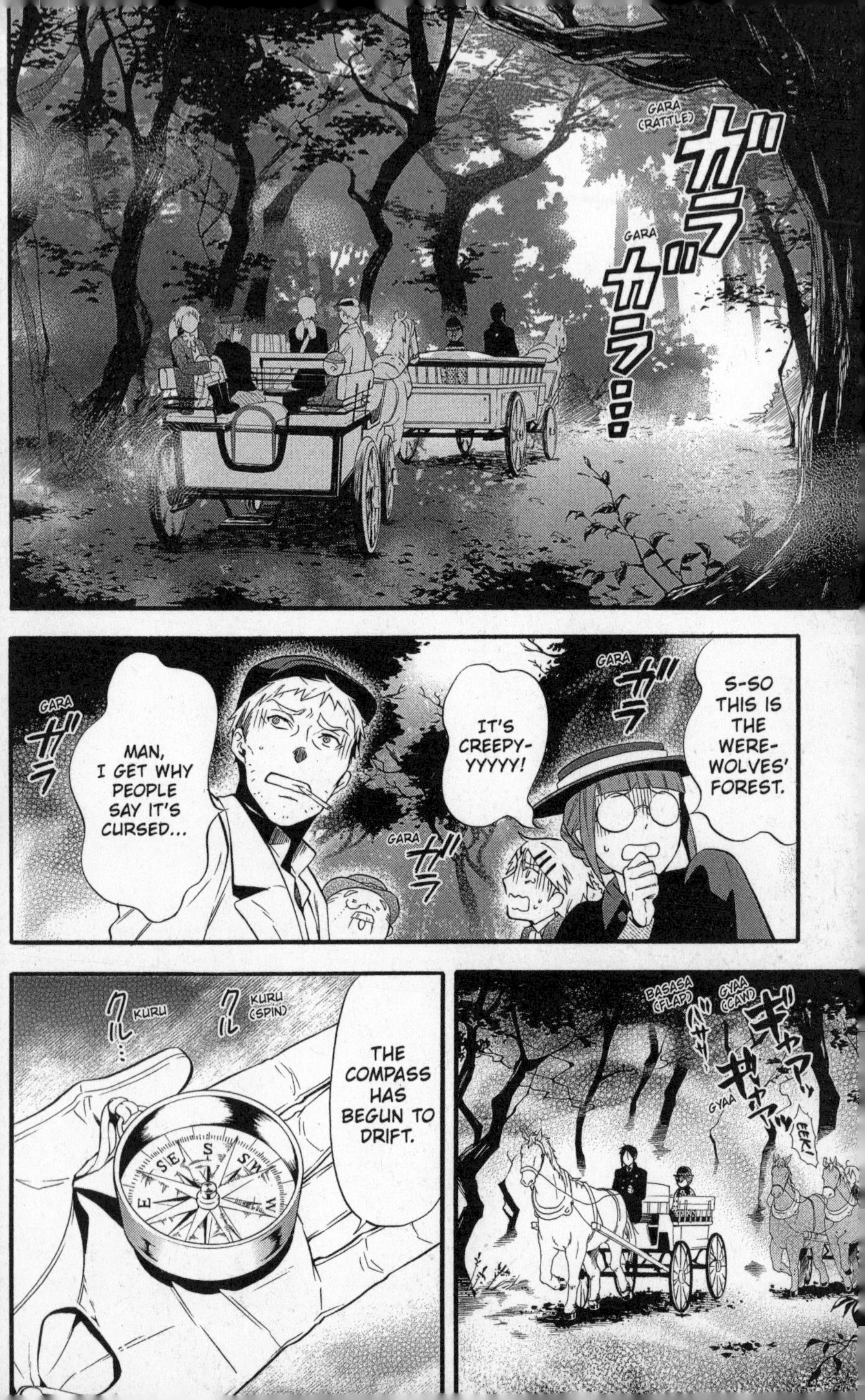
GARA (RATTLE)
ガラ
GARA
ガラ...
GARA
ガラ
S-SO THIS IS THE WERE-WOLVES' FOREST.
IT'S CREEPY-YYYYY!
GARA
ガラ
MAN, I GET WHY PEOPLE SAY IT'S CURSED...
GARA
ガラ
GYAA (CAW)
ギャアッ
BASASA (FLAP)
バサッ
GYAA
ギャアッ
EEK!
THE COMPASS HAS BEGUN TO DRIFT.
KURU (SPIN)
クル
KURU
クル...

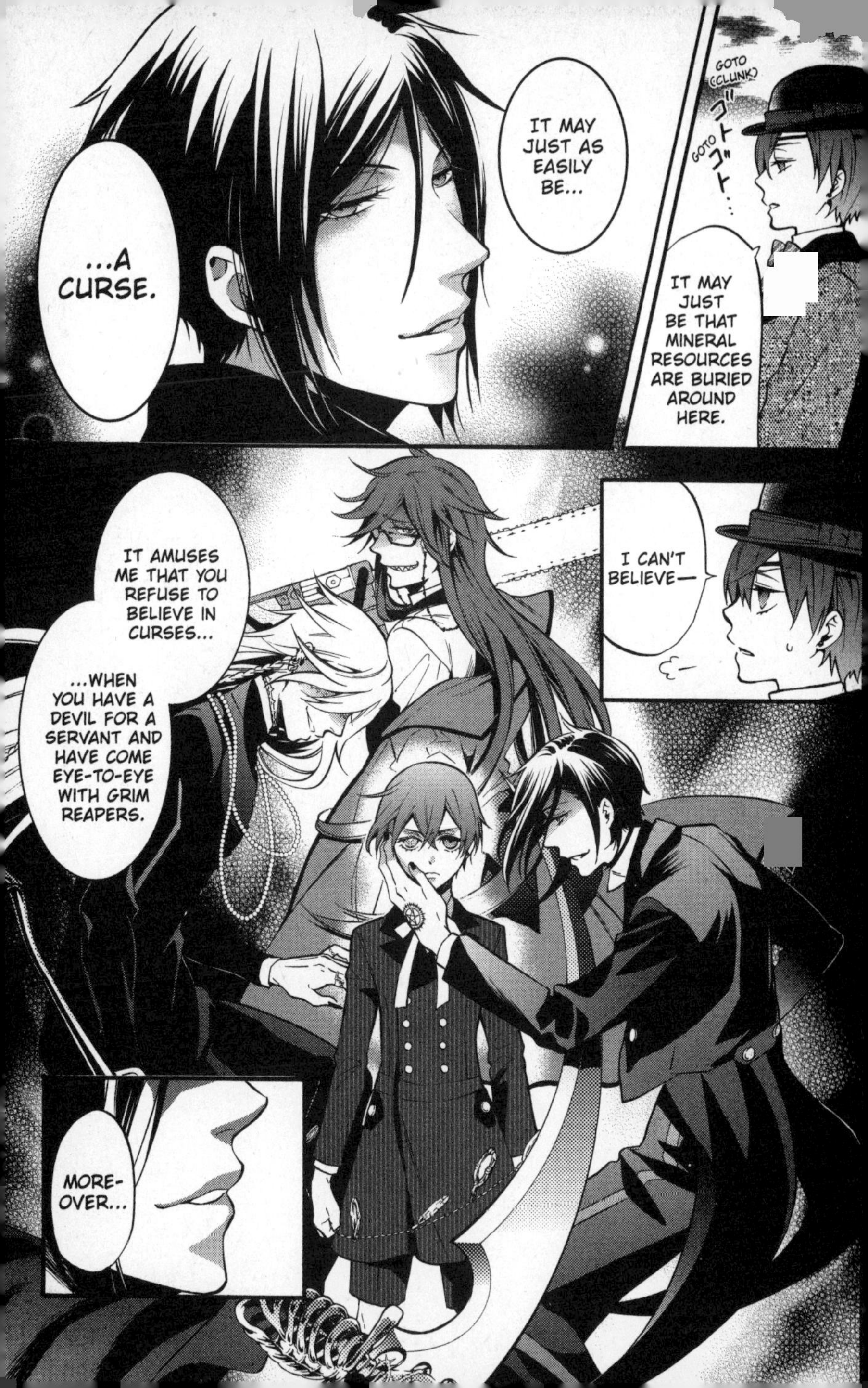
GOTO (CLUNK)
ゴト
GOTO
ゴト…
IT MAY JUST BE THAT MINERAL RESOURCES ARE BURIED AROUND HERE.
IT MAY JUST AS EASILY BE...
...A CURSE.
I CAN'T BELIEVE—
IT AMUSES ME THAT YOU REFUSE TO BELIEVE IN CURSES...
...WHEN YOU HAVE A DEVIL FOR A SERVANT AND HAVE COME EYE-TO-EYE WITH GRIM REAPERS.
MORE-OVER...

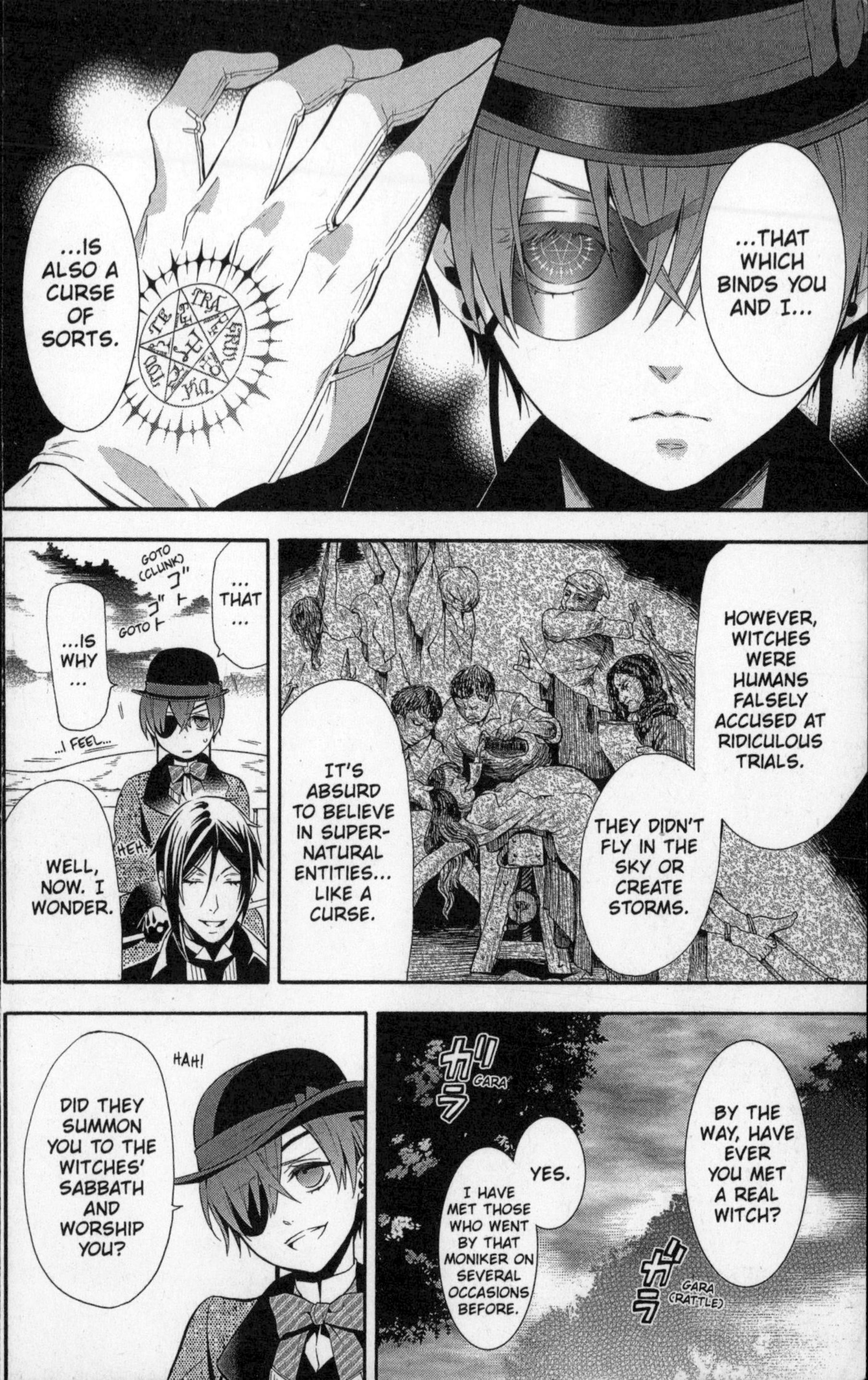
...THAT WHICH BINDS YOU AND I...
...IS ALSO A CURSE OF SORTS.
HOWEVER, WITCHES WERE HUMANS FALSELY ACCUSED AT RIDICULOUS TRIALS.
THEY DIDN'T FLY IN THE SKY OR CREATE STORMS.
IT'S ABSURD TO BELIEVE IN SUPER-NATURAL ENTITIES... LIKE A CURSE.
...THAT...
ゴト
GOTO (CLUNK)
ゴト
GOTO
...IS WHY...
...I FEEL...
HEH.
WELL, NOW. I WONDER.
ガラ
GARA
BY THE WAY, HAVE EVER YOU MET A REAL WITCH?
YES.
I HAVE MET THOSE WHO WENT BY THAT MONIKER ON SEVERAL OCCASIONS BEFORE.
ガラ
GARA (RATTLE)
HAH!
DID THEY SUMMON YOU TO THE WITCHES' SABBATH AND WORSHIP YOU?

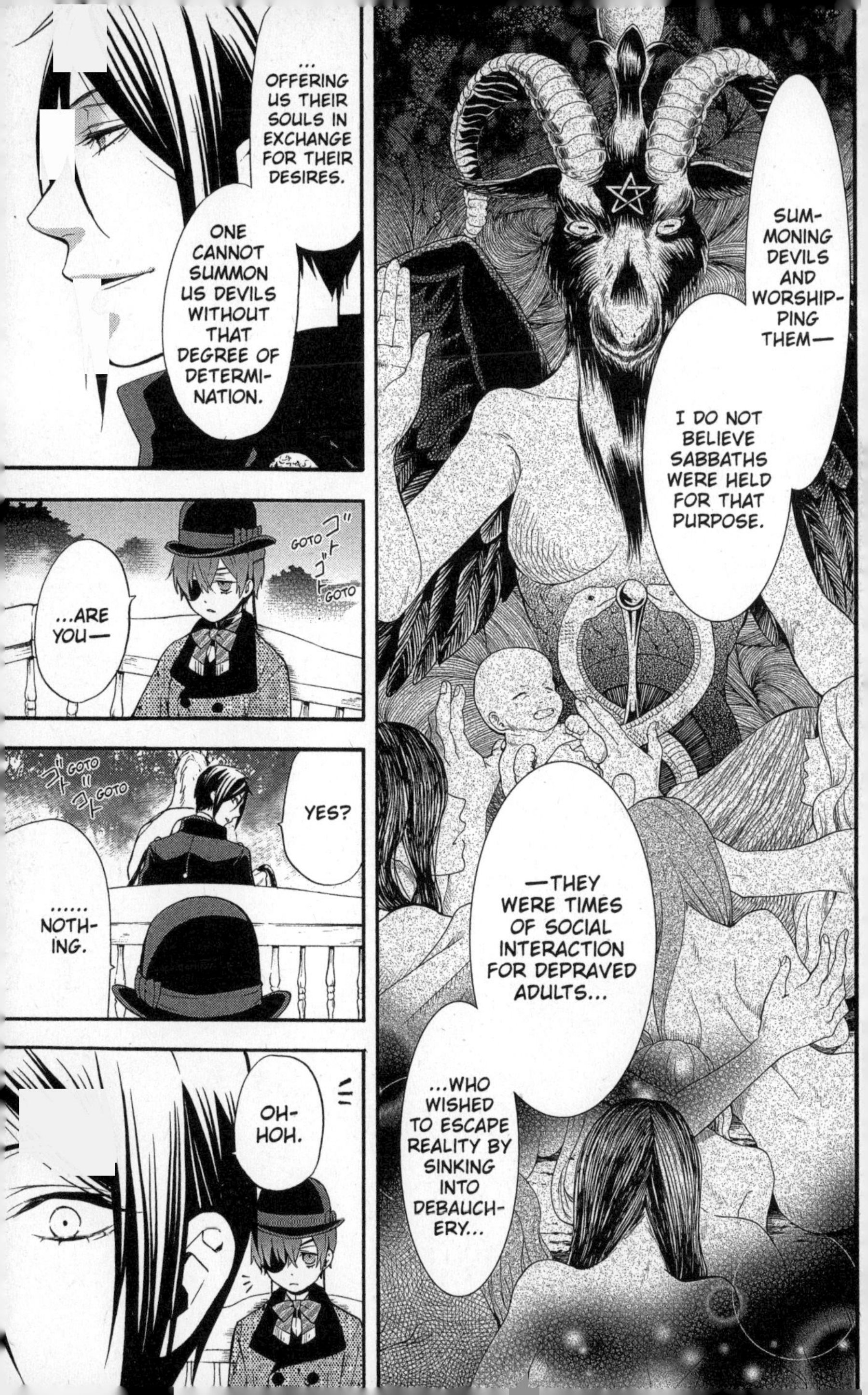
SUMMONING DEVILS AND WORSHIPPING THEM—
I DO NOT BELIEVE SABBATHS WERE HELD FOR THAT PURPOSE.
—THEY WERE TIMES OF SOCIAL INTERACTION FOR DEPRAVED ADULTS...
...WHO WISHED TO ESCAPE REALITY BY SINKING INTO DEBAUCHERY...
...OFFERING US THEIR SOULS IN EXCHANGE FOR THEIR DESIRES.
ONE CANNOT SUMMON US DEVILS WITHOUT THAT DEGREE OF DETERMINATION.
GOTO GOTO
...ARE YOU—
GOTO GOTO
YES?
......NOTHING.
OH-HOH.

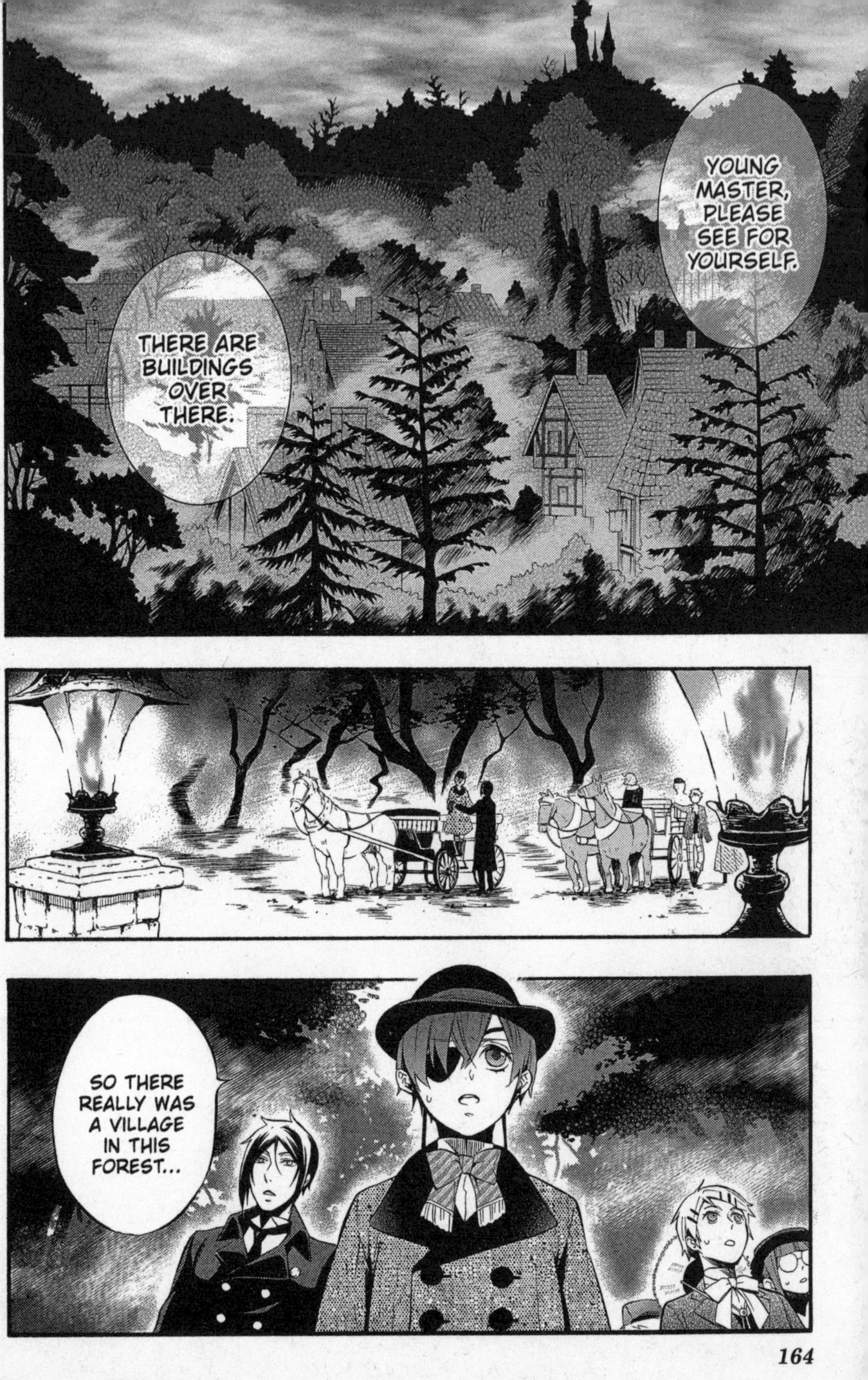
YOUNG MASTER, PLEASE SEE FOR YOURSELF.
THERE ARE BUILDINGS OVER THERE.
SO THERE REALLY WAS A VILLAGE IN THIS FOREST...

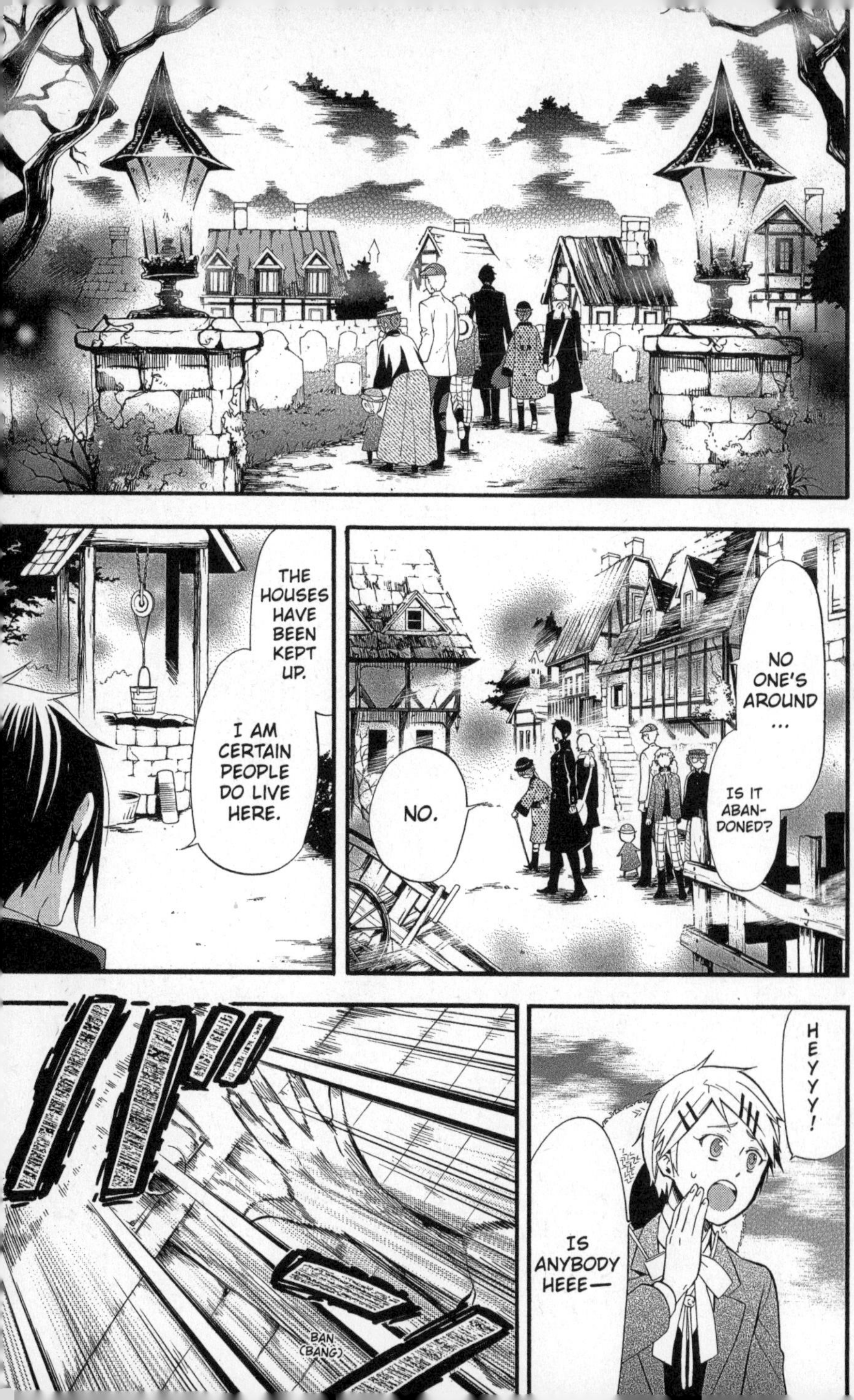
NO ONE'S AROUND...
IS IT ABANDONED?
NO.
THE HOUSES HAVE BEEN KEPT UP.
I AM CERTAIN PEOPLE DO LIVE HERE.
HEYYY!
IS ANYBODY HEEE—
BAN (BANG)

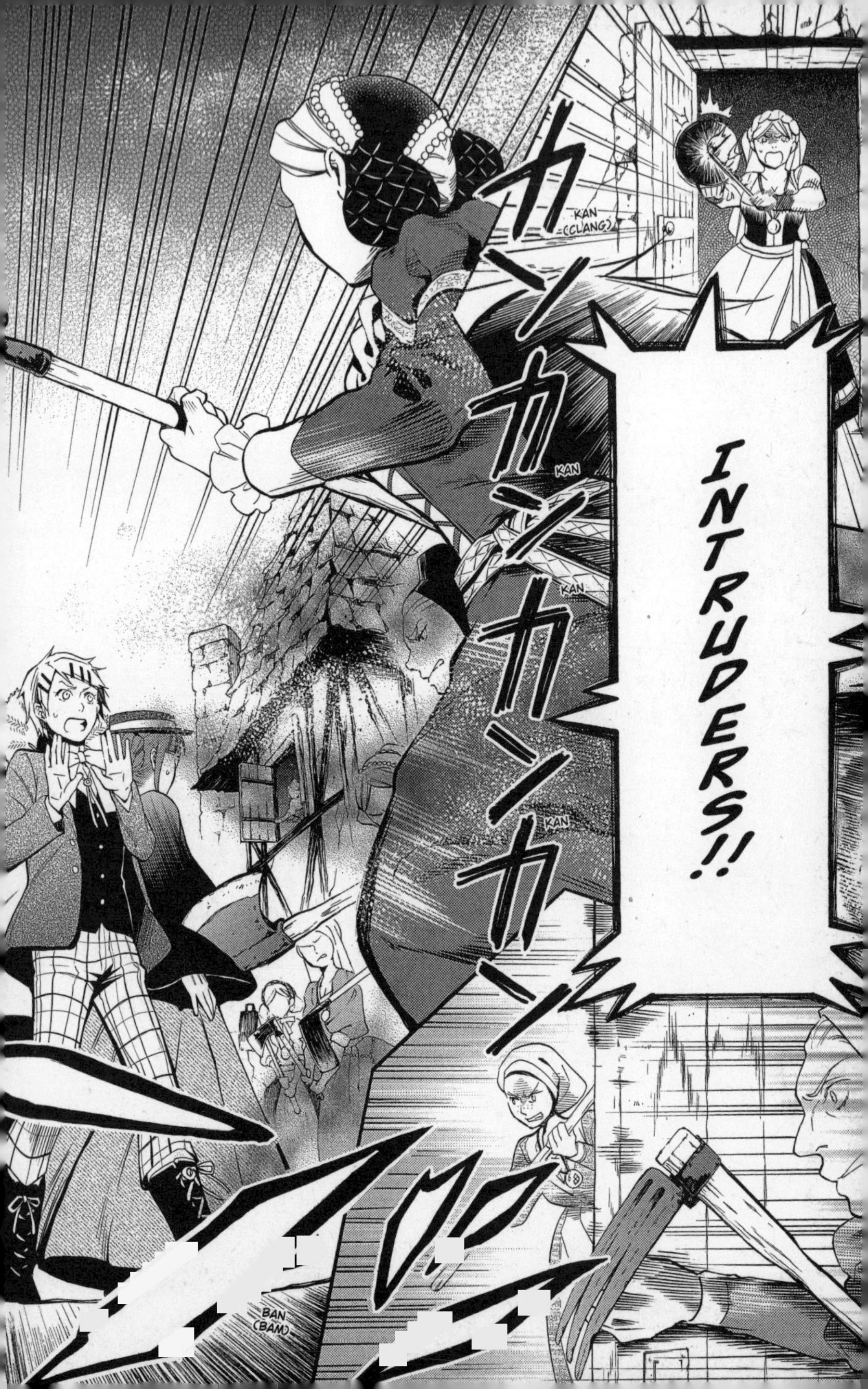
KAN (CLANG)
INTRUDERS!!
KAN
KAN
KAN
BAN (BAM)

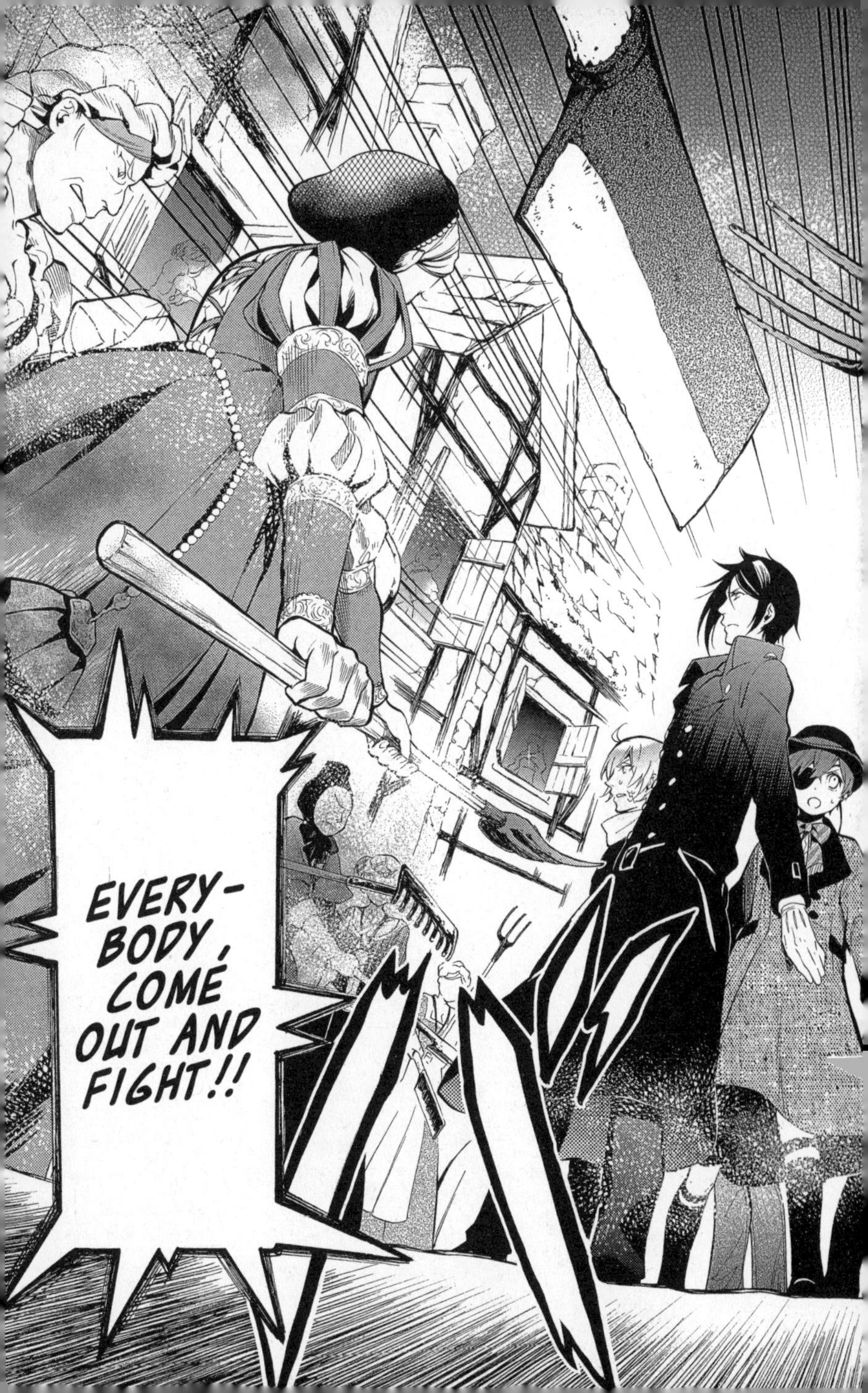
EVERY-BODY, COME OUT AND FIGHT!!

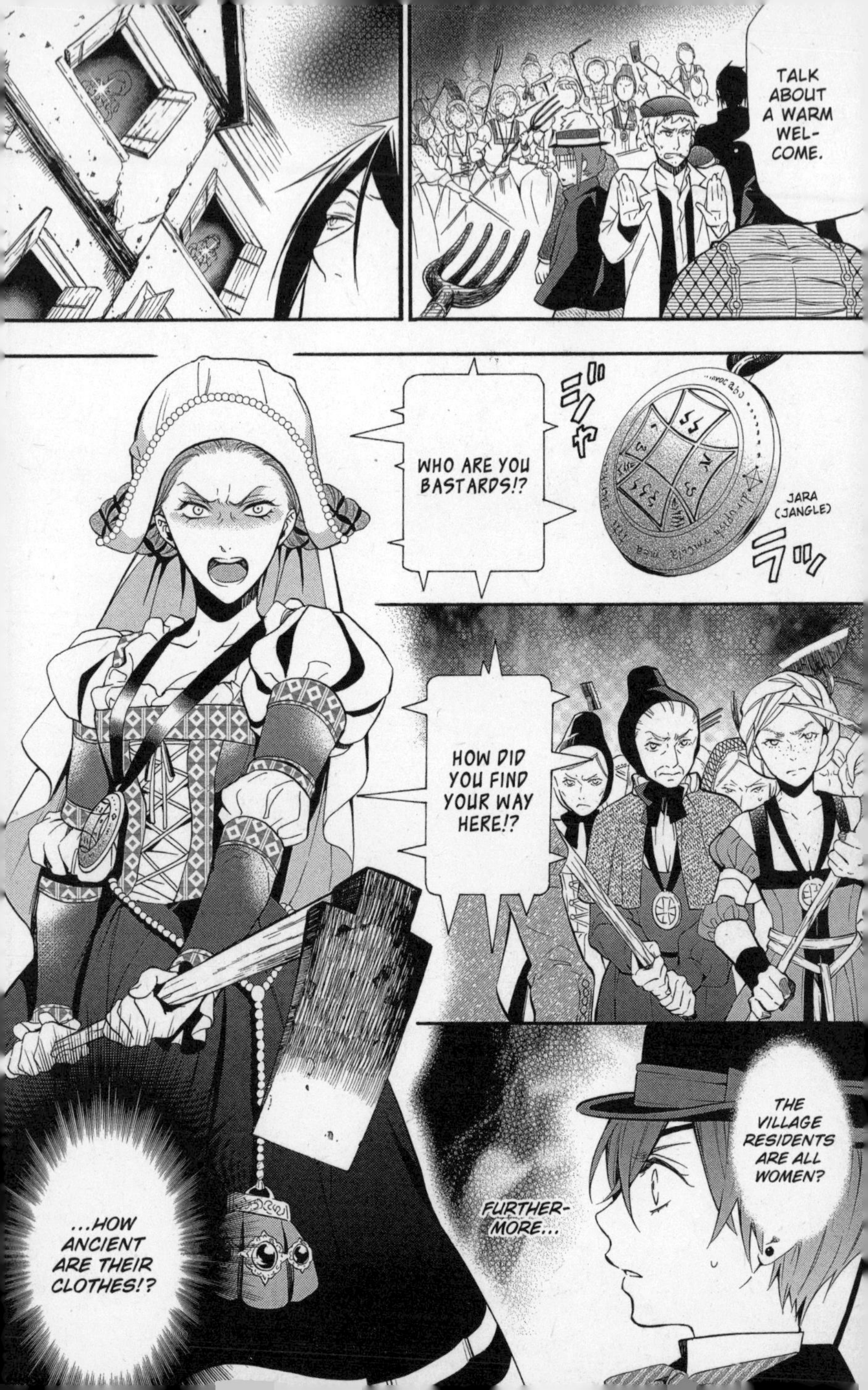
TALK ABOUT A WARM WEL-COME.
WHO ARE YOU BASTARDS!?
ジャ
ラッ
JARA (JANGLE)
HOW DID YOU FIND YOUR WAY HERE!?
THE VILLAGE RESIDENTS ARE ALL WOMEN?
FURTHER-MORE...
...HOW ANCIENT ARE THEIR CLOTHES!?

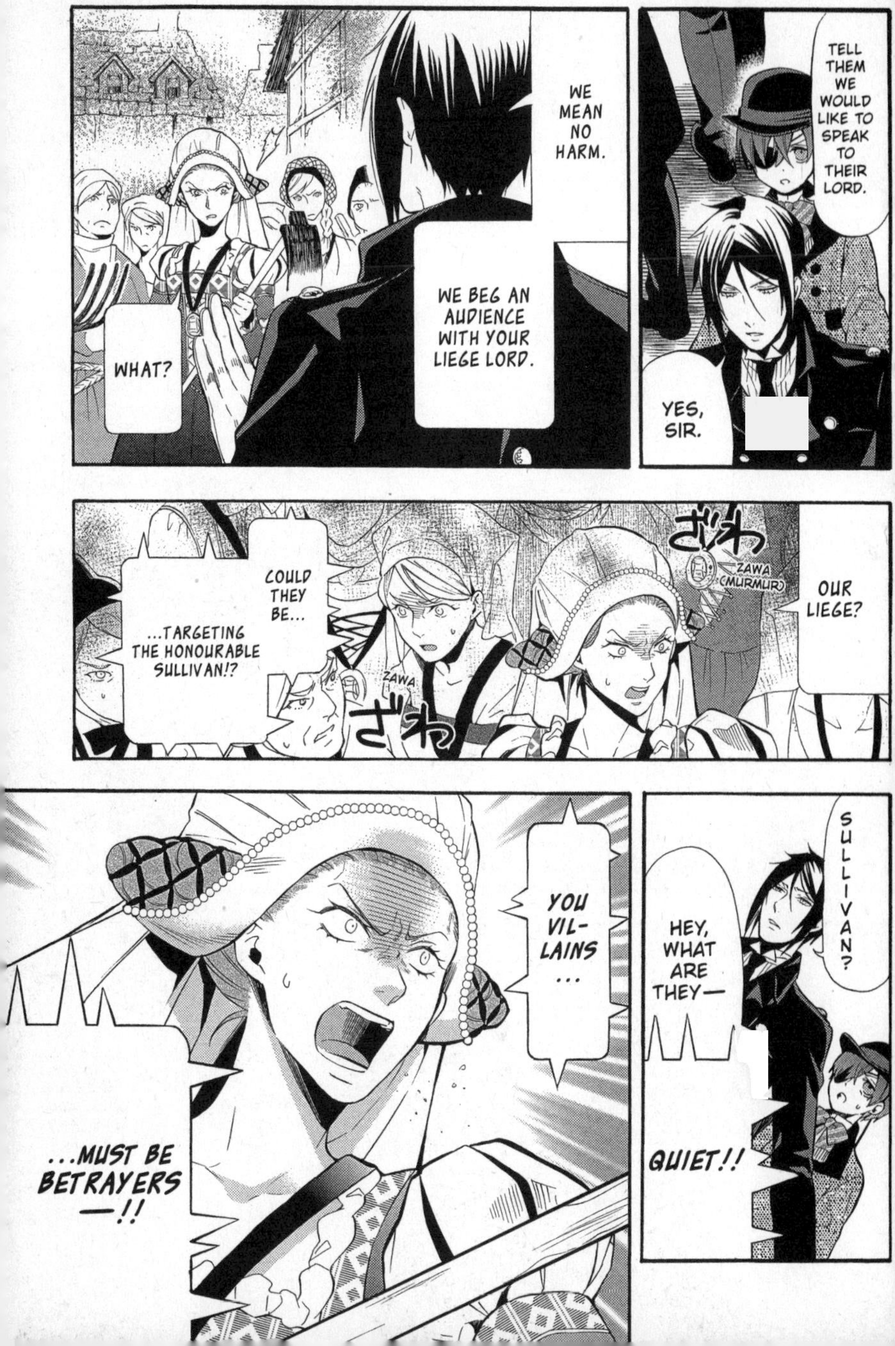
TELL THEM WE WOULD LIKE TO SPEAK TO THEIR LORD.
YES, SIR.
WE MEAN NO HARM.
WE BEG AN AUDIENCE WITH YOUR LIEGE LORD.
WHAT?
OUR LIEGE?
ZAWA (MURMUR)
ざわ
COULD THEY BE...
...TARGETING THE HONOURABLE SULLIVAN!?
ZAWA
ざわ
SULLIVAN?
HEY, WHAT ARE THEY—
QUIET!!
YOU VIL-LAINS...
...MUST BE BETRAYERS—!!

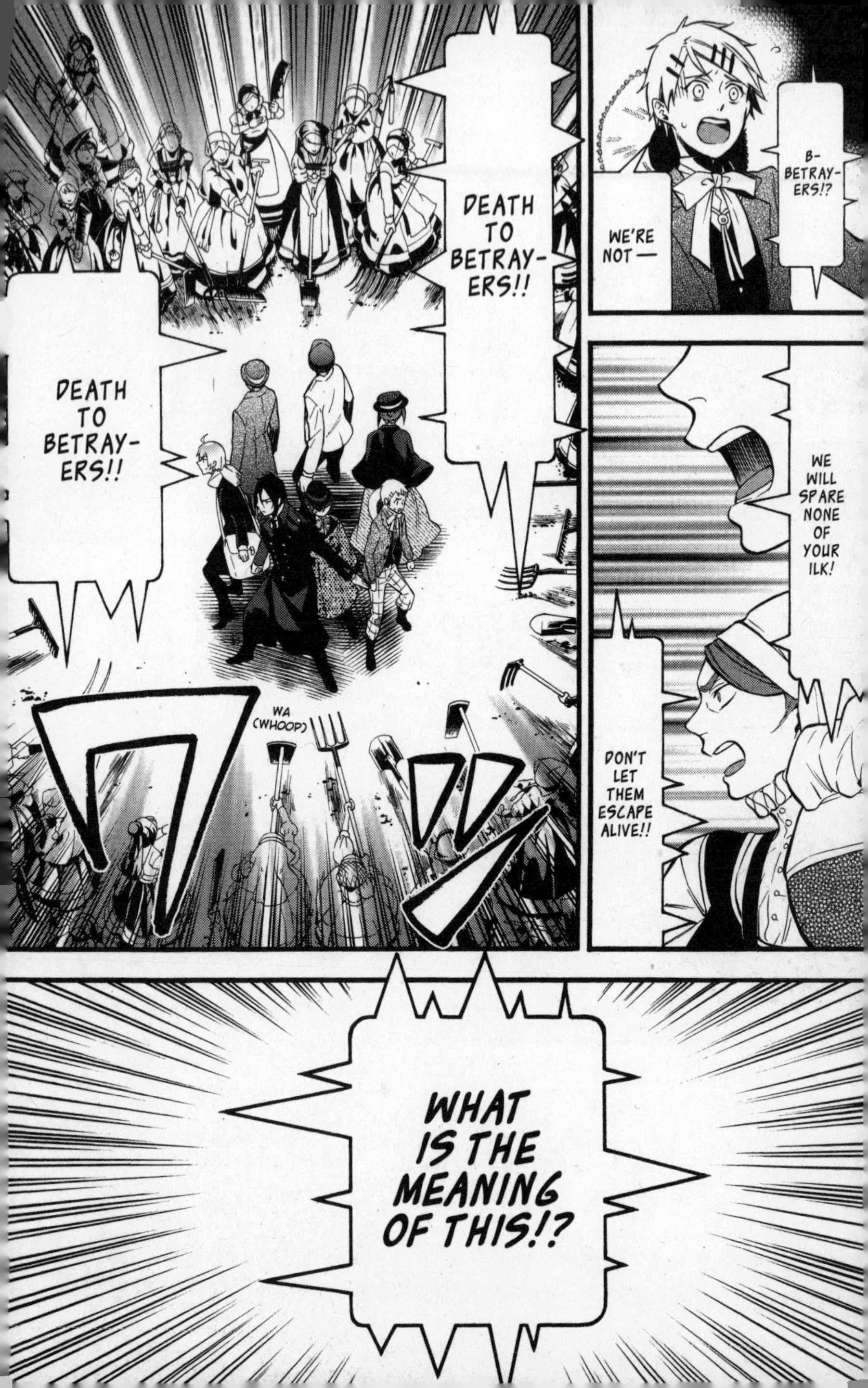
B-BETRAYERS!?
WE'RE NOT—
WE WILL SPARE NONE OF YOUR ILK!
DON'T LET THEM ESCAPE ALIVE!!
DEATH TO BETRAYERS!!
DEATH TO BETRAYERS!!
WA (WHOOP)
WHAT IS THE MEANING OF THIS!?

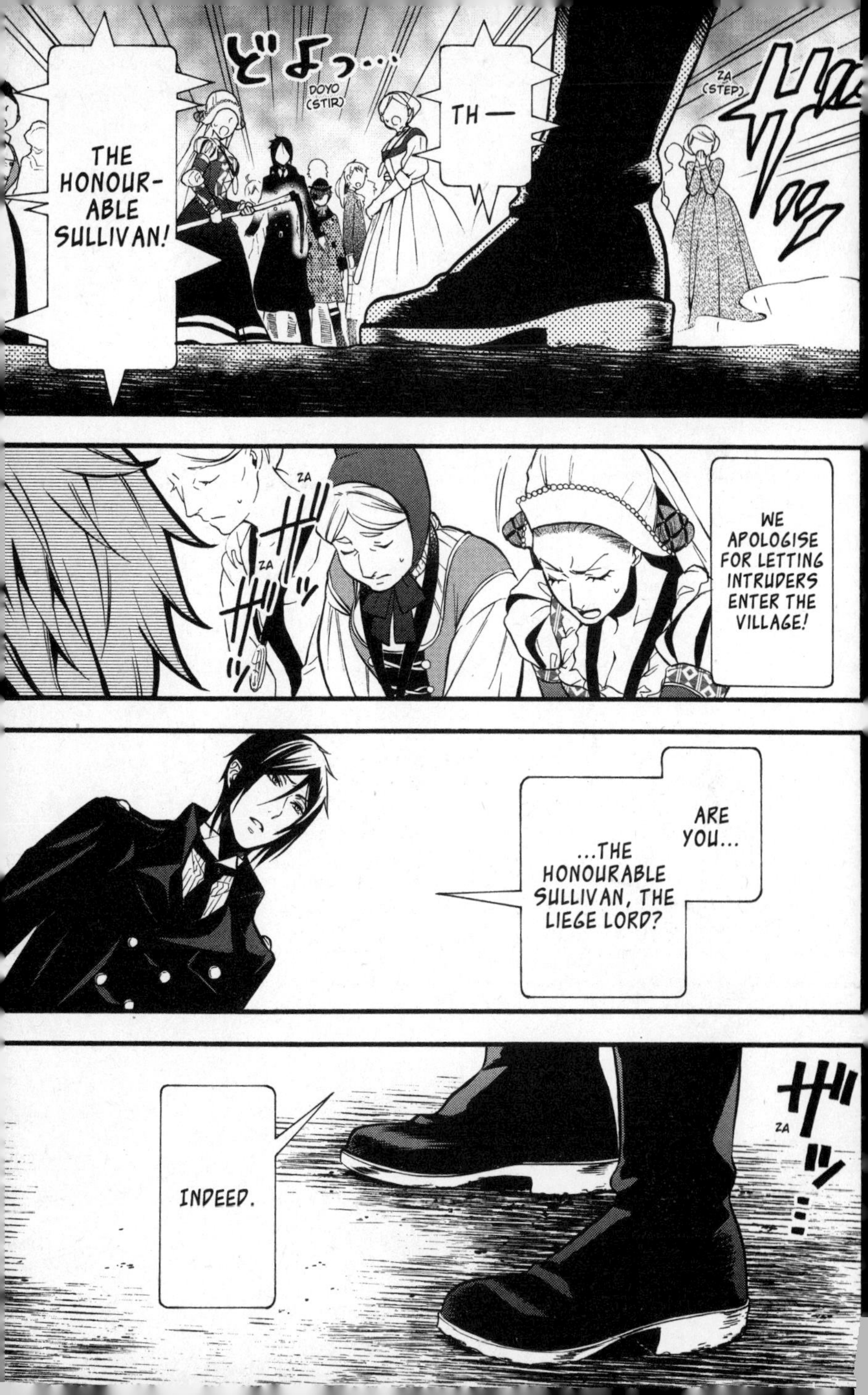
ZA (STEP)
TH—
どよっ…
DOYO (STIR)
THE HONOURABLE SULLIVAN!
WE APOLOGISE FOR LETTING INTRUDERS ENTER THE VILLAGE!
ZA
ZA
ARE YOU...
...THE HONOURABLE SULLIVAN, THE LIEGE LORD?
ZA
INDEED.

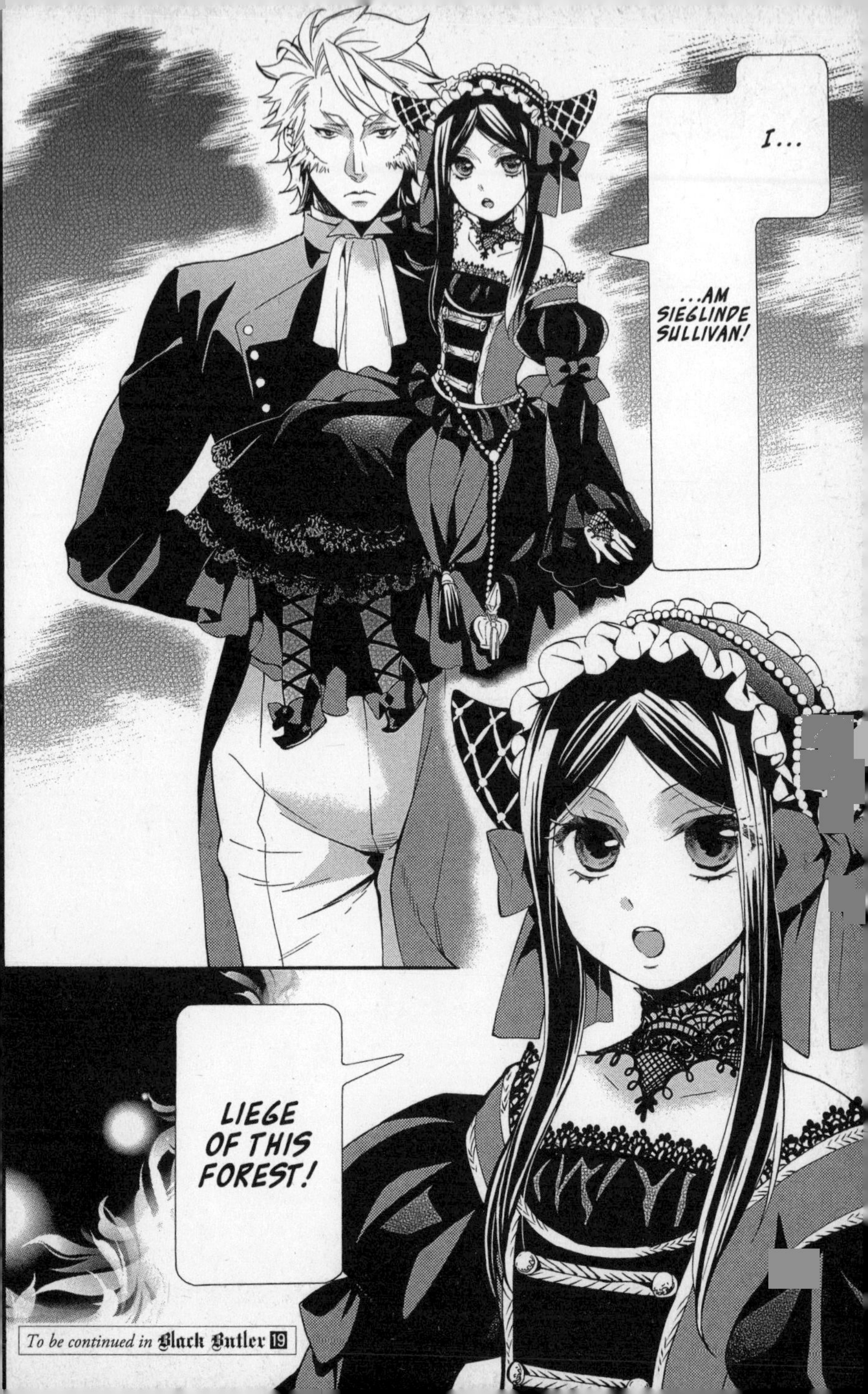
I...
...AM SIEGLINDE SULLIVAN!
LIEGE OF THIS FOREST!
To be continued in Black Butler 19

➤ Black Butler ◄

黒執事

❖

Downstairs

Wakana Haduki

7

Saito Torino

Tsuki Sorano

Chiaki Nagaoka

Asakura

*

Takeshi Kuma

*

Yana Toboso

❖

Adviser

Rico Murakami

Special thanks to You!

Translation Notes

Inside Front and Back Covers

Youkai
Youkai is a word for supernatural creatures found in Japanese folklore.

Karasu tengu
Sebastian is a *karasu tengu*, a mountain *youkai* usually portrayed with black wings, a red face, and a long nose, and dressed like a mountain priest.

Youko
The Undertaker is a *youko*, or fox *youkai*. *Youko* with multiple tails are called *o-saki*. Their tails are said to be their sources of power, so the more tails, the stronger the *youkai*.

Karakasa kouzou
Finny is a *karakasa kozou*. Old umbrellas turn into this *youkai*, and its distinguishing feature is the one leg it hops on.

Tanuki
Mey-Rin is a *tanuki*, or raccoon dog *youkai*, believed to be able to take the form of other beings.

Kappa
Baldo is a *kappa*, a water spirit that looks like child, is green or red all over, has a plate on its head, a tortoise shell on its back, and webbed hands and feet.

Shrine maiden
Ciel is dressed like a shrine maiden. He's holding an *oonusa*, which is used for purification during Shinto rituals.

Page 90
Fortnum & Mason's Royal Blend
First blended for King Edward VII in 1902, this blended tea features leaves from Ceylon and Assam.

Page 105
Micah Clarke
A novel by Arthur Conan Doyle published in 1889 (three years after the first appearance of Sherlock Holmes). This historical novel follows the titular character as he seeks adventure and comes of age. The story takes place during the Monmouth Rebellion of 1685 (an attempt to overthrow the then-King of England, James II).

Page 106
Cherry lips and jap desserts
Two different kinds of old fashioned English candy. The former were scented, cherry-flavoured jelly candies, while the latter were cubes of coconut with a sweet, flavoured coating.

Page 140
"Pleased to meet you" in German
Ciel is trying to say "Ich freue mich, sie kennen zu lernen."

Page 172
Sieglinde
In Richard Wagner's famous three-act opera, *The Valkyrie*, which is itself the second of four operas in *The Ring of Niebelung* cycle, Sieglinde is the mother of the legendary hero of Norse mythology, Siegfried.

Yana Toboso

AUTHOR'S NOTE

The third season of the *Black Butler* anime is to go into production after the live-action movie, an exhibition of my manuscripts is to be held, and multiple artbooks are planned for publication too.

I don't quite know what to do with myself since 2014 is full of happy occurrences, so I'll just draw my manga for now.

And that's how things stand in Volume 18, where a new arc finally begins.

WELCOME TO IKEBUKURO, WHERE TOKYO'S WILDEST CHARACTERS GATHER!!

DURARARA!!

DRRR!! 1

CREATOR
RYOHGO
NARITA

CHARACTER
DESIGN
SUZUHITO
YASUDA

ARTIST
AKIYO
SATORIGI

AS THEIR PATHS CROSS, THIS ECCENTRIC CAST WEAVES A TWISTED, CRACKED LOVE STORY...

AVAILABLE NOW!!

To become the ultimate weapon, one must devour the souls of 99 humans...

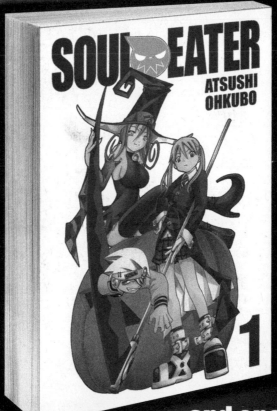

and one witch.

Maka is a scythe meister, working to perfect her demon scythe until it is good enough to become Death's Weapon—the weapon used by Shinigami-sama, the spirit of Death himself. And if that isn't strange enough, her scythe also has the power to change form—into a human-looking boy!

VOLUMES 1-22 IN STORES NOW!

BLACK BUTLER ⑱

YANA TOBOSO

Translation: Tomo Kimura • Lettering: Alexis Eckerman

KUROSHITSUJI Vol. 18 © 2014 Yana Toboso / SQUARE ENIX CO., LTD. First published in Japan in 2014 by SQUARE ENIX CO., LTD. English translation rights arranged with SQUARE ENIX CO., LTD. and Hachette Book Group through Tuttle-Mori Agency, Inc.

Translation © 2014 by SQUARE ENIX CO., LTD.

Yen Press
Hachette Book Group
1290 Avenue of the Americas, New York, NY 10104

www.HachetteBookGroup.com
www.YenPress.com

Yen Press is an imprint of Hachette Book Group, Inc. The Yen Press name and logo are trademarks of Hachette Book Group, Inc.

First Yen Press Edition: October 2014

ISBN: 978-0-316-33622-2

10 9 8 7 6 5 4 3 2 1

BVG

Printed in the United States of America